Decrees of Fourth-Century
Athens (403/2–322/1 BC)

Decree-making is a defining aspect of ancient Greek political activity: it was the means by which city-state communities went about deciding to get things done. This two-volume work provides a new view of the decree as an institution within the framework of fourth-century Athenian democratic political activity. Volume 1 consists of a comprehensive account of the literary evidence for decrees of the fourth-century Athenian assembly. Volume 2 analyses how decrees and decree-making, by offering both an authoritative source for the narrative of the history of the Athenian *demos* and a legitimate route for political self-promotion, came to play an important role in shaping Athenian democratic politics. Peter Liddel assesses ideas about, and the reality of, the dissemination of knowledge of decrees among both Athenians and non-Athenians and explains how they became significant to the wider image and legacy of the Athenians.

Peter Liddel is Senior Lecturer in Ancient History at the University of Manchester. He has published extensively on Greek political history, notably *Civic Obligation and Individual Liberty in Ancient Athens* (2007), as well as on Greek history, historiography and epigraphy. He is co-editor of the *Annual of the British School at Athens*, and serves as co-editor of *Brill's New Jacoby* and as associate editor of *Polis*. He is a founding member of the Editorial Board of the Attic Inscriptions Online project (https://www.atticinscriptions.com/) and is also Co-Investigator in a project to digitally publish Attic inscriptions in UK collections (AIUK).

Decrees of Fourth-Century Athens (403/2–322/1 BC)

Volume 2
Political and Cultural Perspectives

PETER LIDDEL

CAMBRIDGE
UNIVERSITY PRESS

University Printing House, Cambridge CB2 8BS, United Kingdom

One Liberty Plaza, 20th Floor, New York, NY 10006, USA

477 Williamstown Road, Port Melbourne, VIC 3207, Australia

314–321, 3rd Floor, Plot 3, Splendor Forum, Jasola District Centre, New Delhi – 110025, India

79 Anson Road, #06–04/06, Singapore 079906

Cambridge University Press is part of the University of Cambridge.

It furthers the University's mission by disseminating knowledge in the pursuit of education, learning, and research at the highest international levels of excellence.

www.cambridge.org
Information on this title: www.cambridge.org/9781107185074
DOI: 10.1017/9781316882788

© Peter Liddel 2020

This publication is in copyright. Subject to statutory exception and to the provisions of relevant collective licensing agreements, no reproduction of any part may take place without the written permission of Cambridge University Press.

First published 2020

A catalogue record for this publication is available from the British Library.

Library of Congress Cataloging-in-Publication Data
NAMES: Liddel, Peter P. (Peter Philip), 1977– author.
TITLE: Decrees of fourth-century Athens (403/2–322/1 BC) : political and cultural perspectives / Peter Liddel.
DESCRIPTION: Cambridge, United Kingdom ; New York, NY : Cambridge University Press, 2019. | Includes bibliographical references and index.
IDENTIFIERS: LCCN 2018043697 | ISBN 9781107185074
SUBJECTS: LCSH: Legislation – Greece – Athens – History – To 1500. | Democracy – Greece – Athens – History – To 1500. | Constitutional history – Greece – Athens – To 146 B.C. | Athens (Greece) – Politics and government
CLASSIFICATION: LCC KL4361.32.A75 L53 2019 | DDC 340.5/385–dc23
LC record available at https://lccn.loc.gov/2018043697

ISBN 978-1-107-18507-4 Hardback

Cambridge University Press has no responsibility for the persistence or accuracy of URLs for external or third-party internet websites referred to in this publication and does not guarantee that any content on such websites is, or will remain, accurate or appropriate.

Contents

List of Tables	*page* vi
Introduction	1
1 The Social Capital of the Decree	14
2 Appropriation and Aspiration: Decrees in the Pursuit of Political Self-Interest	59
3 The Dissemination of Fourth-Century Athenian Decrees: Local Audiences	109
4 The Audiences of Decrees Beyond Athenian Citizens	159
5 Literary Representations of Athenian Decrees	189
Conclusion	240
Appendix 1 Proposers of Decrees at the Athenian Assembly 403/2–322/1	247
Appendix 2 Literary Inventions	269
Bibliography	273
Index Locorum	300
General Index	306

Tables

1 Comparison between the Literary and Epigraphical Evidence for
  Period 1 (403/2–353/2) and Period 2 (352/1–322/1)   12

2 Epigraphically Attested Early Fourth-Century Decrees which
  are Referred to by the Literary Sources   135

3 References to Extraordinary Inscriptions in Oratory   147

Introduction

In this volume, I offer a new view of the role of the decree as an institution within the framework of Athenian democratic political activity and its legacy. Focusing upon decrees of the Athenian *demos* of the period 403/2–322/1, the perspectives offered in this volume are informed primarily by the literary evidence collected in Volume 1, but also by epigraphic material and literary engagement with documents and decrees of a wider chronological context, particularly those associated with the fifth century.

What makes this volume distinctive is its attempt to contemplate the role of the decree as an institution which, by offering both a rhetorically authoritative resource for narratives of the history of the Athenian *demos* (Chapter 1 below) and a legitimate route for the political self-promotion of individual citizens (Chapter 2 below), came to play an important role in shaping Athenian politics. I seek to determine how awareness and interpretations of decrees circulated among contemporary Athenians in the fourth century, considering the role of epigraphical publication in that process (Chapter 3 below). I assess ideas about, and the reality of, the dissemination of knowledge of decrees among non-Athenians (Chapter 4 below); I also explore their representation in classical literature, seeking to explain how the subject of decrees came to attain a rhetorical presence and a significance to the wider image and legacy of the Athenians (Chapter 5 below).

Over the course of this volume I build upon a number of different modern scholarly developments which deserve mention here: first, scholarly works on Athenian democracy, which have gone some way to placing decrees and activity related to them within the broader frameworks of political institutions and social dynamics;[1] second, the work of those who have emphasised the technical aspects of decrees, the significance of their epigraphical publication, and their literary circulation;[2] third, those who have produced close studies of

---

1 For interpretations of Athenian democratic activity based upon an analysis of the city's institutions (including decree-making institutions), see Rhodes 1972; Hansen 1987, 1999; Lambert 2018: 171–226; on the social dynamics of Athenian politics, see Finley 1966; Ober 1989, 2008.

2 For institutions and Athenian decrees: Hansen 1987: 108-118; Rhodes 1972: 52–87; Schoemann 1819: 129–47; Biagi 1785; for technical aspects of decrees: Rhodes with Lewis 1997; Canevaro 2013; on the significance of their epigraphical publication: Hedrick 1999, 2000; Sickinger 2009; Lambert 2011a (= 2018: 71–92) and 2018: 47-68; on the literary circulation of decrees: Haake 2013.

1

particular types of decree.[3] Particular mention must be made of the work of Stephen Lambert, which has opened up a great variety of historical perspectives on inscribed Athenian laws and decrees (see especially Lambert 2018); several of the avenues of analysis Lambert has opened up are pursued here, in particular those which concern the significance of epigraphical publication and the association between decree-making and political influence. To the angles developed by such approaches, I add those developed in sociological theory, New Institutional analysis, and memory studies.

An account of the premises upon which this study of Athenian decrees in literature is based can be found in the Introduction to Volume 1, and the Inventory of Decrees. References to 'D' and 'DP' in the current volume refer to the entries in the Inventory. In the current Introduction, I outline succinctly the approaches offered in this volume to the analysis of the ancient evidence for decrees.

* * *

In Greece, the decree, as a means by which communities made decisions, and initiated the process of implementing them, emerged towards the end of the archaic period out of the political tendency of the Greek city-states to draw together their male adult citizens to discuss proposals put forward by members of their community and to make enactments as shared decisions.[4] Some classical Greek city-states entitled an unusually high – for a premodern (or indeed a modern) society – proportion of male citizens to a role in politics. Yet comparable decision-making processes are known in other, non-Greek, city-state organisations which featured forms of direct democracy.[5] For instance, the seventeenth-century *rada* (assembly) of the Zaporozhian Cossacks was a decree-making body which voted by acclamation on matters such as the division of income, plunder, mercenary remuneration, hunting and questions of

---

3 Four works which have successfully placed the discussion of particular types of honorific grant in their wider context are: Osborne 1981–3 (citizenship decrees); Ma 2013 (honorific statues); Mack 2015 (proxeny awards); Lambert 2011a (= 2018: 71–92; honorific decrees).

4 For inscribed enactments of archaic Greek city-states, see Koerner 1993; Van Effenterre and Ruzé 1994–5. On decision-making at the Homeric proto-assembly, see Hom. *Il.* 1.1–305, 2.1–182; *Od.*2.1–159 with Hammer 2002 and Raaflaub 2004.

5 For discussion of rule by councils and assemblies 'in which decisions were made by vote after a debate' as a characteristic of the city-state across history, see Hansen 2000: 612 with note 81, pointing to examples of republican forms of political organisation among city-state organisations of the Etruscans, Latins, Italians, Swiss, Dutch, Mzâb, Swahili, Ibadan of the Yoruba, and Banda-Neira of the Malay. For decision-making in the assemblies of Balinese village society, see Hobart 1975: 87–91.

INTRODUCTION

war or peace.[6] In this and the ancient Greek context, decrees were formulated and enacted by groups of men who shared privileged status at an assembly or a smaller council. In the ancient Greek world, the passing of decrees allowed communities to regulate internal matters related to areas such as cult practice and civic organisation, but also enabled them to co-ordinate transactions with other communities (through exchange, honorific transactions, diplomacy and warfare). They were, therefore, important for social co-ordination and co-ordination of interaction with other communities. Yet, as we shall see, the Athenian system of enactment, in which individual initiative played a big part, also meant that the proposal of decrees offered a significant route of political self-promotion.

Decrees appeared in democratic Athens before the fifth century and it is likely that they were made by the assembly even in the pre-Cleisthenic era;[7] the oldest extant Athenian inscription which makes reference to an enactment of the people is *IG* I³ 1 of perhaps the late sixth century, a slab of marble on which is inscribed a decree concerning Salamis.[8] Extant epigraphical evidence suggests that the publication of inscribed decrees by the Athenians accelerated over the second half of the fifth century and reached a peak in the second half of the fourth century.[9] This aspect of the epigraphical habit is a clear demonstration

---

6 On Cossack decision-making, see Longworth 1969: 36-7. For the re-establishment of the *rada* both at the beginning and again at the end of the twentieth century, see O'Rourke 2007: 200–201, 282; caution is necessary about the modern claims about their heritage, given that such developments were at least partially inspired by Cossack ideals of freedom and equality which were, according to O'Rourke 2007: 62, 'the stuff of popular dreams'. On the *veche* (town-meeting) and other 'free institutions' among the city-states of Kievian and Novgorodian Russia of the Middle Ages, Cossack communities and military democracies of South Russia, see Timasheff 2010.

7 For an account (perhaps anachronistic) of a decree (a proposal attributed to a certain Aristion) granting a bodyguard to Pisistratos before his first seizure of power in 561/0, see [Arist.] *Ath. Pol.* 14.1. Herodotus (1.59.4) tells a story about Pisistratus persuading the Athenian *demos* to grant him a bodyguard, but without explaining it as a decree. For another occasion when a fourth-century source describes an incident known from Herodotus' work as a decree, see Chapter 5.2.1 below. Fourth-century sources make frequent reference to decrees of the Persian War era, but these are often thought to be spurious: see Develin 1989: 56, 59, 64, 66; Habicht 1961; cf. discussion below, Chapters 1.5.3 and 5.4.1 with note 113 below.

8 *IG* I³ 1 line 1 contains the earliest epigraphically attested occurrence of the enactment formulae 'ἔδοχσεν τõι δέμοι' ('it was resolved by the people'). For the earliest known use of the term *psephisma*, see Chapter 1.1 note 4 below.

9 For a quantitative survey of the publication of Athenian decrees, see Hedrick 1999; for the relationship between imperial administration and the publication of decrees, see Schuller 1974. For figures of fifth- and fourth-century Athenian decrees on stone, see Table 1, pp. 12–13 below.

of the importance of the decree to the ancient Athenians,[10] who displayed their financial and physical investment in decrees by setting them up them in public places (often at locations with monumental and/or religious significance), and adorned some of them with sculptured reliefs.[11] Such forms of publication are a clear demonstration of the importance of the decree to ancient Athenian culture.

In Athens, the enactment of decrees was generally regarded as indicative of the democratic will of the people, a theme that will be explored in Chapters 1 and 2;[12] more precisely, however, decrees demonstrated the authority of the institutions that enacted them.[13] Indeed, while decrees were prevalent in other Greek democracies,[14] they were the tool of decision-making also in those Greek city-state communities, such as Delphi, which possessed more narrowly restricted institutional bodies or were not conspicuously democratic;[15] decree-making, therefore, was not the exclusive preserve of democratic regimes. Moreover, associated as they were in Athens with individual proposers,[16] decrees were subject also to appropriation by political actors in a number of different ways. By the 330s, Demosthenes was able to make claims about his contribution to the salvation of the Athenian city-state on the basis of accounts of decrees that he proposed; in the same period, decrees are attested as the subject and focus of political competition (see Chapter 2.3 below). It is clear, therefore, that in the second half of the fourth century decree-proposing had become a signifi-

---

10 Rhodes with Lewis (1997) collects the evidence for the enactment of decrees of city-state communities from across the Greek world, drawing predominantly upon epigraphical evidence. The epigraphical publication of Athenian decrees will be explored in more detail in Chapter 3 below.

11 Places of publication: Hölkeskamp 2000; Liddel 2003; Moroo 2016; Lambert 2018: 19–46; see discussion in Chapter 3.3 below. On document reliefs: Lawton 1995; Hagemajer Allen 2003; Moreno 2007: 260–9; Blanshard 2004b, 2007; Deene 2016; Mack 2018. On the history of the *stele* as a documentary form, see Meyer 2013 and Davies 2005.

12 On the relationship between democracy and decree-publishing see Hedrick 1999, 2000 and now Sickinger 2009.

13 However, on the limits to the sovereignty of decrees of the Athenian *demos*, see Chapter 1.3 below.

14 Decrees elsewhere in the Greek world: Rhodes with Lewis 1997: *passim*; democracies outside Athens: Robinson 1997 and 2011; Grieb 2009; Carlsson 2010.

15 Rhodes with Lewis 1997: 126–40. For decrees of (what might be, given that the awards were made by the council alone) oligarchic Erythrai, see RO 56 and SEG XXXI 969; for a decree of oligarchic Miletos, see OR 123 = ML 43. For voting and electoral manipulation at assemblies in oligarchies, emphasising their deployment in supporting regimes, see Simonton 2017: 121–33.

16 The earliest epigraphically attested Attic decree to mention a proposer is *IG* I³ 8 of c. 460–50: Ἀντίβιο[ς εῖπεν· τὰ μὲν ἄλλα καθάπε]ρ Καλλίμαχος' (lines 3–4: 'Antibio[s proposed: other things just a]s Kallimachos (proposed)'): according to this restoration, Kallimachos is revealed as the original proposer, with Antibios the author of a rider. For the attribution of a sixth-century decree to a certain Aristion, see note 7 above.

cant political activity which offered a route (but not the only route) to political prominence.[17] This theme will be explored in more detail in Chapter 2 below.

The interpretations of decrees, their political connotations and the literary representations of them explored over the course of this volume – particularly in Chapters 1 and 2 below – draw extensively upon ancient sources but are informed more broadly by critical perspectives. The approach taken draws upon three related interpretations of human behaviour and aspiration which have been developed in sociological studies. The first is that of symbolic capital, articulated by Pierre Bourdieu in his 1979 *La Distinction: critique sociale du jugement* (*Distinction: A Social Critique of the Judgement of Taste*). This notion emphasises the preponderance among human individuals of aspiration for 'name, renown, prestige, honour, glory, and authority'.[18] The desire for symbolic capital is said to be 'inculcated in the earliest years of life and reinforced by all subsequent experience'.[19] Its demonstration and display equates to the expression of symbolic power.[20] That similar aspirations are espoused by individuals in ancient Greek culture has been extensively demonstrated in modern scholarship;[21] indeed, the widespread public display of symbolic capital in honorific and commemorative contexts (both inscribed and funerary) is well documented.[22] This approach is resonant with the appearance of decrees in political and forensic oratory: in Chapter 2 below I underline the fact that decrees are deployed in political arguments not only for purposes of persuasion but as a demonstration of personal knowledge and political achievement; politicians were able to capitalise on them by deploying accounts, both at the assembly and the lawcourt, of decrees and success in enacting them. In other words, knowledge of decrees could be deployed in the manufacture of political capital. But as will become clear (see Chapter 1 below), this is not the whole picture: decrees were held up not only as records of decisions that were supposed to bolster the profile of particular individuals, but they also could be described in ways which were aimed at communicating a sense of solidarity and shared interests among the people; this is relevant to Bourdieu's notion – related to, but distinct from, that of symbolic capital – of social capital.[23] Bourdieu's sociological methodologies,

---

17 The view that political institutions can provide a focus for political competition and struggle has been established in the field of political institutionalism: see Blyth 2002.

18 Bourdieu 2010: 249. For an exposition of the idea of symbolic capital, see Bourdieu 1977: 171–83.

19 Bourdieu 1977: 182.

20 On the idea of symbolic power, see Bourdieu 1991: 163-70.

21 Cf. Cohen 1991; Herman 2006.

22 Veyne 1976; Gauthier 1985; Whitehead 1983, 1993; Loraux 1986; Tsagalis 2008: 135–213.

23 Social capital: Bourdieu 1998: 70-1.

therefore, form a good basis for articulating the deployment of knowledge and familiarity with decrees as tools related to expressions of individual aspiration and visions of shared ideals.[24] However, another set of theories is helpful in elucidating the significance of thinking about decrees as dynamic institutions – through which human aspirations were framed and managed – in their own right: those which fall under the banner of New Institutionalism.

The term 'New Institutionalism' is used to refer to a broad set of analytical approaches which focus upon the role of institutions in theoretical, comparative and specific political analyses.[25] As defined by North, 'institutions are the rules of the game in society or, more formally, are the humanly devised constraints that shape human interaction.'[26] Put another way, institutions consist of 'the formal rules, compliance procedures, and standard operating practices that structure the relationship between individuals in various units of the polity and economy.'[27] They can consist of formal constraints (rules) or informal constraints (conventions, codes of behaviour).[28] It is widely accepted that the notion of the 'institution' can be helpfully applied to thought not only about 'institutional agencies' (in ancient Athens, assemblies, councils, lawcourts, boards of magistrates), to 'institutional arrangements' (such as concepts of ownership, property, marriage, the *oikos*, or law-making) but also to 'institutional things' (a contract, the *agora*, the decrees of the council and assembly).[29] Of particular

24 Bourdieu's development of such methodologies in the late twentieth century was articulated in a way that is relevant to the interpretation of ancient Greek history; see now, for its re-articulation as a theory of value, Graeber (2001). Earlier pioneers of the idea of symbolic capital include Mauss and Veblen: see Veblen (2006) and Mauss (2006). One early sense of the value of social capital was raised by de Tocqueville, who observed the value of participation for democratic cohesion. See Volume 1, Part 2, Chapter 3 of his 1835 *Democracy in America*: de Tocqueville 2003: 269–87.

25 On New Institutionalism, see March and Olsen 1984, 1989. For an introduction to the revival of the study of institutions in politics, see Thelen and Steinmo 1992: 2; March and Olsen 1989; Lowndes and Roberts 2013.

26 North 1990: 1.

27 Themen and Steinmo 1992: 2.

28 North 1990: 4. On informal constraints, see North 1990: 36–45; on formal constraints, see North 1990: 46–54

29 For this perspective, see MacCormack 2007: 34–7. North 1990: 5 defines such agencies not as institutions but rather as 'organizations'.
For the application of a range of New Institutionalist theories to ancient Greek history, see, for instance, Weingast 2002; Canevaro 2011; Harris 2013a: 12–14; Simonton 2017: 65 with note 295; Blok 2017: 46, 145–6, 199–200. New Institutional economic thought has also been introduced to the study of ancient Greek economics: see Frier and Kehoe 2007 (emphasising the role of rational self-interest); Ober 2015: 5. With characteristic incisiveness, Davies (2015: 241) writes: 'the jury is still out on the adequacy of New Institutional Economics'.

INTRODUCTION

relevance is the Historical Institutionalist approach,[30] which is concerned with assessing the significance of institutionalised rules, practices and procedures in steering political habits (path dependence)[31] over time and emphasising their role in political activity and political change (see Chapter 2 below); it considers also the ways in which accounts of political activity aspire towards demonstrating legitimacy of political decisions (see Chapter 1 below). This volume's underlying position, that the decree can coherently be given centre-stage in an analysis of political activity, takes a view of the decree as an institutional arrangement in its own right.[32] The view that institutions are shaped not only by authoritative rules but are founded upon accepted practices and narratives is also very important.[33] The Athenians certainly possessed formal rules when it came to the making and challenging of decrees (see Chapter 1.2.1 below) and such activities were treated also as standard operating practices; yet the liveliness and breadth of narratives about past decrees in political oratory (Chapters 1 and 2) and other genres (Chapter 5 below) is striking. Such an approach, furthermore, places emphasis upon analysis of political actors' compliance with, and deployment of, these institutions rather than speculations about the personalities of human individuals:[34] this is highly appropriate when analysing a dataset in which a small number of famous men dominate the record but which also indicates the breadth of political participation (see Chapter 2 below).[35]

Finally, New Institutionalism emphasises the importance of strong political institutions in ensuring stability:[36] there was some debate in fourth-century

---

30 On Historical Institutionalism as one of seven forms of institutionalist analysis, see Peters 2005: 71–86 and 2008: 2–5; cf. Steinmo, Thelen and Longstreth 1992; Sanders 2006: 39–55.

31 On the 'path dependence' perspective, which says that forms of institution established at a prior stage in history have a significant impact on the behaviour of rational actors in the future, see North 1990: 93–8; March and Olsen 1984, 1989: 49–51; Thelen and Steinmo 1992.

32 An alternative view might be to consider decrees as a kind of 'transaction', that is a unit of the wider institution of Athenian democracy; this would be to follow the model developed in Avner Greif's study of the ways in which fledging medieval economic institutions (such as merchants' guilds and traders' coalitions) influenced modes of economic and commercial behaviour. Greif defines a transaction as the basic unit of institutional analysis (Greif 2006: 29), and as an action taken when an entity (whether that be a commodity, social attitude, emotion, option or piece of information) is transferred from one individual to another (Greif 2006: 45–6).

33 Lowndes and Roberts 2013: 46–76.

34 Sanders 2006, concluding: 'Historical institutionalists, then, will not be distracted by wishful thinking about different personalities occupying executive power. If HI teaches us anything, it is that the place to look for answers to big questions about class, power, war, and reform is in institutions, not personalities, and over the longer landscapes of history, not the here and now.'

35 Demost, Appendix 1 and Lambert 2018: 65–7.

36 Huntington 2006: 91–2.

Athens about the extent to which the decree-system was an effective way of meeting day-to-day challenges,[37] and individual decrees were open to challenge and dispute through indictment by the *graphe paranomon* process. Regardless, political leaders and the *demos* carried on with the decree-making system throughout good times and bad during and beyond the fourth century:[38] we might presume that there was no public conception of any plausible alternative way of making decisions democratically;[39] this consensus is what underlay the continuity and to a certain degree the strength and constancy of the decree as a decision-making institution. As we will see, there were rules to the systems within which decrees operated (see Chapter 1.2.1 below), but this volume's emphasis on the use of decrees places emphasis on practice (especially Chapters 1 and 2) and narratives about Athenian decrees (Chapters 3, 4 and 5 below).[40]

There is one further critical perspective that has influenced the approach taken to decrees in this volume, particularly that which underscores its assessment of the dissemination of their ideas (Chapters 3 and 4). This is the perspective of memory studies and in particular the notion of collective (or 'social') memory as a significant historical factor in political and human interaction.

---

37 Mader 2006; cf. Chapter 1.2.2 below.

38 For a survey of fourth-century decree-making in relation to geopolitical developments, see Chapter 1.4 below. The decree-making system is epigraphically well attested at Athens throughout the Hellenistic period: see Hedrick 1999; Byrne 2004; *nomothesia* is not, however, attested to have continued in the same way, though the classical distinction between laws and decrees appears to have persisted: see Canevaro 2011. The example of Philon's *graphe paranomon* against Sophokles in 306 suggests that the process continued after 322/1: see Diogenes Laertius 5.38.

39 Decrees may have been enacted even under the non-democratic regimes of late fifth-century Athens by more limited boards or groups of voters. For decrees of the regime 5,000 of 411/10 at Athens, see Develin 1989: 164–5. The honorific decree OR 173 may be one of the regime of Four Hundred; for another example, see [Plu.] *X Or.* 833e–f. Despite the fact that the Thirty were chosen purposefully to frame new laws and a constitution (Xen. *Hell.* 2.3.11) it proves hard to isolate any particular examples within the narrative accounts of their activity (Xen. *Hell.* 2.3–4; [Arist.] *Ath. Pol.* 35–7). At *Ath. Pol.* 37.1–2 it is said that the Thirty ordered its *boule* to pass a number of laws. Kritias' speech at the Council condemning Theramenes refers to decisions made by the Thirty, but calls them 'new laws' and it is far from clear that he was referring to decrees (Xen. *Hell.* 2.3.51). The closest we come to evidence for a decree made by enfranchised citizens under the Thirty is the death sentence against men captured at Eleusis, which was passed by the vote of the hoplites and cavalry who were 'on the list' at an extraordinary meeting at the Odeion attended also by armed Spartan soldiers (Xen. *Hell.* 2.4.9-10); on Kritias' manipulation of this occasion see Simonton 2017: 128–9. Oinobios' decree to recall Thucydides (Paus. 1.23.9) is often associated with the period of the Thirty in 404/3: see Develin 1989: 186. Kritias' decree casting Phrynichos' body out of the city must, however, be placed before the time of the Thirty: Lycurg. 1.113–14. On the abolition of democracy through the decree of the assembly in 411, see Chapter 1 note 101 below and Chapter 5.2.2 below.

40 Practice: Bourdieu 1977.

It is an approach which places emphasis on the potential fluidity of memories of the past especially those which are sustained among collective groups and enunciated in different forms by individuals. Two recent works in Greek history have been instrumental in demonstrating the potential of memory studies to the wider interpretation of Greek history.[41] The approach established by Shear in her *Polis and Revolution* places an emphasis on the view that a society's memory 'might be regarded as an aggregate collection of its members' many, often competing, memories'.[42] Collective memory, for Shear, finds one expression in the setting up of monuments and public documents in commemoration of particular events and processes; yet it is viewers' interaction with such monuments and their reperformance of these memories which is what, according to Shear, perpetuates shared memory.[43] The creation of these memories underpinned the Athenian reconstruction of a unified *polis* in the aftermath of the oligarchic interventions in 411/10 and 404/3; as I shall argue (Chapter 1.5 below), memories of decrees played an important role in the construction of ideas about the harmonious *demos* of the reconciliation of 403/2. Steinbock's 2013 book, moreover, has also underlined the importance of collective memory both in public discourse and social cohesion;[44] for Steinbock, while there existed a 'monolithic group mind',[45] individual Athenians were at the same time free to tweak and adapt versions of the past that suited the case they were making. The presentation of decrees (both Athenian and non-Athenian) is relevant to this picture: Steinbock shows how Athenian discourse played up contradictory Theban decrees at different points in the fourth century. Accordingly, an Athenian wishing to encourage hostility to the Thebans would emphasise the Theban proposal to destroy Athens at the end of the Peloponnesian War (Din. 1.25); those who in the 330s wished to encourage rapprochement would emphasise a Theban decree which had assisted the Athenian democrats (Xen. *Hell.* 2.2.19–20).[46]

Engagement with memory studies highlights the rhetorical significance of claims made about decrees, in particular in the Athenian courts. This is

---

41 Note also the seminal studies of Wolpert (2002), Gehrke (2001) and Bommas (2011); see also the contributions in Marincola, Llewellyn-Jones and MacIver (eds.) 2012; for a detailed discussion of approaches to memory studies, see Assman 1995; Olick 2007, Shear 2011: 6–12 and Steinbock 2013: 7–17.
42 Shear 2011: 7 citing Young 1993: xi.
43 Shear 2011: 11–14; for further explication of dynamism in the treatment of inscribed public documents, see Low forthcoming.
44 Steinbock 2013; cf. Shear 2014: 506–8.
45 Steinbock 2013: 13.
46 Steinbock 2013: 211–79, 280–340.

particularly pertinent in the case of accounts of Persian War era decrees which circulated in the late fourth century. These included the decree of Themistocles and that against the traitor Arthmios: the former is represented by an inscribed version which is generally agreed to be partially fabricated in terms of its historical details;[47] the latter by a series of stories about it which circulated in the oratorical evidence.[48] But the role of social memory is relevant also to the deployment of roughly contemporary fourth-century decrees; as we shall see in Chapter 3 below, social memory was probably more important in terms of the profile of decrees than inscribed or archival versions of them. But when it came to the deployment of contemporary material, orators were apparently more careful to ground their claims in truth than they were in the discussion of fifth-century material: both public awareness of events and the development of an archive from 403/2 meant that, even while orators did not base their claims about a decree closely on scrutiny of the archive, its accessibility meant that their claims could be checked by others.[49] Decrees, therefore, were not merely empty vessels that could be put to use for any political purpose or manipulated in any way possible: their content went some way in structuring the possibilities of their deployment.

It is to the subject of the significance of the decree to political dynamics that I turn in Chapters 1 and 2 below, where I assess the extent to which decree-making and decree-citing might be viewed as social and political practices in their own right and analyse the ways in which those familiar with decrees drew on them in the pursuit of political activity. A guiding principle of this book is the view that the writing of the political history of the decree includes, but should consist of much more than, an account of mechanics and rules; accordingly, I emphasise the role both of decree-making and decree-recalling as a social practice and its significance in oratorical persuasion. Chapter 1 below develops some of the themes initiated in this Introduction, setting out the institutional factors that gave the decrees a negotiable status and exploring their use to make claims about collective achievements and shared values of the *demos*. In Chapter 2 below, I explore the role of the decree in the construction of arguments, the creation of individual political legacies, and assess the depth of knowledge that was deployed in the courts by self-interested politicians. Both chapters demonstrate that Attic orators presumed that their audiences would

---

47 Meiggs and Lewis 1988: 48–52.
48 Meiggs 1972. See also Chapter 5.4.1 below.
49 Olick 2007: 7, 37–54 emphasises that the development and exercise of shared memory was a negotiation between different political challenges and cultural claims, but one constrained by awareness of past events.

be sufficiently familiar with and assured of the authority of decrees to find citation of them credible or convincing. This leads into questions about the sources of knowledge of decrees: in Chapter 3 below I ask how awareness of, and ideas about, contemporary decrees diffused among fourth-century Athenians and set out the implications of the fits and non-fits between the epigraphical and literary record of decrees for an understanding of their inscribed publication. Chapter 4 below looks more broadly at the question of audiences, exploring perceptions and realities of non-Athenian audiences, their identity, their likely points of access to knowledge about decrees, and their reactions to them. In both Chapters 3 and 4 below I underline the role that inscriptions played not in ensuring the dissemination of accurate information about decrees but rather in providing rhetorically useful reference points to some high-profile decrees. Finally, Chapter 5 below assesses the representation of decrees in a range of literary contexts: the relatively high profile achieved by Athenian decrees reflects the reception of a perspective on their cultural and political importance and demonstrates that, having started out as an institutional process, they came to achieve a high cultural status among a range of audiences.

Table 1 Comparison between the Literary and Epigraphical Evidence for Period 1 (403/2– 353/2) and Period 2 (352/1–322/1)

Genre-type of decree	Inscriptions containing decrees: Period 1 (approximate figures)[1]	Inscriptions containing decrees: Period 2 (Lambert's figures)[2]	Decrees attested in the literary record: 403/2–322/1 (Period 1; Period 2)
Attested decrees: total	c. 223+[3]	240	**245** (104; 141)
Number of attested decrees of discernible content	182	199	235 (103; 132)
Honorific: total	126 (69.2%)	180 (90.5%)	80 (32.7%) (38; 42)
Honours for non-Athenians	125 (68.7%)[4]	116 (58.3%)	48 (19.6%)[5] (27; 21)

1 Percentages are those of attested decrees of discernible content; I am grateful to Angelos Matthaiou for his assistance in drawing up a list of inscribed decrees of this period. It is important to note that on occasion inscriptions make mention of several different decrees enacted distinctly: one example is the case of *IG* II³ 1 306, which contains an account of honorific decrees for an outgoing council (lines 24–6) while providing texts of a proposal of Phanodemos (lines 17–23) and the honorific decrees for Phanodemos (lines 4–16) and Eudoxos (lines 27–33, 43–9); another inscription contains a dossier of five decrees for a single individual (Herakleides of Salamis: *IG* II³ 1 367). However, this table measures the number of self-standing inscriptions containing decrees and accordingly counts them as single cases. It does not attempt to include all dedications which include the passing of decrees. Moreover, with the exception of *IG* II² 1629.170–271 (= *IG* II³ 1 370) it does not include decrees referred to in the inscribed accounts of the naval *epimeletai*; decrees in these accounts are the subject of work being undertaken by Adele Scafuro.

2 Figures in this column are based upon Lambert, 2018: 62–4. I have removed laws from Lambert's figures (which originally included both laws and decrees). Excluded also are *dubia et incerta* (*IG* II³ 1 531–72).

3 A minimal figure which excludes those fragments such as those dated by *IG* II² to the period 400–350 (e.g. *IG* II² 87–94) or 400–300 (e.g. *IG* II² 608–11, 629–39) the content of which is so fragmentary as to make their identification as decrees uncertain. The figures here do not include the fragments of the period before 352/1 published by Walbank, 2008 nos. 1–10. Once the new edition of decrees of the period 403/2–353/2 is published, the total figure, including fragmentary decrees, is likely to be higher. Indeed, a higher figure is suggested by Hansen, *The Athenian Assembly*, 110–11, stating the existence of 488 decrees preserved on stone for the period 403/2–322/1, of which he counted 100 as fragmentary. *IG* II² (published in 1913) counted 447 fragmentary and non-fragmentary decrees and laws for the whole period 403/2–322/1 (*IG* II² 1–447).

4 Of these honours for non-Athenians, 61 are proxeny and 9 are citizenship awards.

5 See Appendix 2. This figure consists of 29 citizenship awards, 5 proxeny awards, and a range of other awards (including *ateleia, isopoliteia*, protection and statues).

• Honours for Athenians	1 (0.5%)	29 (14.6%)[6]	31 (12.7%) (11; 20)
• Honours for a deity	0 (0%)	1 (0.5%)	0 (0%)
• Honours for a party whose ethnicity is not known	0 (0%)[7]	34 (17.1%)	1 (0.4%)
Alliances/treaties/war and peace	34 (18.7 %)	11 (5.3%)[8]	39 (15.9%) (19; 20)
Commands/ dispatches/ expeditions/ mobilisation	0 (0%)	3 (1.5%)[9]	35 (14.3%) (13; 22)
Religious regulations	4 (2.2%)	5 (2.5%)[10]	10 (4.1%) (1; 9)
Other domestic arrangements (incl. appointments, constitutional, evacuations, financial, legislative, procedural, regulations)	3 (1.6%)	0 (0%)[11]	51 (20.8%) (31; 20)
Other foreign policy	15[12] (8.2%)	2 (1%)	22 (9.0%) (1; 21)

Fifth-century figures: see Sickinger 1999b and Lambert 2017: 5 note 5: 'Of the ca. 240 total of inscribed decrees from before 403/2 (i.e. the ca. 230 dating to after 454 and the handful inscribed before that), ca. 68 award honours, almost all to foreigners (28%), ca. 54 are treaties or otherwise relate to foreign affairs (23%), ca. 46 are religious measures (19%), ca. 9 are on other topics (4%), ca. 63 are too fragmentary for their subject matter to be determinable (26%).'

The comparison between the literary and epigraphical record for decrees based on this table is discussed in Chapter 3.4 below.

6 This figure includes two decrees of the Athenian *boule*, *IG* II² 1155 lines 1–6 and 1156 lines 36–44.
7 Unidentified honours for the period 403/2–353/2 are assumed to have been honours for non-Athenians.
8 This figure excludes regulations concerning overseas relations: see note 9 below.
9 *G* II³ 1 370 (on the expedition to the Adriatic), 399 (forbidding attack on Eretria), 433 (agreement with Sokles).
10 This figure includes *IG* II³ 1 447 (containing both a law and a decree) but excludes the fragmentary *IG* II³ 1 487, which may perhaps be a lease.
11 The figures in this row do not include inscribed laws.
12 This figure includes some decrees which appear to concern foreign policy but whose precise content is indecipherable.

1

The Social Capital of the Decree

1.1 An Introduction to the Political Faces of the Decree

The ancient Greek word ψήφισμα means, literally, 'a thing voted by ballot'. At the Athenian assembly, *cheirotonia* (the raising of hands) was the usual procedure for voting on proposals (Dem. 20.3) and for candidates in elections (Dem. 4.26); raised hands were counted or estimated by the presiding magistrates known as the *proedroi*.[1] However, it is striking that, in the literary and epigraphical sources, language is sometimes at odds with procedure: whereas, for the most part, the sources refer to *cheirotonia* for the election of officials (Aeschin. 3.13),[2] they use the term *psephisma* (and the verb ψηφίζομαι, 'I cast a ballot') for the voting of decrees.[3] In the classical period, therefore, the term *psephisma* was used in the texts of Athenian inscriptions,[4] the works of historians, the Attic orators and Atthidographers to refer to a decision in the form of a decree, decided by popular vote (see LSJ, s. v. 'ψήφισμα'). Later writers, including lexicographers and commentators on classical texts used the term in the same way.

This study is concerned primarily with decrees enacted by the *demos* at the Athenian assembly. At Athens the Council of 500 made *psephismata* of its own, but their scope was restricted usually to adjusting or re-instituting decisions made at the assembly.[5] Sub-*polis* units – principally, in fourth-century Athens, the demes and tribes – also made decrees, but these would have been decided

---

1 *Ath. Pol.* 44.3; Hansen 1987: 4–32; Hansen 1983: 103–21, 207–26.
2 On the election of magistrates, see [Arist.] *Ath. Pol.* 44.4, 54.3–5, 61.1 and, for its sociological consquences, Taylor 2007a: 323–5.
3 As Hansen (1983: 104 note 2) notes, the Athenians could refer to decisions made in the *ecclesia* interchangeably with the terms ψηφίζομαι and χειροτονέω: see Isoc. 8.52.
4 The word for 'decree' appears first in the form φσέφισμα in mid fifth-century inscriptions. Its earliest appearance in an Athenian inscription (albeit in a heavily restored context) is in the decree concerning cult at Sounion, *IG* I³ 8 (460–50) lines 12–13: ἀ[ναγράφσαντας δὲ τόδε τὸ φσέφ]ισμα ('w[riting up this dec]ree'); the first unrestored appearance is in a decree for the Milesians, *IG* I³ 21 (450/49) line 47: [ἐ]ν στέλει [κα]ὶ τοῖς φσεφίσμασ[ι] ('[o]n the stele [an]d in the decrees').
5 Decrees of the council: see Rhodes 1972: 82–8, 271–5. For examples of decrees of the council attested in literary texts, see Volume 1, Appendix 1. The council also played the role of creating the agenda of the assembly by the formulation of *probouleumata*: see Chapter 1.2 below.

SOCIAL CAPITAL OF THE DECREE

by, and binding primarily upon, members of their communities or those involved in their affairs.[6] While the council was normally involved in the prior discussion of the subject or even the formulation of the substance of the decree, the *demos* at the assembly was the principal body for the enactment of decrees in ancient Athens and in this way possessed powers (within the bounds of law) over matters on which decrees were concerned.[7]

Essential to understanding the political implications of the decree is the fact that whenever there was a consensus among the male citizens of Athens that it was necessary to do something (such as launching an expedition or sending ambassadors) or to initiate any process (legislative, honorific, or related to foreign policy),[8] the route to doing so was through consideration at the council and the proposal of a decree at the assembly.[9] The Athenians, therefore, regularly made decrees not so much out of self-conscious political ostentation but simply because this was how their decision-making process worked.[10] Accordingly, we might think of the decree as a straightforward institutional transaction, that is, a way of getting things done or responding to internal developments and external opportunities and threats. But decree-making involved the initiative of an individual proposer, debate and, ultimately, a vote. Accounts of the process of enactment, their substance and the implications of decrees were widely deployed in Attic oratory in the production of persuasive capital. These will form the subject of discussion in this chapter and Chapter 2 below.

It is reasonable to envisage the existence of two political faces to the decree. On the one hand, their substance – by which I refer to the honours they

---

6 Two well-preserved examples of deme decrees are RO 46 from Halai Aixonides (honouring a priest of Apollo Zoster) and RO 6 from Hagnous (concerned with the duties of the demarch and the lending of deme funds). For further examples of deme decrees, see Whitehead 1986: 374–93. A well-preserved example of a tribal decree is *Ag.* XVI 86 (the tribe of Aiantis honours its *thesmothetes*). For decrees of the tribes see Jones 1999: 178–94; RO 89 is a well-preserved *stele* containing honours for ephebes dedicated by the tribe Kekropis. For decrees of other associations, see Jones 1999: 221–67 and Arnaoutoglou 2003.

7 Decrees, however, were challenged by the process of *graphe paranomon* in the lawcourts which could lead to them being overruled: see Hansen 1974; for the debate about the location of sovereignty in Athens, see Hansen 2010 and Chapter 1.3 below.

8 For the view that debates generally led to consensus decisions among Athenians, see Canevaro 2018. For the initiation of law-making procedures by decree of the assembly, see Canevaro 2016b; certain judicial procedures, such as *apophasis* (see Carawan 1985) and impeachment (see Hansen 1975: 26; Hansen 1987: 188 note 749 and *Ath. Pol.* 43.4) were sometimes initiated at the assembly (but at other times at the council) by individual citizens and then voted on by the *demos* at the assembly. For the wider account of activities of the assembly, see *Ath. Pol.* 43.3–6; Hansen 1987: 94–124.

9 This is a point made by Develin 1989: 23.

10 Hansen (1987: 108) estimates that the Athenians *demos* passed some 300–400 decrees per annum in the period 403–322.

bestowed, the administrative measures they effected, or the diplomatic movements they entailed – was deeply political in the sense that decrees had great impact upon social and political interactions both within Athens and between the Athenians and other communities. On the other hand, the very act of proposing a decree – or recalling one as part of an argument – entails a political performance in its own right, and it is in this sense of symbolic political significance that the current chapter and Chapter 2 below are interested. Such a dual perspective on the decree – both as an institutional and as a symbolic transaction[11] – should not be regarded as contradictory; rather, the two are intertwined and mutually constitutive:[12] it is clear that in the second half of the fourth century, those engaged politically exploited both the institutional ability to propose and attack decrees, but also exhibited awareness of the persuasive significance of knowledge about past decrees. As we will see (Chapters 1.2.2, 1.4 and 2.3 below), given that they could be challenged at the assembly and in the courts, the status and authority of the decree was the scene of negotiation, and the instability of their authority made the decree quite a different rhetorical tool – in some ways more pliable – from knowledge of established law, the criticism of which was far harder to justify.

I shall analyse, over the course of Chapters 1 and 2 below, the deployment of knowledge of decrees in political activity in fourth-century Athens. My starting point in this chapter is to sketch the 'how' and 'why' factors which underscore the significance of the decree as a normative tool of conventional political activity in fourth-century Athens: they consist, first (Chapter 1.2.1 below), of the process of decree-making and the involvement of the Athenian council and the Athenian people; second (Chapter 1.2.2 below) the high, but rhetorically pliable, status and authority of decrees. I then discuss (Chapter 1.3 below) the notion that their proper enactment could be viewed as an expression of appropriate and constitutional behaviour. Their status and authority drove politicians to make use of a 'decree-minded' approach to oratory and politics, which will be explored in more detail in Chapter 2 below. Over the course of the rest of Chapter 1 I examine the deployment of decrees and knowledge about them in the fourth century, setting out the practical and symbolic factors that made

---

11 This distinction between 'institutional' and 'symbolic' transactions maps relatively neatly onto that drawn by some contemporary theorists of Historical Institutionalism between what they describe as the material aspects of institutions (which refer to structure and practices) and the symbolic aspects (which can break with context and take on different connotations); see Thornton, Ocasio and Lounsbury 2012: 11; March and Olsen 1989: 52. For discussion of other senses in which Historical Institutionalism is relevant to the interpretation of decrees, see the Introduction above.

12 Thornton, Ocasio and Lounsbury 2012: 10.

decrees important to the fourth-century Athenians (Chapter 1.4 below) and then exploring their role in evoking portrayals of harmony and crisis as a way of making assertions about the shared values of the people (Chapter 1.5 below). In Chapter 2 below I move on to the ways in which individual politicians made use of decrees in supporting their political interests. As we shall see, while decrees could sometimes be dismissed as the products of self-promoting politicians or the capricious *demos*, engagement with them appears to have become, particularly in the second half of the fourth century, an important instrument for those with political ambitions.

Any study of the decree as a political phenomenon in the history of fourth-century Athens must take on board both the literary and epigraphical datasets.[13] Notwithstanding this book's focus upon literary perspectives on decrees, it is appropriate to close this introductory section by giving a sense of the basic political perspectives that inscribed decrees offer.[14] As we will see, these texts offer insights into the complexity of attribution of responsibility for decrees. Texts of inscribed decrees of the fourth-century Athenians offer a view of them as simultaneously the proposals of individuals, as the decisions of the *demos*, and the product of co-operation between different political institutions; their formulaic presentation gives a view of the processes behind their enactment. In order to illustrate this, we shall look closely at an inscribed document which offers a detailed view of the decisions which led to its production. In 325/4, the Athenians decided to write up on a stone *stele* a dossier of decrees in honour of Herakleides of Salamis, a grain-dealer who had made donations to the people at a time of shortage (*IG* II³ 1 367 (= RO 95)). In this well-known dossier we encounter the proposal which appears to have initiated the process of making these awards:

> Telemachos son of Theangelos of Acharnai proposed (εἶπεν): it is to be decreed by the People (ἐψηφίσθαι τῶι δήμωι): that the Council shall formulate and bring forward to the next Assembly a proposal (τὴν βουλὴν προβουλεύσασαν ἐξενεγκεῖν εἰς τὴν πρώτην ἐκκλησίαν) about Herakleides, for him to obtain whatever benefit he can from the Athenian People. (*IG* II³ 1 367 lines 47–51; translation *AIO*)

According to this passage, Telemachos of Acharnai proposed at the assembly that the Council should make a *probouleuma* which would enable the people to discuss and vote on a proposal of honours for Herakleides; this proposal

---

13 For an epigraphically-informed approach to the Athenian decrees of the period 352/1–322/1, see Lambert 2018.

14 For discussion of the epigraphical publication of decrees, see Chapter 3.3.1–3.3.3 below.

led to the recommendation of his fellow demesman (and likely political collaborator) Kephisodotos at the Council (lines 52–66) that Herakleides be honoured by the *demos*; it was put forward at the assembly by the same Telemachos and the honours were enacted by decree (*IG* II³ 1 367 lines 29–35) in 329/8. The decree added that an envoy was to travel to Herakleia Pontika to request the return of sails that had allegedly been stolen from him by the Herakleots (lines 36–46).

This account gives a public-facing explanation of the decree (to make a return for Herakleides' zealous generosity to the Athenians) and a motivation of the Athenians' enactment of the decree, 'that others may also show love of honour (ὅπως ἂν καὶ οἱ ἄλλοι φιλοτιμῶνται) knowing that the Council honours and crowns those who show love of honour' (lines 64–6). Its details establish also the institutional legitimacy of the decree, showing (to a relatively high level of detail) that it had been approved by both the council and assembly and brought forward by both Telemachos in the assembly and Kephisodotos at the council,[15] apparently in co-operation.[16] It might be viewed as a monument both to Herakleides' character and at the same time the recognition of this by the decree's advocates and the Athenian *demos*;[17] it demonstrates the interaction of the council and assembly in the production of a decree. But while such texts offer us details on the formalities of proposal and enactment and the motivation of honorific reward, they tend to obscure any political backstory to the decree:[18] they represent them as proposals of individuals approved by the collective decision of the people.[19] We are offered no indication of the debate that may have taken place about the award at the assembly or council, nor whether the decision made was unanimous, or carried by a substantial or narrow

---

15 For the role of accounts of appropriate political processes in ensuring legitimacy of political decisions, see March and Olsen 1989: 50.
16 On their co-operation of these two individuals, see Lambert 2018: 178–9. Another example of collaboration is that where Athenodoros made a proposal concerning sacrifices on the basis of advice of Euthydemos, the priest of Asklepios: *IG* II² 47.
17 This is the view of Low 2016: 161–2.
18 For further discussion of this view, see R.G. Osborne 1999. See also Low 2016 on the reticence of inscribed decrees of the fourth century about the details of honorands' euergetic behaviour.
19 Luraghi's view of documentary inscriptions is that 'they expressed the collective will of the political community in a more direct way than any other text that has been preserved from ancient Greece': Luraghi 2010: 248. Low (2016) suggests that the fact that honorific decrees preserved on stone before the 320s rarely give detailed insight into the actions of honorands reflects the control of the *polis* over which aspects of euergetic behaviour were recorded. Low (forthcoming) emphasises the dynamic aspect of inscribed decrees, demonstrating that whereas they represented a collective memory of a decision of the *demos*, they offered the potential to represent the interests of specific individuals or groups other than the *demos*.

majority.[20] Athenian decrees on stone, therefore, present the decision-making process as one which follows particular procedures; its chief aspects consisted of the proposal of an individual, and ratification at the assembly of a decree on a subject that had been placed on its agenda by the council.[21] The name of the proposer at the assembly appears always to have been inscribed on stone versions of a decree even if it was one that had originally been formulated in the council: liability for the outcome of the decree, in this sense, was placed at the feet of its advocate at the assembly rather than the council.[22] Moreover, Athenian inscribed decrees sometimes recorded the name of the councillor formulating the *probouleuma* (*IG* II³ 1 367 lines 52–66) and regularly contain the names of the *proedroi* putting the matter to the vote (*IG* II³ 1 337 (= RO 91) lines 4–6, 28–30; *IG* II³ 1 349 lines 7–8), suggesting that these individuals bear some responsibility for the decree, alongside the proposer at the assembly, on the grounds of their contribution to the formulation and enactment of it. Inscribed versions of decrees, therefore, reflect a balance between individual initiative and popular decision, and the question of liability or political responsibility becomes one open to debate.

On the other hand, as we shall see over the course of this chapter and Chapter 2 below, literary accounts of decrees, considered within their wider narrative and persuasive contexts, tell stories about the political intentions of their proposers, as well as using them to offer perspectives on the policy or even the mentality of the Athenian people. Approaching decrees both as institutional and symbolic transactions (as already noted, this is a distinction drawn from the language of New Institutionalism: see note 11 above), in these chapters I explore the dynamics of the decree as an instrument of conventional political activity and shall attempt to explain the preponderance of the decree in the political life and discourse of the fourth century as well as its implications. One essential ingredient which made the decree politically and rhetorically

---

20 Voting figures are never recorded in Athenian decrees on stone; for discussion of the phenomenon across the Greek world, see Todd 2012. For the argument that most decrees were carried by consensus decisions, see Canevaro 2018, a perspective which makes Athenian democracy appear to behave like a 'unity' rather than 'adversary' democracy (for this distinction see Mansbridge 1983).

21 For an account of the procedure of decree-making, see Chapter 1.2.1 below and, in more detail, Rhodes 1972: 52–81; Hansen 1987: 41–4; and M.J. Osborne 2012.

22 This is an observation I owe to Stephen Todd. On 'probouleumatic' decrees, see Chapter 1.2.1 below. As Rhodes (1972: 71) observes, amendments to decrees might be referred to either – if they made a change to a motion contained within a *probouleuma* – by reference to the council ('τὰ μὲν ἄλλα καθάπερ τῆι βουλῆι': 'in other respects in accordance with the council') or – if they made a change to a non-probouleumatic motion – by reference to a named proposer ('τὰ μὲν ἄλλα καθάπερ ὁ δεῖνα': 'in other respects in accordance with [name of proposer]').

significant was its authoritative status as the consummation of the decision of the Athenian people undertaken by way of a process that followed institutionally-accepted norms (Chapter 1.2 below).

1.2 Decrees: Process, Status, Authority

1.2.1 Process

At the time when popular government was restored during the archonship of Eukleides (403/2), a legislative distinction appears to have been introduced between law (*nomos*) and decree (*psephisma*).[23] From this point, the process of introducing new laws was undertaken by a process of *nomothesia*,[24] but decrees were enacted in a procedure – as we saw in the case of the decree for

---

23 The precise point at which the distinction was introduced is not known, but for Athenian legislative reform (initiated by decree) in that year, see DD 7, 8 below. For the distinction at Athens, see Hansen 1983: 161–76; Ostwald 1986: 523; Todd 1996: 127–9. As Harris 2013a: 163–5 observes, while there was no formal distinction between laws and decrees in the fifth century, few inscribed decrees actually exhibit the characteristic of laws (that is, general rules, applying to large groups of people). Interchangeability between the terms *nomos* and *psephisma* might be observed in the fifth century, see Hansen 1983: 162; note also Ar. *Birds*, 1037–8; *Acharnians*, 532; Thuc. 3.37.3, where Kleon contends that the laws should not be altered in the debate about a decree. But even in fifth-century texts we might observe a hierachical relationship between the two. This might be seen, as Canevaro (2016b: section 3) points out, in the inclusion, in the chorus' account in Aristophanes' *Thesmophoriazusai* (lines 352–71), of impious women, of those who try to make changes to *psephismata* and *nomos*: 'the use of the singular *nomos* opposed to the plural *psephismata* seems to imply some sort of hierarchy between the sphere of the law and as a unified and coherent one, and the individual engagements of the assembly'. For discussion of Aristophanes' parody of decrees (and their relationship to *nomos*), see Chapter 5.5 below.
For the view that the distinction between laws and decrees is relevant also to the enactments of Athenian associations, see Arnaoutoglou 2003: 128–9. For the distinction outside Athens, see Rhodes with Lewis 1997: 498–9. Hansen 1983: 162 note 3 offers reference to older bibliography which maintained that the Athenians frequently disregarded the distinction, e.g. Quass 1971: 71.
24 For a reconstruction, drawing primarily upon Dem. 20.24 and Aeschin. 3.38-40, of the procedure of *nomothesia* (law-making), see Canevaro 2016b (with summary at Harris 2016a: 74–6) and Canevaro and Esu forthcoming: after a preliminary decree was made at the assembly enabling consideration of new laws, proposals were published at the *eponymoi* and were read aloud in three consecutive meetings of the assembly; *nomothetai* were appointed by the assembly; contradictory laws were repealed by a court. Inexpedient laws were subject to being overturned by the procedure of *graphe nomon me epitedeion theinai*. For perspectives on the board of the *nomothetai*, see Rhodes 1984, 2003a; Hansen 1985. For the suggestion that the appointment of *nomothetai* to regulate the constitution was made necessary by the fact that many fifth-century *psephismata* must have 'encroached on the stipulations of the Solonian code', see Ostwald 1986: 410; for *nomothesia* as a special session of the assembly, see Canevaro and Esu forthcoming.

Herakleides (Chapter 1.1 above) – involving the assembly and the council of 500. It is generally accepted that for a decree to be considered legal, its subject or substance had to be put on the agenda of the assembly by the council; otherwise it was liable to the charge of being *aprobouleuton*.[25] The substance of particular decrees was, however, not always discussed in detail at meetings of the council. What appears to have been a new distinction between law and the decree (see Chapter 1.2.2 below) in 403/2 has generally been seen as having the effect of limiting the power of the *demos* at the assembly, but it has been proposed that the change had the effect also of strengthening democracy by ensuring the stability and scrutiny of law.[26] The power of the people to make decrees (within the bounds of law) appears to have continued unchanged.

References to, but not complete accounts of, the process of fourth-century Athenian decree-making survive in passages of Attic oratory and in the formulae of inscribed decrees; the processes have been reconstructed in the work of Rhodes and Hansen; a balanced assessment of the decree-making process underlines the interaction of the council and the assembly in the enactment of decrees.[27] The formal process of decree-making appears to have been initiated usually at the *bouleuterion* where members of the council discussed proposals put to them by the assembly (as they did in the example of Herakleides' honours *IG* II³ 1 367 discussed at 1.1 above) or by members of the council (Dem. 19.185): these discussions resulted sometimes in the passing of an 'open' recommendation, inviting the assembly to make a decision on a related subject as it agreed

---

25 Rhodes 1972: 53, 62; [Arist.] *Ath. Pol.* 45.4 (cf. Dem. 19.185) says that the *demos* was not permitted to vote on matters that had not been previously discussed by the council; the author states that anyone who proposed an *aprobouleuton* decree was liable (*enochos*) to prosecution for illegality (*graphe paranomon*). Harpokration, s.v. 'ἀπροβούλευτον'. However, we should note also the claim evidently made by the opponent of Demosthenes in Dem. 22 that an assembly could propose honours for outgoing *bouleutai* (on the grounds of a law that the assembly could grant it if the council appeared to deserve it) even if this had not been discussed by the council (Dem. 22.5). For discussion see Commentary on D89 below and Liddel forthcoming.

26 Aeschines (3.6–7, 233) saw the rule of law as a bulwark of democracy. For the view that the reform had the effect of reducing the power of the *demos* and ensuring stability, see Ostwald 1986: 524; for the suggestion that it made Athens less democratic, see Todd 1990b: 170; for the proposal that it strengthened democracy, see Rhodes 2010: 68; for the idea that it ensured stability of the laws, see Canevaro 2011, arguing on the grounds that the constitution could no longer be overthrown by a simple vote of the assembly, as happened in 411 ([Arist.] *Ath. Pol.* 29.2–3; Thuc. 8.67.1).

27 Rhodes 1972, 52–81; cf. Hansen 1987, 41–4. De Laix 1973 emphasises the importance of *probouleusis* and the influence of the council on the nature and substance of Athenian decrees. For a view of 'divided power' at Athens which emphasises the interaction between the council and the assembly in the production of decrees at Athens, exploring its implications for the meaning of 'sovereignty' at Athens, see Esu 2018.

was appropriate or requiring it to listen to the appeal of a named individual;[28] alternatively, the council could make a specific recommendation (*probouleuma*) on the wording of a decree, upon which the assembly would vote.[29] Rhodes' designation of this distinction as one between non-probouleumatic and probouleumatic decrees (marked by distinct epigraphical formulae) has rightly gained widespread acceptance among modern scholars; in the ancient sources, however, there is no indication of any hierarchy in the relationship of the two types in terms of their authority and status.[30]

The communication of the agenda and proposals from the council to the assembly was the responsibility of individual office-holders: the *prytaneis* (the tribal contingent of 50 members of the council who were in effect a standing committee for one tenth of the year)[31] were expected to ensure that the Council's specific recommendations were communicated – sometimes in the form of a written draft (Aeschin. 2.68; Xen. *Hell.* 1.7.34)[32] – to the *proedroi* (who, from early on in the fourth century, acted as the presiding magistrates of the assembly)[33] so that they would appear on the agenda of the assembly ([Arist.] *Ath. Pol.* 44.2; *IG* II³ 1 476 line 18); accordingly, the relevant *probouleumata* were then presented to the assembly (see, for example, *IG* II³ 1 325 lines 10–11).[34] When

28 See for instance Dem. 24.11–14 (= D92); Dem. 18.169–74; Rhodes 1972: 58–9. The brief formula of Lycurgus' decree honouring Eudemos of Plataea of 330/29 (*IG* II³ 1 352 = RO 94) suggests that it was a non-probouleumatic decree (in other words did not enact directly what was put to the assembly in a *probouleuma*); the content of the subject of the original *probouleuma* which presumably gave rise to its proposal is, however, not known. An example of a decree which was enacted by the people in response to an open *probouleuma* of known content is Lycurgus' decree allowing the Kitians to acquire land for a sanctuary of Aphrodite: *IG* II³ 1 337 = RO 91.

29 Rhodes with Lewis 1997: 13; Rhodes 1972: 52–81; Rhodes 1981: 543–4. For example of specific recommendations accepted by the assembly (in other words, probouleumatic decrees), see Aeschin. 3.125–7 (= D161) with Rhodes 1972: 60 note 1; *IG* II² 96 = RO 24.

30 For the distinction, see Rhodes 1972: 68; for the formulae of 'probouleumatic' and 'non-probouleumatic' decrees, see Rhodes 1972: 246–66. Lambert (2018: 227–71) shows that for the period 352/1–322/1, the majority of epigraphically attested decrees were non-probouleumatic, which 'confirms the liveliness of the Assembly in late classical Athens as a forum for decision-making' (Lambert 2018: 254). Literary attestations of decrees do not offer the level of detail which would allow for either modification or confirmation of this view.

31 Rhodes 1972: 16–25; Hansen 1987: 35–7.

32 Sickinger 2002 offers a balanced assessment of the degree to which legislative proceedings made use of written documents, acknowledging the 'oral nature of legislative proceedings' (Sickinger 2002: 150; cf. *Ath. Pol.* 54.5) while recognising that 'the seemingly oral environment of the Assembly thus actually revolved around written texts, and new legislation often had a written origin' (2002: 153).

33 Rhodes 1972: 26.

34 The agenda was publically displayed in advance of meetings of the assembly and council, but it is not clear that texts of proposals were (*Ath. Pol.* 43.3–4 with Sickinger 2002: 150). Proposed laws were set out for public display (Dem. 20.93–4).

the assembly received the proposal of the council, it is likely that a preliminary vote (*procheirotonia*) was held to decide whether the *probouleuma* would be scrutinised by the assembly or whether the council's recommendation sufficed and could be accepted without debate (Harpokration, s.v. 'προχειροτονία'; cf. Aeschin. 1.23; Dem. 24.11 = D92 T1).[35] Over the course of deliberation at the assembly, citizens could accept, amend,[36] reject, or propose alternatives to *probouleumata*, though in the case of an open recommendation, individual citizens were free to make positive proposals in response to it.[37] If different proposals were made in response to a *probouleuma*, it is likely that the *proedroi* would have to decide which were to be put to the vote. At this point there was opportunity for debate at the assembly by supporters and opponents of the proposal (Dem. 19.185–6).[38] It appears that the actual content of the text could be finalised either by the proposer himself (on one occasion referred to as the 'draughtsman' [ὁ γράφων] of a decree: Dem 23.70) alone or in association with a secretary.[39] After discussion, the *proedroi* would put the matter to vote (Aeschin. 2.67–8; *IG* II³ 1 324 lines 6–7),[40] and the assembly accepted or rejected the decree as it saw fit.[41] Aeschines' account of Aleximachos' proposal that Kersobleptes might partake in the oaths of the Peace of Philokrates, while it emphasises the obstructive behaviour of Demosthenes, offers a view of the political process that went on over the course of a discussion of a proposal made at the assembly:

> At that assembly, Kritoboulos the Lampsakene, on coming forward, said that Kersobleptes had sent him, asking that he be able to give his oaths to the ambassadors of Philip, and requesting that Kersobleptes be enrolled alongside your

---

35 Hansen 1983: 123–30 takes the view that the *procheirotonia* addressed the question of whether to accept the council's proposal without discussion or to debate on specific recommendations, but for doubt on this matter, see Osborne 2012: 39–40.

36 For an example of a decree where the assembly appears to have amended the motion put to it in a *probouleuma*, see Xen. *Hell.* 7.1.1 = D56; *IG* II² 112 = RO 41 and *IG* II² 212 = RO 64 with Rhodes 1972: 60, 73–4.

37 Hansen 1987: 38–9, 88–93.

38 Cammack 2013 suggests an absence of debate at the assembly, but the likelihood of this is challenged in the papers of Rhodes 2016a and Canevaro 2018. The likelihood that there was substantive discussion of, and debate about, decrees at the assembly is suggested also by the existence of riders added to decrees (see Rhodes 1972: 278–9; Lambert 2018: 249–52). Moreover, the existence of disagreement at the assembly is suggested also by the fact that on one occasion, the Athenians offered a solution to it by proposing alternative courses of action, the choice of which was delegated to the Delphic oracle: see *IG* II³ 1 292 lines 25–30.

39 For the view that a secretary was responsible for the drafting the copy that would be inscribed or deposited in the archive, see Dover 1980; cf. Osborne 2012: 41–2.

40 Hansen 1987: 41–2.

41 Rhodes with Lewis 1997: 13; Rhodes 1972: 52–81; Rhodes 1981: 543-4.

allies. When these words were spoken, Aleximachos of Pelekes gave to the *proedroi* to read a decree (Ἀλεξίμαχος ὁ Πήληξ δίδωσιν ἀναγνῶναι ψήφισμα τοῖς προέδροις) in which it was written that the one coming from Kersobleptes should give oaths to Philip with the other allies. When the decree was read out, and I believe that you all remember this, Demosthenes stood up from among the proedroi and refused to put the decree to vote (οὐκ ἔφη τὸ ψήφισμα ἐπιψηφιεῖν), saying that he would not undo the peace with Philip, and that he did not recognise as allies those who joined only just at the moment that the libations for the sacred matters were being poured; for this opportunity had been presented at a previous assembly. When you gave a shout and ordered the *proedroi* to the platform, the motion was put to the vote forcibly (οὕτως ἄκοντος αὐτοῦ τὸ ψήφισμα ἐπεψηφίσθη). To show that I speak the truth, bring here the proposer of the decree Aleximachos (κάλει μοι τὸν γράψαντα τὸ ψήφισμα) and the fellow-*proedroi* with Demosthenes, and read the statement. (Aeschin. 2.83–5 = D132)

In this case, we can presume that Kritoboulos requested permission from the council to attend and make a request at the assembly; the council presumably discussed this and allowed him to do so; Aleximachos therefore, at the assembly, proposed a decree by handing a written version of it to the *proedroi*. Demosthenes attempted – unsuccessfully – to prevent the decree being put to the vote; the decree, however, appears to have been rejected on the basis of a vote. As well as enacting decrees, the assembly could also reject by vote or take no action about recommendations of the council; it may be the case that proposals could be blocked by *prytaneis* or *proedroi* who did not proceed with expected procedures.[42] After being put to the vote, a decree can be said to have been enacted only after a show of hands at the assembly had been judged by the *proedroi* to constitute a majority;[43] additionally, decrees granting citizenship had to be ratified by the casting of ballots.[44]

---

42 For the view that *proedroi* were entitled to refuse to put a proposal to the vote, see Hansen 1999: 39 with Aeschin. 2.84, but note the objection to this view by Ober 1996: 115–16..

43 Voting: [Arist.] *Ath. Pol.* 44.3 with Hansen 1983: 103–21. Todd 2012 accepts Hansen's contention that votes in the Athenian assembly were estimated rather than counted, but also adds an alternative explanation for the absence of voting figures on decrees: that 'the public recording of votes in the permanent medium of an inscription may be undesirable because it invites losers (particularly those who have lost narrowly) to revisit decisions that have been made' (Todd 2012: 39).
For the view that a proposal might be regarded as an enacted decree if an opponent had given an immediate formal undertaking to bring a *graphe paranomon* see Hansen 1974: 51–2, 1987: 94–107; Todd 1993: 159–60, 298–9.

44 This second vote of ratification was introduced in or shortly after 385/4: Osborne 1981–3 III–IV, 161–6 with RO 33 lines 34–6 and [Dem.] 59.89–90.

SOCIAL CAPITAL OF THE DECREE

The process of decree making, then, was one involving the contribution of the council, a debate and vote at the assembly, and the administrative support of magistrates in the communication of details; but individual initiative played also an important part. The fact that the Athenian institutions and individuals were obliged to undertake such processes in order to introduce their political decisions was the foundation not only of their authority and legitimacy but also of the rhetorical value deployed in the portrayal both of individual political behaviour and the activity of the Athenian *demos*.

1.2.2 Status and Authority

Having described the formal institutional foundations of the decree's authority, we turn to looking at its status in fourth-century Athens and in particular to consider its relationship to law. The first aspect to consider is that in addition to the procedural distinction between law and decree (see Chapter 1.2.1 above), there usually appears to have been a substantive difference: the view that in fourth-century Athens, laws usually referred to general, permanent rules, and decrees referred to short-term directives specific to individuals or situations – never comprehensively articulated in the ancient oratorical sources – has been worked out in most detail in the work of M.H. Hansen.[45] Decrees concerned the award of honours, all aspects of foreign affairs (the making of treaties, the dispatch of expeditions and ambassadors, declarations of war) and short-term issues concerning adjustments to cult, the administration of justice, constitutional procedure, and adjustments to financial management;[46] laws, on the other hand, concerned long-term arrangments concerning religious, general financial issues, constitutional matters, individual behaviour, rights, duties and affairs relating to the grain-supply.[47] *Ad hominem* laws were forbidden (And. 1.88–9 = D8 T1), but decrees could concern individuals (Dem. 8.29). Ancient philosophers reflected on the differences between the two: Plato offered the perspective that a *psephisma* was a political act (δόγμα πολιτικόν) of a fixed duration of time (*Definitions*, 415b11). In the *Nicomachean Ethics*, Aristotle advocated the view that *psephismata* were needed as rules about things about which it was not possible to lay down a universal statement that would be entailed by a law (Arist. *NE* 1137b13–4 and 27–32). Elsewhere, he asserted that

---

45 For the view that the distinction was adhered to with the exception of times of crisis, see Hansen 1983: 161–77 and 1987: 113. For the view that there was erosion of the distinction over the course of the fourth century, see Atkinson 2003. Canevaro 2011: 81 suggests that the distinction was still probably recognised even after the disappearance of *nomothesia* in 322.

46 For summary coverage of the scope of decrees, see Hansen 1987: 110–13.

47 Harris 2013a: 138–74.

the essence of the decree (τὰ ψηφισματώδη) is justice of a conventional but not natural sort (1134b24). What is perhaps striking here is that rather than asserting a straightforward hierarchical relationship between law and decree, Plato and Aristotle shared the view that decrees were less universal as ordinances than were laws. The fact that philosophers and other commentators had an interest in the distinction between law and decree is indicative of the wide impact and cultural resilience of an institutional distinction: [48] indeed, as Canevaro writes, the Athenian understanding of the distinction between law and decree 'must have taken roots in the institutional ideology of the Athenians well beyond its actual implementation'.[49]

Moreover, at Athens there appears to have been a formal subordination of decrees to laws: the orthodox view enunciated by the orators was that laws possessed more authority than decrees (κυριώτερον: And. 1.88–9 (= D8 T1);[50] Dem. 23.87, 218; 24.30; Hyp. *Ath.* 22),[51] and that the proposal of decrees should be carried out in accordance with them (Dem. 20.92; 22.43; 23.86)[52]. It is clear that in fourth-century Athens there were laws which regulated aspects of the honours granted by decrees as well as assembly activity.[53] Moreover, it is significant that, as Harris points out, decrees of the assembly were able to overturn decisions of the courts; but they could not over-ride laws.[54] Their relative authority meant that Andocides was ready to assume that his audience would accept the principle that, given that it was illegal to enforce a law that was not written down, it would also be illegal to enforce a decree that was not written down (And. 1.86).[55]

48 Writing in the second century AD, Aelius Aristides took the view that the greatest difference between law and decree is that 'the laws have discovered once and for all justice and have made this a universal order for all time, but decrees depend upon emergencies' (Aelius Aristides VI *The Opposite Argument* 9, trans. Behr 1981–6).

49 Canevaro 2011: 81.

50 Canevaro and Harris 2012: 116–19 show that the document at Andocides 1.87 is a forgery, reconstructed in all likelihood on the basis of the adjacent text of Andocides and other speeches.

51 Hypereides (*Ath.* 22) even claimed that this was a Solonian law. There is, however, no reason to believe that the process was introduced by Solon: see Hansen 1974: 61, and as Leão and Rhodes 2015: 164 point out the hierarchy could not have been enacted before the distinction between laws and decrees was made at the end of the fourth century.

52 The status of the document at Dem. 23.87 is discussed in the light of these passages by Canevaro 2013: 75–6.

53 Liddel forthcoming, citing *IG* I³ 131, [Dem.] 59.89–92 and other legislation on the award of honorific decrees and assembly activity.

54 Harris 2016a: 80–1.

55 Alternatively, as Stephen Todd points out to me, Andocides might have assumed that his audience would overlook a flaw in his logic: that it might not be necessary to have a decree – as a decision of temporary effect – written down.

SOCIAL CAPITAL OF THE DECREE

Aeschines articulated one strand of reasoning behind the hierarchy of laws and decrees, suggesting that decrees were inferior (καταδεέστερα) because whereas laws were enacted with a singular concern for justice, the assembly and courts were prone to be led astray by trickery and appeals to passion (Aeschin. 1.177–9); elsewhere he complained about illegal proposals and that those *proedroi* who agreed to put such motions to the vote held the position by deceit (Aeschin. 3.3–4); these complaints lead Hansen to suggest that Aeschines was implying that the *proedroi* – who would have passed judgement on the balance of votes – had been accepting bribes to skew the results of the vote.[56] In an important sense, Aeschines' perspectives on the problems with the decree represent a strand in the negative characterisation of the decree – as subject to the manipulations of unscrupulous orators at the assembly – that we encounter also in accounts of late fifth-century political activity.[57]

Accordingly, the existence of a hierarchical relationship between laws and decrees is undeniable,[58] and is underlined both by the fact that, with the exception of a number of forensic speeches (Dem.18, 20, 23) laws were cited with a higher frequency in Attic oratory than were decrees[59] and also in the nature of disputes about them in the courts. While it was acceptable to attack a recently proposed law on the grounds of it being inexpedient (*graphe nomon me epitedeion thenai*: e.g. Dem. 20), established laws and the normative aspects of law and law-making were on the whole not subject to extensive criticism.[60] One of the arguments put forward by Diodorus, in his attack on Timokrates' law about the liberty of state debtors, was that the regularity with which Athens' politicians were proposing laws was damaging to its tried and tested system of laws (Dem. 24.142–3): the idea was that politicians were abusing the system of law-making by using it for their own ends, but there was no criticism of the *established* laws *per se*. Praise of 'the laws' was widespread in Attic oratory: in the *Against Aristokrates*, Demosthenes, challenging Aristokrates' proposal that Charidemos be inviolable, praised the established laws and the supposed intentions of Draco the legislator (e.g. Dem. 23.22–87).

On the other hand, decrees were vulnerable to general attacks, and the speech *Against Aristokrates* is widely critical of honorific decrees passed by

---

56 Hansen 1983: 114.
57 On such literary perspectives, see Chapter 5.2.1 below.
58 Sealey takes the view that decrees offered a weaker norm which had to conform to the laws of Athens: Sealey 1987: 32–4; this is a view upheld by Canevaro 2016b and Gagarin 2011: 185.
59 Harris 2013a: 359-76. On the high profile of law in oratorical argumentation, see Carey 1996.
60 On Athenian legislative conservativism, see Boegehold 1996.

the Athenians.[61] The claim that a decree should be rescinded owing to the fact that it contradicted one or more laws – central to Demosthenes' speeches *Against Androtion* (Dem. 22.8) and *Against Aristokrates* (Dem. 23.18, 22–87) – was presumably widespread in speeches advocating *graphe paranomon* in fourth-century Athens.[62] Moreover, as Mader has pointed out, sections of Demosthenes' symbouleutic oratory are dedicated to criticising the Athenian *demos* for passing decrees upon which it would not act:[63] in the *Third Olynthiac*, for instance, Demosthenes gave an account of the people's decree of 352/1 for an expedition against Philip (Dem. 3.4 = D106) before going on to criticise them for failing to carry out the expedition (Dem. 3.5). What lies at the heart of this hierarchy is the expectation, enunciated by Aeschines (1.178), that whereas laws would be coherent and as unified as possible, aspiring to justice and the common good, the decisions of the assembly and courts were prone to the deceit of individual politicians (cf. Dem. 19.86 = D135; [Dem.] 59.91 = D109).[64] Moreover, the fact that, as Lycurgus observed (1.7), the scope of decrees was rather limited (to trifling issues, concerned with a moment of time), meant that they were treated as lower down in the hierarchy of authority. However, as we will see shortly (Chapter 1.5.3 below), the view that historic decrees might have timeless application rather contradicts this view of decrees as transactions with only ephemeral relevance.

The manifestation of this hierarchy in the rhetorical strategies of ancient orators is reflected in the trajectories of modern scholarly analysis of ancient lawcourt rhetoric. There has been much recent scholarly discussion of the significance of laws (*nomoi*) as rhetorical devices and as evidence in debates about both legal and non-legal matters; while there is debate about the extent to which laws were treated by orators as binding or just persuasive, it is clear that they were cited in a range of contexts: as a basis for legal claims, in the interpretation

---

61 For attacks on Athenian decrees, see Liddel 2016.
62 Sundahl 2003: 140–2. As Sundahl 2003 notes, however, contradictions between decrees and laws became an issue only when they were raised by a proposer: this was hardly a strong form of protection for laws.
63 Mader 2006. For examples of this criticism, see [Dem.] 50.3-7 (= D67); Dem. 3.4 (= D106); Dem. 13.32 (= DD 111, 112); see discussion in Chapter 2.5.2 below. For other criticisms of the Athenian *demos*, see Harris 2006c.
64 For the theme that the demos at the assembly was prone to be misled by demagogues, see Hesk 2000; Ober 1989: 168–9; Kremmydas 2012: 184–5; Canevaro 2016a: 189, pointing also to the theme in Dem. 8.63, 15.16, 19.29–30, 23.96–7; Aeschin. 1.178, 3.35.

of justice, and to construct assertions about character.[65] Interpreting law was not always a straightforward task: as Harris points out, orators sometimes develop novel interpretations of laws for persuasive purposes, though more often juries opted for traditional ones.[66] Law (*nomos*) was undoubtedly enshrined in a respected position, and the attribution of large amounts of particular legislation to law-givers, most prominently Draco and Solon, certainly heightened that esteemed position.[67] Yet the rhetorical significance of the decree, however, has received much less attention in modern scholarship.[68]

There are several reasons, however, not to dismiss decrees as insignificant instrument in political persuasion. The frequency of their occurrence in the literary and epigraphic texts suggests that the fourth-century Athenians made decrees more prolifically (Hansen estimates that some 30,000 decrees of the assembly were passed in the period 403/2–322/1)[69] than they did laws.[70] This meant that there was a bigger selection of contemporary material – enacted

---

65 Compare the perspectives of Harris, emphasising the rule of law (e.g. Harris 1994, 2006b, 2013a) with that of Lanni, arguing that law encouraged rather than coerced compliance (Lanni 2016). For a view of an ideology of rule of law as an aspect of wider democratic discourses and as a way of resolving feuds, see Cohen 1995. Todd (1990a, 1993) and Carey (1996) emphasise the rhetorical potential of laws as evidence. For a review of the different assessments of the rhetorical power of law in Attic oratory, see De Brauw 2001–2: 161–2, demonstrating the ways in which the evidence of law was deployed in the portrayal of character. On the use of laws in speeches and for a broad view of relevance among the Athenians, see Lanni 2006: 64–70. For a list of laws cited by the Attic orators, see Harris 2013a: 359–78. A wide-ranging and balanced discussion of the ways in which the laws were deployed in the courts, with discussion of recent bibliography, is provided by Sickinger 2007.
66 See Harris 2000b, writing of the 'open texture' of Athenian law, and arguing that juries generally opted for traditional interpretations of laws rather than novel ones. For the possibility of non-literal interpretations, see Aviles 2011. Christ 1998: 193–224 emphasises the potential for distortions and manipulation of the law in the courts and the extent to which jurors developed a sense of fairness.
67 Cf. Hansen 1990; Thomas 1994. Many of these claims are clearly anachronistic, such as Solon's association with a *graphe paranomon* at Dem. 24.212 or the misattribution of detailed rules about *nomothesia* to Solon at Dem. 20.90: see Leão and Rhodes 2015: 151–96.
68 For an excellent discussion of the importance of the decree in the rhetoric of conspiracy, see Roisman, 2006: 95–117.
69 Hansen 1987: 108.
70 For the numbers of preserved decrees, see Table 1. For the nine extant inscribed laws of the fourth century, see Stroud 1998: 15–16 (note now the publication of the law concerning repair work on the sanctuary of Artemis at Brauron: *SEG* LII 104); for laws proposed in the period 403/2–322/1, see Volume 1, Inventory B6.1. Lambert 2012a: 59 suggests three possible reasons for the relative scarcity of inscribed laws: there were fewer of them; they may have been inscribed at locations other than the acropolis (and so fewer have been discovered); they were published on non-permanent media; Lambert 2018: 61–2 adds the suggestion that a further factor was that the Metroon by the fourth century had become the place to host physical copies of the laws and there was felt no need to inscribe them.

within living memory – for orators to draw upon in the formulation of arguments. The status of the decree in the lawcourts is indicated by the fact that all Athenian jurors swore to observe both laws and decrees and to judge in accordance with them; orators frequently reminded the jurors of the duty to adhere to them and to vote according to their provisions (Hyp. *Dem*. Fr. 1 col. 1, Din. 1.84; Dem. 19.179; Dem. 24.149 [document]).[71] The pairing of 'laws and decrees' as terms of authoritative reference in these passages reminds us that one of the shared ideals that emerges in Athenian discussion of legislation is that the two institutions were conceived not normally as at odds but rather to complement each other.

The deployment of decrees in the courts was, as we will see, widespread and provides the clearest impression of their importance to political life and litigation. Litigants in the courts insisted, where it suited them, on the importance of imposing both laws and decrees in an appropriate fashion (see Dem. 47.19–20 = D85; see further Chapter 2.2.2.2 below). Decrees were cited also for their persuasive value; indeed, the conventional hierarchy of legislation was undermined when it was rhetorically necessary or convenient for litigants to do so, especially in challenges brought against laws: Demosthenes, arguing that Leptines' law on *ateleia* annulled the favour set in store for the Athenians by their honorary decrees, claimed that some of their laws were no different from, and no newer than, many of their decrees (Dem. 20.92).[72] The law was said to lead to an excess of wickedness (*kakia*) and contradicts the treaties (*sunthekai*) implied by the proviliges granted to Leukon (Dem. 20.36–7). Demosthenes' statements should be appreciated within their rhetorical context: they were designed to underline his argument that Leptines' law subverted the salutary impact of Athenian honorific decrees. It must be considered as an aspect of his wider rhetorical view that the passing of honorific decrees supported the interests of the Athenian community by encouraging euergetic behaviour.[73] It is clear that, when it was rhetorically useful to do so, it was publicly acceptable to emphasise the importance of the decree: in the case

---

71 For a list of references to the oath, see Harris 2013a: 353. For discussion of its application, see Harris 2013: 101–37; on its content, see Canevaro 2013: 175–80, suggesting that the document of the oath at 24.149 is a reconstruction or forgery. For discussion of the pledge to vote in accordance with the laws and decrees of the Athenians, see Harris 2006a: 159.

72 Dem. 20.92: 'ψηφισμάτων δ' οὐδ' ὁτιοῦν διαφέρουσιν οἱ νόμοι, ἀλλὰ νεώτεροι οἱ νόμοι, καθ' οὓς τὰ ψηφίσματα δεῖ γράφεσθαι, τῶν ψηφισμάτων αὐτῶν ὑμῖν εἰσίν'. Isocrates claimed that the laws were full of confusion and contradiction: Isoc. 12 *Panath.* 144, though the display-oratory context of this speech means that it was possible for the author to say things that a democratic audience might have found objectionable.

73 See Chapter 2.5.1 below; Liddel 2016.

SOCIAL CAPITAL OF THE DECREE

against Leptines' law abolishing honorific exemption, Demosthenes amassed the evidence of decrees to make a case against his legislation (see Chapter 2.4.1 below). Later in the fourth century, Lycurgus' decision (Lycurg. 1.127; see D19 Commentary) to cite the late fifth-century decree of Demophantos rather than the contemporary law of Eukrates (*IG* II³ 1 320 = RO 79) as a paradigm of how the Athenians treat traitors suggests that decrees could attract as much persuasive capital as laws.

The physical investment on decrees that the Athenians of the fourth century undertook also is indicative of their high status.[74] It is clear that while the Athenians did not attempt to inscribe on stone every single decree that was passed by the assembly,[75] the large numbers of stone inscriptions that survive indicate that the Athenians frequently did so:[76] this would have incurred substantial costs, with the price of inscribing such decrees in the fourth century regularly being 20 or 30 *drachmai*, a sum which may have included the cost of supplying and preparing the stone.[77] By the 360s money for inscribing costs was regularly drawn from a special fund for expenses incurred by the provisions of decrees (not just those pertaining to publication) known as τὰ κατὰ ψηφίσματα ἀναλισκόμενα τῶι δήμωι ('the monies expended by the people in accordance with decrees').[78] Athenian investment in decrees is shown also by the fact that in the fourth century the Athenians charged particular magistrates with the management of them. From the 340s onwards,[79] there is evidence for a secretary deemed to have responsibility for decrees

---

74 For the importance of inscribed decrees in terms of religiosity, dissemination of messages, and imperial ambition, see Lambert 2018: 19–46.

75 See discussion in Chapter 3.3 below; Lambert 2018: 47–68; *pace* Osborne 2012, who argues, unconvincingly, against the orthodoxy that only a minority of decrees were published on stone: see especially Osborne, 2012, 33–4 note 2.

76 For the period 352/1–322/1, some 280 inscribed decrees survive in some form of preservation: see *IG* II³ 1 292–572 and Table 1.

77 For occasional larger sums, see Osborne 2012: 50 note 99. For the cost of inscribing, see Loomis 1998: 121–65. For discussion of other costs, including that of the stone and its transportation, see MacLean 2002: 13–14. For the view that the costs even of reliefs on inscribed decrees were covered by the issuing body that passed them, see Deene 2016; for the Athenians charging allies for the inscription of decrees, see Low 2005: 100–1.

78 First attested in 367/6: RO 35 with commentary at p. 173; *IG* II³ 1 327 lines 15–18; 453 lines 35–41. See also, for payment out 'of the amount set aside according to decree' ('τῶν κατὰ ψηφίσματα μεριζομένων'), see *IG* II³ 1 298 lines 41–2; 355 lines 50–2; 411 lines 26–7. For discussion see Rhodes 2013: 216–17, with reference to the debate about the sources of payment expenditure for Athenian decrees at 216 note 88; cf. Osborne 2012: 50.

79 Develin 1989: 21.

(γραμματεύς ... ἐπὶ τὰ ψηφίσματα: *IG* II³ 1 306 C lines 34–7).[80] Moreover, there was a prytany secretary who, according to the author of the *Ath. Pol.*, had the duty of ensuring that an official text of a new decree was recorded ([Arist.] *Ath. Pol.* 54.3), and – on occasions when epigraphical publication was decided – was charged with arranging for its publication on stone (e.g. *IG* II³ 1 473 lines 13–14), and with abolishing inscribed texts which contradicted laws (RO 25 lines 55–6). From 363/2 the prytany secretary held the office for a year, rather than a prytany, at a time, which suggests that the growing amount of detail required more expertise than would be garnered in little more than a month (Rhodes 1972: 135–8); we should not think of a professional requirement, given that, as the author of the *Ath. Pol.* (54.3) states, this officer was at his time appointed by sortition, though he had previously been appointed by lot. In the later fourth century an *anagrapheus* (recorder) appears also to have been responsible for the recording of state documents, which probably included papyrus documents in the archive (see *IG* II³ 1 469 lines 13–15). It is likely that public employees (*demosioi*) were responsible for the physical incising of the texts on stone slabs.[81]

Having established the scope and limitations of the institutional authority of the decree and its status among fourth-century Athenians, we turn to perceptions of the decree that are suggested by the treatment of them in contemporary literature. The perceived association between good forms of decree-making and the right way of doing democratic politics (Chapter 1.3 below) was a theme that underscored the status of the decree as a tool of normative political activity but, as we will see, some counter-arguments reveal a level of disquiet about the way that the decree represented the power of the people.

1.3 Decrees and Democracy

The author of the *Athenaion Politeia* stated that one characteristic of the Athenian democracy of his own time was that the people were in charge of everything (ἁπάντων κύριος) and that they administer matters through their

---

80 Rhodes 1972: 137–8 discusses this secretary and asserts that it was an office distinct from the secretary of the council; cf. *Agora* XV 58 lines 76–85; there is, however, no evidence on how its duties were separate from those of the principal *grammateus*. Harpokration, s.v. 'γραμματεύς' describes the secretary as the one who keeps guard over the passed decrees (τὰ ψηφίσματα τὰ γενόμενα) and makes copies of all the other decrees (τὰ ἄλλα πάντα ἀντιγράφεται).

81 For the involvement of a public slave (*demosios*) in making inventories, see *IG* II² 120 lines 11–19 with Rhodes 1972: 98, 141–2 and 1981: 601.

SOCIAL CAPITAL OF THE DECREE

control of decrees and the lawcourts (*Ath. Pol.* 41.2).[82] This is rather a summary and over-generalised analysis of the location of power within the Athenian state: emphasising the power of the *demos*, it ignores the place of the laws and marginalises the council. Yet it demonstrates that rule by decree could be viewed as an important element of the power of the people, perhaps inasmuch as they were able to undermine or even to challenge the rule of law. The extent to which we should recognise a distinction between the power of the people at the assembly and that in the lawcourts is the subject of a long-running debate between Hansen and Ober. Hansen's view seeks to find a stable location of sovereignty in the lawcourts and does not see the courts as embodiments of the assembly; alternatively, Ober's allows for the location of sovereignty in the hands of the people in whichever capacity they met.[83] An alternative to their perspective is that of Harris, which emphasises the rule of law in Athens.[84] Along the same lines of thought, Apollodoros ([Dem.] 59.88) reminds us that the sovereignty of the people was restricted by laws which the *demos* itself enacted.[85]

What is the place of decrees of the assembly in the debate about sovereignty? It is very clear that activity surrounding decrees is a central aspect of the question of sovereignty, but it seems that there was a tug of law between the decrees of the assembly on the one hand and the laws and the people at the lawcourts on the other: as we have seen, the people at the assembly possessed the power

---

82 [Arist]. *Ath. Pol.* 41.2: 'The people has made itself supreme in all fields; they administer matters by decrees of the assembly and by decisions of the lawcourts in which the people are supreme' ('ἁπάντων γὰρ αὐτὸς αὑτὸν πεποίηκεν ὁ δῆμος κύριον, καὶ πάντα διοικεῖται ψηφίσμασιν καὶ δικαστηείοις, ἐν οἷς ὁ δῆμός ἐστιν ὁ κρατῶν').

83 Hansen's view – set out originally in Hansen 1974: 19–21, expanded in Hansen 1978 and re-iterated in Hansen 2010, esp. 526 – is that there was a substantive distinction between the courts and the assembly and that the courts were the location of sovereign power in the fourth century. For the view – that of the majority of scholars – that sovereignty was in the hands of the people, see Ober 1996: 107–22, asserting at 117 that the term *demos* could constitute a synechdocal reference to the whole citizen body while at times also taking in a narrower term of reference to the people gathered at the assembly. Ober criticises Hansen's emphasis on institutions in his analysis of the location of sovereignty and instead focuses upon the citizenry's power over discourse. For the important observation of the lack of consensus among ancient writers on the question of the location of power, see Blanshard 2004a.

84 See Harris 2013a and Harris 2016a; for earlier statements of the 'rule of law' thesis see Meyer-Laurin 1965; Ostwald 1986; Sealey 1987. Lambert (2018: 157–70) notes an increased emphasis on the rule of law in Athenian inscriptions after the defeat at Chaironeia.

85 [Dem.] 59.88: 'The Athenian people is supreme over all things in the city, and has the power to do as it pleases, but it held the gift of citizenship to be so fine and sacred a thing that it made laws to which it must abide whenever it wishes to make someone a citizen' ('ὁ γὰρ δῆμος ὁ Ἀθηναίων κυριώτατος ὢν τῶν ἐν τῇ πόλει ἁπάντων, καὶ ἐξὸν αὐτῷ ποιεῖν ὅ τι ἂν βούληται, οὕτω καλὸν καὶ σεμνὸν ἡγήσατ' εἶναι δῶρον τὸ Ἀθηναῖον γενέσθαι, ὥστε νόμους ἔθετο αὑτῷ καθ' οὓς ποιεῖσθαι δεῖ, ἐάν τινα βούλωνται, πολίτην').

to make decrees without consultation of the lawcourts, but at the same time the lawcourts possessed the power to overturn or uphold those decrees referred to them through the *graphe paranomon* process on the basis of the question of their legality or illegality.[86] This process upheld the principle that laws possessed higher authority than decrees and that decrees were bound within the limits of the law; yet, on the other hand, the *demos* created the context for law-making by acting as the body that initiated – by way of a decree – the process of *nomothesia*.[87] Furthermore, recent work by Esu (2018 Chapter 2) has emphasised the place of a third party, the Athenian council, in the balance of powers: not only did the council possess the power of *probouleusis*, but the assembly was able, by decree, to designate specified powers to decrees of the council.

The statement at *Ath. Pol.* 41.2 about sovereignty reminds us of the fact that the people had the potential, at points, to exercise sovereignty by voting on decrees which concerned areas unbounded by the laws of the city, such as the formulation of treaties or the exercise of foreign policy.[88] By accepting that it was at the point of the vote on decrees, whether upon their enactment in the assembly or on their rejection when challenged in the courts by *graphe paranomon*, that the *demos* exercised its powers, we can posit the occurrence of moments of sovereignty of the people both in the lawcourts and in the assembly.[89] This is manifested in the evidence for the regulation of the sovereignty of the *demos*, in terms of the processes of *graphe paranomon* and *graphe me epitedeion thenai* held in the courts, in terms of those decisions pertaining to areas (such as public finances, jurisdiction, and some matters pertaining to the constitution and religion) which usually fell under the scope of law and which were subject to scrutiny by way of the process of *nomothesia* (involving the intervention of the *thesmothetai* (Aeschin. 3.38) and repeal of contradictory legislation in the courts: Dem. 24.35–6). But in

---

86 Hansen 2010: 528; Sundahl 2003; Harris 2018: 66 note 138. Esu 2018 emphasises the idea that the courts, by way of the *graphe paranomon*, contributed to the principle of the sovereignty of law while also upholding by majority vote decrees that the courts deemed legal.

87 On the process of nomothesia, see now Canevaro 2016b; for the view that nomothesia was undertaken as a special session of the assembly and the nomothetai as a special instantiation of the assembly, see Canevaro and Esu forthcoming; this view has important implications for the sovereignty of the Athenian assembly. On re-activating old laws: see Dracon's law (*IG* I³ 104) or the account of Aristophon's revival of the Solonian law on taxation for foreigners: Dem. 57.31–3, 34. For discussion of decrees which contain provisions for legislation, see Lambert 2018; Hansen 2017: 270–5.

88 On the scope of decrees, see Chapter 1.2.2 above

89 Cf. the idea of 'floating sovereignty', which emphasises the external limitations on statist sovereignty, outlined in Kostakopoulou 2002 and Jovanović and Henrard 2008. For critique of the usefulness of the term 'sovereignty' to classical Athens, see Pasquino 2010; Davies 1994b. Esu 2018 suggests replacing it with the perspective of 'divided power'.

terms of declaring war, diplomacy, and making rewards, the people was sovereign through its decrees.

To return to [Aristotle]: given his expression of disappointment that the late fifth-century Athenians failed to observe their laws properly (*Ath. Pol.* 26.2), his statement may, admittedly, be indicative of a critical view of their classical form of democratic government.[90] In work firmly attributed to Aristotle, however, it is not so much the decree itself, but rather the excessive assignment of power to decrees, which is identified as problematic: Aristotle made a close connection between unconstitutional decrees and undesirable and extreme forms of government.[91] In his analysis of the general idea of democracy in the *Politics*, he shows how extreme democratic societies make use of decrees in an undesirable or unconstitutional way: he says that one symptom of mob-rule was that of decrees over-riding laws, a condition brought about by demagogues (1292a 6–11).[92] In such a situation, the *demos* seeks to exercise monarchic rule and becomes despotic (15–17). Aristotle equates this with the tyrannical form of anarchy, because despotic control is imposed over the better classes, and the *psephismata* become the equivalent of commands (*epitagmata*) of a tyrant (20).[93] This is inappropriate to a proper *politeia* given his principle that it is impossible for a decree to be a universal rule and means that a state in which decrees rule over everything cannot be defined as a *demokratia* (32–6). What may lie behind Aristotle's opinion is the view that in an extreme democracy,

90 This is the view of Rhodes 1981: 489, 512; cf. Harris 2016a: 73 note 2.
91 Aristotle also made observations about the significance of decrees in other communities: in what may be a fragment of Aristotle's *Constitution of the Megarians*, Plutarch noted that the Megarian extreme democracy enacted a decree (*dogma*) according to the terms of which the poor received back again the interest which they had paid their creditors (*palintokia*: Plu. *Mor.* 295c–d). On Megara as a literary paradigm of extreme democracy, see Forsdyke 2005. For the argument that the Megarian sections of Plutarch's *Greek Questions* derive from Aristotle's *Politeia of the Megarians*, see Giessen 1901: 461–3 with Aristotle fr. 550 Rose.
92 For Aristotle's wider concern that, in an extreme democracy, the authority of laws and magistrates is undermined by decrees, see *Politics* 1292a1–37, 1293a9–10. For the view that a good form of democracy was one that was law-abiding, see Hdt. 3.80; Eur. *Suppl.* 403–50; Dem. 22.51; Aeschin. 1.4–5, 3.6; Harris 2013a: 3–18.
93 Unconstitutional decrees were associated also with tyrannical forms of government: according to [Aristotle], the Thirty were established by a decree of Drakontides, which the people were forced to approve: [Arist.] *Ath. Pol.* 34.3; cf. Lysias 12.73. The non-Athenian evidence suggests that the proper constitutional use of decrees appears to have been important in distinguishing good kingship from demagogy or tyranny. Dio Chrysostom, in his speech *On Agamemnon* or *Kingship*, claimed that something that distinguished the king from demagogues was that the latter (unlike the former) bring before the popular assembly measures that have not been passed by the council (56.10). Part of Polybius' criticism of Kritolaos as a tyrant was that he brought forward a *paronomon* decree that said that generals should have absolute power (Plyb. 38.13.7).

the council lacks any power (Arist. *Pol.* 1299b30–1300a4); accordingly, in such a scenario, the people would enact whatever forms and types of decree for which advocates at its meetings were able to make a persuasive case. At least in the fourth century, this is an unrealistic scenario: it is unlikely that it was ever the usual practice for Greek states to pass decrees without any consultation of their councils at all.[94]

But this critique of the democratic connotations of the decree is not enunciated in the oratorical texts.[95] What we find in the speeches is that problems with decrees are identified not with them as manifestations of popular sovereignty, but with their vulnerability to the conspiracy and intrigue of self-interested individuals. Aeschines, for instance, claimed that Philokrates and Demosthenes collaborated to exclude Kersobleptes from swearing the oath of the alliance with Philip II of Macedon by surreptitiously inserting a clause giving Athens' allies the privilege into the decree just before it was put to the vote (Aeschin. 3.73–4; cf. 2.82–90 = D131). Procedural problems loom large in oratorical critiques of decrees: among the most effective ways of attacking a decree in the Athenian lawcourts were the claims that it contradicted law (Dem. 23) or that its subjects had not been considered by the council (Dem. 22.5–6).[96]

The discourse of Athenian politics at times placed emphasis on correct political procedure, a view enunciated most clearly in Aeschines' tendency to align his own cases with descriptions of good practice (e.g. Aeschin. 1.33–5; 3.3–12). The democratic legitimacy – and sense of shared sentiment – of the process of decree-making is asserted in the standard form of the enactment formula which appeared in the prescripts of Athenian decrees, 'the council and the people resolved' ('ἔδοξε τῆι βουλῆι καὶ τῶι δήμωι');[97] such a formula emphasised the role of the collective decision of the demos in indicating the formal creation of a decree. Aeschines thought it appropriate in his speech *On the False Embassy* to describe the way in which decrees were passed with the explicit approval – by way of voting through *cheirotonia* at the assembly – of the *demos* (Aeschin. 2.13; 3.3; cf. Ar. *Eccl.* 263–7;

---

94 *Probouleusis* across the Greek world: Rhodes with Lewis 1997: 475–501. For decrees whose critics claimed they had not been considered by the council (*aprobouleuta psephismata*), see Rhodes 1972: 53, 62 and 1981: 544.

95 For discussion of some of the criticisms of decrees found in the lawcourts, see Liddel 2016.

96 There are many examples of decrees said to have been unconstitutional: see Hansen 1974 *passim*. For more discussion of the attacking of decrees, see Chapter 2.3 below.

97 On this and other enactment formulae, see Rhodes 1972: 64 and Rhodes with Lewis 1997: 4. For the importance of demonstrating that decisions were made in appropriate ways for establishing their legitimacy, see March and Olsen 1989: 49.

[Arist.] *Ath. Pol.* 30.5).[98] Moreover, his assertion that the laws forbade the introduction of falsehoods into the decrees of the Athenians (Aeschin. 3.50) is another indication of how they might be construed as a politically upstanding form of political transaction.

No literary author ever alleged that decrees were unique to democratic forms of government, but there certainly was a tendency to identify government by decree of the people as a central feature of democracy: Aeschines classified the government of Oreos (earlier known as Histiaia) on Euboia as a democracy on the basis of the observation that 'everything is done there by decree' ('δημοκρατουμένων τῶν Ὠρειτῶν καὶ πάντα πραττόντων μετὰ ψηφίσματος': 3.103).[99] Furthermore, we also encounter in the literary sources the view that correct decree-making procedure was to be identified with democracy; this was something suggested by Demosthenes' claim that the process of *probouleusis* was something that distinguished democracy from oligarchy or monarchy:

> For in these polities [oligarchy and tyranny], as I see it, everything is done promptly by word of command; but with you, first the Council must be informed, and must adopt a provisional resolution (προβουλεῦσαι δεῖ), and even that not at any time, but only after written notice given for heralds and embassies; then the council must convene an assembly, and this must happen at the point which is directed by the laws. (Dem. 19.185)

Demosthenes then goes on to highlight the role of the best orators in prevailing and overcoming ignorant and dishonest opposition, as well as ensuring that arrangements are made so that the provisions of the decree can be put in place (19.185–6). What, therefore, the oratorical analyses of decree-activity appear to emphasise is the notion that openness and adherence to constitutional procedures were essential in the process of constructing a sound decree. Indeed, we should note that Aeschines celebrated the Athenian tendency to write down and to protect the substance of their enactments (Aeschin. 3.50, 75–6). To the literary evidence we can add the observation that inscribed decrees in Athens appear to have become more standardised and detailed in their prescripts

---

98 The act of voting does not appear explicitly in the enactment formula in Athenian decrees (which uses 'ἔδοξε' ('resolved') rather than, e.g., 'ἐψηφίσθη' ('voted')), but the act of voting is sometimes referred to in the motion formula, which Rhodes with Lewis (1997: 5) describe as 'an infinitive dependent on the "N said" in the prescript', which 'calls on the enacting body to approve the motion put to it'; for instance, *IG* II³ 1 333 lines 8–9 calls on the assembly to resolve the decree ('ἐψηφίσθαι τῶι δ[ήμωι ἐπαινέσαι μὲ]ν Ἀρχιππον': 'be it decreed by the people to praise Archippos') on the basis of the council's report; see also *IG* II³ 1 367 (= RO 95) line 47 discussed in Chapter 1.2.1 above. Rhodes (1972: 65) observes that in motion formulae 'δεδόχθαι' ('be it resolved') and 'ἐψηφίσθαι' ('be it voted') were interchangeable.

99 On democracy at Oreos, see Robinson 2011: 175–6.

38   DECREES OF FOURTH-CENTURY ATHENS

and enactment formulae over the course of the fourth century,[100] suggesting a growing effort at ostensibly demonstrating adherence to appropriate levels of procedure.

In addition to a strong rhetoric of respect for procedures surrounding enactment, there was also a clear idea of the right way of attacking a decree: Aeschines and others suggest that the procedure to indict unconstitutional proposals (*graphe paranomon*) was central to the conception of proper democratic behaviour. Aeschines claimed – in the course of a speech in support of the *graphe paranomon* against the honours for Demosthenes – that after the restoration of democracy in 403/2 it was said that the abolition of this mechanism was what had caused the fall of democracy (3.191); he complained, as a way of convincing his audience of the severity of their predecessors, that the jurors no longer took the process as seriously as had their ancestors (3.192–4).[101] As we shall see later (Chapter 2.4 below), the record of having launched a *graphe paranomon* against an unconstitutional decree could be referred to in claims about political service.

In conclusion, we can observe that in their right form, decrees appear to be conceived of as a staple of orderly government and careful adherence to good procedure. Properly formulated, they could be construed as expressions of the will of the *demos*[102] but the process of *probouleusis* at the council oversaw their formulation and that of *graphe paranomon* in the courts tested their legality. It will come as no surprise, therefore, that decrees could be seen as upholding core values of the Athenian *demos* (see Chapter 1.5.1 below) and that participating in the decree-system could be construed as appropriate political behaviour (see Chapter 2.2 below). At the same time, however, we should recognise a vein of scepticism expressed by Aristotle about the political impact of decrees which underlined the dangers that they posed when they became too powerful or were enacted without appropriate constitutional scrutiny. Such views are reminiscent of the debate reported by Xenophon on the fate of the generals after the battle of Arginusae in 406: some claimed that Kallixenos' proposal (on which he is alleged to have taken bribes) to make a decree that the generals be tried

---

100 Henry 1977: 1–49. Athenian decrees start to record their month and day of enactment in the second half of the fourth century: Rhodes and Osborne 2003: 149.

101 [Aristotle] *Ath. Pol.* 29.4 associated its abolition with the oligarchic coup of 411; cf. Thuc. 8.67.2; Dem. 24.154. Indeed, the association of it with a virtuous form of democracy is suggested by Xenophon's report that it was over-ridden at the debate in the aftermath of the battle at Arginusae (Xen. *Hell.* 1.7.12–13). The author of the *Ath. Pol.* (40.2) took the view that Archinos' *graphe paranomon* against the decree of Thrasyboulos admitting to citizenship all those who had come back together from Peiraeus (D5) was a praiseworthy indication of his statesmanship. For discussion of the connection between democracy and *graphe paranomon*, see Hansen 1974: 55–61.

102 Luraghi 2010.

as a board and not individually was unconstitutional, but others responded that it was right for the people to do as they pleased (Xen. *Hell.* 1.7.9–12; see Chapter 5.2.1 below).[103] It is an account that suggests the existence of contentious views about the rightful extent of the power of the decree and the danger that decree-making might be swayed by selfish politicians in their own interest. We must take into account, however, that this debate is reported in the work of an author who had reservations about Athenian democratic norms;[104] nevertheless, given that decrees were the subject of debate and voting in the assembly, it therefore follows that contradictory opinions would have been expressed about the concept of the decree.

So far I have offered an account of the enactment of decrees and the origins and limitations of their authority (Chapter 1.1–1.2), and have made a case for the potentially close association, in oratorical texts, of correct democratic behaviour with the proper enactment of a decree (Chapter 1.3). As we shall see in Chapter 2 below, this image coincided with, and to a large extent, underlay, the tendency of politicians of fourth-century Athens to be what we may reasonably describe as 'decree-minded': in other words, to make use of familiarity with decrees, proposing them, attacking them, interpreting them and applying them in their political rhetoric; in short, to be mindful of the value of decrees in their accrual of symbolic capital through political activity.[105] But this image is also important to the construction of decrees as expressions of shared Athenian values and sentiments in relation to the promotion of ideas about the social capital of the *demos* as a community, which is the subject of Chapter 1.5 below.[106] First, however, it is necessary to consider the perceived geopolitical context of the decrees that we are dealing with.

1.4 Fourth-Century Geopolitics and the Profile of Athenian Decrees: Practical and Symbolic Aspects

Thus far, it has become clear that, despite an institutionalised subordination to law in fourth-century Athens (Chapter 1.2 above), the decree as a political

---

103 On Xenophon's account of the trial of the generals, see Chapter 5.2.1 below.

104 Xenophon as a critic of democracy: see Seager 2001; Christ 2012: 138. For a more positive appraisal of Xenophon's view of democracy, see Gray 2004: 169–71; Farrell (2016; forthcoming). For his interest in the rule of law, see Gray 2007: 9–10. See the discussion at Ferrario 2017: 66–71, suggesting that while Xenophon frequently casts democracy in a bad light in the *Hellenika*, his main reservation is about the capacity of the people to govern effectively without effective leadership.

105 On Bourdieu's notion of symbolic capital, see Introduction, p. 5 above.

106 On Bourdieu's notion of social capital, see Introduction, pp. 5–6 above.

transaction possessed significant potential authority on the grounds of its close association with proper democratic procedure (Chapter 1.3 above). The prominence of decrees to political matters is manifested both in their practical and symbolic aspects (see Chapter 1.1 above). The practical aspects must be viewed in the light of their perceived historical context, and so in what follows I shall set out a brief account of Athens' history as it is represented in literary references to decrees. It must be stressed that this is an account which inevitably emphasises those decrees which are prominent in the literary record: therefore it constitutes a view of their history that reflects the preoccupations of the literary sources and should not be taken as an straightforward account of Athenian history; my interest here is in elucidating the geopolitical features of Athenian decree-making of this period that are highlighted in literature. A full analysis of the history of Athenian interstate relations in this period would necessitate thorough engagement with epigraphical sources and is beyond the scope of the current work.

Over the duration of the fourth century, the Athenian *demos* faced up to a changed and shifting geopolitical reality: this is manifested in the fact that, in the aftermath of Athens' defeat in the Peloponnesian War, she was no longer the unchallenged military authority of the area of Greece and the Aegean. It became clear that Athenian power was not able to match the city's former ambitions.[107] This had an impact upon the type of decrees that were passed at the Athenian assembly in the fourth century, which reflected Athenian attempts to deal largely on a case-by-case basis with the military threats she faced and to make the most of the occasional opportunities that she enjoyed. Before 395, Athenian decree-activity appears to have focused upon internal reconstruction: the Athenians based their restoration of institutions at the end of the fifth century on the enactment of decrees (DD 1, 2, 7, 8, 9, 10, 11, 19; cf. Chapter 1.5.1 above), deployed them to recognise the contribution of those who had assisted in the restoration of democracy (DD 3, 5, 6, 15, 18), and repayed debts to outsiders (DD 12, 13). But from the mid 390s the Athenians restored their alliances and walls by way of decrees (DD 20, 21, 22); moreover, in the years and decades after the defeat of the Spartans at Knidos in summer 394, the Athenians used decrees to seal alliances with other communities (DD 29, 30, 33, 36, 45, cf. DP 20, 21, 27), to negotiate peace terms (DD 25, 26, 51, 52, 53; cf. DP 18, 39), to pursue military campaigns (DD 34, 44, 50, 55), to manage their own military officials (DD 37, 48), to offer shelter to groups of exiles (DD 31, 32, 40, 41, 49) and to honour both citizens and foreigners who made contributions to the prosperity

---

107 Badian 1992; for the rhetorical theme that Athenian decrees were passed in vain, see Mader 2006 and discussion in Chapter 2.5.2 below.

and security of the city (DD 23, 24, 28, 35, 42, 43, 46, 47, 54) as a way of encouraging others to act in similar ways.[108] Over the course of the period from the early 360s to the mid 350s the Athenians appear to have pursued a similar line, using decrees for diplomatic purposes (DD 81, 90), to make alliances and peace agreements (DD 58, 63, 79, 80, 83, 87), to dispatch military expeditions (D56, 60, 67, 82), to pursue interests in territories outside Attica through the grant of honours (DD 58, 59, 61, 62, 70, 72, 73, 74, 75, 76, 77, 78, 84, 94, 100, 103, 104, 204), to support Athenian interests outside the city in other ways (DD 64, 65, 66, 205, DP 47), to commend good behaviour of Athenian citizens (DD 89, 102), and to improve both public finances (DD 57, 68, 85, 86, 88, 91, 92) and military organisation (DD 67, 69).

As late as 353/2 BC, Diodorus, speaker of Demosthenes *Against Timokrates*, talks in front of an audience of jurors about how Athenian laws and decrees had in the past secured Athenian interests and achieved goals, such as protecting communities, punishing enemies and bringing about peace (Dem. 24.92–3). But another style of argument – known from the assembly speeches of Demosthenes (such as the *Third Olynthiac* of 349/8) – was much more negative about the legacy of Athenian decrees, criticizing the *demos* for failing to live up to the promise of its decrees in terms of military action (e.g. Dem. 3.4–6, 14–15; cf. Chapter 2.5.2 below). Yet proactive aspects of Athenian policy are highlighted in the literary sources decrees even down to the time of the defeat at Chaironeia in summer 338: dated to this period are decrees dispatching ambassadors (DD 116, 117, 125, 140, 142, 144, 148, 162), launching military expeditions (DD 106, 108, 111, 112, 129, 143, 154, 155, 157, 158, 159, 162), making alliances and arranging peace (D113, 130, 131, 132, 141, 147, 149, 151, 152, 153, 163), celebrating victories (D105, 165), granting awards to foreigners (DD 109, 110, 120, 209), honouring citizens (DD 114, 118, 124, 128, 134, 136, 146, 156, 166, 221), initiating adjustments to public finances (DD 115, 164) and concerning Athenian settlers outside Athens (DD 150, 20; cf. DP 52, 63). The growing proliferation of honorific decrees is noticeable. As the fourth century went on, the Athenians appear to have faced up to the fact that even such decrees as they passed were often rendered insignificant by the limits to their capabilities. Defeat at the hands of rebellious allies in the Social War in 355, the failure to stall Philip's progress either at Olynthos in 348 or through the Peace of 346 (D130) or on the battlefield at Chaironeia in 338 demonstrate that the power behind their

---

108 For Athenian honours for grain dealers see Engen 2010; for inscribed honours for Athenians, see Lambert 2011a.

decrees had further subsided.[109] This is visible in the rhetoric that surrounded the decrees of the period from the early 340s (see Chapter 2.5.2 below) but also in the substance of those decrees which suggest Athenian attempts to cope with crisis: there are decrees managing the use of disputed sacred territory (D107), arranging the evacuation of the countryside (D135), dealing with the Delphian Amphictyony (D161), directed against those who threaten merchants (D207); other decrees, relating to the scrutiny of the citizen body (D137), concerning public works (D138), the powers of the Areopagus (D214) suggest a decree of introspection.

The period after the defeat at Chaironeia saw the Athenians use decrees to manage a range of further crises (DD 167, 168, 183, 237, 238; cf. DP 69 and see Chapter 1.5.2 below), military organization (DD 170, 176; cf. DP 72), domestic matters (DD 193, 194, 195, 196, 200, 226), religious affairs (DD 237, 240, 241), external demands (D186, 202) and perceived acts of aggression (D191). While decrees were still deployed to dispatch emphassies or to make peace (DD 170, 171, 172, 185, 188, 201), and perhaps even to make alliances and prepare for war (DD 184, 192, 199), decree-making appears to have been focused much more upon the dispensation of honours to Athenians (DD 179, 181, 187, 189, 190, 222, 228, 229, 230, 234, 245) and foreigners (DD 173, 174, 175, 177, 178, 180, 182, 196, 227, 231, 232, 235, 236, 243, 244). Indeed, as Lambert has recently observed, the fact that there are no epigraphical records of the Athenians making bilateral treaties in the period from the defeat at Chaironeia until the death of Alexander demonstrates Athens' weaker hand in interstate diplomacy; on the other hand, the Athenians used honorific decrees in the period after Chaironeia as a tool to promote good relations with the Macedonian regime and their allies.[110] At the same time, the necessity of encouraging euergetic behaviour among non-Athenians, as well as civic-minded office-holding among Athenians, as a means of promoting the interests of the city became more stark; both the literary and the epigraphical pictures suggest that the passing of honorific decrees as a tool of Athenian interests was deployed more extensively.[111] Such matters, I sug-

---

109 For developments of that era in Athenian politics and notions of citizenship in the late fourth century, see Mossé 1989; Hakkarainen 1997; Humphreys 2004: 77–129; Liddel 2007: 98–102; Scholz 2009; Azoulay and Ismard 2011.

110 Lambert 2018: 7, 96–9.For the possibility of a bilateral alliance with the Thebans in 335/4, see D184 (cf. also D171).

111 Engen 2010 makes a case for the significance for the Athenian grain-supply of honorific decrees in the wider the period after the Sicilian expedition to the end of the fourth century. On the relationship between decrees and her changed place in the world, see Lambert 2011a, 2011b and Liddel 2016. Changes in the types of decrees being passed at the assembly are discussed by Lambert 2018 93–111.

SOCIAL CAPITAL OF THE DECREE

gest, combined with Athenian insecurity about the power and impact of their decrees, go some ways to explaining the profile of the decree in political life in the second half of the fourth century.

The symbolic prominence of the decree is suggested by its profile in extant lawcourt speeches in which the citation of decrees played a prominent role in the construction of social and political values; in these speeches, decrees were a subject of focus. In his speech *Against Leptines* of probably 355/4,[112] Demosthenes attacked Leptines' law of the previous year which had withdrawn from honorands all exemptions from liturgies related to festivals. He challenged the law on the basis of his claim that it was not expedient (ἐπιτήδειος: see Dem. 20.83, 95) and stripped the people of the right to make awards as they saw fit (Dem. 20.2–3, 102–3). In making his argument,[113] Demosthenes drew extensively upon knowledge of fifth- and fourth-century Athenian honorific decrees to support an argument about how the Athenian honorific system – threatened by Leptines' law – enabled the *demos* to encourage foreign benefactors to treat the Athenians favourably,[114] adding that honorific inscriptions represent a memorial of the character of the city and provide examples for those who want to do good to the city (Dem. 20.64).[115] Second, in 331 Lycurgus the orator placed strong emphasis on decrees in his speech supporting the impeachment of the runaway Leokrates. In particular, decrees were held up as offering paradigms of the harsh treatment of traitors and other offenders.[116] Furthermore, we can point to epigraphic tendencies of that particular era: the Athenians published decrees on stone in the second half of the fourth century more prolifically than

112 Kremmydas 2012: 33.
113 For an assessment of the logical nature of the rhetoric of this speech, see Kremmydas 2007b.
114 For the decrees cited in this speech, see Dem. 20.35–7 (= D39), 20.55 (= D41), 20.41–8 (decree for Epikerdes of Cyrene; cf. *IG* I³ 125), 20.52–4 (decree for Corinthians), 20.59 (= D40). 20.68–71 (= D23), 20.84 (= DD 46, 47, 62), 20.131–3 (= D103, 104), 20.148 (= D12) and West 1995. See also the discussion of the deployment of decrees in this speech in Chapter 2.4.1 below.
115 This view of the importance of the honorific system to the functioning and prosperity of the Athenian community was not unique: see also Andocides 2.23, Dem. 18.120, Xen. *Poroi* 3.11 with Liddel 2016: 349–50 and Lambert 2018: 75
116 Decrees in Lycurgus' speech *Against Leokrates*: Lycurg. 1.16 (= D167b), 1.36–7 (= D167c), 1.41 (= D167a), 1.53 (= D168) 1.113 (Kritias' decree against Phrynichos), 1.120–1 (against those who moved to Dekeleia), 1.117–18 (establishment of pillar of traitors), 1.122 (decree against those executed in Salamis, 1.124–7 (= D19) 1.146 (= D240). For the date of the speech, see Harris 2013a: 233 note 54 and Harris 2013a: 233 note 54, citing Lycurg. 1.45 (in the eighth year after Chaironeia, that is, seven years after 338, i.e. 331; cf. 58, 145). Engels (2008: 113) prefers the date of 330. On the notion of the good citizen in this speech, see Scholtz 2009. As Grethlein (2014: 340–4) points out, there is also considerable emphasis on mythological parallels in this speech; cf. Brock 1998.

at any other time in their history;[117] moreover, as Habicht argued in 1961,[118] it was probably in the second half of the fourth century that the Athenians created documentary versions of what they believed to have constituted patriotic documents and decrees from the era of the Persian Wars, in some cases writing them up on stone and so symbolically engraving them into the public memory.[119] It is from this point, therefore, that the Athenians demonstrably regard historical decrees as possessing political and rhetorical significance in setting standards of ideal behaviour, particularly in respect to the community's treatment of those who carry out benefactions on its behalf or those who commit crimes against it (see Chapter 1.5.3 below). Negative characterisation of Athenian decree-activity certainly does not disappear in the fourth century, as Demosthenes' attack on the inanity of unfulfilled decrees in his symbouleutic oratory demonstrates.[120] But such characterisation – expressed as it was in arenas of public debate – far from undermining the idea that knowledge of them was important for political rhetoric, actually suggests the existence of a lively contest about their significance. Indeed, there was a counter-argument to Demosthenes' position: that decrees could be made effective by a combination of decision and action (D82 T1; D191).

Perceptions of Athens' changed geopolitical position in the late fourth century may go some way to explaining the heightened profile of the decree in the political contests of the late fourth century.[121] Moreover, it might also explain the changes in genres of decree that were prominent, in particular the growing proliferation of inscribed honorific decrees for Athenians in the second half

---

117 Hedrick 1999: 304; the increased proliferation of epigraphical publication of decrees in the Lycurgan period is noted also by Lambert 2010.

118 Habicht: 1961.

119 Inscribed fifth-century patriotic documents written up possibly in the late fourth century include the Themistocles decree: ML 23 , recited by Aeschines in 348 (Dem. 19.303), the Oath of Plataea (RO 88 lines 21–51) and Arthmios decree: see Meiggs 1972 and discussion in Chapter 5 below. In his speech against Neaira, Apollodoros claims that the decree regarding the Plataeans was set up in the acropolis near the temple of the goddess ([Dem.] 59.104–6): we cannot be certain whether his reference to the inscription was to a genuine fifth-century document or one written up in the following century. Against the authenticity of the document at 59.104, see now Canevaro 2010.

120 Mader 2006; see Chapter 2.5.2 below. For other negative characterisations of the substance of decrees at both the lawcourts and assembly, see Chapter 1.3 above and Liddel 2016: 348–52.

121 This impression of the raised profile of the decree may also be a result of speech-survival and the fact that dating from the 350s and later there are several *graphe paranomon* speeches which make extensive use of decrees, and in particular honorific decrees, in their line of argument. See also, for the influence of factors relating to survival of speeches on modern impressions of fourth-century history, Lane Fox 1994: 141.

SOCIAL CAPITAL OF THE DECREE

of the fourth century.[122] It is likely that the crisis in funding at the end of the Social War in 355 provoked debates about the relationship between decrees and the raising of finances: such are the arguments which arise in Demosthenes' speeches 20 (*Against Leptines*) and 23 (*Against Aristokrates*) of 352 (on the date, see Volume 1, D94 Date), both of which make prolific use of honorific decrees in their argumentation (see Chapter 2.1 below). But the fact that there is one earlier speech – Andocides' *On the Mysteries* of late 400[123] – which makes extensive use of decrees in its argumentation shows that their deployment was not restricted to the late fourth century.[124] What we can perhaps conclude is that the detailed engagement with decrees – and specifically with honorific decrees – was a phenomenon that became more common after the Social War, but was not restricted to that period: decrees were a feature of political life throughout the fourth century.

Having made a case for the importance of decrees in realities and percep-tions of fourth-century Athenian political and geopolitical activity I shall turn, in the next stage of this chapter, to the orators' deployment of them, exploring the ways in which knowledge about decrees, and the deeds of proposing and attacking them, were key means of developing an image of Athenian shared values (Chapter 1.5 above) and for accruing individual political capital in the Athenian assembly and lawcourts (Chapter 2 below). It is worth underlining at this point – at the risk of anticipating the conclusions of Chapter 3 – that there is little to suggest that the publication of decrees on stone would have automat-ically led to widespread detailed knowledge of them; while the comprehensive storage of decrees at the Metroon evidently provided a resource upon which those seeking particular documents would have been able to draw,[125] famili-arity with the language of decrees was something that was learned primarily

---

122 On the point of inscribing honorific decrees in the second half of the fourth century, see Lambert 2018: 71–91; on the proliferation of various types of decree in the fourth century see above, Table 1 and Chapter 3.3 below.

123 For the dating of the speech to the second half of 400, see Makkink 1932: 32–5 and MacDowell 1962: 204–5.

124 Decrees in Andocides *On the Mysteries*: 1.8 and 71 (decree of Isotimides), 1.27–8 (decrees of Kleonymos and Peisandros), 1.81, 90 (= D1), 1.81 (= D2), 1.76-80 (decree of Patrokleides), 1.82, 85 (= D7), 1.88–9, 93 (= D8), 1.95– 6 (= D19). For discussion of the inauthenticity of the documentary versions of the decrees which appear in some manuscripts of the text, see Canevaro and Harris 2012, Harris 2013–14; Canevaro and Harris 2016; cf. Sommerstein 2014b; Hansen 2015; 2016; Carawan 2017. As Sickinger 2002: 162 –7 demonstrates, the citation of decrees took place in political debates also of the fifth century too; he points to Euryptolemos' speech in the Arginusae debate (Xen. *Hell.* 1.7.16–33) and Pericles' references to the Thirty Years' Peace and the Megarian decree (Thuc. 1.140.2; 1.141.2–3).

125 Archive at the Metroon: Aeschin 3.187, Din 1.86. Generally, see Sickinger 1991, 1999b and Chapter 3 below; on the storage of laws, see Sickinger 2004.

through socialisation and political participation.[126] My working hypothesis (to which we shall return in Chapter 3.2.3 below) is that orators aspired to exploit, augment and manipulate their audiences' awareness (however sketchy it was) of past decrees when deploying them in argumentation.

1.5 Decrees and the Representation of Harmony and Crisis Management

1.5.1 Athens After the Thirty: Decrees and Memories of Reconciliation

Athenian orators at times sought to emphasise any single decree's association with its proposer: this is a theme to be explored in depth over the course of Chapter 2 below); alternatively, decrees could be read as expressions of the will of the community of citizens as a whole. At this point I begin consideration of how orators undertook to do this in two particular ways: first (1.5.1) I look at the decrees drawn upon in narratives about the establishment of harmonious arrangements associated with the restoration of democracy during the archonship of Eukleides of 403/2;[127] second (1.5.2) I look at the deployment of decrees to represent accounts of shared sentiments in the face of crisis, particularly in the aftermath of the Athenian defeat at Chaironeia in 338. Finally (1.5.3) I assess the implications of the orators' citation of historical decrees for the view of decrees as transactions with long-lasting significance.

Shear's 2011 *Polis and Revolution* marks an important step forward in the understanding of ways in which the Athenians reconstituted democracy after its restoration in 403/2 C. The re-institution of popular government, she argues, was based on legislative reforms and a form of epigraphical publication and monumentalisation which aimed to envelop its audience in a feeling of democratic restoration.[128] Such a process can be identified also in the significant

---

126 For assumed familiarity with particular documents, see Richardson 2015.

127 For an early view of the reconciliation as an example of forgiveness and unity, see Dorjahn 1946. The definitive study of the politics of the reconciliation is now Shear 2011: 188–322; for details of the decrees concerning the reinvention of the Athenian political system, see DD 1–8. For a view of the success of the Athenian reconciliation and its classical and Hellenistic legacy, see Joyce 2016. For the wider themes of *homonoia* in accounts of classical Athenian history, see Christ 2012: 50–67. On the idea more broadly, see Funke 1980: 13–26; Christ 2012: 50–67; Gray 2015: 39–41; 2018: 144–5.

128 Shear 2011: 296 note 30; on the inscriptions which emphasised the return to democracy, see Shear 2011: 162: 'inscriptions all reminded the readers of what it meant to be Athenian and what being democratic entailed ... the memory created, consequently, will function as a "national" memory to unify them.' For another approach to memory (and forgetting) in the post-oligarchic reconciliation, see Loraux 2002 and Wolpert 2002 (concentrating on the relevant speeches of Lysias).

amount of decree-making activity undertaken in the aftermath of the revival of democracy (see DD 1–19); moreover, in the years after the restoration of 403/2, a number of honorific decrees of the era before 404 were re-inscribed on stone.[129] In investing in the creation of such inscriptions,[130] the Athenians were showing that they were ready to re-affirm privileges that had been abolished in the time of the Thirty:[131] restoration of the fifth-century honorific record was an important aspect of the restoration of democracy. Moreover, our literary sources suggest that this year was one of the busiest in terms of not only the initiation of the revision-process of Athenian laws but also the enactments of decrees by the Athenian assembly: some 19 of the 245 decrees firmly attested in the literary record can reasonably be placed in that year or thereabouts,[132] and as many as eight inscribed decrees can reasonably associated with the year 403/2.[133] However, close examination of the literary records (for which, see Inventory D1–19) shows that few of these decrees are unproblematic in terms of their dating and content: there is a lack of clarity in these testimonia in terms of the content, status and date.[134] The reason for this lack of clarity is that accounts of these decrees of the period were put to use in strongly rhetorically charged contexts, some of which, as we will see, have an interest in creating a rose-tinted account of the decrees of those years.[135]

Andocides, in *On the Mysteries*, made reference to a number of the decrees of that year relating to the reorganisation of Athenian legislation (DD 1, 2, 7, 8, 19). He did so in support of a claim – central to a wider argument protesting his innocence – that, given the revision of laws introduced by the decree of Teisamenos of 403/2 (And. 1.82-4), the earlier decree of Isotimides which excluded him from the agora and the temples of Attica was invalid (1.8) and did

---

129 *IG* II² 1; 6 lines 11–15; 9; 52 lines 4–8; 66; *Agora* XVI 37 lines 7–15, 39. For an outline of these reinscribed decrees, see Lambert 2018: 145–6.

130 It is worth noting, however, that on at least one occasion the funding of the inscription was to be funded by the honorand: *IG* II² 6 lines 14–16.

131 In addition to destroying inscribed honorific decrees, the Thirty were associated with the destruction of inscribed records of enemies of the democracy (cf. the story of Leodamas: Arist. *Rhet.*, 2.23.25 = 1400a32–6).

132 See Volume 1, Inventory A Checklist.

133 *IG* II² 1–7; *SEG* XXVIII 45 (cf. D15) and, more controversially *SEG* XXVIII 46 (cf. D17).

134 For the difficulties in reconstructing the reconciliation agreement, see Loening 1987.

135 For modern discussions of the reconciliation, see Quillin 2002, Wolpert 2002, Lanni 2016: 179–99 (at 198, emphasising its 'expressive and persuasive effect'); on the amnesty legislation, see Carawan 2013: 171–202 (taking the view that the pledge 'not to remember ills' applied to specific reconciliatory agreements; Joyce 2016, on the other hand, makes a case for the traditional view that the pledge was a wide-ranging promise not to seek retribution of any kind); for another broad interpretation see Gray 2015: 87.

48 DECREES OF FOURTH-CENTURY ATHENS

not affect him (1.71). At the same time he emphasises the sense of popular unity expressed through these decrees:

> After your return to Athens from Piraeus, though it was possible for you to take revenge (γενόμενον ἐφ' ὑμῖν τιμωρεῖσθαι), you decided to let bygones be bygones (ἔγνωτε ἐᾶν τὰ γεγενημένα). You prioritised the preservation of Athens over personal vengeance, and it was resolved not to revive accusations against one another for what had happened. On resolving this you appointed twenty men (εἵλεσθε ἄνδρας εἴκοσι) ... You organised a meeting of the assembly, discussed the matters, and voted that the laws were to be examined (ἐψηφίσασθε δοκιμάσαντες πάντας τοὺς νόμους), then those which were scrutinised would be written up at the Stoa. (And. 1.81–2 (cf. D1 T2 and D2 T1), trans. MacDowell 1998, adapted)

In this passage, the emphasis upon the second person plural, that is, the Athenian male citizens (cf. D23 T2; D41 T1; D46 T2), as agents behind the decree, is striking: Andocides stresses the role of his audience, in initiating the reconciliation and reconstitution of the laws. This is a reasonable claim to make: a significant proportion of his audience would have been aware of the constitutional changes undertaken by the Athenians just three years previously. Elsewhere in his speech he emphasised *homonoia* and amnesty (And. 1.108–9). Of course Andocides, speaking in his own defence, had a reason for portraying the harmoniousness of these changes: what he wanted to do was to stress the success of the reconciliation, which was such that the pre-Euclidian decree of Isotimides, with which he was threatened, was no longer valid. But the perspective appears to have been echoed in other oratory: a number of other speeches, which reach out to a wider historical perspective, underline the paradigmatic nature of the legislation in the aftermath of the Thirty.

Recollections of the democratic reconciliation were founded upon knowledge of decrees in the work also of other orators. Isocrates – a speaker with serious reservations about the democratic process – was hardly a natural advocate of the power of the decree: in his *Areopagitikos*, dated usually to the period after the Social War, he argued that morals – not decrees – underlay the smooth running of a community:

> Those who are rightly governed, on the other hand, do not need to fill their porticoes with letters (οὐ τὰς στοὰς ἐμπιπλάναι γραμμάτων), but only to cherish justice in their souls; for it is not by decrees, but by morals, that states are well directed (οὐ γὰρ τοῖς ψηφίσμασιν ἀλλὰ τοῖς ἤθεσι καλῶς οἰκεῖσθαι τὰς πόλεις), since men who are badly reared will venture to transgress even laws which are drawn up with minute exactness (τοὺς ἀκριβῶς τῶν νόμων ἀναγεγραμμένους τολμήσειν παραβαίνειν), whereas those who are well

SOCIAL CAPITAL OF THE DECREE 49

brought up will be willing to respect even simple norms (καὶ τοῖς ἁπλῶς κειμένοις ἐθελήσειν ἐμμένειν). (Isocrates 7 *Areopagitikos* 41 tr. Norlin adapted)

However, later in that same piece (7.68–9) he recalled the decision of the Athenian people to repay debts incurred by the Thirty (D13 T1) as a 'beautiful and great testimony of the fairness of the people' (κάλλιστον καὶ μέγιστον τεκμήριον τῆς ἐπιεικείας τοῦ δήμου), and as a vital stage in the establishment of *homonoia* at Athens.[136] Isocrates appears to make reference in such a positive way to this decree[137] in order to rebut the criticism levelled against him for his anti-democratic views (7.70).[138] His view of this particular decree was re-asserted, in the context of the law-courts, also by Demosthenes in the *Against Leptines* (20.11–12 = D13 T2), who also wanted to make a point about it illustrating the trustworthy *ethos* of the Athenians which contradicts the legislation of Leptines he is attacking. For Demosthenes, this decision forms part of a much wider view on the credibility of Athenian decrees and the argument that Leptines' law, by cancelling awards of exemption (*ateleia*), will do much to damage this reputation. What these deployments of decrees have in common, however, is that they place emphasis on the unity of the Athenians and the view that the legislation of that year was worthwhile.

The positive view of the decrees of 403/2 surfaces again in the 330s: Aeschines, in his attack on Ktesiphon's honours for Demosthenes (D179), cited the reward for the democrats of Phyle (D15) to exemplify honours bestowed in an appropriate manner upon a deserving people. In this case, Aeschines drew upon the contrast between the 'good' decree rewarding the democrats and the 'shameful' decree of Ktesiphon for Demosthenes, saying, 'if this resolution is good (εἰ τοῦτ' ἔχει καλῶς), the other was bad (ἐκεῖνο αἰσχρῶς). If they were worthily (κατ' ἀξίαν) honoured, this man is unworthy (ἀνάξιος) of the crown that is proposed' (Aeschin. 3.188).[139] The threat was that Demosthenes' decree would bring shame on the Athenian people, an argument we encounter in other critiques of decrees.[140] But here the mode of citation is slightly different, with the speaker emphasising also the role of the proposer (ὁ τὸ ψήφισμα νικήσας) Archinos (3.187 = D15 T1), in order to juxtapose his diligence with the illegal-ity of Ktesiphon's proposals. Clearly in this case the role of the proposer bears particular significance for the rhetorical deployment of the decree, and suggests

---

136 *Areopagitikos* 69: 'καὶ γάρ τοι διὰ ταύτην τὴν γνώμην εἰς τοιαύτην ἡμᾶς ὁμόνοιαν κατέστησαν.'
137 For Isocrates' presentation of the decision as a decision of the assembly, see D13 Commentary.
138 This is the suggestion of Usher 1999: 305.
139 On the rhetoric of shame associated with decrees, see also Chapter 2.4.1 below.
140 Dem. 23.142 = D59 T1; Dem. 23.172 = D81 T1.

that his involvement in the reconciliation after the fall of the Thirty contributed to the emergence of a positive reputation.[141] But the reward was described still as one 'which you [i.e. the *demos*] gave' (ἣν ἔδοτε δωρεάν) to the honorands (3.187): the role of the individual as proposer of a noble decree is combined with that of the *demos* as gracious donor of the reward.

A further paradigm which is drawn out of the decrees of this era in the law-courts arises in Lycurgus' citation of the decree of Demophantos against political usurpers (which he places in the era after the Thirty: see Lycurg. 1.124–6 = D19 T3) as an example of paradigmatic harshness: he urged the Athenians to replicate these standards by condemning the runaway Leokrates (127), telling the Athenians that they had sworn in this decree to kill such a traitor.[142] In this and the other rhetorical contexts, orators attempted to direct the opinions of their audience by using decrees to portray a picture of paradigmatic harmony and unity and steadfastness against common threats.[143] The accounts amount almost to a (re-)foundation story of democracy according to which Athenian harmony was recreated through the votes of the assembly. Perhaps the strength of the decrees lie in their enduring relevance: even if they were enacted at some point 70 years before the orator was speaking, they could still be presented as contemporary and authoritative. This was done easily with decrees because, as enactments of the people, they could be presented as their own decision which bore lasting consequences.

This optimistic perspective was not restricted to oratory: as I note in Volume 1 (D1 Literary Context), the most detailed account of the terms of the reconciliation is that which appears in the *Ath. Pol.*'s account of the events of 404/3–403/2 (D1 T1), and the author does so to support his claim that the Athenians behaved with moderation and fairness towards even those who had been responsible for previous disasters (*Ath. Pol.* 40.2–3).[144] Such a classical perspective gave rise to a wider praise of the decree for the amnesty: it was held up by Plutarch, in his *Precepts of Statecraft*, as an example of the type of act through which statesmen could improve the characters of their contemporaries (Plu. *Mor.* 814a–b).[145] But

---

141 For his political acts, see Hansen 1983: 38.

142 'διομωμόκατε δ' ἐν τῷ ψηφίσματι τῷ Δημοφάντου κτενεῖν τὸν τὴν πατρίδα προδιδόντα καὶ λόγῳ καὶ ἔργῳ καὶ χειρὶ καὶ ψήφῳ'. For discussion of the date and content of this decree, see D19.

143 See Dem. 19.276–9 (= D27 T2) for citation of a decree putting ambassadors to death as an example of the way in which Demosthenes wanted the Athenians to treat those responsible for the Peace of Philokrates. The treatment of Arthmios and Kallias who negotiated peace with the Persians is cited in support of the same argument (Dem. 19.268–72) as is the decree against those who betrayed the Olynthians (Dem. 19.267 = D119 T1).

144 Elsewhere, the reconciliation was held up as an achievement which demonstrated Athenian wisdom: Aeschin. 2.176–7.

145 On the rhetoric of the success of the Athenian reconciliation, see Gray 2015: 87–90, 177.

it was an idealising view of the past: we should remember that it is clear, as Shear highlights, that in 403/2 there was not a complete consensus on the mode of reconciliation. We know about a number of proposals of that year the rectitude of which was challenged,[146] and the accounts that we have of these disputes contradict the impressions of concord that are expressed in Andocides' and others' accounts of the decrees of that year.[147]

So far, we have seen that the history of decrees was deployed by orators to contribute towards a vision of unity after a period of adversity: in this way, knowledge of decrees was used to generate a feeling of social capital which emphasised the contribution of the people to the creation of a post-crisis reconciliation.[148] The names of proposers, we should note, usually do not loom large when decrees are cited to this end. When we look at the representation of decrees of the second half of the fourth century, we encounter also their deployment in the creation of narratives about a rather different political atmosphere, but nevertheless one that was, according to one view, addressed by the people's decrees.

1.5.2 Decrees and Social Cohesion in the Face of Crisis

Fourth-century Athenians were painfully aware of the difficulties that they faced in negotiating their place in the world at the time of the emergence of Philip of Macedon's power over Greece (cf. Chapter 1.4 above); this feeling was particularly acute in the aftermath of the Peace of Philokrates in 346, after which they had effectively abandoned their Phokian former allies to their enemy. Portrayals of crisis were an important feature of narratives about the year during which the Peace was agreed: Aeschines, in his speech *On the False Embassy* (Aeschin. 2.73), cited the emergency decree of Kephisophon recalling an Athenian general on campaign (D129) as a way of evoking the crisis under which the Athenians made the peace of Philokrates; he claimed that:

> things were so precarious and dangerous (σφαλερὰ καὶ ἐπικίνδυνα τὰ πράγματα) that Kephisophon of Paiania, one of the friends and accomplices of Chares, was forced to propose a decree (ἠναγκάσθη γράψαι ψήφισμα) that Antiochos, the commander of the dispatch-boats, should set sail quickly and should seek out the general commanding our forces.

---

146 For disagreements about the mode of reconciliation in 403/2, see Shear 2011: 260, 312; for *graphe paranomon* against decrees of that year, see D5 (Thrasyboulos' proposal = Hansen 1974 no. 4), D17 (Theozotides' proposal = Hansen 1974 no. 5). For the rejected proposal of Phormisios, see D4.
147 For other accounts of the decrees of 403/2, see DD 1–13.
148 On wider claims about *homonoia* in Athenian self-perceptions, see Christ 2012: 50–67.

The decree was recited to demonstrate the circumstances during which the debate on the peace of 346 was undertaken: accordingly, Aeschines attempted to deflect responsibility for making the peace away from himself and the other envoys sent to Philip. Knowledge of decrees, therefore, was deployed in the rhetorical construction of crisis and necessity. On one hand this was a reflection of the fact that crisis and perception of crisis was an important driver of policy in the fourth-century assembly. Yet, as we shall see, it is an indication of the interest that individual orators had in evoking memories of crisis and the role of the decree as a community-sanctioned means of dealing with emergencies.

Some 10 decrees in the literary record are associated with the year of the archonship of Chairondas (338/7), in other words the ten-month period after the Athenian disaster at Chaironeia in August 338 (see DD 167–76). This survival rate points to the possibility that more decrees were passed during years of crisis in an attempt to meet perceived external threats; but it is just as likely that decrees undertaken in reaction to crisis were more likely than those of other times to become lodged into public memory because they were instrumental in the description of a critical point in history. In his prosecution of the runaway Leokrates of 331, Lycurgus drew widely upon examples from mythology,[149] and history both ancient and contemporary. In particular, he made use of decrees of that year to heighten this feeling of crisis, citing at 1.16 the decree evacuating the countryside (= D167b) and at 1.36 a decree that the council should go down to the Piraeus armed (= D167c); he emphasised that the latter was passed as a consequence of the risks (κίνδυνοι) that the city faced up to at the time. He cited also Hypereides' decree (later overturned – though Lycurgus did not acknowledge as much – as illegal) which enfranchised those without citizen rights (1.41–2 = D167a), and held it up in contrast to the Athenian claim to be 'autochthonous and free'. At 1.53 he accounted for the decree declaring that anyone leaving the city would be a traitor (= D168), saying that it was inspired by the people's sense of horror (ὁ δῆμος δεινὸν ἡγησάμενος) at what was happening. In one of the more allusive and roundabout arguments he puts forward, towards the end of the speech against Leokrates, Lycurgus had a decree on piety read out, and he claimed that Leokrates' behaviour threatened to destroy the principles which it entailed (Lycurg. 1.146 = D240).[150]

---

149 Brock 1998; Grethlein 2014.On the date of Lycurgus' speech, see note 116 above.
150 There is evidence – in the form of references made by later writers to his speeches – to show that Lycurgus drew upon his knowledge of decrees also in other, non-extant, speeches: see fr. 58 Conomis (fifth-century crown of foliage for Pericles); fr. 31 Conomis (decree on priestess' seal) = D241; fr. 19 Conomis (crown for Kallisthenes) = D244; fr. 20 Conomis (statue for Epikrates) = D189.

Lycurgus' presentation of these decrees on one level reflects one aspect of the reality of crisis after Chaironeia. The fact that Hypereides' decree about enfranchising those who lacked citizen rights (D167a) was indicted as illegal shows that there were disputes about the right way to meet the challenges the Athenians faced. Yet even if decrees did not solve the problems that the Athenians faced, according to Lycurgus, they showed how the people shared in the crisis. Lycurgus' portrayal of the situation and emphasis on the dangers faced by the Athenians was of course rhetorically important for his argument against the defendant Leokrates who, he claimed, ignored the depth of crisis that faced Athens and therefore deserved to be punished as a traitor. Lycurgus wanted also to make the point that the Athenians – through decisions of the *demos* – were able to live up to the challenges of such crises: he did this in order to convince the people that the condemnation of Leokrates would be in tune with their past record of dealing with crisis. The same view is communicated also by Lycurgus' elaboration of decrees against traitors in earlier times of crisis,[151] describing, for instance, the decree against a traitor at Salamis in 480 as 'an admirable decree, worthy of your ancestors', which revealed the nobility (εὐγένεια) of the Athenians.[152] It is, however, striking that he offers up this historic decree as symbolising Athenian virtue, whereas contemporary decrees are reflections of Athens' precarious position.

1.5.3 Decrees as Historical Paradigms of Athenian Values

Lycurgus was not alone among the politicians of the fourth century in drawing upon historical decrees in the illustration of the virtues of the Athenian people and their tendencies to face up to crisis: Demosthenes, Aeschines and Dinarchus too drew upon decrees of the Persian War, like that against the traitor Arthmios, in the construction of their arguments; their references to an inscribed version of it strongly suggest that the Athenians at some point in this

---

151 Lycurgus made use also of past decrees of the Athenians, including Kritias' decree condemning Phrynichos as a traitor and a subsequent decree against his supporters (112–15), the decree ordering the destruction of the bronze statue of Hipparchos son of Charmos (117–18), the decree condemning Athenians who withdrew to the Lakedaimonians at Dekeleia during the Peloponnesian War, and the decree against a traitor at Salamis in 480 (122). For discussion of the reliability of Lycurgus' accounts, see Rhodes and Osborne 2003: 444–5. Lambert has made a case for a related phenomenon, the tendency of epigraphical decrees to connect with the past: see Lambert 2018: 115–53.

152 Lycurgus may be alluding to a story about the stoning of Lykidas who had proposed that the Athenians accept terms with the Persians after Salamis (Hdt. 9.5), a version of which episode may be alluded to by Demosthenes (18.204). For Herodotus' version of the episode, see Chapter 5 below.

54 DECREES OF FOURTH-CENTURY ATHENS

era even fabricated a version of it on the acropolis.[153] In particular, Demosthenes in his speech defending his conduct as an ambassador to Philip, maintained that the treatment of Arthmios represented paradigmatic Athenian harshness towards traitors:

> You hear, men of Athens, the record which declares (τῶν γραμμάτων λεγόντων) Arthmios son of Pythonax, of Zelea, to be enemy and foeman of the Athenians and their allies, him and all his kindred. His offence was conveying gold from barbarians to Greeks. Hence, apparently, we may conclude that your ancestors were anxious to prevent any man, even an alien, taking rewards to do injury to Greece; but you take no thought to discountenance wrongs done by your own citizens to your own city. Does anyone say that these words (τὰ γράμματα) have been set up just anywhere? No; although the whole of our citadel is a holy place, and although its area is so large, the inscription stands at the right hand beside the great brazen Athene which was dedicated by the state as a memorial of victory in the Persian war, at the expense of the Greeks. In those days, therefore, justice was so venerable, and the punishment of these crimes so meritorious, that the retribution of such offenders was honoured with the same position as Pallas Athene's own prize of victory. Today we have instead mockery, impunity, dishonour, unless you restrain the licence of these men. (Dem. 19.271–2 trans. Vince and Vince adapted)

The citation of the example of Arthmios deserves note: the deployment of historic decrees was a practice which enabled orators in both the assembly and lawcourts to enhance the well-established tendency to look towards historical examples for examples of paradigmatic behaviour with the institutional authority of the decree.[154] Past decrees could be presented as timeless, and applicable outside their immediate contexts; they developed a rhetorical fiction by which, as Wolpert suggests, the rule of the people was presented as transcending time and place:[155] this is why Apollodoros was able to cite a fifth-century decree for the Plataeans to make a point about the value of Athenian citizenship ([Dem.]

---

153 Dem. 9.41–3, 19.271–2; Din. 2.24–5; Aesch. 3.258; of these only Dinarchus makes it clear that it was an enactment voted by the people. For a full account of the testimonia for the Arthmios decree, see Meiggs 1972: 508–12 and Habicht 1961: 18–19; on the deployment of it in making claims about the relevance of past decrees, see Low forthcoming. For the other Persian war era decrees cited by Attic orators, see Chapter 5.5.1 below with note 113.

154 The tendency to cite Persian war era decisions in the lawcourts stretches back at least as far as the start of the fourth century: see Andocides 1.107 citing the decision of the Athenians to restore exiles and re-instate disenfranchised citizens before Marathon. On the uses of the past in fourth-century oratory, see Nouhaud 1982, Rhodes 2011; Hesk 2012, Grethlein 2014; Westwood 2017. On the uses of the past in fourth-century Athenian decrees, see Lambert 2018: 115–70.

155 See Wolpert 2003.

59.104 cf. D49 T2); this is why also the Athenians appear to have re-inscribed decrees from the Persian wars in the second half of the fourth century as examples of virtuous conduct in the face of external threats.[156]

Moving slightly closer to a decree of a contemporary period, Dinarchus (1.39–40 = D44 T1), in his discussion of those politicians who behaved in a way equivalent to the reputation of the Athenians (contrasted to the behaviour of Demosthenes on receipt of Harpalos' money), says that Kephalos' decree of winter 379/8, proposing that the Athenians should march out to help the exiles who had fled Thebes, lived up to the ancestral reputation of the Athenians;[157] Dinarchus in this way praised the proposer, but his emphasis on the fact that the Athenians had fulfilled the decree bolstered the point that they had on this occasion lived up to the reputation of their ancestors. Such a simultaneous praise of proposer and past Athenian habits is reminiscent of Aeschines' discussion of Archinos' decree rewarding the democrats of 404/3 (see Chapter 1.5.1 above).

Finally, we should also point out that particularly in the late fourth century there is a tendency in argumentation to intermingle contemporary with past decrees. Demosthenes, for instance, cited old cases alongside decrees passed within the lifetime of his audience as examples of penalties imposed by the Athenians (Dem. 19.276 = D27 T2). Moreover, Hypereides, in his prosecution of Athenogenes, offers another example of a decree illustrating the good nature of the Athenian *demos* when he points to its reward of citizenship to Troizenians as illustrating the people's readiness to remember another community's good deed during the Persian Wars (D175).[158] His argument was that the behaviour of his opponent, Athenogenes, contradicted not only the substance but also the spirit of Athenian decrees. But in the case of Hypereides' citation it is actually impossible to tell whether or not a decree being cited is historical or contemporary, and it is not altogether clear that the audience would have been any more enlightened. The myth of continuity – the impression that the Athenians made decrees back in the fifth century in the same way, and to the same effect, as they did at the time of speaking – underscored the rhetoric in

---

156 Habicht 1961; see Chapter 1.5.3 above and Chapter 5.4.1 below.

157 The view that an Athenian decree was an indication of Athenian good character is suggested also by Demosthenes' claim that accepting Corinthian exiles was a deed of *kaloi kagathoi* men: see Dem. 20.54 (= D41) and discussion in Kremmydas 2012: 189–90 (on *philoxenia*) and Canevaro 2016a: 287. For the view that Kephalos' decree in assistance of Theban exiles in 379/8 was in tune with Athenian character, see Din. 1.39 (= D44).

158 Demosthenes in the *Against Leptines* points to honorific decrees – of both the fifth and fourth centuries – as an indication of Athenian readiness to return favours: see Dem. 20.64. For a list of the decrees he cites, see note 114 above.

56 DECREES OF FOURTH-CENTURY ATHENS

such contexts.[159] In effect, this oratorical emphasis on the timeless relevance of some decrees[160] contradicts the widely held view that decrees were enactments which had only a restricted duration of relevance (cf. Chapter 1.2.2 above). At the same time, we must remember the malleability of this aspect of the decree, given that some advocates emphasise their contemporaneity: Aeschines 1.81 (D138 T1), for instance, used decrees to focus his audience's attention on the present in his discussion of Timarchos' career, urging them to focus on what happened at a particular assembly meeting.[161]

While, of necessity, Attic orators and politicians built arguments upon decrees that had been enacted in the past, the fact that they could be portrayed as enactments of 'you, the people' meant that they possessed an enduring value. Accordingly, as tools of argument, they could be used to build a bridge between past and present, and to hold the people, or individual proposers, responsible for those past decisions that have given rise to a current scenario or dilemma; this, perhaps, has broader implications: recent studies have placed emphasis on the role of the past in the creation of social memory; what I suggest is that the past and present decrees were co-opted in the construction of the past and ideas about morality, blame, identity and Athenian self-interest, a combination which has been underplayed in contemporary studies on the construction of social memory.[162]

1.6 Conclusion

Over the course of this chapter I have explored the nature and limits of the authority of the Athenian decree (Chapter 1.1–1.2 above) and the relationship between perceptions of the decree and democratic norms (Chapter 1.3 above). I explained the profile of the decree in the context of literary accounts of Athens' fluctuating geopolitical situation in the fourth century (Chapter 1.4 above).

159 On the importance of myth-making in the success of particular institutions, see Meyer and Rowan 1991.
160 This is an aspect discussed also in Chapter 2.4.1 below.
161 Aeschin. 1.81 = D138 T1: 'I omit mention of many of those things which happened long ago, but I want to remind you of what happened at that assembly, when I proclaimed this prosecution of Timarchos. When the Areopagus council appeared before the assembly in relation to the decree which this Timarchos made about the dwelling-houses on the Pnyx ('κατὰ τὸ ψήφισμα, ὃ οὗτος εἰρήκει περὶ τῶν οἰκήσεων τῶν ἐν τῇ Πυκνί'), it was Autolykos, a member of the Areiopagos, who made the speech, a man who, by Zeus and Apollo, lived his life with honour, with piety and was worthy of that institution.'
162 On the 'past-connectedness' of Lycurgan-era epigraphical publishing habits, see Lambert 2018: 115–53. Lambert 2012b emphasises the way in which the democratic system was generally regarded as the creation of the era before the fifth century.

Towards the end of this chapter (Chapter 1.5 above) I underlined the role that decrees played in oratorical portrayals of the group psychology of the *demos* of Athens – past and present – and its reaction to particular developments; these images were evoked, ultimately, as part of the wider construction of arguments. Nevertheless, they emphasise the collective role of the *demos* in using decrees: this is perhaps why Lycurgus omits to mention that the decree on enfranchisement (Lycurg. 1.41 = D167a) was overturned by *graphe paranomon*. Speakers, then, held up decrees to represent a mainstay of social cohesion in the face of crisis which offered telling juxtaposition with the behaviour of an opponent. It is striking that speakers drew upon both contemporary and historical decrees (see esp. Chapter 1.5.3 above) to present universal norms: in this sense they went way beyond the rather limited view represented in the sources (see Chapter 1.2.2 above) that they were restricted to the implementation of short-term and specific measures. There is, of course, no straightforward answer to the question of whether decrees really did underpin social cohesion: probably it was the case that some of them appeared, to the Athenian demos at particular moments in time, to do so (that is how they came to be passed at the assembly: Canevaro 2018), whereas others were divisive[163] or, like the decree of Theozotides (D17), perceptibly prioritised the interests of particular groups.[164] What is, however, revealing about the extent of orators' deployment of decrees is that they presumed that their audiences would respond to arguments which drew upon them; this, then, is strongly indicative of the high profile of the decree among the Athenian people in the fourth century.

When the Athenian assembly enacted a decree, it represented a collective decision; but of course, as we have noted (Chapter 1.1 above), such decisions had their origins in proposals of individuals. Accordingly, decrees were dynamic in the sense that they had the potential to be represented either as a collective contribution of the demos or as a contribution of an individual proposers. As we will see (in Chapter 2 below), the fact that decrees were proposed by particular individuals meant that credit (or symbolic capital) for them could be accrued – or liability attached to – those individuals. Before we turn to that line of investigation, it is appropriate to introduce some ancient debates about the liability for

---

163 The evidence for decrees that were challenged in the lawcourts can be found in Hansen 1974, a collection of material pertaining to the *graphe paranomon* in classical Athens; these challenges were undertaken no more than a year after their original proposal at the assembly: Giannadaki 2014.

164 For the view that the pursuit of social capital can reproduce inegalitarian structures and practices, see Bourdieu 1986. Yet it can also be a force which introduces measures which place heavier financial burdens on the rich: see, for instance, Demosthenes' proposed law on trierarchic support at Dem. 18.102 (cf. D160).

decrees. This debate was first noted perhaps by Thucydides in the fifth century, in his account of points at which the people expressed anger at the politicians whose proposals they had approved at the assembly (Thuc. 2.61.2, 64.1; cf. 8.1.1): Pericles' response to this was to say that the problem lay not with his policy but the people's implementation of it (Thuc. 2.61.2). Later on in Thucydides' work, Diodotos, in his challenge to the Athenian decree against the Mytileneans of 427, complained that the Athenians would be more careful what they voted for if both proposer and voters were subject to the same penalties (Thuc. 3.43.4–5).[165] A similar dynamic is visible in the sources for fourth-century political rhetoric: the dual potential of the decree was skilfully put to use by Demosthenes in the courts of 343. Speaking against Aeschines and Philokrates for their role in shaping the terms of the Peace of Philokrates, Demosthenes casts his audience's mind back to two earlier decrees, those of Diophantos (D105) and Kallisthenes (D146) as a way of juxtaposing the Athenians' reaction to victory and defeat, respectively:

> Take and read the decree of Diophantos and that of Kallisthenes, so that you might know that, when you did your duty, you were thought worthy of acts of sacrifice and of praise, both at Athens and among other peoples; but that when you were led astray by these men, you brought in your children and women from the countryside and you voted to make the sacrifices to Herakles within the city walls, even while there was peace. (Dem. 19.86)

In this passage Demosthenes wants to hold up a virtuous decree (that of Diophantos, celebrating victory) with a hopeless one (that of Kallisthenes, evacuating the countryside): in order to do so, he associates the first decree with dutiful action and sacrifice by the people, but the latter with the Athenians being misled by its politicians. Accordingly, Demosthenes asserts both the social capital of shared decision-making and also the fact that it was sometimes undermined by the will of feckless politicians. At this point I will move on to explore the deployments of decrees by individual politicians, in the advocacy of their personal political interests, and in the construction of their own political identity.

---

165 For more discussion in Thucydides about liability for decrees, see Chapter 5.2.1 below. The question of responsibility is discussed also in Finley 1962: 3–4.

2

Appropriation and Aspiration: Decrees in the Pursuit of Political Self-Interest

2.1 Introduction

We have shown already (Chapter 1.1–1.3 above) that, despite their institution-alised subordination to law in fourth-century Athens, decrees as a political transaction offered a great deal of persuasive capital on the grounds of their close association with proper democratic procedure. Decrees were deployed to portray the Athenian community's management of reconciliation and its reaction to crisis as a way of grounding arguments about shared values with which the audience would sympathise (Chapter 1.5 above). But such portrayals were deployed primarily in support of the cases of litigants, and they must be understood in that context. Accordingly, at this point I turn to assess the role of the decree in the pursuit of individual political self-interest.

Modern studies of ancient democracy have not thoroughly explicated the relevance of decrees to an assessment of political activity in ancient Athens: over the course of the late twentieth century, a number of scholars have set out models for assessing the activity of Athenian politicians and their interaction with the assembly in the democratic era, but most – with the exception of M.H. Hansen and more recently S.D. Lambert – have done so without close consideration of the significance of the proposal of decrees or the deployment of knowledge of about them.[1] In this chapter, I attempt to redress this imbalance: I shall argue that politicians in the Athenian lawcourts, drawing upon the institutionally-normative basis of decrees (established in Chapter 1.2 and 1.3 above), deployed them extensively in the construction of arguments about themselves and about their opponents; in so doing they contributed to the proliferation of

---

1 Works exploring the relative significance of political leadership and popular contribution include the following: Finley 1962; Connor 1971; Mossé 1989; Rhodes 1986, 2000; Pope 1988; Taylor 2007a, 2007b; Ober 1989; 2008: 124–30, 180; Yunis 1996. For analysis of the significance of proposal of decrees in political activity and profile see Hansen 1989: 1–127, illustrating the breadth of political participation but emphasising the dominance of expertise and leadership; for the epigraphical picture, see Lambert 2018: 171–226, emphasising the spread of political power and influence between multiple individuals.

what we might call decree-minded argumentation among Athenian political actors. Their importance in political life is clearly demonstrated in the fact that orators frequently attempted to generate rhetorical leverage from knowledge of decrees or of practices related to them. This has already been illustrated by reference to the way that the orators use decrees to illustrate the shared values of the Athenian *demos* (Chapter 1.5 above); this chapter, however, will focus upon the role that decrees played in the assessment of individual political activity. After exploring the claims that the Athenians made about the reliability of the decree as evidence (2.2.1), I will look at the deployment of decrees in the portrayal of good and bad human behaviour (2.2.2). At that point, I make a case for the significance in the fourth century of familiarity with decrees and the decree-making and decree-breaking processes for the accrual of symbolic capital (2.3–2.4). In Chapter 2.5, with a view to asking how far expertise in decrees was the preserve of an elite, I will assess the evidence for close attention to the language of decrees and claims made about the proposers' intention and actual consequences of decrees.

2.2 Decrees as Evidence in the Lawcourts

2.2.1 The Reliability of the Decree

It is already well established that laws could be usefully deployed as evidence in a number of ways in the Athenian courts (see Chapter 1 note 65 above). It is noteworthy that Aristotle did not describe decrees among his types of 'inartificial proofs' (*atechnoi pisteis*), but it is possible that he was not trying to distinguish them from laws, which constituted one of the five types that he discussed at length (*Rh.* 1375a22–b25).[2] Yet decrees, evidently, possessed a potentially high status as the bases of arguments in the courts, as proofs of 'fact' that were difficult to dispute. Aeschines, who observed that the preservation of public documents meant that the people were able to probe the political legacy of unscrupulous turncoats (3.75), articulated the view that the decrees of Athens offered insight into the true nature of his opponents: emphasising that the laws forbade the inscription of falsehoods into public decrees (ἐν τοῖς δημοσίοις ψηφίσμασι: 3.50), he juxtaposed the constancy of decrees, standing as they were drafted, with the misleading spoken words of the sycophants (Aeschin. 2.66). Aeschines himself was in the habit of citing decrees in his speeches to support the claim that he was speaking the truth (e.g. Aeschin. 2.46 (= D128 T1), 2.73

---

2 On Aristotle's deployment of these proofs in relation to argumentation, see Carey 1994.

DECREES AND POLITICAL SELF-INTEREST

(= D129 T1), 3.93 (= D147 T1)).[3] He was not alone in championing the idea that the value of decrees was lodged in their nature as true records of things that really had happened:[4] Apollodoros, too, in the speech against Neaira, asked the secretary to read out the fifth-century decree for the Plataeans in order to make the law about Athenian citizenship completely clear ([Dem.] 59.104 = D49 T2) and to demonstrate that he was telling the truth;[5] the example underscored his view on the moral implications of the privilege of citizenship which had been abused by Neaira. Such value attached to decrees meant that they were sometimes held up as evidence in the support of arguments alongside witness-statements (e.g. [Dem.] 50.3 = D67; [Dem.] 50.13 = D70); a decree could itself represent a witness in its own right (Dem. 23.16 = D94 T2).

The idea that decrees were reliable as pieces of evidence was one that underscored their use in accounts of historical situations (see Chapter 1.5 above), but it also enabled their use in the verification of assessments made in the lawcourts of individuals' behaviour. As several extant speeches demonstrate, decrees formed the substance of considerable proportions of the evidence offered in a number of high-profile political contests fought in the second half of the fourth century. The example *par excellence* is the ongoing confrontation between Aeschines and Demosthenes, played out in the lawcourts in 343 and then again in 330, in which they deployed knowledge of decrees, both contemporary and historic, as ammunition in personal and political debate (see Chapter 2.2.2 and 2.3 below). In short, I will make a case for the view that politicians in the late fourth century were able to profitably undertake a 'decree-minded' approach to politics. In the following sections, I will discuss the substance and expression of this decree-mindedness; I will show how exhibiting and deploying knowledge about decrees, proposing them and attacking them were key ways of accruing self-promoting symbolic capital in the Athenian lawcourts. Decrees appear to have worked well as pieces of evidence in those speeches where orators

---

3 The same strategy was used by the speaker at Dem. 23.151 = D64.

4 Hegesippos, for instance, maintained that the existence of a decree emending the Peace of Philokrates undermined Philip's claims that he had never agreed to it ([Dem.] 7.18–19 = D130). For other applications of decrees as proofs, see Dem. 18.115; 19.161.

5 [Dem.] 59.104: 'From your decrees the law will become plain to all and you will know that I am speaking the truth' ('ἐκ γὰρ τῶν ψηφισμάτων τῶν ὑμετέρων καταφανὴς πᾶσιν ἔσται ὁ νόμος, καὶ γνώσεσθ' ὅτι ἀληθῆ λέγω'). On the inauthenticity of the document that appears subsequently in some versions of the text, see Canevaro 2010: it omits two important provisions which Apollodoros claimed it included; it is, therefore, possible either that the text that appears on the page is defective or that Apollodoros is misleading his audience; the former solution is preferable.

attempted to build logical, well-informed arguments.[6] At the same time, it should be noted that extant texts suggest that reference to them in assembly oratory appears to have been made relatively infrequently (see Chapter 2.3.1 below).

2.2.2 Decrees and Dynamics of Behaviour

A key aspect of persuasion in the Athenian law-courts was to represent oneself or one's client in the best possible light and one's enemies in the worst possible way.[7] It has already been shown that law (and other types of evidence) could be used in character portrayal in Attic oratory.[8] Decrees too contributed to such characterisation, and did so in two ways: on one level, honorific decrees were deemed to offer proof of public-spirited character (Chapter 2.2.2.1 below); on another level, exploration of the dynamic between regulatory decrees and human performance (Chapter 2.2.2.2 below) was also relevant to the judicial assessment of those involved in disputes. These two themes will be the focus of discussion in Chapter 2.2.2 as I explore the ways that decrees were used as evidence; the question of characterisation will be revisited in the discussion of decree-making legacy of specific individuals (Chapter 2.3 below).

2.2.2.1 *Announcement and Recital of Honours*

Aristotle defined honour (*time*) as the token of a reputation for doing good (σημεῖον εὐεργετικῆς δόξης) and wrote that those who have done good are justly honoured (*Rh.* 1361a28–9). He defined a number of different parts of honour: it included sacrifices, monuments (*mnemai*) with words and without words, privileges, grants of land, front seats, public burial, state maintenance (*Rh.* 1361a34–6). Claims made by Xenophon and Demosthenes that the Athenians were particularly amenable to honour and reputation (Xen. *Mem.* 3.3.11; 3.5.3;

---

6 For the view that orators in the courts (in contrast to those in the assembly) emphasised logical and the appearance of being well informed, see Bers 2013; Harris 2017b also downplays the role of exaggerated emotional persuasion in the courts. For the role of emotional persuasion in the assembly, see Sanders 2016; Gotteland 2016 notes that Demosthenes offers a critique of emotional persuasion in his prologues, while paradoxically deploying emotional arguments as a way of demonstrating his dedication to the city's interests.

7 On the importance of characterisation in the Athenian courts, see Dyck 1985; Spatharas 2011; Adamidis 2017; for characterisation and self-presentation in the Athenian assembly, see Kremmydas 2016. Hunter 1991 explores the politics of reputation and Wohl 2009 the rhetoric of citizenship.

8 For the role of law in characterisation, see de Brauw 2001–2 and Adamidis 2017: 154–5; for other types of evidence, see Todd 1990a.

Dem. 18.66, 203) should not be read out of context, but it is tempting to hypothesise that they reflect the fact that the Athenians were particularly interested in the question of how to recognise euergetic activity. Indeed, not only literary texts (e.g. Demosthenes 20 *Against Leptines*) but also the inscriptions of fourth-century Athens provide abundant evidence that honorific awards were being bestowed by decree of the assembly.[9] The passing of honorific decrees, therefore, was clearly an important medium for the official communuication of the token of honour.

In fourth-century Athens, the fact that honorific transactions carried such weight meant that they were an important part of public life: a large proportion of those decrees which survive in the literary and epigraphical sources are some form of honorific decree, and the proliferation of them expanded particularly in the second half of the fourth century (see Table 1). Many such decrees were set up on stone in prominent places, which constituted an enhancement of the award.[10] However, the decree was not merely a lapidary honour: there was also an oral element to such awards, which went beyond their proposal and discussion at the council and assembly.[11] For example, in his response to Aeschines' claim that proclamation of Ktesiphon's honours for him at the theatre was illegal (Dem. 18.120–2; Aeschin. 3.32–6, 43; cf. D179), Demosthenes revealed a view on why honours were announced in public places: announcement provided, he argued, glory (*zelos*) for the honorand and stimulus for all those listening to doing services for the city (Dem. 18.120).[12] Elsewhere he took the view that worthwhile recipients of honours would give their lives for the city, rather than bringing shame upon the awards that were granted to them (Dem. 20.82).

---

9 For a linguistic survey of honorific awards, see Henry 1981; for awards of the period 352/1–322/1 see Lambert 2012a: 3–47, 93–183.
10 On the point of inscribed honorific decrees, see Lambert 2011a (= Lambert 2018: 71–92); for places of publication see now Lambert 2018: 19–46 citing past scholarship at 20. For detailed discussion of the significance of places of publication of decrees, see Chapter 3.3 below.
11 On the announcement of honours in the theatre, see Hanink 2014: 120; Ceccarelli 2010; Wilson 2009; Wilson and Hartwig 2009; Lambert 2018: 54. See further note 12 below.
12 This was a response to Aeschines' argument that honorands should be content with the admiration of the people (Aeschin. 3.33); he claimed the existence of a law which stated that honours could be announced only at the council and *ecclesia* on the Pnyx (Aeschin. 3.32–48); this was contradicted in a law cited by Demosthenes allowing the announcement of honours in the theatre if the *demos* decreed it (Dem. 18.120–1). See the discussion in Harris 1994: 142, arguing that Aeschines did not have a legally valid case against the announcement of the honours at the theatre; cf. Liddel 2007: 170–4. Honorific decrees are known to have been enacted at the assembly which took place at the theatre after the festival of Dionysia: see *IG* II³ 1 344, 345, 346, 347, 384. On this meeting of the assembly, see Lambert 2008: 52–3 and Harris 2013b: 211–13, 222.

64   DECREES OF FOURTH-CENTURY ATHENS

Despite the contentiousness of the question of where honorific decrees for citizens could legally be proclaimed in fourth-century Athens, it is likely that announcement – at the assembly or at the theatre of Dionysos – was normal. It was an ostentatious expression of the fact the honorand had been granted the token of honour as outlined in Aristotle's *Rhetoric*. But honorific decrees could also be discussed as a way of conspicuously asserting how one had behaved in the interests of the wider community. The oratorical citation of honorific decrees suggests that they offered value to those who aimed to make a case about their own good behaviour and the community's recognition of it. This is a phenomenon attested from the late 360s onwards, in Apollodoros' speech (preserved as [Demosthenes] 50) *Against Polykles* in which he attacked his opponent for not taking up his trierarchic service; in that speech, he reminded the audience of his own euergetic service, telling them that in order to ensure that he did not neglect to follow the orders which the people sent him, he pledged his estate as security to two lenders in order to fund the remuneration of his sailors. Accordingly, the people praised him and granted him dinner at the *prytaneion* as a reward; he had the decree read out, telling the jury that he did so to illustrate the truth of the matter (Dem. 50.13 = D70).[13]

It is hardly surprising that the reading out of honorific decrees was a practice in which Aeschines and Demosthenes engaged in their disputes in both 343 and again in 330: they read out or referred to honorific decrees passed in their honour in those speeches in which they gave an account of their public careers. Aeschines in 343 explained and read aloud the honours that he was awarded for his participation at the battle of Tamynai (Aeschin. 2.169–70 = D114) in order to support his assertion that he was not, as Demosthenes claimed, a hater of the people (*misodemos*) but a hater of wickedness (*misoponeros*), and that he encouraged others to emulate activities that were good and salutary to the city (2.171). It is clear that the reading of honorific decrees in one's favour was a practice that offered clear ammunition in the whitewashing of one's own character and career; for Demosthenes, too, the reading of honorific decrees passed

---

13 [Dem.] 50.13: 'Pledging my estate to Thrasylochos and Archeneos as security for the 30 *mnai* which I borrowed from them and paid to the sailors, I set out to sea, so that nothing of the things which the people had ordered me might be neglected. And the people, hearing of this, both praised me, and invited me to dinner at the *prytaneion*. And to show that I am telling the truth, a witness statement of these things and the decree of the people will be read to you. WITNESS STATEMENT. DECREE.' (ὑποθεὶς δὲ τὸ χωρίον Θρασυλόχῳ καὶ Ἀρχένεῳ, καὶ δανεισάμενος τριάκοντα μνᾶς παρ' αὐτῶν καὶ διαδοὺς τοῖς ναύταις, ᾠχόμην ἀναγόμενος, ἵνα μηδὲν ἐλλείποι τῷ δήμῳ ὧν προσέταξε τὸ κατ' ἐμέ. καὶ ὁ δῆμος ἀκούσας ταῦτα ἐπῄνεσέν τέ με, καὶ ἐπὶ δεῖπνον εἰς τὸ πρυτανεῖον ἐκάλεσεν. καὶ ὡς ταῦτ' ἀληθῆ λέγω, τούτων ὑμῖν ἀναγνώσεται τὴν μαρτυρίαν καὶ τὸ ψήφισμα τὸ τοῦ δήμου. ΜΑΡΤΥΡΙΑ. ΨΗΦΙΣΜΑ.'). There is a notable absence of any comparable decree from the evidence offered in support of the speaker's liturgical claims in earlier speeches such as Lys. 21.1-12.

in his honour not only offered parallels to those aspects of Ktesiphon's proposal which were under attack from Aeschines (Dem. 18.83 (= D156), 222–3 (= D166)) but also re-iterated his argument about how he was worthy of praise.

The same practice is attested elsewhere in other apparently high-profile cases: in the speech *Against Neaira* of the late 340s, perhaps Theomnestos was making a point about the deserved status of his *synegoros* Apollodoros when he opened the speech with an account of the citizenship decree granted by the Athenians in recognition of his father's service to the city ('διὰ τὰς εὐεργεσίας τὰς εἰς τὴν πόλιν': [Dem.] 59.2 = D42).[14] Litigants generally, however, seem to have been relatively restrained in their discussion of decrees in their own favour; more often their citation was not about self-adulation – which might, given Aeschines' warnings against the moral consequences of granting *charis* to those who seek it (Aeschin. 3.180), have run the risk of appearing excessive – but about illustrating particular parts of their argument. Indeed, oratorical discussion of them suggests that the enactment by the people of these honours was as highly valued as were the good deeds behind them, and this may reflect the reluctance of inscribed honorific decrees of the fourth century to offer details of the actions of honorands.[15] Accordingly, Euxitheos in his speech *Against Euboulides* mentions the decree passed in his honour by his fellow demesmen apparently to illustrate the conspiracy against him in the deme: his enemies had had the inscribed version of it chiselled out as a way of undermining him (Dem. 57.65); there was no need for him to offer any justification for the award. At the same time, his claim about the legitimacy of his citizenship would certainly have been bolstered by the status implied in his reminiscence of this decree. The citation of honorific decrees illustrates also one aspect of a wider theme: the rhetorical deployment of accounts of the relationship between individual good behaviour and the Athenian decree. In what follows I explore how this was worked out with respect to accounts of non-honorific decrees.

2.2.2.2 Conforming – and not Conforming – with Decrees

There exists scholarly debate on the question of legislative enforcement in ancient Athens. A balanced view is that the enforcement of laws was heavily reliant upon the readiness of individuals, as magistrates, or at some points as

---

14 As I note in D42 Literary Context, the speaker is also explaining his family connection to Apollodoros.

15 Before the 320s, epigraphically published details about the deeds of honorands for which they were being honoured were usually brief and formulaic: see Low 2016.

66 DECREES OF FOURTH-CENTURY ATHENS

citizens, to implement their provisions as they interpreted them:[16] this is because the judicial and executive processes of the Athenians were set in motion only on the initiative of magistrates and individual citizens (in the assembly and council). The heavy reliance upon individual activity for the enforcement of decrees too (see Chapter 3.2.1 below) meant that, in accounts of obedience and public performance, there was political capital to be gained from exploring the relationship between Athenian decrees and human activity. The speaker of Demosthenes 47, justifying his efforts to exact state property from Theophemos, claims that he was obedient to a decree of the council which ordered him as a successor trierarch to recover in any way possible the ship's equipment retained by his predecessor Theophemos; accordingly, he vividly describes his demand for the gear, in accordance with the decree, which he appears to have wielded in his hand (ἔχων τὸ ψήφισμα: 47.34; cf. 47.20 = D85).[17] This is an example of a rhetorical strategy widely deployed,[18] an account which presented one man's behaviour as the virtuous performance of the orders of a decree, while representing his opponent's as its infringement. Orators argued also that they or their clients had gone beyond the requirements of a decree: in his account of his own investment in trierarchic activity, [Apollodoros] (Dem. 50.3–7 = D67)

16 Modern scholars have placed different weightings on each of these factors: on Athenian 'self help' in enforcement of the law, see Hunter 1994; Harris challenges Hunter's view, and emphasises the role of magistrates in the enforcement of laws and decrees: see Harris 2007, 2013a: 26–59, 349–52. Herman, meanwhile, has made a case for an internalised code of self-restraint combined with a limited coercive state apparatus: see Herman 2006. An alternative view is that of Lanni 2012, 2016, emphasising the role of legal institutions in encouraging (rather than coercing) compliance with the law; Gottesman 2014: 67 suggests that popular sentiment in the assembly and courts would have determined how far legislation and decrees were imposed, but largely ignores the role of magistrates; Wallace 2012 points out that the Athenians did not always successfully enforce their laws; the same would have applied to decrees, as Demosthenes acknowledged: Mader 2006 and Chapter 2.5.2 below.
17 Dem. 47.33–4: 'And after many speeches, the Council replied with a decree that the secretary shall read to you, that we were to make the recovery in any way we could. Decree. Well then, when this decree had been passed by the Council and no one brought in an indictment against it for illegality but it became operative, I then approached Euergos who is present here, the brother of Theophemos (for I was unable to find the latter); and with the decree in hand I began by demanding the equipment and told him to inform Theophemos.' (trans. Scafuro 2011, adapted) ('καὶ πολλῶν λόγων γενομένων ἀποκρίνεται ἡμῖν ἡ βουλὴ ψηφίσματι, ὃ ἀναγνώσεται ὑμῖν, εἰσπράττεσθαι τρόπῳ ᾧ ἂν δυνώμεθα. Ψήφισμα. γενομένου τοίνυν τοῦ ψηφίσματος τούτου ἐν τῇ βουλῇ, καὶ οὐδενὸς γραφομένου παρανόμων, ἀλλὰ κυρίου ὄντος, προσελθὼν Εὐέργῳ τουτῳὶ τῷ ἀδελφῷ τοῦ Θεοφήμου, ἐπειδὴ τὸν Θεόφημον οὐχ οἷός τε ἦν ἰδεῖν, ἔχων τὸ ψήφισμα πρῶτον μὲν ἀπῄτησα τὰ σκεύη καὶ ἐκέλευσα αὐτὸν φράσαι τῷ Θεοφήμῳ.')
18 In Dem. 47.19, the speaker underlines that he was 'obeying your decrees of the people and council and law' ('ψηφισμάτων δὲ ὑμετέρων δήμου καὶ βουλῆς καὶ νόμου ἐπιτάξαντος'). See also Dem. 51.4 (= D76 T2).

DECREES AND POLITICAL SELF-INTEREST

claimed that he had done markedly better than Aristophon's ineffective decree on enrolment.

A similar tactic emerges in an attempt to challenge an opponent's claims about good behaviour: Apollodoros spoke of his rival, the reluctant trierarch Polykles, being 'forced by you and your decrees' to take over the command of a ship ([Dem.] 50.29 = D69: 'ἐπειδὴ ὑφ' ὑμῶν καὶ τοῦ ψηφίσματος τοῦ ὑμετέρου ἠναγκάσθη ἐπὶ τὴν ναῦν ἀπιέναι'); this was a way of undermining the possibility that his opponent would have done something public-spirited of his own volition. Immediately before that, in the same speech, the speaker claimed that he had paid the costs of the expedition voted by the people in advance (Dem. 50.8 = D68), in other words, in compliance with a decree.

Other orators made much of the converse argument, that the behaviour of an opponent contradicted the provisions of a decree: this is what Demosthenes at 19.278 says about the behaviour of the ambassadors (including Aeschines and Philokrates) on the Second Embassy to Philip: the exclusion of the Phokians from the Peace of Philokrates directly contradicted an earlier decree of the Athenians which had made friendship and alliance with them (Dem. 19.61–2 = D87). Disobedience to orders contained within decrees was held up as part of an attack on the characters of opponents in the courts. In his prosecution speech charging Ergokles (a general who served under Thrasyboulos on his expedition in the Northern Aegean)[19] with embezzlement and receiving bribes, Lysias (28.5 = D38 T1) maintains that the Athenians had required, by decree, that he and his magistrates present accounts of what they had taken from the cities. Ergokles' response to the request – which was to maintain that the people were again acting as sycophants and longing for their old laws (*archaioi nomoi*: probably a reference to the fifth-century habit of exacting tribute) – is held up as symptomatic of his behaviour and is intended to prejudice the jurors against him. Ergokles' reaction to the decree could be seen as a reflection not only of his dishonesty but also his arrogance towards the commands of the people. Such criticisms could also be made against non-Athenians: one of the accusations that Demosthenes (Dem. 23.149–51 = D64) brought against Charidemos was that he had disobeyed the orders of the Athenian decree about the hostages at Amphipolis, thereby undermining Athenian attempts to recover that territory.

A further aspect of the deployment of claims based on decrees consists of the attempt to create logical support for a wider argument about human conduct. In his second speech *Against Stephanos*, Apollodoros claimed that

---

19 See Hansen 1974: 88.

the testament of his father, Pasion, had been forged by his rival Phormio; in support of this position, he formulated an argument on the basis of the date of the award of citizenship to Phormio, granted ten years after the death of his father:

> Phormio became an Athenian during the archonship of Nikophemos, in the tenth year after our father died. And so, how could my father, not knowing that he would become an Athenian, have given him his own wife in marriage, and would both have outraged us and shown contempt towards that gift which he received from you, having contempt for the laws? ([Dem.] 46.13 (= D72))

His claim is that the date of the gift of citizenship indicates that his father would never have bequeathed to him his widowed wife in marriage, given that he did not know that Phormio would have become an Athenian a decade later.[20] The effectiveness of the argument is dependent on the consensus that the dating of decrees can be reliably ascertained. There are other more roundabout uses of decrees of limited relevance to the case in hand, including those which build upon a view of the intentions of the proposer and the likely implications of the decree: Demosthenes cited, approvingly, Timarchos' decree (which he described as forbidding the export of arms to Philip (19.285–7 = D122)) to demonstrate that Aeschines' intention, in destroying the career of Timarchos (on a charge of sexual misconduct), was not to improve the behaviour of the Athenians. The implication of Demosthenes' line of argument was that Timarchos' decree would, conversely, improve the Athenians.

Having established some of the ways in which accounts of the interface between decrees and human activity was used to offer perspectives on human behaviour in forensic oratory, in what follows (Chapter 2.3 below) I set out to explore the extent to which the act of proposing decrees played a role in the positive representation of individual political activity.

2.3 Making Decrees: 'Decree-Mindedness' and Political Activity

2.3.1 Proposing Decrees

In this section I assess the significance of the act of proposing decrees as an aspect of political self-promotion. A considerable proportion of the business of

---

20 On this occasion Phormio did not deploy the language of Athenian decrees when talking about the citizenship award, but the strength of claims made on the basis of the date of a citizenship award was surely rooted in the fact that the jurors knew that such awards could be granted only by decree of the people and that decrees were firmly dated – in documentary (cf. Aeschin. 2.58, 89) and epigraphical form – by particular archonships.

the council and assembly must have been dedicated to the proposal, discussion, and enactment of decrees.[21] Yet this is hardly reflected in extant symbouleutic oratory: as Hansen observes, it offers relatively little clear evidence on the proposal of decrees. While a considerable amount of assembly time must have been dedicated to the discussion of decrees that had been proposed, Hansen argues that only one surviving Demosthenic symbouleutic speech, the *First Philippic* (see D108) and a couple of pseudo-Demosthenic speeches ([Dem.] 7 (cf. D144)[22] and 17 (cf. D192)), directly advocate a decree being proposed.[23] This may be owing in part to the processes behind survival: as Trevett (2011: 19) suggests, most assembly speeches were made extemporaneously (or at least aspired to appear so) without reference to a prepared text and perhaps without the kind of planning that detailed reference to a decree would entail. Moreover, Demosthenes or his political advocates may have revised or released for publication mostly those speeches which advocated policy broadly rather than those which advocated particular decrees on the grounds that the latter were more susceptible to political critique.[24] It is clear, however, that Demosthenes made recommendations about aspects of policy in other speeches too: in the *Third Philippic* he gave advice to the *demos* about taking immediate military action (Dem. 9.19), dispatching embassies (Dem. 9.71–2) and supporting those Athenians in the Chersonese with funds (Dem. 9.73);[25] at the close of

---

21 For the view that the preponderance of non-probouleumatic decrees in the period 352/1–322/1 suggests the vigour of the assembly and liveliness of democracy, see Lambert 2018: 227–71.

22 Hegesippos, the speaker of [Demosthenes'] speech 7, ends his reply to Philip with the statement that he intends to make a proposal about how the Athenians will respond to Philip ([Dem.] 7.46).

23 For this observation, see Hansen 1989: 283–6.

24 For the view that Demosthenes may have made drafts of his assembly speeches before he gave them, see Edwards 2016: 30. Trevett 1996b argues that Demosthenes' symbouleutic speeches remained mostly unpublished until after his death; this is a view followed by MacDowell 2009: 7–8. On the other hand, Yunis (1996: 243) thinks of the publication of speeches as an important part of Demosthenes' career and Tuplin suggests that he did so to justify his policies. On the factors influencing the selection and arrangement of surviving symbouleutic oratory, see Tuplin 1998, suggesting that an editor carefully selected and arranged the speeches. Worthington 1991 suggests that the extent of revision was limited and that they were based on drafts of what he had intended to say to the assembly.

25 The final paragraph of the speech includes the statement 'these are the things I propose' ('ταῦτα γράφω': 9.76), but it is not clear that such recommendations were put to the vote as a decree. MacDowell (2009: 349) takes the view that the 'text appears to have been written in order to introduce a specific proposal, though the wording of the proposal is not preserved', while acknowledging that the speech is about 'policy towards Philip in the longer term, and its conclusion is that they should prepare for war'.

On the Peace he offered guidance about avoiding war (Dem. 5.24–5).[26] In the speech *On the Chersonese* Demosthenes attempted to persuade the Athenians to exonerate the actions of Diopeithes and make war against Philip (Scholion on Demosthenes 8.2 Dilts); the speech closed with a general recommendation about raising money, keeping a force together, sending out ambassadors and punishing those who undermine the interest of the community (Dem. 8.76).

It may be worth noting that orators at the assembly do make occasional reference to decrees of the past in their argumentation: the decree of Arthmios, for instance, was cited as an example of Athenian ancestral *ethos* (Dem. 9.42–6).[27] But when citing contemporary decrees they seem rarely to associate them with their proposers, tending to lay responsibility for them at the feet of the *demos* at the assembly who enacted them (e.g. Dem. 3.4–6).[28] References to past decrees were sometimes very vague, as were Hegesippos' claims about how the decree of Philokrates damaged Athenian interests at Amphipolis that were set out 'in past decrees': there is no indication exactly when exactly they were passed ([Dem.] 7.25 = D140 T2). We should add that, in assembly contexts, it seems that individuals rarely boast straightforwardly of their own proposals: even as he responded to his rivals' criticism of his own reluctance to make proposals, Demosthenes in *On the Chersonese* talked of his benefactions rather than his proposals (Dem. 8.68–73). For an assessment of the role of decrees in politics and self-promoting political activity we are, once again, heavily reliant on their citation and discussion in forensic oratory (for the projection of 'decree-mindedness' in the courts, see also Chapter 2.3.2 below).

One essential ingredient which made the decree politically and rhetorically significant is its authoritative status as a transaction of the Athenian people (see Chapter 1.2 above); but its association with, and appropriation by, individuals meant that the decree was reproduced in the pursuit of personal political interests too. Speakers at the lawcourts were likely to name the proposer of a

---

26 These recommendations are noted by Harris 2017c. We should note also the specific recommendations made in the *First Olynthiac* for expeditions to be sent to Chalkidike or to ravage Philip's territory: Dem. 1.17–18. Another speech which amounts to a general discussion of policy in terms of finances and military organisation is [Demosthenes] 13.

27 For further discussion of the presentation of decrees at the assembly, see Chapter 3.2.1 below.

28 References to decrees in assembly oratory: D60 (= Dem. 15.9), D106 (= Dem 3.4), D112 (= [Dem.] 13.32), D141 (= Dem. 7.30–1), D142 (= [Dem.] 12.6). In his attack on the policy of Timotheos, Demosthenes criticised a policy presented in a speech rather than associating it explicitly with a decree: Dem. 8.74–5. Hesitancy to make reference to past decrees by reference to proposers may well be another example of an 'informal rule' of oratory at the assembly; for others such informal rules see Harris 2017b; for Demosthenes' self-presentation in symbouleutic oratory, see Kremmydas 2016. For the role of argument from emotion in symbouleutic oratory, see Sanders 2016.

decree on occasions when they were attempting to make a point (positive or negative) specifically about the proposer. This ties in with a useful perspective, emphasised by New Institutionalist analysis, which is that political institutions are very much formed by the broader human environment, and once they have taken shape they themselves start to become influential on the choices and strategies of human individuals.[29] Ambitious individuals, both aware of accounts of the history of an institution and presented with opportunities for engagement with it, internalise the conception that the institutional route is an effective means of self-promotion and self-interest. Accordingly, institutions, as systems of normative rules and beliefs, channel the social and political behaviour of the political class.[30] Engagement with them leads analytically minded individuals to ask critical questions about their functioning and rectitude.[31] Yet institutional practices are founded not only on authoritative rules but are modelled upon both accepted practices and also the stories that are told about them.[32] As we will see in this section, Athenian politicians were led to engaging with decrees (sometimes normatively, sometimes critically) not because they were bound to by a set of rules but because to do so was a widely accepted practice, accounts of which loomed large in popular discourse.

There were many ways of being a citizen in Athens. Many may have found a route through life rarely partaking in political activity, leading them to be branded as *idiotai* (private citizens).[33] Some, like Isocrates, took a route into public life which was essentially critical of mainstream political values;[34] others may have engaged in profile-building exercises by spending money ostentatiously rather than through political engagement.[35] Some citizens were involved

---

29 Ostrom 1986: 5–7.
30 Greif 2006: 30.
31 Gray 2015: 15–16.
32 Generally, for the way in which political institutions shape actors' behaviour through systems of rules, practice, and narrative, see Lowndes and Roberts 2013: 46–76, articulating the view that 'actors understand how they are supposed to behave through observing the routinized actions of others and seeking to recreate those actions' (Lowndes and Roberts 2013: 57); for a view of the ways that institutions influence action by way of the narratives told about them, see Lowndes and Roberts 2013: 63.
33 Political quietism: Christ 2006; Carter 1986.On *idiotai*, see Rubinstein 1998; on the difficulty in distinguishing between active and passive citizens, see Mossé 1979.
34 Too 1995.
35 Lysikrates son of Lysitheides of Kikynna is an example of an individual who had a high profile in Athens through choregic sponsorship (he was the victorious sponsor of the Akamantis tribe in the boys' dithyramb in the Dionysia of 335/4 (*IG* II³ 4 460) and the dedication of a tripod, but does not seem to have been politically engaged; see discussion of his homonymous father and his family at *APF* 9461. The bibliography on Athenian euergetism is huge, but see most recently Domingo Gygax 2016.

in public life principally through activity at the lawcourts;[36] others would have taken centre-stage at the assembly or at the council when they engaged in debates at those arenas.

The privilege of proposing decrees was one reserved for Athenian citizens, and was removed from those who had been punished by *atimia* (Joyce 2018: 58 note 77) including those who had been prostitutes or debtors (Dem. 22.29, 33). It is clear that making decrees was a central aspect of the activity of the meetings of the assembly. How important was the act of proposing a decree to Athenian political life? Lambert observes, in a recent statistical and socio-economic analysis of the proposers attested on inscriptions of the period 352/1–322/1, that the epigraphical 'statistics for proposers of laws and decrees do not perhaps indicate that the ordinary Athenian had as much political influence as someone of wealth and prominence; but it does suggest that, whether wealthy or not, it was an essential aspect of Athenian democratic culture that political power and influence should be spread between multiple individuals'.[37] The literary evidence for decrees supports such an inference, while adding the nuance that association with activity surrounding decrees could have both positive and negative connotations (see Chapter 2.4.2 below).

The breadth of participation – emphasised by Lambert by reference to the epigraphical material[38] – is reflected also in the literary evidence for decree-proposal. Of the total of 245 decrees attested in the literary sources, 141 of them (that is, about 58 per cent) are attributed to named proposers, of whom there are 61 unique individuals (see Appendix 1). The spread of literary decrees is interesting: a disproportionately large number – as many as 40 of them – are attributed to Demosthenes, whose name is attested only once in the epigraphical record as a proposer of a decree.[39] But significant numbers are attributed to other prominent politicians, most of whom are attested as proposers also in the

---

36 For diverse assessments of the wide range of forms of enmity in the lawcourts (which according to some scholars spilled over into violence outside them), see Rhodes 1986; Cohen 1995; Christ 1998; Johnstone 1999; Rhodes 1998; Todd 1998; Herman 2006; Alwine 2015.

37 Lambert 2018: 202–3.

38 See Lambert 2018: 171–226, observing that 54 different proposers of decrees are known for the period 354/3–322/1, and emphasising also that they derived from a spectrum of different political backgrounds. For a list of the 91 epigraphically attested proposers for the whole period 403/2–322/1, see Appendix 1. The phenomenon of widespread fourth-century engagement with decree-making is in tune with Taylor's observations on the breadth of political participation in the fourth century generally: see Taylor 2007a, 2007b.

39 Lambert 2018: 185–7 discusses the factors behind the high number of decrees attributed to Demosthenes in the literary sources.

inscriptions: Demades (at least 9 literary decrees), Aristophon (7),[40] Philokrates (6), Lycurgus (possibly as many as 5),[41] Hegesippos (4), Euboulos (3 or 4), Hypereides (2 or 4), and the less-well-known Philippides (3). Timarchos, who is said to have proposed more than one hundred decrees (Aeschin. 1 *hypothesis*) is associated with 2 examples, as are 5 other politicians. According to the literary evidence, therefore, there were Athenians who seem to have prolifically proposed decrees and appear to have founded a reputation on them. It is plausible that some of the prolific proposers acted as advocates of particular political factions in the assembly: some scholars, for instance, have suggested that Aristophon was the advocate of an ambitious Athenian foreign policy of the first half of the fourth century represented on the field of battle by the generals Diopeithes and Chares.[42] Others, such as Athenodoros, the proposer of a decree concerning sacrifices at Piraeus proposed on the recommendation of Euthydemos, the priest, appear to have acted as advocates of cult interest groups (*IG* II² 47).[43] But it is perhaps revealing also that the vast majority of proposers attested in the literary evidence, that is 43 of the 61 (= 70.5 per cent), are associated only with a single proposal in the literary dataset.[44]

In terms of their social background, 41 per cent (25 of 61) of the literary-attested proposers are identified by Davies, in his *Athenian Propertied Families* (*APF*), as members of the liturgical classes. When we look at the epigraphical record for the same period, a slightly lower proportion (26 of 87, that is 29.9 per cent) are identified as members of the liturgical classes.[45] It is clear, therefore, that the literary evidence places slightly more emphasis on the decrees proposed by the elite (and in particular the activity of Demosthenes!), but is still not wildly out of tune with the epigraphical evidence. On the whole, it seems

---

40 Aristophon is said to have been acquitted 75 times for making illegal proposals (Aeschin. 3.194), a story which indicates either that he was an extremely prolific proposer of decrees or that it was the type of story that could be told in the courts with a reasonable hope of being believed. Hansen suggests on the basis of this anecdote that Aristophon may have proposed up to 225 decrees. On Aristophon and the accuracy of this figure, see Oost 1977; Whitehead 1986.

41 For the suggestion that Lycurgus was responsible for 'hundreds of decrees' see Lambert 2018: 188–9 note 52.

42 See Oost 1977; Whitehead 1986; Salmond 1996.

43 For examples of decrees made on the advice of religious functionaries and other officials, see Rhodes 1972: 43.

44 Of these, there is reason to believe that one, Kephalos, was engaged in the proposal of many more decrees: for Aeschines' response to his boasts about this, see Aeschin. 3.194 and b, Chapter 2.3.2 below.

45 This figure is based on the testimonia analysed in Hansen 1989: 34–72. Lambert's survey of the epigraphical evidence for the period 354/3–322/1 shows that 38 per cent of epigraphically-preserved proposers were of the liturgical class: Lambert 2018: 190.

that the literary evidence tells the same story as the epigraphical evidence: the coexistence of a number of proposers from a wide socio-economic background with an elite who were frequently involved in proposing decrees. The act of proposing a decree appears therefore to have been a manifestation of both high- and low-profile political activity.

For a balanced picture of Athenian politics we must consider the fact that not all Athenian citizens, even those with an active public life, would have engaged in the activity of proposing decrees: indeed, of those 373 individuals listed by Hansen in his 'Inventory of *rhetores* and *strategoi* of the period 403/2–322/1',[46] only 22 per cent (82) of them are attested as proposers of decrees of the assembly.[47] Decree-proposing was a significant part of political activity and underscored its principles of participation, but it was very far from being the only way of making a political career; if one wanted to become prominent, it was not enough just to propose decrees.[48] At the same time, however, we should acknowledge the significance of the fact that of the prominent political actors of the fourth century, even those who are not attested to have proposed a decree undertook some political activity which would have led to some association with decree-making or decree-challenging processes: Agyrrhios and Meidias are known to have proposed laws (the initiation of which process involved decrees of the assembly); three other prominent non-proposers, Iphikrates, Chabrias and Timotheos were recipients of an honorific decree.[49] Even Aeschines, who emphasised that he himself had not made proposals about the peace with Philip (Aeschin. 2.160), was deeply implicated with the politics of decrees, famously attacking the decree honoring Demosthenes (Aeschin. 3).

A relevant insight which is offered in contemporary Insitutionalist thought is Ostrom's view that while institutions do not shape the behaviour of human actors, they can channel it in particular ways.[50] This perspective applies not so much to those who were politically unengaged, but rather to those who were eager to raise their profile in the city through political activity. Indeed, when we look at those involved in the political sphere, even those who – like

---

46 Hansen 1989: 69.
47 Hansen 1989: 102.
48 Indeed, very few of those who are attested to have proposed only one decree of the assembly are otherwise known: see Lambert 2018: 190 and Hansen 1989: 34–72.
49 These observations are based on the lists in Hansen 1989: 34–72. Perhaps the only prominent Athenian who does not appear to have had dealings with a decree was Chares, though even he may have launched his *eisangelia* against Pheidiades by way of a decree: see Hansen 1976 no. 114.
50 Ostrom 1986: 5–7.

Aeschines – were not connected with the proposal of decrees in any source, whether epigraphical or literary, involved themselves with the wider consequences of decree-activity by attacking others' decrees. In that sense, then, Ostrom's insight is helpful: in ancient Athens political ambition generally necessitated some engagement with the widely pervading culture of decrees and their consequences.

2.3.2 Political Presentations of Proposals

At this point, I turn to explore the extent to which the proposal of a decree could be construed as a political act which possessed value beyond its immediate substance. And more broadly, I ask what forms of engagement with decree-activity had implications for the development of political profile in fourth-century Athens? Lawcourt oratory, as we have seen, provides a great deal of information about fourth-century perspectives on the decree; however, one of the clearest expressions of the possibility of aspiring to political capital, or a raised political profile, in the process of decree-proposing, emerges in a philosophical text: Plato, in the *Phaedrus*, identified the written words of an honorary decree as a manifestation of a conventional speech of a politician:

> Socrates: The name of the commender (ὁ ἐπαινέτης) is written first in the writings of the politician ... the author (ὁ συγγραφεύς) says 'the council resolves' or 'the people', or both, and X proposed, mentioning his own name with dignity and praise. (Pl. *Phdr.* 258a–b)[51]

Plato went on to claim that the main body of a proposal amounts to an attempt at displaying wisdom and a vain aspiration to immortality (*Phdr.* 258c). His remark, while it overlooked the role of the council, people and magistrates in the enactment of a decree (see Chapter 1.2.1 above), underlines the significance of one aspect of the form of the decree – the mention of the proposer's name – to argue that the politicians with the highest opinions of themselves are those most anxious to attach their names to any form of composition. It contributes to his view that such politicians are no better than the speech-writers (*logopoioi*) who he criticises.[52] One view, taken by Rhodes with Lewis, is that Plato's argument displays a 'wonderful perversity';[53] it should certainly be seen in the

---

51 Pl. *Phdr.* 258a–b: Σωκράτης: ἐν ἀρχῇ ἀνδρὸς πολιτικοῦ [συγγράμματι] πρῶτος ὁ ἐπαινέτης γέγραπται ... 'ἔδοξέ' πού φησιν 'τῇ βουλῇ' ἢ 'τῷ δήμῳ' ἢ ἀμφοτέροις, καὶ 'ὃς <καὶ ὃς> εἶπεν'– τὸν αὐτὸν δὴ λέγων μάλα σεμνῶς καὶ ἐγκωμιάζων ὁ συγγραφεύς.

52 On the status of *logopoioi* at Athens, see Gottesman, 2014: 83–5.

53 Rhodes with Lewis 1997: 4 note 9.

76   DECREES OF FOURTH-CENTURY ATHENS

context of Plato's wider critique of democratic political activity.[54] As already noted (2.3.1 above), straightforward boasts of decrees do not occur in symbouleutic oratory. But given that we have seen praise of historical proposers deployed in the Athenian lawcourts (cf. Aeschines' presentation of Archinos (Aeschin. 3.187 = D15) and Dinarchus on Kephalos (Din. 1.39 = D44)), it seems reasonable to assess the question of whether the proposal of decrees carried with it some sense of political capital: did the act of making a proposal serve to promote the reputation of the proposer? Epigraphical evidence offers an affirmative response to this question.

It was indeed the case that draft proposals (Aesch. 1.188; 2.68) and inscribed decrees bore the name of their proposer usually at the end of their prescripts (see Chapter 1.1 above on the decree for Herakleides of Salamis), and in some inscribed decrees of the 330s a whole line was dedicated to the name of the proposer.[55] Lambert takes the view that the increasing proliferation of inscribed decrees in the 330s and 320s, among them a significant proportion proposed by two politicians of the era (notably Lycurgus and Demades),[56] is indicative of 'an increasing tendency to regard successful proposing of decrees in the Assembly, prominently displayed on inscribed *stelai*, themselves erected by the decision, and at the expense, of the Assembly, as an expression of political influence'.[57] This is borne out both by the literary testimonia and the epigraphical evidence.

A dedication and dossier of decrees of 343/2 inscribed on a base from Athens offers an indication of the recognition and profile that could be granted to proposers of decrees. This base consists of a dedication to Hephaistos made by the Athenian council after it had been crowned by the people for its excellence and justice; on its front and left-hand and right-hand inscribed faces it contains also five decrees (one of the People and the other four of the Council). Prominently inscribed on the front face of the base beneath the dedicatory formula is a decree of the Council granting honours to Phanodemos of Thymaitadai; the award was made on the grounds that he had spoken and acted best and incorruptibly on behalf of the Athenian Council and People (*IG* II³ 1 306 lines 4–16). It seems to be the case that the words and deeds being honoured here consisted

---

54 The view that Plato had some positive things to say (Monoson 2000) about democracy or that he was critical but not wholly negative (Saxonhouse 1996: 87–114) is not incompatible with the view of him as a critic of the workings of democracy: see Ober 1998: 156–247 and Allen 2010.

55 Lambert 2018 189 with note 53; this became a more common practice after 307/6: Henry 1977: 63–6; Tracy 2000; Lambert 2015: 5–6.

56 For proposers of decrees attested in the literary record, see Appendix 1.

57 Lambert 2015: 5–6; Lambert 2018: 171–204. For the view that the setting up of a decree on a *stele* represents a political statement in its own right, see Culasso Gastaldi 2014b.

of the proposal of a decree which was written up on the left-hand face of the base: this included the provision to set up a dedication to Hephaistos and Athena Hephaistia (lines 17–23) and to write up the honours which the assembly had previously bestowed upon the Council for its having managed the City Dionysia well (lines 22–3, 24–6): there is a clear appreciation of the significance not only of writing up honours but of the value of Phanodemos' proposal. At the same time, however, the most prominent lettering on the block is reserved for the dedicatory formulae of the Council (lines 1–3).

This suggestion of the high valuation of the proposer appears to be part of a wider theme which finds its expression in language: indeed, the successful proposal of a decree was, on occasion, described with the verb νικάω ('I am victorious': Aeschin. 3.63, 68 (= D127 T4); *IG* II² 77 line 8[58]); similarly, the individual who carried a motion could, on occasion of his success, be referred to as ὁ νικήσας (that is, the victor in a debate: [Arist.] *Ath. Pol.* 45.4 and Lysias F130 lines 72–82= D17 T2), which suggests that success in passing a decree could be construed as a victory in a contest.

The literary record of decrees supports this high profile of individual proposers in relation to their decrees. As noted above, some 58 per cent of fourth-century decrees attested in the literary record are done so in association with one of 61 named proposers,[59] and some – but not all – fifth-century examples cited by later sources were associated with individual names.[60] The high political valuation of the proposer is a theme promoted in the speeches of Demosthenes. More decrees of Demosthenes are preserved in the contemporary literary sources than those of any other Athenian politician (see Appendix 1). This is, to a large extent, owing to the fact that he himself refers to his own decrees prolifically in those speeches in which he defended his political activity

---

58 In *IG* II² 77 line 8 the subject of the verb ἐνίκησε is not stated.

59 See Appendix 1 for a list of all those Athenian decrees of the period 403/2–322/1 which are associated in the literary evidence with named proposers.

60 However, decrees were sometimes associated – in both lawcourt oratory and also in later literature – with prominent fifth-century historical figures including Kallias (e.g. Dem. 19.273 with the testimonia collected in Fornara 1983 no. 95), Kritias (Lycurg. 1.112-15), Pericles (see Chapter 5.2.3 below), Themistocles (Dem. 19.303 and ML 23) and Miltiades (Dem. 19.303; Ar. *Rh* 1411a = D82 T2; Plut. *Mor.* 628e; Nep. *Milt.* 4; see D82 Commentary). For decrees associated with the family of Aristeides, some of them attributed to Aristeides the Elder (Plu. *Arist.* 27.2; Dem. 20.115) and others Lysimachos the son of Aristeides (Plu. *Arist.* 27.1; Aeschin. 3.258; Nep. 3.3), see Domingo Gygax 2016: 177–8. Later rhetoricians, such as Aspines, were fond of associating prominent historical figures with decrees: see Chapter 5.5 below. For the tradition on the decree of Syrakosios against the satirising of named individuals, see Scholiast to Aristophanes *Birds* 1297; it was associated with Syrakosios by Phrynichos (fr. 27 K-A) and Eupolis (fr. 220 K-A); cf. Atkinson 1992. A certain Antimachos is associated with a decree forbidding the satirising of the people: see Suda s.v. Ἀντίμαχος' (Adler *alpha*, 2683).

78 DECREES OF FOURTH-CENTURY ATHENS

(Dem. 18 and Dem. 19), but also because they were attacked in the speeches of his opponents (Aeschin. 2 and 3; Din. 1). It is notable that only one of his decrees is extant in epigraphical format (*IG* II³ 1 312), which is an indication that the literary record over-states the proliferation of his decrees in the politics of the 340s and 330s.[61]

Demosthenes, therefore, uses accounts of his own decrees strikingly to substantiate claims about his own political contribution:[62] this tendency is particularly clear in speech 18 where he uses accounts of his own proposals to demonstrate that he was a politician worthy of Ktesiphon's honorary decree for him:[63] he recalls the embassies and expeditions dispatched on the basis of his proposals of the 340s, emphasising that whereas Aeschines remembers some of his proposals, he forgets others (Dem. 18.79 = DD 139, 148a, 154, 155). He reminded the audience of his record of creating positive alliances for the Athenians (Dem. 18.237 = D149; 18.301–3 = DD 147, 151, 152) and dispatching forces (Dem. 18.80, 88 = D158). He recited a number of decrees that he himself had proposed before the battle of Chaironeia after the fall of Elateia to Philip in spring 338,[64] and claimed that they made the danger which had befallen the city 'pass away like a cloud' (188). He took pride in his decrees because they made the city safe (248), ensured the security of the corn-supply, and secured the friendship and alliance of Byzantium, Abydos and Euboia (18.301–2 = DD 151, 152):

> All these achievements were accomplished by my decrees and my political acts (*politeumata*). Whoever will study them, men of Athens, without jealousy, will find that they were rightly planned and honestly executed; that the proper opportunity for each measure was never neglected, or ignored, or thrown away by me ... [65]

---

61 Lambert (2018: 185–7) has discussed the factors behind the prominence of Demosthenes' decrees in the literary record, underlining the very high profile of Demosthenes in the surviving oratory of the period, which may have been owing to his nephew Demochares' promotion of his uncle's posthumous reputation; cf. Asmonti 2004.

62 But fifth-century politicians may also have been ready, over the course of their public speeches, to point out the significance of their public acts: Thucydides' Alcibiades in the Sicilian debate, for instance, calls upon the Athenians to consider his public acts (*ta demosia*: Thuc. 6.16.6).

63 For extensive discussion of the use of decrees in Demosthenes 18, see Harris 1994; for their use in establishing chronology, see Clarke 2008: 292–3.

64 For instance the decrees appointing *nomothetai* (D160), and a decree (D162) which launched ships against Philip and made the alliance with Thebes.

65 Dem. 18.303: 'ταῦτα τοίνυν ἅπαντα πέπρακται τοῖς ἐμοῖς ψηφίσμασι καὶ τοῖς ἐμοῖς πολιτεύμασιν, ἃ καὶ βεβουλευμέν', ὦ ἄνδρες Ἀθηναῖοι, ἐὰν ἄνευ φθόνου τις βούληται σκοπεῖν, ὀρθῶς εὑρήσει καὶ πεπραγμένα πάσῃ δικαιοσύνῃ, καὶ τὸν ἑκάστου καιρὸν οὐ παρεθέντ' οὐδ' ἀγνοηθέντ' οὐδὲ προεθένθ' ὑπ' ἐμοῦ.

A sense of his own decree-mindedness emerges also in his attacks on Aeschines for not making proposals or failing to indict those of others (Dem. 18.139–40, 222–3, 235). At points he offers not just boasts of having made decrees but talks about details of their provisions: when defending his record in the year before Chaironeia, he read out some particulars of his decree on the ambassadors to be dispatched to Thebes:

> Afterwards, I order you to select ten ambassadors, and to grant them the author-
> ity, together with the generals, to decide when it is necessary to march out there
> (sc. Thebes) and on the conduct of the campaign. (Dem. 18.178 = D162 T2).

As Yunis suggests, Demosthenes offered such specifics in order to demonstrate the seamlessness of the connection between his policy and the decrees through which it was expressed,[66] and as a way of demonstrating his power and significance in forging an alliance with the Thebans. Accordingly, he presented agreement of an alliance with Thebes before Chaironeia as the consequence of his own ambassadorial mission rather than, as his rivals appear to have suggested, as the result of Athenian military pressure (Dem. 18.209–15).[67] His description of the fear faced by the Athenians both before (18.173: 'ἐν αὐτοῖς τοῖς φοβεροῖς') and after (Dem. 18.248: 'ἐν αὐτοῖς τοῖς δεινοῖς καὶ φοβεροῖς') the Athenian defeat strikes a chord with Lycurgus' description of its immediate aftermath of Chaironeia (see Chapter 1.5.2 above), but unlike Lycurgus he was more interested in emphasising his own role rather than the contribution of the people to address the situation. A strong sense of his own decree-mindedness emerges in the claim that he himself did not speak without making a proposal in the immediate aftermath of the fall of Elateia (Dem 18.179). Yet Demosthenes earlier in this speech had also to recognise that Athenian decisions before Chaironeia had not been successful in resisting Philip:[68] accordingly he attempted to deflect Aeschines' claims that he had embroiled the city in hostility (Dem. 18.79–80) by underlining the fact that there were other proposers who, before Chaironeia, affected policy by making decrees (Dem. 18.75 = DD 213, 215, 216, 217, 218).

Demosthenes made use of a similar strategy when it came to defending his record after the defeat of Chaironeia, speaking of his proposals for military changes and repairs to the fortifications (Dem. 18.248 = D169). In his discussion of his decree to dispatch a force to Byzantion, he acknowledges that the

---

66 Yunis 2001: 209.
67 For the view that Demosthenes exaggerated his role in setting up the alliance with Thebes before Chaironeia, see Guth 2014.
68 On the balance that Demosthenes in *On the Crown* struck between defending his own record and acknowledging Athenian failure, see Yunis 2001.

people's forces prevented the Hellespont being taken by Philip, but emphasises that this was carried out under the directives of his decree (Dem. 18.88 = D158). Overall, much of Demosthenes' *On the Crown* – as he made a case in support of Ktesiphon's honours – amounts to an exercise in self-aggrandisement, and his own record in proposing decrees played an important part in this. It is a speech which enunciates more clearly than any other extant text the idea that the political leader bears a social obligation to formulate and advocate policy at the assembly.[69] What is more, Demosthenes' readiness to recite his own proposals contributed to the development of his political reputation and his historical legacy.[70] While the speeches he made at the assembly tend not to make explicit associations between individual politicians and their decrees, in the *Second Philippic* he offers a firm association between appropriate political activity and proposing decrees, criticising those politicians who shrink from making proposals or offering advice, being wary of incurring the displeasure of the people (Dem. 6.3). Moreover, in the *On the Chersonese* he pre-empts those whom he anticipates will reproach himself for cowardice if he fails to make a proposal (Dem. 8.68), turning the criticism against those who participate irresponsibly or vexatiously (8.69).

Demosthenes was not alone in accruing capital from the decrees with which he was associated, but the weight placed on such argumentation by other orators is unclear. In the speech *Against Neaira*, Apollodoros' co-speaker, Theomnestos, as part of his account of the ongoing conflict between Apollodoros and Stephanos, introduces Apollodoros as the proposer, in spring 348, of a probouleumatic decree on the use of surplus money. His description of the proposal underlines Apollodoros' adherence to procedure ([Dem.] 59.4–6 = D115). While Themnestos emphasised the unanimous popular support of the proposal (claiming there was an absence of votes against the use of surplus for military funds) as a counterweight to Stephanos' undeniably successful indictment of the decree, his presentation does not, however, indicate a clear implication of Apollodoros taking pride in it. In fact, when we reflect on the substance of this decree – that the people should decide by vote whether the surplus of state funds should be used for military purposes or for the theoric fund – what stands out is the cautiousness of the proposal. Whereas it is likely that

---

69 Cf. Liddel 2007: 250–3.

70 Pseudo Lucian's *Encomium of Demosthenes* clearly associated him with decree-making and other political acts (Lucian, *Dem. Enc.*18, 37, 45); Plutarch's anecdote about Philip, in the aftermath of Chaironeia, going about drunk among the bodies of the dead and reciting, in metre, the start of the Demosthenes' decree, 'Demosthenes, son of Demosthenes, of Paiania, proposes in this way …' is also indicative of the literary phenomenon of associating Demosthenes with stories about decrees: Plu. *Dem.* 20.3: see Chapter 5.2.3 below.

Theomnestos' presentation of Apollodoros' decree may have aimed to make it appear less controversial than it actually was ([Dem.] 59.4–5), it appears to be the case that Apollodoros stopped short of making a positive proposal on the use of surplus funds; perhaps, as Trevett suggests, Apollodoros' proposal may have been a 'calculated attempt to test the public acceptability of a policy of increasing investment on the military side of things at the expense of the theoric fund'.[71] Apollodoros' cautiousness in proposing a substantive decree may be indicative of his relative lack of political experience.

On the other hand, the representation of the high-profile politician Demades, in a speech of dubious authenticity, as pointing to his own decree making peace with Alexander as made well and expediently (καλῶς καὶ συμφερόντως) in defence of his political career ([Demades], *On the Twelve Years* 14–15 = D188 T1) may well reflect arguments that he actually deployed. Evidence for straightforward boasts about the success of one's proposals can be found in Aeschines' report in 330 on the less famous Kephalos (known as the proposer of only one literary decree of the period, D44: see Appendix 1) who garnered *philotimia* from the claim that he had been the author of more decrees than anyone else, but yet had never been charged in a *graphe paranomon* for making an unconstitutional proposal; to Aeschines this represented a more reverent boast than Aristophon's claim that he had been acquitted seventy-five times in a *graphe paranomon* (3.194).[72] But the claim that Aeschines attributes to Kephalos is something of an exceptional one, and we cannot rule out the possibility that he invented it: if this was the case, then the passage is still interesting not so much as a window into the reality of Kephalos' political activity but rather as a demonstration of the kinds of claims that might be made in front of a jury. Given the negative reputation that was at points attached to the decree at the end of the fifth century (see Chapter 5.2.1 below), it is perhaps hardly surprising that, as we have seen, it was not until the second half of the fourth century that it became viable for public figures to make such boasts in terms which made the proposer eclipse the role of the people in the enactment of the decree. On the other hand, in his extant assembly speeches, Demosthenes highlighted the role of the people in making decrees;[73] moreover, in his description of the role he played in the making of the Peace of Philokrates, Aeschines stressed that he had specifically not proposed a decree in relation to it (Aeschin. 2.160): it is clear, therefore, that there is plenty of variation in politicians' attitudes towards decrees.

---

71 Trevett 1992: 146.
72 On Aristophon, see note 40 above. For other politicians who faced multiple *graphai paranomon*, see Hansen 1974: 25
73 Mader 2006; see Chapter 2.5.2 below.

At this point, I return to considering less prolific proposers. As already noted (Chapter 2.3.1 above), the vast majority of proposers attested in the literary evidence, 70.5 per cent of them, are associated only with a single proposal, and a significant proportion (59 per cent) of literary-attested proposers are not known to have held significant wealth. How do we explain this apparently wide spread of decree-proposing activity across the population? It is plausible to think that less prominent citizens may have aspired to be associated with prominent politicians by supporting decrees that represented their interests or policy: this is one possible implication of Apollodoros' complaint about individuals, such as Stephanos, who allow their names be inscribed at the head of motions formulated by others ([Dem.] 59.43). There is limited evidence for proposals being made by two individuals jointly: a decree on pirates is presented in the accounts of the naval *epimeletai* as proposed by Lykourgos Bouta(des) and Aristonikos: *IG* II² 1623 line 280–3 (cf. also D166a). Another possibility is that prominent individuals may have asked others to make proposals on their behalf as a way of getting their policy through without having to face the direct opposition of their political rivals. But the evidence for this is contentious,[74] controversial (see Aeschin. 3.159 with Commentary at D223) or late (Plu. *Arist.* 3.4; Plu. *Dem.* 21.3; Plu. *Per.* 7.7–8; Plu. *Mor.* 811c–13a). At other times, collaboration between individuals in the formulation of decrees may have been undertaken by two individuals who collaborated on relatively equal terms.[75] It is better, then, with Lambert, to conclude that the multiplicity of proposers (attested also in the epigraphical evidence) points to the broad spread of political engagement in late fourth-century Athens.[76] It seems, therefore, that the institution of the decree was one which facilitated wide and meaningful participation in Athenian democratic politics.[77]

We might add to this impression the observation that the inscribed record of honorific decrees from the 340s onwards indicates that the Athenians became

---

74 Aeschin. 3.125–8 (= D161) claimed, as part of his attack on him, that Demosthenes coerced a councillor to put together a *probouleuma* concerning Athenian attendance at the meetings of the Delphian Amphictyony before himself putting it to the vote at the assembly. For allegations about decrees being proposed in return for bribes or as political favours see note 103 below.

75 See discussion in Chapter 1.1 above, of *IG* II³ 1 367, in which the fellow-demesmen Kephisodotos and Telemachos collaborated in the formulation of honours for Herakleides of Salamis.

76 Lambert 2018: 201–4. Cf. Hansen 1991: 145, underplaying the political significance of those proposers associated with a small number of decrees.

77 See Taylor 2007b, observing that in the fourth century there was widespread political participation among the non-wealthy and those from non-urban demes; Taylor (2007a: 339–40, 2007b: 76–7) notes that proposers of decrees came from demes widely dispersed across Attica.

more ready to honour those who had played even a relatively minor, or an administrative, role in civic activity.[78] The Athenians were ready to value even a small contribution to political activity when the circumstances were right. But we must emphasise that there was no mechanism to ensure the raised profile of a proposer; there was nothing to stop a decree and its proposer falling into obscurity: the fame of Demosthenes' decrees survives principally because the speeches in which he defended his political career are extant; that of Lycurgus survives owing to the epigraphical legacy of his decrees. It was up to the individual to exploit the potential of political capital offered by the act of proposing a decree either by ensuring that his decrees were inscribed or by talking about them in other political or litigious contexts. Accordingly, we again draw attention to the fact that no politically ambitious individual would have restricted his political engagement solely to activity associated with decrees, especially given that decrees were always open to attack.

Indeed, the most extensive deployment of decrees and knowledge about decrees appears to have been undertaken in the course of those cases related to acts of challenging decrees and laws, in the processes known respectively as *graphe paranomon* and *graphe nomon me epitedeion theinai*.[79] In the next section, therefore, I will assess the significance to our understanding of decree-mindedness of claims about decrees in speeches relating to these processes.

2.4 Decrees in the Construction of Arguments

2.4.1 Challenging Decrees and New Laws

Whereas making proposals could form the basis of a claim to fame (see Chapter 2.3 above), the other side of the coin was the fact that every decree was liable to be challenged by the indictment that it was illegal, the claim that it was damaging or disadvantageous to the city, or that the honorand was unworthy (*graphe paranomon*);[80] this meant that the proposer, by making a decree, ran the risk of his proposal being attacked. While the spectrum of possible punishments

---

78 See, for instance *IG* II³ 1 301, 305, 311, 323, 327, 469; Lambert 2011a.
79 For the distinction between the two procedures, see Hansen 1974: 44–8, 1983: 171–5; MacDowell 2009: 152–3, observing that a *graphe paranomon* might plausibly be used against a newly proposed law, but that in practice this does not seem to have happened. Further on the process see, highlighting its significance as a political process, Yunis (1988) and, emphasising its relationship to the rule of law, Sundahl (2003) and Harris 2018: 66 note 138.
80 Yunis 1988 argues that both a legal and political plea was necessary to successfully overturn a decree by way of *graphe paranomon*; MacDowell 2009: 154 is less certain; for the view that it was oriented against illegality, see Harris 2018: 66 note 138.

ranged from execution to a symbolic fine of 25 *drachmai*,[81] alongside impeachment (*eisangelia*), it was one of the most effective ways of attempting to embarrass, or disrupt the policy of, a political adversary within a year of their proposal (Dem. 23.104):[82] Aristophon was allegedly mocked (κεκωμῴδηται) for supporting what was later deemed to have been an illegal decree relating to Keos (Scholion on Aeschin. 1.64 (Dilts 145); see D66). The fact that the proposer of any decree at the Council or Assembly took such a risk is a further indication that making decrees was something considered important for the creation of one's own political legacy. As we shall see below, over the course of those speeches which were made against or in support of claims about the legality of proposed laws and decrees, decrees were cited extensively as evidence: two such speeches, Demosthenes' *Against Leptines* (Dem. 20) and *Against Aristokrates* (Dem. 23)[83] made widespread deployment of decrees.

It is possible that some, like Theokrines, the opponent of Apollodoros in Demosthenes 58, may have used such indictments against unconstitutional decrees as a springboard for raised political profile: his opponent claimed that he described himself as on guard against illegality (Dem. 58.45–7; cf. Dem. 24.11–14). Indeed, the procedure was invoked sometimes in descriptions of the expectations that the Athenians had about political behaviour: Dinarchus suggested that Demosthenes had failed in his duty as a politician given his reluctance to indict Demades for his numerous unconstitutional proposals (Din 1. 100–1 = D187 T1). As already noted (see Chapter 1.3 above) Aeschines in his *Against Ktesiphon* went so far as to suggest that the *graphe paranomon* was central to a conception of proper democratic behaviour and called upon the jurors in the course of such a trial to consider themselves as securing democracy and punishing those who were against the laws (Aeschin. 3.8). Indeed, he argued that the *graphe paranomon* was just about the only reputable democratic process remaining in Athens (3.5, 75), given that standards of orderly procedure had been set aside at the assembly (Aeschin. 3.3). As a constitutionally normative mode of polemic political activity, using the *graphe paranomon* was considered an appropriate way of attacking the enactment of a political enemy (Dem. 21.182–3 = DD 210, 211; [Dem.] 25.37 = D237 T1): certainly it was a more

---

81 Hansen 1974: 53. For the prosecutors' allusion to the possibility of the death penalty, see Hansen 1974 nos. 12 and 14, but neither of the relevant passages demonstrate that it was in fact imposed (Dem. 22.69 and 23.62). As MacDowell 2009: 155 points out, those who had been convicted three times in a *graphe paranomon* would be disenfranchised.

82 Hansen 1974: 24–5, 53. For the view that a *graphe paranomon* would have to be launched within a year of a decree's proposal, see Giannadaki 2014.

83 For the reputation of Demosthenes 20 in antiquity, see Kremmydas 2012: 62–4 and Chapter 5.4 below; for that of Demosthenes 23, see Papillon 1998.

acceptable mechanism than the chisels used by the demesmen who obliterated an honorary decree set up for the speaker of Demosthenes 57 (57.64). On the other hand, those who attacked decrees using the process were liable to the criticism that they were sycophants motivated by the hope that they would be bribed by their opponents to withdraw the indictments (Dem. 58.34).

It is relevant to our understanding of the nature of Athenian politics that cases against particular new laws and decrees drew extensively upon a knowledge of decrees. In the speech attacking Aristokrates' proposal to make anyone who killed Charidemos liable to arrest (D94), Euthykles (the speaker) offered a largely negative survey of Athenian honorific activity. His argument was supported by a narrative which recounts the damage done to the reputation of the Athenian *demos* by its readiness to grant honorific decrees to those who did not deserve them.[84] He did his best to underline, by reference to a knowledge of Athenian honorific habits and to claims about the inflation of awards granted to non-Athenians, Athenian anxieties about their dispensing of honorific decrees for citizens. He expatiated on the mistakes that the Athenians had made in granting awards to unworthy and despicable foreign honorands: he pointed to the example of Kotys as someone to whom the Athenians gave citizenship contrary to their interests. In citing this example he was careful to place the blame at the feet not of the Athenian people but of the (unnamed) proposer, asserting that such was 'the act of men of unsound mind to propose such decrees and to give such awards to these men' and emphasising that the people who enacted it believed the honorand to be a well-wisher: 'you would not have done that had you believed him to be your enemy' (Dem. 23.118 = D43). The behaviour of another honorand, Philiskos (Dem. 23.141 = D59) was said to be even worse, including the mutilation of free-born boys, the insult of women, and uncivilised conduct. Even in the *Against Leptines*, where Demosthenes mostly defended the Athenians' record of granting awards by decree, he acknowledged that the people were sometimes deceived into making bad decrees (Dem 20.3), drawing upon a theme which underlined the susceptibility of the people to be deceived by demagogues.[85]

Honours for Athenians came in for criticism too: Euthykles says that through their hyperbolic awards also to Athenian military leaders (pointing

---

84 For more detailed discussion of the decrees see Liddel 2016: 350–2. For the decrees in Demosthenes 20, see Chapter 1.4, note 114) above; for the decrees in Demosthenes 23, see Dem. 23.12 (= DD 77, 78), 23.16 (D94), 23.104 (D71), 23.116 (= D73), 23.118 (= D43), 23.141 (= DD 59,74), 23.145 (= D84), 23.149 (= D64), 23.172 (= D81), 23.173 (= D83), 23.175 (= D80), 23.202 (= D61), 23.203 (= D75).

85 Hesk 2000; Ober 1989: 168–9; Kremmydas 2012: 184-5; Canevaro 2016a: 189, pointing also to the theme in Dem. 8.63, 15.16, 19.29-30, 23.96-7; Aeschin. 3.35.

to Timotheos, Iphikrates and Chabrias), the *demos* had deprived itself of honour (*time*) for particular victories (23.198); in past times, on the other hand, referring to the battles of Marathon and Salamis, they rewarded great leaders not with bronze statues but by choosing them as leaders (Dem. 23.196–7).[86] But Demosthenes' emphasis in this speech was on honours for non-Athenians and he warned too against the inflation of awards for foreigners which meant that the old honours no longer sufficed (23.199–201). Contemporary practice was held to stand in contrast to the restrained fifth-century Athenians who drew the line at awards of citizenship for Meno of Pharsalos and Perdikkas of Macedonia (23.199–200). While Demosthenes' speech targeted individual examples in his criticism of Athenian honorary decrees for non-Athenians,[87] it is clear that he was arguing that the system as a whole is extremely problematic; but the blame for this he placed – as he did the decree for Kotys – at the feet of contemporary Athenian politicians, who are said to drag the system through the mire and make it contemptible (23.201). It is perhaps significant that in this speech Euthykles did not reveal the name of the decrees' proposers, perhaps because he did not wish to provoke a reaction from those responsible for them; the *demos* was in these cases held to be the party responsible for the decrees.

His argument extends to the point that the Athenians undermined the awards for deserving men, by making grants to the unworthy too (Dem. 23.202), drawing the conclusion that Athenians' reputation was damaged by such awards: 'what is really terrible is, not that our counsels are inferior to those of our ancestors, who surpassed all mankind in excellence, but that they are worse than those of all other peoples.' (Dem. 23.211). Accordingly, Demosthenes claimed that the honorific tendencies of the contemporary Athenians – led astray by their leaders – was undermining the honorific system and reputation of the Athenians established long ago. Moreover, he argued that those honorands who desired Athenian citizenship for the personal advantages that it brought rather than out of an admiration for Athenian character and customs would not be champions of Athenian interests (Dem. 23.126).

Contrastingly, Demosthenes' case against Leptines' law abolishing *ateleia* argued – as already noted: see Chapter 1.4 above – that his legislation would undermine the favour accrued to the Athenians by their decrees for their benefactors (20.64). He drew upon decrees from the fifth and fourth centuries extensively to make a case about the damage that the law would do to the

---

86 For the treatment of honorific decrees in oratory, see Liddel 2016.

87 Other decrees cited negatively in this speech: citizenship for Kersobleptes (Dem. 23.141 = D74); honours for Euderkes (Dem. 23.203 = D75); citizenship for Simon and Bianor of Thrace (Dem. 23.12 = D77 and 78); protection for Charidemos (Dem. 23.16 = D94).

DECREES AND POLITICAL SELF-INTEREST

Athenian honorific system;[88] in doing so, Demosthenes took the guise of a defender of Athenian decrees and their legacy. As part of his argument about the shame that the Athenians would feel at the withdrawal of decrees if they were to accept Leptines' law (20.60), Demosthenes holds up – among other decrees – the example of the offer of refuge to political exiles from Corinth after the Peace of Antalkidas, asking his audience whether these decrees should stand as authoritative:

> Later, when the peace with the Spartans was brought about, that is the Peace of Antalkidas, they (sc. the Corinthians who were sympathetic to Athenian interests) were exiled by the Spartans because of what they had done. By receiving them you did a deed of noble and good men ('ἔργον ἀνθρώπων καλῶν κἀγαθῶν'), for you voted for them what they needed. Shall we now examine whether these grants should remain valid? For it is shameful even to ask the question, if anyone were to hear how the Athenians are examining whether it is necessary to allow the benefactors to keep the grants they have been given. These things should have been scrutinised and decided about long ago. Read out also this decree to them. DECREE. These are things you voted for those Corinthians who went into exile because of you. (Dem. 20.54–5)

To abolish these decrees – by upholding Leptines' law – would be to bestow shame on the Athenians who had originally acted as noble and good men; the idea that stripping Athens' honorands of their privileges is a shameful act which amounts to deception (Dem. 20.9) is deployed a little later in the speech (Dem. 20.60 = DD 31, 32).[89] Such an appeal was powerful because by drawing on decrees of the past (Demosthenes in this speech appears to have avoided citing decrees made over the course of the decade prior to his speech)[90] it made a case for the timeless relevance of Athenian decrees.[91] Accordingly, as Wolpert argues, it placed a moral burden onto the shoulders of the jury to preserve the status quo which had been established by the people in past times:[92] in this case, it applied to the balance of Athenian honorific relations. As well as making moral appeals, like those which made a case for the necessity of avoiding shame, the same speech also makes an argument about decrees on the basis

---

88 For the view that this amounted to a subversion of the orthodox hierarchy of laws and decrees, see Chapter 1.2.2 above.

89 For claims that bad decrees bring shame upon the Athenian people, see Aeschin. 1.188 (D15) and Dem. 23.142, 172 (DD 59, 81) with discussion in Chapter 1.5 above. For claims about shame as foundations of civic obligations, see Liddel 2007: 149–50.

90 The latest decree cited is that for Klearchos (D62) of the period 366–362. For a list of the decrees cited in the speech, see Chapter 1.4 note 114 above.

91 The timelessness of decrees is also discussed in Chapter 1.5.3 above.

92 Wolpert 2003.

of the practicalities of Athenian interests: Demosthenes emphasised also the role that rewarding citizens (as well as foreigners) in encouraging good public service (Dem. 20.67–87). But the speech's emphasis on decrees is remarkable when we consider that the Athenians had the power to indict a new law or decree on the basis that it contradicted a law,[93] but not on the basis that it contradicted a decree. Demosthenes places decrees at the centre of his argument on the grounds that Leptines' law was unacceptable because it contradicts not the exact provisions but the spirit of so many Athenian decrees.[94] On this occasion and also the speech *Against Aristokrates* it is perhaps relevant that Demosthenes emphasised the interests of the city (Dem. 20.1; Dem. 23.1–2) rather than his personal interest in the debate, which means that his argument is logical and places emphasis on examples of decrees rather than personal slander. Knowledge of decrees, then, emerges as an important tool for those constructing logical arguments.

Finally, no discussion of honorific decrees in *graphe paranomon* cases can be complete without reference to the recrudescence, in 330, of the dispute about the crowning of Demosthenes proposed by Ktesiphon's decree (Aeschin. 3 and Dem. 18: see D179).[95] Aeschines' argument focused on allegations he made about the illegality of the decree (see D179 Commentary) but asserted also that the decree was proposed shamefully (Aeschin. 1.188 with discussion in Chapter 1.5 above). In these speeches, the orators combine polemic and logic, drawing widely upon decrees. In his defence of Ktesiphon's proposal, Demosthenes cited Aristonikos' decree for himself not just to boast of his own achievements (cf. Chapter 2.2.2.1 above), but as a precedent for the proclamation of a crown at the theatre (18.83 = D156) and the decrees of others as evidence that men who are liable to audit could be crowned (18.114–15).[96] Aeschines, on the other hand, cited honorific decrees which he claimed the Athenians all agreed to be for deserving benefactors (the democrats from Phyle, Chabrias, Iphikrates and Timotheos) in his assault on Demosthenes' worthiness (Aeschin. 1.88 = D15; Aeschin. 3.243 = D46 T4). Moreover, Aeschines – as he did elsewhere – used

---

93 Hansen 1974.

94 For the view that this speech goes some way to subverting the hierarchical relationship between decrees and laws, see Chapter 1.2.2 above. On the logic of the argument that runs throughout the speech, see Kremmydas 2007b.

95 A parallel, but less famous case, is that of the rivalry between Lycurgus and Demades: Lycurgus launched an attack on Kephisodotos' proposal to honour Demades with a statue (D187), and he cited the achievements of Pericles in the fifth century presumably as a way of comparing the modesty of Demades' achievements (Lycurg. fr. 58 Conomis).

96 At 18.114–15 he mentions honours for Diotimos (D190), Nausikles (D228) and Charidemos (D229).

DECREES AND POLITICAL SELF-INTEREST   89

decrees in a detailed way in an attempt at demonstrating the illegality of the crowning of Demosthenes: he held up Demosthenes' decree on the repair of the city walls as evidence to prove that he had held an office, and accordingly not yet rendered accounts, when Ktesiphon made the proposal (Aeschin. 3.27 = D176).[97]

2.4.2 Blame and Liability

We have already seen (Chapter 2.4.1 above) that the act of challenging decrees, as well as decree-making, appears to have been a potential source of political capital in Athenian forensic oratory, while it is clear that knowledge of decrees was a useful tool in the construction of such cases. At this point we add the suggestion that holding political rivals to account for their decree-proposing activity was also an important tool of political invective. This view of responsibility may have been what underscored Lycurgus' argument, in his speech *On Administration*, that the Athenians should subject proposers of decrees to *dokimasia* (Conomis fr. 18 1b).[98] Whereas the *stelai* of discredited or obsolete decrees could be destroyed,[99] memories of rejected decrees could be perniciously revived by rivals of their proposers. Hypereides, evidently responding to criticisms of his enemies,[100] had to explain the emergency enfranchisement decree that he had proposed after Chaironeia by asserting that it was not he but the Athenian defeat on the battlefield – in other words, circumstance – that had proposed it (D167b T6= [Plu.] *X Or.* 848f–9a). In the debate on the conduct of the embassy to Philip in 343, Aeschines and Demosthenes traded arguments about the responsibility for the decrees that shaped the Peace of Philokrates, and in particular their implications for the treatment of the Phokians and Kersobleptes of Thrace, the Athenians' allies. Demosthenes claimed that Aeschines was responsible for persuading the people to accept the details of Philokrates' decree on the Peace (19.47–50, 113; cf. D134). Aeschines, correspondingly, made

---

97 Harris 1994 and Harris 2017 demonstrate thoroughly that Aeschines' claims about the illegality of Ktesiphon's decrees are empty. On the charges against Ktesiphon's decree and Demosthenes' response, see Harris 2017, summarised at D176 Commentary.

98 According to Suda, s.v. 'δοκιμασίαν ἐπαγγεῖλαι' (Adler *delta*,1329) the law on *dokimasia* subjected active politicians and those who had proposed a decree to the process. Another passage suggesting suspicion of those who proposed decrees is Suda, s.v. 'Πανδελετείους γνώμας' (Adler *pi*,171), alleging that a certain blacksmith Pandeletos was known as a sycophant, proposing decrees, and spent his time hanging around the courts.

99 Bolmarcich 2007, arguing that the act of destroying a *stele* would have to be enacted by decree.

100 The fragmentary preservation of this passage makes it impossible to know precisely to what sort of criticisms Hypereides was replying.

a case for Demosthenes' responsibility for the Peace of Philokrates on the basis of an argument that his proposals led up to it (Aeschin. 2.176 = D124; Aeschin. 2.53, 109, 3.63 = D126; Aeschin. 2.67 = D127); he reminded the audience of Demosthenes' responsibility for putting to the vote Philokrates' decree on swearing oaths which led to the exclusion of Kersobleptes (Aeschin. 3.73–5 = D131) as well as his vain attempt to block the putting to the vote of Aleximachos' decree which would have allowed him to give oaths to Philip (Aeschin. 2.83–5 = D132). In the same speech his attacks on Demosthenes' policy extended to other decrees: he claimed also that his alliance with the Thebans betrayed the interests of the Athenians (Aeschin. 2.141; cf. D184).

In his case against Ktesiphon's honours for Demosthenes, Aeschines again attempted to turn Demosthenes' proposals against him: he re-iterated his responsibility for the Peace of Philokrates (Aeschin. 3.54), argued that his decrees after the Peace were those which provoked war with Philip (Aeschin. 3.83 = D146; Aeschin. 3.55 = D159 T1; Aeschin. 3.125-8 = D161), that they had the effect of surrendering opportunities that the city had (Aeschin. 3.92–3 = D147) and asserted his hypocrisy and cowardice by proposing a shrine for Pausanias (Aeschin. 3.160 = D182). Aeschines drew upon his decrees also to disparage the character of his rival, pointing to his decree leading to the arrest of his former guest-friend Anaxinos as an indication that he was a murderer of his host (ξενοκτόνος: Aeschin. 3.223–4 = D145). In response, Demosthenes (18.69–70, 75) argued that he did not bear sole responsibility for formulating Athenian policy against Philip of Macedon in the run-up to Chaironeia, pointing to the proposals of Philokrates, Diopeithes, Aristophon, Euboulos and others (D213, 215–17).

In other political speeches we see a similar combination of attacks on decrees pertinent to the subject of the case and decrees more generally relevant to the reputation of the opponent. In his speech against Demosthenes for his involvement in the Harpalos affair, Dinarchus put into the mouth of its speaker accounts of Demosthenes' decrees on the detention of Harpalos and empowerment of the Areopagus (DD 193, 195, 214), and the deification of Alexander (Din. 1.94 = D198).[101] He claimed that in the period after Chaironeia Demosthenes failed to improve the city either 'by decree or by law' (1.96) and attacked his policy by having his decrees read out aloud (Din. 1.78–80 = D170) and pointing out the contrast to the advice from the oracle at Dodona. He made allegations about the inconsistency of his policy on the basis of knowledge of his opponent's decrees, claiming that Demosthenes at one time made a proposal forbidding anyone to believe in any but the accepted gods, but at another

---

101 Similar attacks on the decree of Philokles concerning Harpalos' money were made in Dinarchus' speech *Against Philokles* (D196).

DECREES AND POLITICAL SELF-INTEREST

time said that the people must not question the grant of divine honours (1.94 = D198).[102]

Not only did the content of decrees come under attack in the courts, but there were claims also about corruption in the process of their enactment; their critics emphasised the workings of surreptitious factors in the process: as we have already established, Aeschines warned that one reason that decrees were inferior to laws was that the people sometimes passed decrees in circumstances when they had been misled by deceit and trickery (Aeschin. 1.178–9).[103] Apollodoros, meanwhile, criticised certain awards as unworthy by claiming the 'individual requesting' the decree had misled the people ([Dem.] 59.91 = DD 109, 110). Moreover, it appears to have been a fairly common way of slandering the proposer of a decree to claim that a citizen had been bribed or persuaded to propose it as a favour or for some self-interested motive;[104] it was, of course, surely frequently the case that the proposal of a decree was motivated by an individual's desire to return a personal favour or secure a networking connection. But the problem we face is that such claims – such as that of Dinarchus about Demosthenes' support of honours for bankers and grain-dealers (Din. 1.43 = D227) – is that they are situated within wider attacks on their proposers. Yet the claims are a reflection of the Janus-faced issue of the allocation of responsibility for the decree and its consequences to the *demos* or the proposer.

Critiques of Athenian decree-practice were, however, evidently not limited to the speeches made in the courts. There is some evidence in the Demosthenic symbouleutic corpus for criticism of past decrees of the *demos*. In [Demosthenes] 13 (*On Organisation*), an assembly speech made in support of spending financial surplus on military matters, the author draws upon examples of decrees deployed elsewhere by Demosthenes, in an attack on Athenian honorific habits: it is likely that the editor of the published version

---

102 The turning of an opponent's decrees against him can be found in Demosthenes *Against Theokrines*, where the accusation of inconsistency is set against Moirokles, one of Theokrines' fellow-speakers: Demosthenes claims that his advocacy of Theokrines will contradict his own decree (Dem. 58.53 = D207). See also Dem. 20.148, where it is argued that Aristophon's support of the proposal to abolish honorific exemption was, given that he was a recipient of it, hypocritical.

103 On the stated intention of decrees and their manipulation, see Chapter 2.5.2 below.

104 For claims about the proposal of decrees and laws by those influenced by bribes or interested in the giving or return of favours see Aeschin. 3.125; Dem. 20.132; 23.146–7, 201–3; 24.66–7, 201–3; 58.35; [Dem.] 59.43; Din. 1.41–3; Hyp. *Dem.* fr. 6 col. 25; cf. Hansen 1974: 54, 1989: 97 note 12. See also DD 148b, 212, 227, 231, 234, 236.

of the speech revised or condensed the passages of the *Against Aristokrates*.[105] [Demosthenes] 12 is a one-off document, which purports to be a letter sent by Philip to the council and people of Athens but which may have been penned by an Isokratean fabricator; what is interesting for our purposes is that on at least three occasions it critically cites Athenian decrees, accusing the Athenians of hypocrisy ([Dem.] 12.8–9 = D74 T1; 12.6 = D142; 12.8–9 = D204) and claiming that no-one cared a jot about Athenian decrees (12.9). Whatever the identity of its creator, he seems to have been aware of Athenian sensitivity about the image of their decrees. It is notable, however, that discussion of decrees in symbouleutic oratory rarely appears to have entailed the naming of the proposer; in the context of the assembly, the emphasis appears to have been on the liability of the demos or its current responsibility to living up to past expectations ([Dem.] 7.25 = D140 T2).

Criticism of decrees in forensic oratory appears to have focussed, for the most part, upon decrees applied to named individuals in relatively recent times. There appears to have been little reason to call attention to problematic decrees of the period before 403/2 except perhaps for reasons of specific argumentative strategy (e.g. Andoc. 1.8). Part of the reason for this is that criticisms of individual decrees are concentrated (in assembly speeches) on those decrees that went unfulfilled in recent times and (in lawcourt speeches) on those decrees which constituted, or were associated with, the policy of a political opponent. We can draw the conclusion at this point that decrees introduced into speeches in the Athenian lawcourts offer a view of portrayals of the dynamics of the Athenian *demos'* behaviour (see Chapter 1.5 above) and in the portrayal of good and bad citizen conduct (2.2). Political capital was accrued also over the course of the processes of decree-making (2.3) and decree-challenging (2.4). The fact that experience and knowledge of decrees offered a potent source of evidential persuasion in the lawcourts and assembly for individual politicians supports the hypothesis outlined earlier: the prevalence of a decree-minded mentality in the politics of the fourth century. At this point I want to turn to a related question: to what degree can this decree-mindedness be thought of as a skill? And if it does amount to a skill, how exclusive was it? What degree of attention did fourth-century orators pay to the content of decrees?

---

105 [Dem.] 13.21–5 with Dem. 23.196–202 with Liddel 2016: 351 note 77. For criticism at the assembly of the *demos'* failure to fulfil the intentions of decrees, see Mader 2006 and discussion in Chapter 2.5.2 below.

2.5 Close Attention to Decrees?

2.5.1 Expertise

It has been observed that over the course of the fourth century there was an increase in the amount of detail that appears in the prescript of Athenian decrees, with elements such as the patronymic of the proposer, the date within the prytany, and the number of the prytany being introduced to inscribed texts.[106] How far can we talk about 'expertise' or even 'professionalism' as a requirement of the secretary? While the growing level of detail in the prescripts of inscribed decrees may explain the change in 363/2 in the term of office of the prytany secretary from one prytany to a whole year,[107] there is no indication that there was anything like a requirement of any exclusive type of professionalism: as the author of the *Ath. Pol.* (54.3) states, this officer was at his time appointed by sortition, though it had previously been appointed by election.[108] As noted already (Chapter 1.2.2 above), from the 340s there is reference to an office with responsibility for decrees (*ho grammateus epi ta psephismata*), who presumably had some role related to overseeing the enactment of decrees and the writing down of their texts, but there is nothing to say that these were experts or specialists.[109]

There is some evidence for the deployment of expertise in the drafting of documents in the classical period: in fifth-century Athens the Athenians commissioned *ad hoc* boards, known as *syngrapheis*, to contribute towards the composition of decrees with elaborate formulae;[110] in the fourth century, we occasionally see officials being required, over the course of decrees, to draw up more detailed specifications than were contained in the version published on stone (e. g. *IG* II³ 1 292 lines 68–9). On occasion, proposers appear to have sought advice from a religious official on the subject of a decree (*IG* II² 47).[111] Proposers, then, certainly consulted those with expert knowledge or

---

106 Rhodes 1972: 138; Henry 1977.

107 Rhodes 1972: 137–8.

108 As Rhodes 1972: 138 writes of the fourth-century situation, 'professional expertise was not yet thought necessary, or the office would not have been made sortitive, but dissociation from the *boule* and a longer period of tenure suggest an improvement in efficiency and perhaps a slightly fairer spreading of the state's burdens'; cf. RO p. xxi; cf. Lambert 2018: 188 note 52. On the secretary, see Chapter 1.2.2 above. For prejudice against experts, see Todd 1996; Ismard 2015.

109 Rhodes 1972: 138; Brillant 1911: 97–108. One might contrast the situation in modern legislative practice where the wording of legislation is drafted by unelected civil servants: Ober 2008: 219 with Huber and Shipan 2002.

110 Rhodes with Lewis 1997: 27, 494.

111 For other examples of proposers taking advice from office-holders, see Rhodes 1972: 43 note 6.

experience in the language of decrees when drafting proposals. It cannot be assumed, however, that the act of handling the language of the initial proposal would have required expertise beyond that which any individual would have obtained through participation in political processes or through consultation of an expert.[112] The anecdote that Lycurgus employed an Olynthian expert to draft his decrees ([Plu.] *X Or.* 842c) is, in all likelihood, based upon a slander that he may have faced in the course of opposition to a proposal: the author of the *Lives of the Ten Orators* probably gleaned this from a now lost oratorical attack on Lycurgus.[113] A balanced assessment of the subject says that the drafting of the text of a decree was an activity that was undertaken through collaboration: the process of finalising the text of a decree involved the input of the council, a proposer and a secretary as well as the magistrate commissioned to have the text written up on a *stele* (see Chapter 1.2.2 above). On at least one occasion Demosthenes appears to have collaborated with a *bouleutes* in order to produce a *probouleuma* which he would carry at the assembly (Aeschin. 3.125–8 = D171). Such a collaborative mode of drafting meant that few citizens would have been ruled out of activity relating to the proposal of a decree.

There is, however, literary evidence for close attention to the language of drafting from at least the 420s onwards:[114] Thucydides claimed that the clause in the Peace of Nicias permitting the Athenians to adjust its terms made the states of the Peloponnese worry that the Spartans were planning to enslave them with the aid of Athens (Thuc. 5.29.2–3). We cannot pretend that the perspectives of that historian into fifth-century documents offer us a straightforward insight into the level to which Athenians in the assembly and lawcourts in the fourth century engaged with the language of decrees. But also in the early fourth century there is some evidence for argumentation based on close attention to the text of a decree: this occurs in Lysias' speech 13, *Against Agoratos*,

---

112 For the idea that a grasp of political language would have been widespread, see Harris, 2006b: 429 following the view of Willi 2003. On participation as an educative experience in the field of politics, see Ober 1998, esp. 161–2. On financial expertise see Davies 2004 and Kallet-Marx 1994 (focussing on its deployment at the Athenian assembly); cf. also Moreno 2007, esp. 213 on the deployment by elite politicians of knowledge about the grain-supply.

113 For a similar assessment of this passage, see Roisman and Worthington 2015: 200; cf. Lambert 2018: 188 note 52, suggesting that the anecdote points to the possibility of an 'increasing professionalisation' of decree-drafting in this era.

114 Rhodes 1972: 277.

DECREES AND POLITICAL SELF-INTEREST

in which the speaker points out that Agoratos was never declared to be an Athenian in the decree praising the assassins of Phrynichos.[115]

Oratorical texts extant from the period after the Social War suggest that politicians were making points on the basis of words that appeared in the texts of decrees. Yunis suggests that Demosthenes' quotation in the *de Corona* of technical aspects of his decree about marching to Eleusis in 339/8 (Dem. 18.178 = D162 T2) aimed at 'creating a seamless connection between his advice and the *demos*' decree'.[116] Some years earlier, in his commentary on the peace with Philip, Demosthenes demanded that the audience appreciate the gulf between the praise and fine-sounding phrases which appear on the decree and Philokrates' rider, which provided that the Athenians would coerce the Phokians to adhere to the terms of the peace (Dem. 19.47–9 = D130 T9). Indeed, it was obvious by the 340s that interstate disputes were discussed in terms of the phraseology of decrees and agreements: the original version of the Peace of Philokrates appears to have deemed it permissible for all parties 'to keep what they held' ('ἔχειν αὐτὸν ἃ εἶχεν'): this went on to form the basis of Philip's contention that Amphipolis was rightfully his (Dem. 7.25–6). At [Dem.] 7.18, 23–9, Hegesippos refers to a promised amendment to the Peace, contradicting this view saying 'that each side should retain its own possessions' ('ἑκατέρους ἔχειν τὰ ἑαυτῶν'), to which Philip denied agreeing (D140 T1).[117] One view of this debate might be to suggest that it was not just the politicians and their critics in the Athenian lawcourts and assemblies who paid close attention to the words of decrees, but Athens' rivals beyond the confines of the *polis* too: the reception of decrees outside Athens will be discussed in more detail in Chapter 4.2 and 4.3 below. But at the same time, we must not exaggerate the implications of a political exchange that centred upon a short phrase: in ancient Athens, just as it is in the modern world, it is possible to

---

115 Lys. 13.72: 'That Agoratos did not kill Phrynichos is clear from the terms of the decree. Nowhere does it say, "Agoratos is to be an Athenian", as it does for Thrasyboulos and Apollodoros. And yet if he really killed Phrynichos, then it would necessarily have been recorded that he was to be an Athenian, on the same inscribed stone where this is said about Thrasyboulos and Apollodoros. But by offering bribes to the proposer, some people arranged to have their own names added to the inscription as "benefactors". The following decree will prove that I am telling the truth.' (trans. Todd 2000) There is textual debate about over the inclusion of 'and Apollodoros' on both occasions in this passage; see Todd 2007: 526 note 8 and below, p. 134 n. 84. On this decree, and its relation to the inscribed honorific decree for Phrynichos' assassins, see ML pp. 260–3, OR pp. 500–5 and Todd 2007: 515–16; see also discussion in Chapter 5.2.2 below.

116 Yunis 2001: 209.

117 On this phrase, see Rhodes 2008: 24–7.

96 DECREES OF FOURTH-CENTURY ATHENS

make claims about the interpretation of political slogans without a firm grasp of their full connotations.

On the domestic front, politicians, with some attention to the texts of decrees, criticised their content in order to score points against rivals or undermine their political activity: as part of his critique of the directives given to the Second Embassy to Philip, Aeschines singled out the vagueness (τὸ ἀφανές) of the instructions of the people for the ambassadors to do whatever good they were able ('πράττειν δὲ τοὺς πρέσβεις καὶ ἄλλ' ὅ τι ἂν δύνωνται ἀγαθόν': Aeschin. 2.104). He claimed that the instructions had been obscurely drafted deliberately so that the ambassadors could retreat in case they failed to persuade Philip to rebuild the Boiotian towns: of course, what Aeschines claimed in 343 was obscure may possibly have been candid to the people in 347/6; moreover, these words constituted standard formulaic decree language. Aeschines also attacked Demosthenes' decrees in his speech of 330, criticising the decree creating alliance with the Thebans by claiming that through its phrase 'if any city revolts from the Thebans, the Athenians are to help the Boiotians in Thebes', Demosthenes had betrayed the Boiotians by handing them over to the Thebans (Aeschin. 3.142 = D163).

At other points it is possible to detect a level of disingenuousness in oratorical descriptions of decrees; in such cases orators place emphasis on general awareness of specific decrees rather than detailed knowledge of their content. In his account of the activities of the Second Embassy to Pella, which was sent to organise the swearing of the oaths of the Peace of Philokrates (according to which key Athenian allies would be left out of the agreement), Aeschines claimed that Demosthenes had praised the returning ambassadors in a decree of Skirophorion 346 (Aeschin. 2.121–2): he aimed to make a point about the hypocrisy of Demosthenes who was, in 343, attacking the conduct of the ambassadors. However, the status of this decree is controversial. Demosthenes, in his account, was keen to maintain that the consequence of his report (*apangelia*) on the activity of the embassy was that, unprecedentedly, the council did not offer the returning ambassadors a vote of thanks or dining at the *prytaneion*. Demosthenes maintains that a *probouleuma* was made by someone in response to his report (19.31), and he has it read out to the court. He maintains, however, that it bestowed no praise on the embassy, and anyway was not read out to the assembly (19.34–5). We are left, therefore, with an apparent contradiction. One possible solution is that Demosthenes did indeed make such a decree, and the passage in which he denies having made it (interestingly, he does not accuse Aeschines of lying) was inserted in a

DECREES AND POLITICAL SELF-INTEREST

later published version of the speech as part of his defence of his reputation.[118] But a preferable view is that of Harris, who takes the view that the council did not propose the bestowal of honours because they were aware of the disagreement among the ambassadors, and that the *probouleuma* mentioned by Demosthenes was non-committal on the question of honours:[119] according to this view, Aeschines presented a misleading view of Demosthenes' proposal as if it amounted to a formal proposal.[120]

Aeschines' deployment of decrees, at other points, was less controversial but simply offered an attack on their nature rather than their substance: for instance, he attacked Ktesiphon's honorific decree for its ἀλαζονεία (false pretence) and κόμπος (pomp);[121] meanwhile, one inspired composition of Demosthenes was said to be 'longer than the Iliad' while being 'more empty than the speeches that he is accustomed to deliver and the life that he has lived'.[122] It is important to recognise that his description of Demosthenes' use of decrees is one which was designed to make a case for a gap between the will of the people and the content of the decree and has no need for close engagement with minutiae. Criticism of the length of Demosthenes' decree may have

---

118 On issues concerning the revision of forensic texts for publication, see Worthington 1991. Worthington 1991: 67 makes observations about other factual errors in the 19th speech, such as the claims (19.154) that Aeschines and other ambassadors delayed in Athens so that the king would have time to seize forts in Thrace. MacDowell (2000: 23–4) suggests that the versions we have of some speeches represent 'a copy of what the speech-writer prepared in advance' in the form of notes, but that in other cases what we have is 'a copy of what was prepared after the trial for distribution to readers. This may or may not incorporate material written beforehand, which the writer has revised with additions and deletions.'

119 Harris 1995: 91.

120 Another example of Aeschines' misleading presentation of proposals is at 3.67, where he presents Demosthenes' proposal that the *prytaneis* call a meeting of the assembly for 8th Elaphebolion, as if it were passed. As Harris 2006b: 94 observes, it is unlikely that this decree was passed. See also Harris 1989: 134–5, observing that Aeschines misleadingly claimed that Demosthenes forced the assembly to accept a proposal of Philokrates by having Antipater address the assembly (Aeschin. 3.71–2; cf. 2.65–6) and told a misleading story about the exclusion of Kersobleptes from the treaty (3.73–5; cf. 2.83–6). Misleading descriptions of decrees can be found also in speeches attributed Demosthenes: the claim that Aristokrates' decree protecting Charidemos empowered him who arrested him to torture, maim and collect money was a tendentious interpretation: see Harris, 2018: 37 note 5.

121 Aesch. 3.237: 'If you turn to the second part of the decree, in which you have dared to write that he is a good man and "constantly speaks and does what is best for the Athenian people," omit the false pretence and the pomp of your decree, deal with real acts and show us what you mean.' ('εἰ δὲ ἥξεις ἐπὶ τὸ δεύτερον μέρος τοῦ ψηφίσματος, ἐν ᾧ τετόλμηκας γράφειν ὡς ἔστιν ἀνὴρ ἀγαθός, καὶ "διατελεῖ λέγων καὶ πράττων τὰ ἄριστα τῷ δήμῳ τῷ Ἀθηναίων," ἀφελὼν τὴν ἀλαζονείαν καὶ τὸν κόμπον τοῦ ψηφίσματος ἅψαι τῶν ἔργων, ἐπίδειξον ἡμῖν ὅ τι λέγεις.')

122 Aesch. 3.100: 'ταῦτα δ' εἰπὼν δίδωσιν ἀναγνῶναι ψήφισμα τῷ γραμματεῖ μακρότερον μὲν τῆς Ἰλιάδος, κενότερον δὲ τῶν λόγων οὓς εἴωθε λέγειν, καὶ τοῦ βίου ὃν βεβίωκε.'

been an attempt to make his audience laugh at it: it was perhaps reminiscent of the joke in Aristophanes' *Clouds* (1016–19), that under the influence of the Worse Argument, Pheidippides 'will have in the first place, a pallid complexion, small shoulders, a narrow chest, a large tongue, little hips, great lewdness, a long decree ...'.[123]

Naturally, the closest attention to the content of decrees came in those compositions which were directed against their substance in the shape of indictment for illegality (*graphe paranomon*). In such cases it is highly likely that the prosecutor would have scrutinised the archival copy of the decree being attacked. Demosthenes' speech on Aristokrates' decree for the inviolability of Charidemos attacked its drafting particularly closely, pointing out that the decree failed to specify whether the murderer of Charidemos would still be liable to seizure had they killed him when he was acting in opposition to Athenian interests (23.16–17 = D94 T2).[124] It seems to be the case that the full political mileage in attacking a decree could be unleashed by its detailed recitation. Aeschines, in addition to expressing exasperation at Ktesiphon's praise of Demosthenes as the one who 'does and speaks the best things for the Athenians' (3.50, 92), emphasised another vein, the procedural performance of a decree, when he re-enacted the drama of the herald reciting the decree for Demosthenes in order to amplify the connotations of an honorific decree for someone he rated unworthy of such distinction (Aeschin. 3.153–5).

The fact that we never, in extant forensic oratory, encounter the claim that an opponent is lying about the straightforward substance of a decree is revealing: it suggests either that litigants were for the most part truthful about the contents of decrees or, alternatively, that they lacked the will to check the claims made by their opponents. Indeed, not even Aeschines, who accused Demosthenes of having lied to the assembly in spring 340 about resources available to the Athenians and of being an adept liar (Aeschin. 3.97–9), claimed that Demosthenes misrepresented the content of decrees.[125]

Earlier I asserted that while proposers might have drawn upon expertise in the drafting of the formulaic or detailed aspects of a proposal, this would have been something available to them through knowledge gleaned through participation in the political process and consultation of experts. We have seen,

---

123 See discussion in Chapter 5.3.2 below.

124 Demosthenes elsewhere in that speech argued against the legality of the decree on the basis of its wording (23.90-1; cf. 23.27, 34, 36, 84).

125 For discussion of the slander about sophistry and mendacity that went on between Demosthenes and Aeschines see Hesk 2000: 213–14, 231–41.

furthermore, the ways in which knowledge of the substance of decrees bore rhetorical potential in the development of political argumentation and invective. There is, however, little evidence to support the idea that orators were putting to use any kind of privileged expertise in decree-making: the level of technical knowledge implied in these attacks was not high and could have been achieved simply by engagement with the decree-making processes of the council or assembly;[126] at times (particularly when advocating an indictment for illegality), however, consultation of the archive would have been necessary. We will return to questions about the dissemination of knowledge of Athenian decrees in Chapter 3 below. However, at this point, I want to explore another means by which the orators appear to have engaged in the rhetoric of decrees: their attempts to emphasise or subvert the intention behind a piece of legislation.

2.5.2 Manipulation of Intention and Consequence

The sociologists March and Olsen, in their work on political institutions, have emphasised the role of stating legitimate intentions in ensuring the authority of political decisions.[127] This is a perspective which can be found in the evidence for Athenian decrees. Even if decrees sometimes drew upon past examples or made connections with episodes in Athenian history,[128] it was in their nature to be concerned with future consequences: as Harris has observed, by reference to Demosthenes' speech *Against Timocrates*, Athenian decrees went potentially into effect from the day when they were passed, and did not normally have retroactive action (Dem. 24.41–4):[129] generally, they offered instructions which required immediate (αὐτίκα μάλα) or subsequent (τὸ λοιπόν) action.[130] The future-facing nature of decrees seems to be amplified by the fact that they often stated explicitly forward-looking intentions:[131] even Hegesippos' decree which specifies that the council is to hand to the people a *probouleuma* concerning those who have in the past made expeditions in the land of the Eretrians states

---

126 Cf. Harris, 2006b: 429
127 March and Olsen 1989: 49–51.
128 Lambert 2018: 115–53.
129 Harris 2006b. The fact that the Athenian assembly sometimes acted as a court (for instance, in some cases of *eisangelia*) suggests that it was not in principle against taking decisions about the past: I owe this point to Stephen Todd.
130 'αὐτίκα μάλα': Rhodes 1972: 280. On references to action to be taken subsequently to the passing of a decree, referred to by the phrase 'τὸ λοιπόν', see Harris 2006: 425–7.
131 Lambert 2011a; on exhortatory intentions in honorific decrees, see Miller 2016.

that this is to be done 'so that they shall render justice in accordance with laws' (*IG* II³ 1 399 lines 7–10).[132]

Statements concerning intention contained in the wording of Athenian decrees fall into three categories. First, there are those which express a general intention of the decree, which is often related to its publication, and aim to publicise the generosity, altruism, or the public reputation of the legislative body. This is often framed in terms of a hortatory clause:[133] in the decree for the grain-merchant Herakleides of Salamis, for instance, we find the stated intention – pointedly using repetitively the language of *philotimia* – that the honorand is crowned 'so that others also may behave in an honour-seeking way (φιλοτιμῶνται), knowing that the council honours and crowns those who behave in an honour-seeking way (φιλοτιμουμένους)' (*IG* II³ 1 367 lines 64–6; trans. AIO); this was linked at other times to the hope that other cities might continue to be friendly to the Athenians, as was expressed in an honorific decree for the city of Pellana in the Peloponnese (*IG* II³ 1 304 lines 16–18). Second, non-honorary decrees might state a general intention which refers to the subject of that decree: the decision about whether or not the Athenians should cultivate the sacred land on the border between Eleusis and Megara of 352/1, once made, would aspire towards piety and the avoidance of *asebeia* (impiety), so 'that relations with the two goddesses may be as pious as possible and in future no impiety may be done concerning the sacred land and other sacred things at Athens' (*IG* II³ 1 292 lines 51–3). Third, non-honorary decrees might also state a local intention which might refer to a specific proposal/idea laid out on a decree: the same decree tells us that Athenian magistrates are to be present at the discussion of the sacred land at the city Eleusinion 'so that they may place the boundaries as piously and fairly as possible' (*IG* II³ 1 292 lines 15–16).[134] Another example which illustrates the second and third types of hortatory clause is the decree concerning sacrifices at the Asklepieion in Piraeus (*IG* II² 47) which contains two stated intentions: so that the preliminary sacrifices might be offered' according to the advice of the priest (lines 25–8) and so that the Athenians might distribute as much meat as possible (lines 32–3).

What did Athenians think about the intentions of their decrees? It is clear from the literary record that Athenians made appeals to the audience by

---

132 The view is widespread: Cohen 1995: 52 uses Dem 24.72–6 as evidence that democratic governments do not apply laws retrospectively; Harris (2018: 147 note 145) observes, on the basis of the same passage, the principle that once a case was decided it could not be brought to court again.

133 Henry 1996. See, for analysis, Lambert 2011a; Miller 2016.

134 On stated intentions that can be found on inscribed Athenian laws, which generally emphasise public interest, see Liddel 2007: 111–14.

reference to the ideas about intention stated on decrees. At times it was expedient to emphasise their consonance with community interests. The speaker of Demosthenes 47 suggests that the decree concerning the collection of naval material that he produced (D85 = Dem. 47.20) was introduced 'so that the equipment for the ships might be recovered and kept safe for the city'.[135] Orators were also ready to assert forward-looking motivations of honorific decrees, the likes of which we encountered in the epigraphical evidence. In Andocides' assembly speech advocating his return from exile, we read perhaps the earliest oratorical presentation of such a motivation,[136] notwithstanding a sense of reservation about the readiness of the Athenians to bestow honours:

> I often see you bestowing civic rights and substantial grants of money upon both slaves and foreigners from every part of the world, if they prove to have done you some service. And you are acting wisely in making such gifts; they engender the greatest possible willingness to serve you (οὕτω γὰρ ἂν ὑπὸ πλείστων ἀνθρώπων εὖ πάσχοιτε). (Andoc. 2.23, trans. Maidment 1953)

Such a perspective, which views honorific decrees as increasing Athens' chance of receiving benefactions in the future, was central to the argument of Demosthenes' case for honours in the de *Corona* (Dem. 18.120), and was also expressed in Xenophon's *Poroi* (3.11).[137] At other times, though, orators, as Isocrates did in his encomium for Evagoras (Isoc. 9 *Evagoras* 57 = D24 T1), made claims about honorific decrees as a straightforwardly fair return to those who had done good for the Athenian community: this constituted an expression of morally upstanding reciprocity conceptually separate from the interests of the city. In the *Against Leptines*, for instance, Demosthenes argued that, were Leptines' abolition of *ateleia* to be accepted, then the likes of those Thasians who handed their island over to the Athenians would be deprived of the things

---

135 Dem. 47.20: "ἵνα εἰσπραχθῇ τὰ σκεύη ταῖς ναυσὶ καὶ σᾶ γένηται τῇ πόλει.' It is impossible to know whether these words were included in the text of the decree or whether they were introduced by the speaker.
136 It is plausible to read hortatory intention in the second of the inscribed Herms cited at Aeschin. 3.184. This text is viewed by Petrovic as that of an authentic epigram: Petrovic 2013. The importance of hortatory intentions (often implied rather than explicitly-stated) is widely recognised in the study of archaic poetry, some of which was epigrammatic: see, e.g., Irwin 2005: 17–34, 63–81; Day 2010: 280; Petrovic 2010: 214.
137 Xenophon recommended that the Athenians should write up the names of benefactors as a way of raising income (*Poroi* 3.11; cf. Liddel 2007: 164); he advised also that the Athenians make awards to merchants so that they would benefit Athens for the sake of both honour and profit (*Poroi* 3.4); Engen's study has shown how Athenian honorific decrees were used by the Athenians to engage their benefactors in a system of gift-exchange and thereby to foster relationships (Engen 2010: 217).

given to them (Dem. 20.58, 60).[138] Demosthenes took this argument further, appealing to the stated intentions of honorific decrees, suggesting that the inscribed versions of them stand as a memorial to the generous character of the city and proofs of this to those who wish to do good things for the Athenians (Dem. 20.64):

> You have heard the decrees ... it is fitting, therefore, to allow these inscriptions to hold good for all time, that as long as any of the men are alive, they may suffer no wrong at your hands, and when they die, those inscriptions may be a memorial of the character of the city, and may stand as examples to all who wish to do us a service, declaring how many benefactors our city has benefited in return.[139]

Stated intentions appear, therefore, to have had a strong appeal to the speakers. But they were open to dispute, both by speakers who wished to dispute the morality (Aeschin. 3.180; Dem. 23.196–201) and practical efficacy (Dem. 23.111–14, 118–19, 138, 141) of the Athenian honorific system, and also by those speakers who wanted to read collusion and conspiracy into their rival activities:[140] in Demosthenes' 24th speech, attacking Timokrates' law on the liberty of public debtors, the speaker claimed that Epikrates' decree (D93) bringing forward the date of the commission of the lawmakers (*nomothetai*) to the 12th of Hekatombaion was drafted not, as it claimed, so that it would arrange for adequate funds to be channelled to the Panathenaic festival so that it would be celebrated as handsomely as possible (ὡς κάλλιστα) but in collusion with Timokrates so that his law would bypass the normal route for the introduction of a law and accordingly could be enacted by them without any significant opposition:

> You noticed as the decree was being read out how craftily its author held out the excuse of the budget and the pressing needs of the festival in order to eliminate the time appointed by law when he proposed that the legislation be passed on the next day. His aim, by Zeus, was not to ensure that the festival be as splendid as

138 There are plenty of other examples in that speech where honours are presented as fair exchange for someone who has done a good service: this, for instance, is stressed in Demosthenes' account of the shelter they offered for the Corinthians who had held out for the Athenians in the Corinthian war (Dem. 20.52–4); Epikerdes of Cyrene, who fed Athenian prisoners in Sicily, is held up as another worthy donor (Dem. 20.414). Cf. the implications of reward and reciprocity in the discussion of the reward to the Troizenians at Hyp. *Athenog.* 3 (= D175).

139 Dem. 20.64: 'ἠκούσατε μὲν τῶν ψηφισμάτων .... προσήκει τοίνυν τὰς στήλας ταύτας κυρίας ἐᾶν τὸν πάντα χρόνον, ἵν᾽, ἕως μὲν ἂν τινες ζῶσι, μηδὲν ὑφ᾽ ὑμῶν ἀδικῶνται, ἐπειδὰν δὲ τελευτήσωσιν, ἐκεῖναι τοῦ τῆς πόλεως ἤθους μνημεῖον ὦσι, καὶ παραδείγμαθ᾽ ἑστῶσι τοῖς βουλομένοις τι ποιεῖν ὑμᾶς ἀγαθόν, ὅσους εὖ ποιήσαντας ἡ πόλις ἀντ᾽ εὖ πεποίηκεν.'

140 Cf. Roisman 2006: 95–117.

DECREES AND POLITICAL SELF-INTEREST

possible, for there was nothing left to be done, and no funds to be provided, but that this law now on trial be enacted and go into effect for their benefit without anyone noticing in advance and lodging an objection. (Dem. 24.28 = D93 T1, trans. Harris 2018)[141]

This, the speaker claims, is one element of Timokrates' plot to exempt his associates from paying their debts to the city.[142] The allegation of self-serving motivations can be observed elsewhere: in an *endeixis* following a *graphe paranomon* the speaker (Epichares) of Dem. 58.30 (D209) mentioned the claim of his rival, Theokrines, that the speaker's father had plotted to force Charidemos to return to his natural father's family and to revoke the inheritance that Aischylos had left for him by the wording of the honorific decree he had proposed; allegedly, the decree had named Charidemos the son of Ischomachos (his natural father) rather than as the son of Aischylos (his adoptive father).[143]

---

141 Dem. 24.28: ἐνθυμήθητε {ἀναγιγνωσκομένου} τοῦ ψηφίσματος ὡς τεχνικῶς ὁ γράφων αὐτὸ τὴν διοίκησιν καὶ τὸ τῆς ἑορτῆς προστησάμενος κατεπεῖγον, ἀνελὼν τὸν ἐκ τῶν νόμων χρόνον, αὐτὸς ἔγραψεν αὔριον νομοθετεῖν, οὐ μὰ Δί' οὐχ ἵν' ὡς κάλλιστα γένοιτό τι τῶν περὶ τὴν ἑορτήν (οὐδὲ γὰρ ἦν ὑπόλοιπον οὐδ' ἀδιοίκητον οὐδέν), ἀλλ' ἵνα μὴ προαισθομένου μηδενὸς ἀνθρώπων μηδ' ἀντειπόντος τεθείη καὶ γένοιτο κύριος αὐτοῖς ὅδ' ὁ νῦν ἀγωνιζόμενος νόμος.'

142 For other examples of allegations made about self-serving motivations for proposals of decrees, see Chapter 2 note 104 above.

143 Dem. 58.30–1 (D209 T1): 'When he prosecuted him for making an unconstitutional proposal, in the accusation he brought against my father, he said that a conspiracy had been formed against the boy who was the subject of the decree, according to which it was promised that Charidemos, son of Ischomachos, be awarded free meals in the *prytaneion*. For he (sc. Theokrines) alleged that, if the boy were to return to his father's home, he would lose all the estate that his adoptive father, Aischylos, had given to him. This was a lie, and no such thing has ever taken place to an adopted person. He claimed also that Polyeuktos, the husband of the boy's mother, was responsible for all of this, because he wanted to take some of the boy's property. The judges were indignant at the things that were said, and though they held the decree in itself and the gift to be legal, they thought the boy would be deprived of his property. And so they fined my father ten Talents as being in concert with Polyeuktos, and they thought that Theokrines was actually helping the boy.' ('τοῦ γὰρ πατρὸς κατηγορῶν, ὦ ἄνδρες δικασταί, ὅτε τὴν τῶν παρανόμων αὐτὸν ἐδίωκε γραφήν, ἔλεγεν ὡς ἐπιβεβουλευμένος ὁ παῖς εἴη περὶ οὗ τὸ ψήφισμα γεγραμμένον ἦν, ἐν ᾧ τὴν σίτησιν ἔγραψεν Χαριδήμῳ ὁ πατὴρ τῷ Ἰσχομάχου υἱῷ, λέγων ὡς, ἐὰν ἐπανέλθῃ εἰς τὸν πατρῷον οἶκον ὁ παῖς, ἀπολωλεκὼς ἔσται τὴν οὐσίαν ἅπασαν ἣν Αἰσχύλος ὁ ποιησάμενος αὐτὸν υἱὸν ἔδωκεν αὐτῷ, ψευδόμενος· οὐδενὶ γὰρ πώποτε, ὦ ἄνδρες δικασταί, τοῦτο τῶν εἰσποιηθέντων συνέβη. καὶ τούτων πάντων αἴτιον ἔφη Πολύευκτον γεγενῆσθαι τὸν ἔχοντα τὴν μητέρα τοῦ παιδός, βουλόμενον ἔχειν αὐτὸν τὴν τοῦ παιδὸς οὐσίαν. ὀργισθέντων δὲ τῶν δικαστῶν ἐπὶ τοῖς λεγομένοις, καὶ νομισάντων αὐτὸ μὲν τὸ ψήφισμα καὶ τὴν δωρεὰν κατὰ τοὺς νόμους εἶναι, τῷ δὲ ὄντι τὸν παῖδα μέλλειν ἀποστερεῖσθαι τῶν χρημάτων, τῷ μὲν πατρὶ δέκα τάλαντων ἐτίμησαν ὡς μετὰ Πολυεύκτου ταῦτα πράττοντι, τούτῳ δ' ἐπίστευσαν ὡς δὴ βοηθήσαντι τῷ παιδί.'). For discussion, see Roisman 2006: 116–17.

One connotation of the forward-looking nature of decrees was that once an audience had become familiar with their content, it was relatively easy for orators and historians not only to elaborate the intentions of decrees but also to compare or contrast them with their actual or probable consequence. Accordingly, Euthykles, speaker of Demosthenes 23, in his case against Aristokrates' decree for the inviolability of Charidemos (a mercenary fighting for the Thracian king Kersobleptes: D94), claimed that Aristokrates' proposal would deprive the Athenians of an honest and effective safeguard for the Chersonese. Showing favour to Kersobleptes through this Charidemos risked distancing his enemies from Athens: if Kersobleptes attacked the Athenians they would be less likely to have the support of those he may have wronged (105).[144] Early on in the speech, he asserted to the audience the importance of deliberating about not only the intentions of the decree but also its consequences:

> If it is your desire to learn the truth about this business, and to give a righteous and legitimate verdict on the indictment, **you must not confine your attention to the mere phrasing of the decree, but also take into consideration its probable consequences** ... You must not be greatly astonished if we convince you that his decree also is so worded that, while apparently offering some personal protection to Charidemos, it really robs our city of an honest and effective safeguard for the Chersonese.[145]

In assembly oratory, whereas it was possible to emphasise the potential of the Athenian decree for resisting hostile powers,[146] Demosthenes in the *Third Olynthiac* offered a potential contrast between stated intention and actual outcome, telling the people that:

---

144 However, the main emphasis of his speech is not this conspiracy theory: much of the rest of the speech is spent discussing what the decree fails to specify, rather than what it actually says (23.22–99), that the decree is unconstitutional, undeserved (6–7, 19, 89, 184) and contrary to the interest of the state (100–22, 189–90). He also attacks the desirability (113) of what he claims to be the concealed intention of the decree, after arguing that it forms a part of a plot to make Kersobleptes the sole ruler of the Thracian kingdom (23.9, 15). For discussion, see Roisman 2006: 116–17.
He insists that (58–9) the decree throws the Athenians into uncertainty about what might happen in the future, as it will deprive anyone maltreated by Charidemos of legal deserts and gives Charidemos licence to do as he pleases (67).
145 Dem. 23.2–3: 'δεῖ δὴ πάντας ὑμᾶς, εἰ βούλεσθ' ὀρθῶς περὶ τούτων μαθεῖν καὶ κατὰ τοὺς νόμους δικαίως κρῖναι τὴν γραφήν, μὴ μόνον τοῖς γεγραμμένοις ἐν τῷ ψηφίσματι ῥήμασιν προσέχειν, ἀλλὰ καὶ τὰ συμβησόμεν' ἐξ αὐτῶν σκοπεῖν.... προσήκει μὴ πάνυ θαυμάζειν, εἰ καὶ τοῦτο τὸ ψήφισμ' ἡμεῖς οὕτω γεγραμμένον ἐπιδείξομεν ὥστε δοκεῖν μὲν Χαριδήμῳ φυλακήν τινα τοῦ σώματος διδόναι, τὴν ὡς ἀληθῶς δὲ δικαίαν καὶ βέβαιον [φυλακὴν Χερρονήσου] τῆς πόλεως ἀποστερεῖν.'
146 See, for instance, Dem. 8.74–5 = D82 T1; see also Dem. 23.104 (D71) emphasising the *dunamis* of the Athenian decree concerning Miltokythes.

DECREES AND POLITICAL SELF-INTEREST

a mere decree is worthless without a willingness on your part to put your resolutions into practice. If decrees could automatically compel you to do your duty, or could accomplish the objects for which they were proposed, you would not have passed such an array of them with little or no result, and Philip would not have had such a long career of insolent triumph. (Dem. 3.14–15)[147]

We close this chapter, therefore, with Demosthenes urging the assembly to take up his policy of strenuous resistance to Philip on the basis of the argument that their decrees are useless – the irony of which may well have coincided with Philip's cynical claim that no-one cared about Athenian honorific decrees (if we are right to think that the author of his letter – at Dem. 12.9 – correctly gauged Philip's views).[148] Demosthenes was attempting to empower himself by criticising the Athenians' decree-making habits. In so doing, he poses as a critic of the decree system in order to motivate the audience into action.[149] He was probably right that the Athenians had not always lived up to the aims of their decrees.[150] Even in the early 350s, speakers could present decrees of the Athenians as ineffective in places where it was rhetorically useful to do so (e.g. [Dem.] 50.3–7 = D67). However, by the time of the speech *Against Diondas*, disillusionment,

147 Dem. 3.14–5: ‘ὅτι ψήφισμ' οὐδενὸς ἄξιόν ἐστιν, ἂν μὴ προσγένηται τὸ ποιεῖν ἐθέλειν τά γε δόξαντα προθύμως [ὑμᾶς]. εἰ γὰρ αὐτάρκη τὰ ψηφίσματ' ἦν ἢ ὑμᾶς ἀναγκάζειν ἃ προσήκει πράττειν ἢ περὶ ὧν γραφείη διαπράξασθαι, οὔτ' ἂν ὑμεῖς πολλὰ ψηφιζόμενοι μικρά, μᾶλλον δ' οὐδὲν ἐπράττετε τούτων, οὔτε Φίλιππος τοσοῦτον ὑβρίκει χρόνον.' For other Demosthenic criticism of Athenian decree-making see Mader 2006 with Dem. 4.20, 30, 46; 7.29; *Exordia* 21.3, 48.1. This line of thinking is emphasised on the speech *On Organisation*, where Demosthenes states that ‘such is the state of our public affairs that if anyone read out your resolutions and then went on to describe your performances, not a soul would believe that the same men were responsible for them both' ([Dem.] 13.32). He points to the decree against the Megarians, when they appropriated the sacred *orgas*, and on behalf of the Phleiasian exiles, as examples of principled hostility which led to action of no account (13.32; cf. DD 111, 112), offering the point that ‘Your decrees accord with the traditions of Athens, but your powers bear no relation to your decrees' (13.33).

148 [Dem.] 12.9 (‘Philip's letter'): ‘And you act like this even though you well know that nobody who receives such gifts from you cares a jot for any of your laws or decrees'. (‘καὶ ταῦτα σαφῶς εἰδότας ὅτι τῶν λαμβανόντων τὰς δωρεὰς τὰς τοιαύτας οὐδεὶς οὔτε τῶν νόμων οὔτε τῶν ψηφισμάτων οὐδὲν φροντίζει τῶν ὑμετέρων.') For Plutarch's view that Philip mocked Demosthenes' decrees on the bloody battlefield at Chaironeia, see Plu. *Dem.* 20.3.

149 Mader 2006 suggests that Demosthenes' tendency to present the *demos* as politically paralysed and gripped by symbolic action was a strategy for moving the audience to endorse his own more strenuous policy. Demosthenes explained the slowness of the Athenians to act in his speech *On the False Embassy* on account of their need to collect the means for expeditions (Dem. 19.185–6).

150 There is epigraphical evidence for unfulfilled promises on Athenian decrees: in their honours for the exiled Arybbas of the Molossi, the Athenians pledged to recover for him his ancestral kingdom: *IG* II[3] 1 367 lines 42–7; as Lambert (AIO website) observes, this was never done and the honorand died in exile (Justin 7.6.12).

born of the realisation of the Athenians' weak geopolitical position (cf. Chapter 1.4 above), had set in: Hypereides maligned the standard of the Athenians' decrees, claiming that whereas their former decisions were on a par with the ancestors of the Athenians, their current ones were equivalent to that of the Megarians and Corinthians, and he attacked Demades' resistance to the people's desire to expunge particular clauses (Hypereides, *Against Diondas*, 20–21 Horváth).[151] What is suggested is a disenchantment born of Athenian weakness, expressed by way of a criticism of their decrees; we will return to the Athenian concern about the image of their decrees in non-Athenian contexts in Chapter 4 below.

2.6 Conclusion

Formulating a general theory about the deployment of the decree in political contexts is a challenging task because public figures engaged with decrees, decree-making processes, and accounts of them in different and sometimes contradictory ways. While the form of deployment with the details of Athenian decrees fluctuates, orators were capable of paying close attention to their language, the procedures that surrounded their implementation, and their implications. Decree-making, decree-challenging, and decree-interpreting were important sources of symbolic capital for the politically ambitious in the Athenian lawcourts. More specifically, we have seen the ways in which knowledge of decrees was deployed in order to sway the people to make particular decisions in the lawcourts, by offering memories and interpretations of the recent and not-so-recent past and to attack political enemies. At the assembly, when orators cited decrees, they tended to do so with the intention of criticising the *demos* for mistakes in past policy, and appear to have avoided naming fellow politicians as proposers. In doing so, speakers assumed that their audiences were familiar with the culture of decree-making and the importance of its workings to the interests of the city.

Over the course of the preceding two chapters, I hope also to have established some of the reasons for the preponderance of the decree in political life: their rhetorically negotiable status (in particular when compared to laws), the perception of them as an appropriate route for political activity, the accessibility of the decree-making process to citizens, their forward-looking nature and the rhetorical pliability of their stated intentions and actual consequences. Orators drew upon them owing to the degree of authority they offered, but also the fact

---

151 For the possibility that this is a reference to the Megarians and Corinthians caving in to Philip's demands after Chaironeia, see Horváth 2014: 153–4.

that they loomed large in the practices of politics and the stories that were told about politics. As we have seen, decrees of the people could be used to summon up an image of Athenian harmony and unity (Chapter 1.5.1 above), but also to evoke an atmosphere of crisis and crisis-management (Chapter 1.5.2 above). Reminiscences of decrees could be used, therefore, to generate a sense of the shared purpose of the Athenian people, as a way of expressing social capital; at the same time, they were used by individuals as evidence in the assessment of individual human behaviour (2.2) and were widely deployed in the construction of politically relevant arguments (2.3); by proposing and attacking them, orators generated self-interested symbolic capital (2.4). Individual orators showed the ability to engage closely with the language and stated intention of decrees, but not to an extent that would necessitate a level of expertise beyond that which the civically engaged individual would have obtained through political and social activity (2.5). Once again, as we saw in Chapter 1, both contemporary and non-contemporary (chiefly fifth-century) decrees could be cited in the formulation of arguments, and Demosthenes does not seem to have had any reservations about deploying them in speeches challenging the law of Leptines and the decree of Aristokrates.

The accessibility of this system to male Athenian citizens (see Chapter 2.3 above) was one manifestation of a positive political freedom to which many of them had access,[152] though it was a system open to manipulation by individuals with an overlapping set of characteristics: ambition, knowledge, eloquence, and being well connected. But we have seen also – especially in the speech *Against Aristokrates* (see Chapter 2.4 above) – that there existed a rhetoric which emphasised systemic problems with the way that the Athenian people dispensed honours by way of decree. Thus challenges to institutional norms in the shape of criticism of decrees may have offered persuasive capital to a politician seeking it. It is a tendency which, perhaps, offers a further insight into the nature of the institution of the Athenian decree: it offered the capacity for individuals and groups to highlight the problems of accepted practices and to deviate from expected norms.

To return to the subject of the dynamism of institutions: as we have seen, decrees served as passive agents or receptacles of ambition. They were subject also to the processes of interpretation, distortion, and dispute. The decree-system offered proposers both the means of initiating political developments and also the opportunity to exploit the memory of their achievements; to their local and wider audiences they could act as souvenirs of virtuous or mistaken

---

152 See now Campa 2018, emphasising positive freedom as 'self-mastery' rather than political participation.

political activity or as receptacles of historical memory. As vehicles for broader political, moral, euergetic and aspirational transactions the decree-system of fourth-century Athens, I suggest, opened up a unique moral economy of its own, one which is revealed in the literary and epigraphical texts pertaining to Athenian political life. But to fully explain their preponderance in political transactions requires assessment at this point of the Athenian politicians' sources of information about decrees, to which I will now turn. In Chapter 3 below, I ask how awareness about contemporary decrees diffused among fourth-century Athenians and set out the implications of the fits and non-fits between patterns of preservation of decrees in the epigraphical and literary records for an understanding of the inscribed publication of decrees.

3

The Dissemination of Fourth-Century Athenian Decrees: Local Audiences

3.1 Introduction

In Chapters 1 and 2 above I have explored the deployment of knowledge about, and accounts of, decrees in political and litigious contexts. At this point I come to assess the ways in which perspectives on recent and contemporary decrees diffused among fourth-century Athenians. I will test the hypothesis that whereas accounts of some Athenian decrees were disseminated through formal institutional mechanisms, those of others were spread by informal means. Accordingly, knowledge of Athenian decrees was often inexact and unevenly distributed throughout the population. I address the question of how knowledge about, and understandings of, fourth-century Athenian decrees circulated among those Athenians (primarily political orators but also historians) who made reference to them in their works; I shall assess how Athenian public knowledge of decrees was informed or facilitated by involvement in political and litigious processes, the informal circulation of knowledge and access to decrees in the public archive (Chapter 3.2 below); I shall explore the relevance of epigraphical publication in terms of its likely audience, its authority and its impact upon the literary reception of decrees (Chapter 3.3 below). A comparison between the range of decrees preserved in the literary record with those in the epigraphical record (see Table 1) will foreshadow discussion of the implications for understanding the relationship between the Athenians' decree-making institutions and their epigraphic habit (Chapter 3.4 below). I conclude by emphasising the largely social nature of the processes through which awareness of decrees was disseminated among Athenians. The fact that literary texts are often very quiet about their sources of knowledge of decrees makes this endeavour a challenging one, and so the first task in this chapter, therefore, is to set out the contexts in which news about decrees was disseminated.

3.2 Diffusion of Athenian Decrees

3.2.1 Institutional and Informal Interaction

As already noted (Chapter 1.2.2 above), it appears to have been the prytany secretary who had responsibility for ensuring that an official text of a decree was recorded ([Arist.] *Ath. Pol.* 54.3), probably in the archive (see Chapter 3.2.2 below). But beyond the meeting of the assembly in which they were enacted, we should not assume that there was any systematic attempt to spread news of decrees evenly through the citizen population of about 30,000 adult males.[1] Instead, the extensive individual participation of citizens in the activities of civic institutions was vital to the spread of ideas about decrees.[2] For those citizens of fourth-century Athens involved – even in a limited capacity – in political activity or litigation, probably the most important way of getting to know about decrees was through hearing them being formulated as preliminary decrees (*probouleumata*) and debated at the *bouleuterion*,[3] read out and discussed in speeches at the assembly,[4] and challenged and advocated in the lawcourts; at such venues, active individuals were engaged with decrees as interested participants involved in a debate about them,[5] as officials involved in the administrative aspects of enactment,[6] or were exposed to presentations of them as citizens whose role in the process of enactment was to pass judgement when the proposal was put to the vote.

The extant sources of the fourth century enable some access to understanding how new decrees were presented before an audience of citizens at the assembly:[7] Demosthenes' *First Philippic* is the clearest example of a speech extant in

---

1 On the population of fourth-century Athens, see Van Wees 2011; Hansen 1988: 14–28.

2 Hansen (1980) suggests there were some 700 magistrates (in addition to the 500 *bouleutai*) selected annually. For a large-scale assessment of the way in which political participation at Athens contributed to the dissemination of knowledge, see Ober 2008, taking the view that formal institutions promoted the cascade of knowledge throughout the citizen body (Ober 2008: 180 note 19). Whereas Ober talks about a 'cascade' of knowledge, in this current chapter I place emphasis on the subjectivity of the accounts of decrees that were disseminated.

3 For the dissemination of knowledge at the council and its role in giving political experience to citizens, see Gomme 1962: 85; Ober 2008: 152–5.

4 On the role of the assembly in disseminating news, see Hansen 1987: 27, Lewis 1996: 98–123; Ober 2008: 163–4, writing of the 'aggregation' of knowledge.

5 For debate at the assembly, see, for instance, Dem. 19.185. On discussion of proposals at assemblies, see Rhodes 2016a. For the view that debates generally led to consensus decisions among Athenians, see Canevaro 2018.

6 On the process of enactment and the drawing up of the text of proposals, see Chapter 1.2.1 above.

7 There are, moreover, examples of speeches attributed to politicians proposing decrees in the work of Thucydides: Thuc. 1.140–5; 3.36–49; 6.8–26.

the corpus of Attic oratory which consists of an argument for a specific proposal under discussion at the assembly (D108);[8] it gives us a view not only of the details of Demosthenes' proposal to organise a mission against Philip (see D108 TT 1–5), but also of the spectrum of intertwined types of argument that were deployed in support of the proposal: these were based on claims about external threats (Dem. 4.6–10, 17–18), practical recommendations (13–22, 28–33), Athenian reputation (3–5, 42), the notion of duty (13, 50), emotional appeal (29, 39–40, 44–6), promises of improved predicament (34, 51) and criticism of past policy (40–2). Demosthenes elsewhere describes how advocates of decrees at the assembly have to speak against those opponents who were motivated by ignorance or dishonesty (Dem. 18.185). Xenophon's *Hellenika* also reports upon some speeches which purport to have been spoken in support of specific proposals: he records a debate that took place in the Athenian assembly in 369 about the terms of alliance with the Spartans, with the orator Kephisodotos persuading the Athenians that the fairest policy was to allow the Spartans and the Athenians to hold the command for periods of five days at a time (Xen. *Hell.* 7.1.14 = D56 T3; cf. 7.4.4 = D63 T2).

Orators at the assembly, therefore, would have combined details of the decrees that they were advocating with elements of logical and emotional argumentation. It seems likely, therefore, that the process of discussion of, and debate about, decrees at the Athenian assembly would have significantly contributed to public perceptions of the substance of such decrees and the rationales behind them.[9] In the case of honorific decrees, announcements would also have contributed to their dissemination: proclamations took place at the council and assembly (Aeschin. 3.32–6) and public knowledge of them within Athens would have been promoted also by public proclamation at the theatre of Dionysos during the Dionysia – if the assembly voted to allow it (Dem. 18.120–1) – in front of both Athenians and non-Athenian visitors.[10]

---

8 On the proposals (both in the form of specific decrees and broad policy advice) preserved in symbouleutic oratory, see Chapter 2.3.1 above.

9 On the basis of the statistical proliferation of non-probouleumatic decrees in the period 352/1–322/1, Lambert (2018: 237–68) makes a strong case for the vitality of the assembly in this period.

10 On the legality of Demosthenes' claim about the possibility of announcing honorific decrees at the theatre, see D179, Harris 1994 and Chapter 2.2.2.1 above. Reckonings of the attendance of performances at the Great Dionysia have ranged between 5,000 and 17,000: see Vatri 2017: 12. Hanink 2014: 98 suggests a seating capacity of 16,000. On the social makeup of those attending the theatre, see Robson 2017: 69–74; on the assemblies that took place after performance festivals, at which decrees were discussed and enacted, see Lambert 2008: 52–3 and Harris 2013a: 211–13, 222.

While there is little evidence to say that texts of past decrees were read frequently to the people at the assembly in the course of speeches,[11] incidental references to decrees in public contexts were also important for the raising of their public profile: as we have already noted (Chapter 2.2 above) other extant assembly speeches in the Demosthenic corpus, in which the speaker advocates general issues of policy, discuss the implications of past decrees over the course of their argument. In *On Organisation* ([Demosthenes] 13), the speaker draws attention to the gap between the stated intention of the Athenians' decrees and their actual performances, pointing to recent Athenian decrees against the Megarians and that in support of Phleiasian exiles ([Dem.] 13.32 = D111 T1; D112). Such strategies of argumentation would have contributed to public perceptions of past Athenian decrees while also, in this case, developing an overall interpretation and the rhetorical theme that the pledges made in Athenian decrees often went unfulfilled.[12] However, if we follow the view of Johnstone, that the structure and acoustics of the assembly-place at the Pnyx meant that it was often hard to hear precisely the words of speakers at the *bema*,[13] it seems unlikely that forms of communication even in this institutional setting would have enabled a straightforward cascade of information about decrees. Moreover, as Lewis points out, the limited capacity of the Pnyx auditorium and socio-economic pressures on individual citizens which affected their ability to attend meant that the assembly 'could never be the sole or even the principal way in which information was disseminated'.[14] Furthermore, references to past decrees in assembly speeches were often vague (see the 'past decrees' referred to at [Dem.] 7.25 = D140 T2). Many citizens would, therefore, have learnt about the decisions of the assembly second hand.

Other institutions were significant too to the spread of accounts of Athenian decrees; the Athenian council of 500 was particularly important, for it was in the enclosed venue of the council chamber that proposals were discussed, opinions about them were exchanged, and *probouleumata* to be placed on the agenda of the assembly were formulated.[15] But the fact that, as inscribed records suggest, citizens rarely appeared to have served more than once during their adult lives meant that this aspect of participation was hardly a systematic

---

11 On the infrequency with which documents were read out in extant assembly oratory, see Hansen 1987: 170 note 572. For references in symbouleutic oratory to decrees, see Chapter 2.3.1 above.

12 On the rhetoric drawn from accounts of unfulfilled decrees, see Mader 2006 with Chapter 2.5.2 above.

13 Johnstone 1996.

14 Lewis 1996: 119; for the debate about the capacity of the Pnyx auditorium, see Hansen 1996 and Stanton 1996.

15 For the involvement of the council in the formulation of decrees, see Chapter 1.2.1 above.

way of disseminating knowledge about decrees.[16] However, it is quite plausible, as Rhodes suggests, that members of the public would have been able to hear the proceedings of the council when it discussed decrees, either by being present inside the *bouleuterion* as it met, or by listening carefully from outside.[17]

The other major institution of the Athenian democracy was its judicial system and in particular its lawcourts, which were manned by up to 6,000 jurors drawn from a wide social spectrum.[18] Decree-related discussions in the Athenian law-courts must have contributed greatly to the spreading of public awareness of decrees: such discussions took place over the course of debates about decrees that were being challenged as illegal (the procedure known as *graphe paranomon*).[19] A significant proportion of the decrees preserved in literary texts – often those about which the most details are preserved – were referred to as evidence in those speeches which relate to such trials (e.g. Aeschin. 3; Dem. 18, 23) or indictments of laws (the *graphe nomon me epitedeion thenai*: Dem. 20, 24) or other speeches which purport to address matters of public concern (e.g. [Dem.] 59): they indicate clearly that awareness of a significant number of decrees would have been disseminated among the litigants and jurors at such trials.[20] But as with their presentation at the assembly, the interpretation of the intention or impact of decrees that were presented in such contexts would have been highly subjective, directed by the speaker's advocacy or criticism of the enactment under discussion.

Decrees were discussed also at the level of local institutions – in the meetings of demes and tribes – where they had implications for matters under discussion: it is clear from Demosthenes' speech *Against Euboulides* that the implications of the assembly decree on *diapsephisis* (= D137) were raised in the course of the deme assembly of the Halimousians and that his fellow demesmen

---

16 For the inscribed evidence of bouleutic and prytanic lists, see Meritt and Traill 1974. For suggestions on the high extent of participation in the council, see Hansen 1991: 249; Stockton took a view of wide participation: 1990, 85–6: 'Every year, 500 new *bouleutai* had to be found, so even if, *per impossibile*, every *bouleutes* served twice in a lifetime, over any 25-year period, 6,250 men would be needed – in reality, the number required must have been more like 10,000 at least.' On the demographics of Athenian councillors, favouring the better-off, see Rhodes 1972: 5–6.

17 For discussion of the question of whether citizens who were not *bouleutai* were permitted to attend meetings of the council, see Rhodes 1972: 40, 80. Some sessions may have effectively been closed off however, given that the council may have plausibly operated without the knowledge of the assembly, pointing to the council's dispatch of Demainetos' trireme in 395 (see *Hell. Oxy.* 6.1 = DP 5).

18 Rhodes 1981: 691; Todd 1990a; Hansen 1991: 1856.

19 *Graphe paranomon*: see Hansen 1974 and Chapter 2.4.1 above.

20 See Liddel 2016 on Demosthenes' deployment of honorific decrees of the past in forensic oratory.

voted to expel from their lists some of its members possibly as a response to its directives (Dem. 57.6, 26).[21] While knowledge of decrees, therefore, would have proliferated among those who were engaged in political or litigious activity, it would not have been restricted to those groups. Presumably decisions of the people were discussed also in contexts in which citizens engaged in a wide range of civic activities: on occasions when, for instance, they participated in arbitration or took part on embassies or military expeditions as soldiers or rowers; their implications were discussed over the course of family disputes also (e.g. Dem. 58.30–1 = D209). Accounts of decrees of the Athenian assembly were disseminated also through discussions of them that took place outside formal institutional contexts:[22] that the business of the assembly would be the subject of day-to-day conversation is strongly suggested by Theophrastos' critique of the Talkative Man who reports news from the assembly to his associates (*Characters*, 7.7) and also of the Boorish Man who discusses assembly activity with his farm labourers (*Characters*, 4.3; see discussion in Chapter 4.3.1 below). But such orally transmitted accounts of assembly activity – as were those discussed within institutional settings – were of course open to the effects of distortion and rumour and would not have been straightforward windows into the content of decrees. Those with an interest in specific decrees may have pursued the imposition of their directives in non-formal contexts: on at least one occasion, it seems to be the case that a decree was relevant to the attempt of a private individual to resolve a dispute to his satisfaction: we have already discussed (Chapter 2.2.2.2 above) the way in which the speaker of Demosthenes 47 describes how, when giving an account of his attempts to recover ship's equipment from his trierarchic predecessor Theophemos, he proffered in his hand a copy of the decree (presumably obtained from the archive) which supported his claims (ἔχων τὸ ψήφισμα: 47.34; cf. D85). For our current purposes what is important about this episode is that it illustrates one way in which perspectives on decrees would have been spread through their implementation.

Decrees might be enforced – and knowledge of them disseminated – by individuals functioning as magistrates in official capacities. Generals and heralds were among those charged with disseminating announcements about the commands of the council and assembly (Andoc. 1.45; Dem. 18.169; D143 T1 = Plu.

---

21 For the view that demes formed a link between individuals and *polis* institutions, see Osborne 1985: 88–92.

22 Ober (1989: 148) suggests that rumour and gossip were important to the dissemination of information about politics; on the circulation of political knowledge through informal discussion, see now Gottesman 2014: 16, 60, 75 and Livingstone 2016: 56–60; on gossip and the rhetorical significance of claims about gossip more generally, see Hunter 1990 and Eidinow 2016: 171–262.

Phoc. 15.1–2). In cases where decrees required the summoning of an Athenian individual overseas, it is likely that a *kleter* (summoner) was appointed to deliver a summons (cf. Thuc. 6.61.4–7).[23] A decree might appoint commissioners of enquiry (*zetetai*) for the sake of finding out information relevant to its provisions (e.g. D91 T1 = Dem. 24.11). Any individual or board charged with the responsibility of enforcing a decree would have contributed to the dissemination of knowledge about it: in a decree inscribed within a *stele* bearing accounts of the overseers of the Athenian dockyards for the year 325/4 (*IG* II³ 1 370), we read of Athenian arrangements for the dispatch of a colonising expedition to the Adriatic. The decree contains provisions for the selection by the people from all Athenians of ten men, to be known as the 'dispatchers' (*apostoleis*), who are to have responsibility for the sending of the colony according to the specifications set out by the *boule* (lines 82–8): it seems to be the case that they were to be given the responsibility of ensuring that ships and equipment were released in time and that the trierarchs were to muster with their ships as set out in the decree so that the colony was sent out as quickly as possible (lines 1–21). There are other occasions too where Athenian officials were responsible for putting the effects of a decree into action. In Athenodoros' decree concerning sacrifices at Piraeus (*IG* II² 47), overseers (*epistatai*) of the Asklepieion were appointed with the task of undertaking sacrifices and providing money for the building work (lines 28–32) while religious officials (*hieropoioi*) were to take care of the festival and the distribution of meat (lines 32–8). In Androtion's decree collecting arrears of *eisphora*, a clause was added which ordered the Eleven, the Receivers (*apodektai*) and their assistants to accompany Androtion in his tax-collecting activities (D88 TT 1, 3). The decree of Philokrates concerning the sacred *orgas* of 352/1 (D107) gave rise to guidelines about delineating the consecrated area: according to the sources (D107 TT 1, 2), the Eleusinian magistrates Lakrateides the hierophant and Hierokleides the *daidouchos* were to mark out the disputed boundary; accordingly, they were effectively charged with the diffusion of the impact of the decree among Athenians and Megarians alike.[24] At the start of the Demosthenic speech *On the Trierarchic Crown*, the speaker claims that the *demos* ordered the treasurer (*tamias*) to grant a crown to the trierarch who was first to ready his trireme for sea ([Dem.] 51.1 = D76 T1). The assembly could also order other bodies to embark on formal investigations

---

23 Harrison 1971: 85-6; Todd 1993: 125.

24 The inscribed document *IG* II³ 1 292 = RO 58 (which I suggest (D107 Commentary) refers to developments subsequent to Philokrates' decree) emphasises the involvement of the *basileus*, the hierophant, the *daidouchos*, the Kerykes and the Eumolpidai in the placing of the boundaries (lines 12–15).

of matters, as it did when it ordered the Areopagus in summer 324 to investigate the scandal surrounding the money brought to Athens by the Macedonian treasurer, Harpalos (DD 194, 195).

While there was no systemic attempt to ensure that knowledge of Athenian decrees were disseminated evenly across the citizen-body, we might reasonably suppose that awareness of decrees would have diffused among politically involved citizens who had an interest in them through the routes we have discussed (at political meetings, via informal means, and through magistrates); such knowledge and understanding would, depending on the circumstance of the conversation and factors influencing its spread, have been of uneven depth and accuracy. But knowledge of Athenian decrees was not something that would have been restricted to Athenian citizens, which will be the subject of discussion in Chapter 4 below.

3.2.2 The Quest for Knowledge: Using Documents, Collections and Archives

Thus far we have considered the possibility that awareness of decrees would have been promoted by their discussion in institutional and private contexts. We have already argued that knowledge of decrees was a potentially important tool in rhetorical contexts (see Chapter 2 above). At this point it is necessary to ask whether, for the sake of their deployment in particular contexts, some Athenians, in particular those who were pursuing political or judicial agendas within institutional settings, actively sought detailed knowledge about decrees. One problem we face when answering this question, however, is that those who draw upon the evidence of decrees in litigious contexts, perhaps because they wanted to deflect the possibility of prejudice against those deemed to be 'experts' in Athenian law,[25] say little about the sources of their knowledge of decrees and virtually nothing about non-inscribed documentation.

Antiquarian decree-collecting reached a new height at the end of the fourth century with the appearance of Krateros' work *Sylloge Psephismaton* ('The Collection of Decrees') and Apellikon, another collector of decrees.[26] While the references to decrees in literary sources earlier in the fourth century

---

25 Todd 1996, 115, 131; Ismard 2015. At Lysias 30.27, Nikomachos, who had been involved in the administration of constitutional reform as an *anagrapheus*, was dismissed as a *hypogrammateus*, or an 'under-clerk'; see also Dem. 19.249 for Demosthenes' description of Aeschines' work as a *grammateus* and *hypogrammateus*. For other prejudice against experts, see Dem. 35.40–3; Isae. 10.1.

26 On Krateros see Higbie 1999; *BNJ* 342 and Chapter 5.4.3 below; on Apellikon, see Chapter 5.4.3 below.

demonstrate some interest in decrees (see Chapter 5 below), there is little evidence to say that private individuals collected knowledge about decrees for reasons other than persuasion in rhetorical contexts. It is possible to speculate that some politically engaged citizens of fourth-century Athens possessed personal collections of documentary versions of decrees;[27] however, evidence is scarce.[28] Demosthenes, a prolific proposer of decrees, referred to his own proposals in defence of his honours, and while it is plausible to think that he drew upon personal records or at least those he had collected in advance of his case being heard (e.g. Dem. 18.79 = D139), at the same time it is not impossible – given the rather low level of detail with which he outlines decrees – that he recited them from memory. In this case Demosthenes' aim was to highlight the wider implications of his decrees – that is, reminding the audience of those public acts which he held to justify Ktesiphon's honours – and had little need to recite details that would necessitate significant research into their content.

It seems to have been the case, however, that the city's archival resources were at the disposal of those citizens who wished to secure detailed knowledge of the substance of the city's decrees.[29] Access to texts of decrees was greatly facilitated by the establishment, at the end of the fifth century, of an archive holding public documents in the west side of the agora in the former *bouleuterion* at the Metroon, the sanctuary of the Mother-Goddess.[30] Reference to the

---

27 Other possible sources of knowledge about decrees might include family archives or petitions put together by those proposing awards for individuals, though the evidence for such sources is not altogether compelling for the classical period: see Gauthier 1985: 100–2.

28 The fact that the Athenians had a generally negative attitude towards documentary bureaucracy (see Todd 1996) goes some way to explaining their reluctance to talk about personal collections of documents; Theophrastus' *Man who has lost all sense* (6.9) describes a person who arrives at a trial loaded with a box of evidence and holding strings of documents pertaining to his case.

29 For citizen access to the archives of the city, see Sickinger 1999a: 158–70. In the speech *Against Leokrates* 66, Lycurgus imagines a citizen entering the Metroon and illegally erasing a law.

30 For the view that a public archive was established in the period 409–406, see Boegehold 1972. But evidence for the writing up in the fourth century of decrees which were enacted as early as the 420s suggests that there was some organised archive in the last quarter of the fifth century (OR 161, a decree of Alkibiades of 422/1). For earlier scholarship, see Todd 1996: 123 note 27 and MacDowell 2000: 258. On the Metroon see Sickinger 1999a: 161–7; cf. 186: '[the] Athenians with some frequency may have sought from the Metroon texts of state documents by which they pursued or protected their interests.' For an important challenge to the idea that litigants were easily able to consult written versions of laws, see Lanni 2004; for a more optimistic view of the accessibility of texts of laws, see Sickinger 2004. Pritchett (1996: 14–39) took a very strong view on the existence of organised archives even in the fifth century, and argued that copies of decrees of the Athenians, in the fifth century, would have been kept in the *bouleuterion* (1996: 34); for a critique of the view that this represents an 'archive' in the modern sense, see Thomas 1989: 75. For a re-statement of the view that there were 'archival' documents in the fifth century, see Faraguna 2017: 258.

post-403/2 re-inscription of decrees destroyed by the Thirty (see Chapter 1.5.1 above) and a written account of a decree (*biblion*: RO 2 line 61) in the possession of the secretary of the council strongly suggests that this resource, from the end of the fifth century at the latest, contained reference copies of decrees of the assembly. An optimistic portrayal of the use of this archive is outlined at one point in Aeschines' speech of 343, *On the False Embassy*, in which he praised the Athenians for preserving for all time their decrees, together with their dates and the names of those who put them to vote, in a public archive (Aeschin. 2.89: ἐν τοῖς δημοσίοις γράμμασι);[31] he offered the view that this constituted a practice (*pragma*) of assistance to those who were the victims of slander in a public place. The availability of decrees in such an archive constituted a resource not only for those who had suffered at the hands of a wrongdoer, but offered a facility for those wishing to strengthen or substantiate defences of their own political activity – or attacks on that of others – by reference to a decree.

Some recent scholarship has made a case for the growing profile of public and private written documents, both inscribed and archival, in the fourth-century courts.[32] While oratorical references to the storage of decrees in the archive are relatively rare, there are enough of them – most of which were made in the second half of the fourth century – to suggest that, by the 340s, there was widespread awareness of the availability of decrees deposited there;[33] moreover, in certain contexts, it seems that it was rhetorically advantageous to make assertions about drawing upon the resource in the construction of an argument: Demosthenes, in his account of the Third Embassy to Philip (see DP 60), had the secretary recite a decree from the archive in the Metroon ('ἐν τοῖς κοινοῖς τοῖς ὑμετέροις

---

31 Aeschines appears to have been particularly adept at exploiting his knowledge of documentary material: Sickinger 1999a: 121; cf. Harris 1995: 30; but note the reservation of Lane Fox 1994: 140–1 about the depth of Aeschines' expertise; on his occasional disingenuousness in citing decrees, see Chapter 2.5.1 above.

32 Sickinger 2002; Rydberg-Cox 2003; Higbie 2017: 172–8. Gagarin 2011: 188: 'Forensic speakers can speak of a decree as an oral proposal rather than a written text (e.g., Dem. 18.75). But Demosthenes and other later orators also regularly refer to writing decrees and speak of decrees as written by someone, and the common expression for the activity of public figures in the assembly is "speaking and writing" (e.g., Dem. 18.66), that is giving oral advice and proposing decrees orally, but also putting those decrees in writing before they are approved.' Thomas (1989: 94), while downplaying the extent of the actual consultation of written documents, suggests it became more frequent over the course of the fourth century BC: 'the slow realization of the use of documents and archives for later consultation ... It is only by the mid-fourth century that we begin to find explicit recognition of the importance of past documents as records to be consulted – and with that, detailed examination of precise wording to elicit new information.' See also, on the proliferation of written documents in classical Athens, Thomas 1989: 41–4; Cohen 2003; Higbie 2017: 241, identifying 'document-mindedness'.

33 For decrees at the Metroon, see Sickinger 1999a: 162–3.

γράμμασιν ἐν τῷ Μητρῴῳ') which mentioned Aeschines (Dem. 19.129).[34] Yet, in this case, the fact that Demosthenes, in the passages that follow the reading of the decree, passes over it without close comment, suggest that he made claims about reference to the archival resource as a way of establishing the authority of what he was claiming, but without drawing out the detailed implications of the decree.

At points it seems to be the case that claims about decrees were not good enough as proofs of their content and they needed to be reinforced with evidence that would be regarded as authoritative by its audience: Demosthenes, in his speech *Against Leptines*, tells his audience to ask his opponents to 'show' (δειξαῖ) them decrees granting exemption to those they claimed were unworthy of it (Dem. 20.131): the implication is that the jury would ask to have them read out by a secretary in court. References in other speeches of Demosthenes and Aeschines demonstrate that they would arrange for documentary versions of decrees to be read out as proofs in court by the secretary at specific points over the course of a speech (e.g. Dem. 19.86 = DD 105, 135; Aeschin. 2.170 = D114; Dem. 19.267 = D119; Aeschin. 2.19 = D124).[35] But, again, on such occasions, orators do not appear to have been particularly interested in the close details of these decrees: the readings of the decrees were not followed by close discussions of their content. It seems to be the case that having a secretary read a decree out loud was something that was done, for the most part, to underline a broader rhetorical point about the existence of a decree: Demosthenes had the decrees of Diophantos and Kallisthenes read out loud in the court of 343 in order to support a wider argument about the consequences of the conduct of Athenian politicians (Dem. 19.86 = DD 105, 135) rather than to make a precise case about the substance or directives of these decrees. Elsewhere, Dinarchus, in attacking Demosthenes' decree proposing that the Areopagus investigate the affair concerning Harpalos' money (D195), claimed that his rival's decree was to be kept (presumably at the archive) 'beside the Mother of the Gods, who is the guardian of all the written agreements in the city' ('παρὰ τὴν Μητέρα τῶν θεῶν, ἣ πάντων τῶν ἐν τοῖς γράμμασι δικαίων φύλαξ τῇ πόλει': Din. 1.86). On this occasion, Dinarchus emphasises the sacred value of the archive to support his insistence that the people uphold Demosthenes' decree and implement it against its proposer.

Documentary versions – presumably obtained from the archive – do on occasion appear to have been proffered as proofs of decrees (Dem. 47.34; Dem.

---

34 MacDowell 2000: 258 suggests that this was a reference to a decree ordering the deletion of Aeschines' name from a public list of some kind.

35 For the process according to which documents were prepared for public reading in the assembly, see Sickinger 1999a: 167; Thür 2008; Canevaro 2013: 1. For the election of a secretary to read documents to the assembly and the council, see [Arist.], *Ath. Pol.* 54.5.

120 DECREES OF FOURTH-CENTURY ATHENS

20.131 = D103, 104a–b). But only on rare occasions do orators appear to have engaged in archival research for the sake of detailed argument. Demosthenes uses documents widely in the speech *Against Leptines*.[36] In composing this speech he appears to have prepared, in advance of his speech, a list of Chabrias' military accomplishments (Dem. 20.78): it is plausible that he probably drew upon research into different public documents, including decrees, naval lists and public accounts.[37] A little later in the speech he asks a secretary to read out an honorific decree for Chabrias, his words suggesting that the official responsible would have to search through a dossier of documents pre-selected by the orator for deployment during the trial: 'Take now also the decree voted for Chabrias; look for it, seek it out, for it must be here somewhere' (Dem. 20.84).[38] But even in this speech, in which Demosthenes refrains from personal slander against Leptines and relies instead on a rational argument based on the evidence of decrees,[39] Demosthenes does not engage at a high level of detail with the provisions of the decrees that he has read out; however, he certainly quotes lines from decrees, such as the statement, on the inscribed honours for Konon, that he had 'freed the allies' (Dem. 20.69 = D23 T2). Yet only occasionally is it possible to detect a level of engagement with the language of decrees which suggests that orators may have looked at documents in the archive: as we have seen already (Chapter 2.5.1 above), orators sometimes drew upon close knowledge of decrees in their argumentation. On such occasions – in the debates about the honours for Charidemos (D94), of the Peace of Philokrates (D130), and the terms of Demosthenes' crowning (D179) – the nature of disputes meant that detailed engagement with the content of the decrees was important for the construction of an argument. But these were exceptions rather than the rule in terms of the style of reference. Perhaps it was the case that orators referred to the archive in the hope that it would give their claims about decrees authority among an audience who had a high level of respect for the record-keeping abilities of the city.

3.2.3 Decrees in Public Memory and Narratives

While, as we have seen, speakers did indeed make assertions and drop hints about their deployment of archival material in the accrual of knowledge about decrees, it seems likely that those who consulted this resource would have

---

36 West 1995; Kremmydas 2012: 62-4.
37 For the view that this was compiled on the basis of Demosthenes' perusal of public documents but also oral accounts, see Kremmydas 2012: 325; Canevaro 2016b: 317.
38 Dem. 20.84: 'λαβὲ δὴ καὶ τὸ τῷ Χαβρίᾳ ψήφισμα ψηφισθέν. ὅρα δὴ καὶ σκόπει· δεῖ γὰρ αὔτ' ἐνταῦθ' εἶναί που.'
39 On the logical nature of argumentation in Demosthenes 20, see Kremmydas 2007b.

had already at least some sense of the kinds of decree that they were looking for. There are, therefore, considerable social aspects to the circulation of knowledge about decrees. Assertions about collective memory – real or fabricated – of decrees appears to have played an important part in the proliferation of accounts of them. These assertions probably were not unfounded: we have already set out the likelihood (see Chapter 1.5 above) that orators, when talking about decrees, would have built upon memory or awareness of decrees – however inexact – among their audience, aiming to augment and manipulate it in different ways.

In their construction of arguments, orators make claims about their audience's memory of decrees or request that they recall certain decrees: when, in the *Third Olynthiac*, Demosthenes reinforced his point about the Athenians' tendency to pass decrees but leave them unfulfilled, he told his audience to 'remember' (μέμνησθ', ὦ ἄνδρες Ἀθηναῖοι) that they had voted to launch an expedition when Philip was in Thrace besieging Heraion Teichos (Dem. 3.4 = D106). His words amount to the claim that the decree already was present in the Athenians' collective memory in which Demosthenes shared. Claims about shared memory should not always be accepted straightforwardly: in the case of the decrees granting citizenship to the Olynthians, Apollonides and Peitholas ([Dem.] 59.91 = DD 109, 110), Apollodoros' claims that those listening would remember the honorands and the fact that their honours were confiscated by a decision of the people in the lawcourts seem rather disingenuous. It is out of the question that Apollodoros was inventing such decrees for the sake of his argument: the accessibility of the archive to Athenian citizens would have made the outright fabrication of a decree politically dangerous.[40] But scarcity of other references to these honorands in public oratory suggests that they were as obscure as they were infamous[41] and that, on this occasion, the collective memory of these awards and their confiscation was one which Apollodoros was attempting

---

40 For the view that the development and exercise of collective memory was a negotiation between different political challenges and cultural claims, but one limited by awareness of past events, see Olick 2007: 7, 37–54. Indeed, claims in political oratory about falsification and manipulation of public records are extremely limited: for some examples of tampering with public records, see Higbie 2017: 172–8 and Calhoun 1914: 140–2, citing Dem. 37.34, 57.60, 62; [Dem.] 58.41; Aristophanes, *Clouds*, 764; *Knights*, 1369-70; [Dem.] 44.37; Lys. 16.7. It appears to have been the case that falsification of private documents was more widespread: see Calhoun 1914.

41 However, the *graphe paranomon* brought against the decree for these Olynthians was known to Aristotle: Arist. *Rh.* 1410a 17ff (= D110 T2), recalls an argument brought against the honorands.

to construct (or at least exaggerate) for the sake of his argument.[42] But at other times, where orators cite a well-known decree (such as those for Timotheos: D47 TT 1–3, where the decree is cited only in passing in three separate oratorical contexts) it seems much more likely that they were taking advantage of an already existing collective awareness of a decree (e.g. Dem. 20.159 = D19 T2).[43] As we will see in Chapter 3.3 below, references to inscribed versions of decrees draw upon a similar line of argument: that the document being cited is one which is already lodged in the popular conscience.

Claims about decrees were often presented within narrative accounts of political activity associated with their proposer, and awareness of them was based probably upon wider orally preserved narratives. Examples of decrees that were embedded by speakers in wider accounts of the past can be found in the speeches of Aeschines. In his speech *Against Timarchos* his mention of his opponent's proposal about dwelling-houses on the Pnyx forms an element of his account of what happened when it was discussed at the assembly (Aeschin. 1.181= D138). In his second speech, Aeschines told the story of the rejected proposal to allow Kersobleptes to take the oaths of the Peace of Philokrates by recalling the procedure through which it was put to the vote against the will of Demosthenes (Aeschin. 2.83–5 = D132). His account was based on the testimony of its proposer Aleximachos (Aeschin. 2.85), as presumably no copy of a rejected proposal was available in the archive. In the same speech, Aeschines quoted the words of Demosthenes, setting out his proposals about the treatment of ambassadors from Philip before going on to ask the secretary to read out the decree granting a truce for them (Aeschin. 2.53 = D126). In this case, Aeschines appeared to present the archive version as a way of backing up a claim about a remembered decree.[44] Elsewhere, speakers combined witness statements with decrees as a way of making a case about the intentions of the proposals that they were describing (Aeschin. 2.19 = D124 T2; Hyp. *Ath.* 33 = D175 T1).

When we look beyond oratory, at historians' accounts of decrees, they often are uninterested in the close detail of their substance. While sometimes Xenophon showed awareness of democratic procedure, as he did in the case of the debate about the procedure to punish the generals after the battle of

---

42 A comparable example is Demosthenes' (23.118 = D43) assertion that the Athenians know well the decree for Kotys of Thrace (ἴστε γὰρ δήπου πάντες').

43 Conversely, orators could also exploit for their lines of argument the obscurity of an honorand, as Euthykles did in the case of Euderkes (Dem. 23.203 = D75).

44 For similar practices, where a description of the decree in the narrative of a speech is followed up by the reading out of a documentary version, see also Andoc. 1. 82 = D7; Aeschin. 2.73 = D129; Aeschin 3.92–3 = D147 and Aeschin. 3.100–2 = D148b.

LOCAL AUDIENCES FOR DECREES

Arginusae,[45] his interest in decrees emerges in relation only to his understanding of debates at the assembly and military adventures. Accordingly, in his account of the background to the peace of 375 (Xen. *Hell.* 6.2.2 = D48), he refers to a decree only as part of his explanation of the recall of Timotheos:

> Two of the Athenian ambassadors, sailing immediately from there (Sparta), in accordance with a decree of the city ('κατὰ δόγμα τῆς πόλεως'), told Timotheos to sail homewards, as there was now peace.

The non-documentary basis of Xenophon's knowledge of decrees is in this case highlighted by his use of language that is not normally associated with Athenian decrees (δόγμα τῆς πόλεως) to describe the decree that recalled Timotheos.[46] Just as with the orators, the historian's knowledge of the decree was lodged within a wider narrative which Xenophon recounts; his sources for this narrative may well have been oral. There are, however, some historiographical accounts of Athenian decrees where it seems, from the level of detail offered, that an author or his sources have ultimately drawn upon an archival source.[47]

Knowledge of decrees, therefore, circulated among fourth-century Athenians and others in a number of ways which arose from both active engagement and passive exposure to their details. In certain contexts, archival research offered detailed substantiation of knowledge of detailed aspects of decrees among those who undertook it but there is little strong evidence to prove that it was a standard source of knowledge for those seeking to construct detailed arguments. Certain orators do, in the second half of the fourth century, attempt to seek rhetorical advantage by referring to the archive. Yet they often appear to appeal to decrees that they claimed were common knowledge: at times claims about this knowledge may have been based on simply rhetorical construction, but at other times – as we shall see in 3.3 below – they appear to have been based on their monumental existence in reality. At this point, it is appropriate to measure the significance of epigraphical publication in the dissemination of perspectives about – and the public profile of – decrees. To do so requires some initial consideration of the wider significance of the epigraphical publication of decrees.

---

45 On Xenophon's account of decrees after Arginousai, see Chapter 5.2.1 below.

46 The possibility that this might refer to a *dogma* of the Spartan assembly is raised at D48 Commentary. For discussion of Xenophon's rather limited use of documents, see Bearzot 2014.

47 This is surely the case with the author of the *Athenaion Politeia*'s account of the ratification of the reconciliation and amnesty of 403/2 BC ([Aristotle] *Ath. Pol.* 39.1–6 = D1 T1. On the sources of the *Athenaion Politeia* and for more detailed assessment of decrees in historical narratives see Chapter 5.2 below.

3.3 Inscribed Decrees and their Uses

3.3.1 The Implications of Epigraphical Publication

For historians of the twentieth and twenty-first centuries, much of what is treated as primary evidence for the enactment and substance of classical Athenian decrees consists of the extant versions inscribed on marble slabs, deriving primarily from the acropolis and, less frequently, other city-centre locations such as the agora;[48] there survive more than 500 in varying states of preservation from the period 403/2–322/1 BC (see Table 1). The majority of inscribed decrees of fourth-century Athens were set up as free-standing *stelai* dedicated to a single decree, but on occasion they were incorporated into other documents (e.g. *IG* II³ 1 370),[49] appeared within dossiers of decrees (*IG* II³ 1 367),[50] or were written upon a dedication (*IG* II³ 1 306; *IG* II³ 4 3).[51] The work of Lambert on the selectivity of publication of *stelai* of Athenian state decrees of the fourth century has contributed to the understanding of the broader significance of the epigraphical publication of decrees:[52] he has observed that certain types of decree do not regularly get inscribed (decisions to dispatch military expeditions, embassies, minor honours such as the award of foliage crowns to Athenians) and that it follows that the positive decision of the Athenians to inscribe any single decree can be viewed, therefore, as an act that was of itself significant; it was primarily those decrees which had enduring importance (awards of citizenship and proxeny, religious regulations, treaties, and, from the 340s, honours for Athenians) that were normally inscribed.[53]

Moreover, the significance of the places of publication at which inscribed decrees would be set up has been studied in extensive detail by Lambert and others: the alluring – and reasonable – assumption behind analysis of them is that decisions about where they would be put on display were motivated by knowable factors.[54] It is clear that the majority of inscribed Athenian decrees

---

48 For the development of the *stele* as the form of publication of decrees, see Meyer 2016.

49 *IG* II³ 1 370 is written up within an inscribed set of accounts of the naval *epimeletai*. Another example is *IG* II² 47, which contains an inventory of medical supplies followed by a decree concerning cult activity at the Asklepieion in Piraeus. Some decrees make provisions for the inscription of earlier, uninscribed decrees, as does RO 31 (= *IG* II² 107) of 368/7, arranging for the writing up of a decree responding to an enquiry of the Mytileneans (lines 21–22, 35–60) of the previous year.

50 For dossiers of decrees, see Rhodes with Lewis 1997: 24–7.

51 Lambert 2018: 23 note 18.

52 On selectivity of publication, see also Chapter 3.4.2 below.

53 See Lambert 2018: 47–68.

54 For places of publication, see Detienne 1998; Hölkeskamp 1992 and 2000; Osborne 1999; Richardson 2000; Liddel 2003; Shear 2007, 2011; Moroo 2016; Lambert 2018: 19–46.

LOCAL AUDIENCES FOR DECREES 125

of the fourth century were set up on the acropolis. The motivation behind this tendency seems not to have been to ensure democratic accountability or to enable individuals to read inscribed texts,[55] but rather to draw upon the potential of the site as a religious, elevated, conspicuous, and monumentally adorned public space. Meyer offers the view that such *stelai* might be interpreted as offerings to the gods.[56] Moreover, it is tempting to think that they were set up on stone as a way of bestowing general divine attention to, approval of, or protection over the provisions they specified, or even that they demonstrated the religious underpinnings of political authority.[57] This divine aspect appears to be very much an epigraphical perspective on decrees: with the exception of the occasionally-enunciated view that the Mother of the Gods offered some kind of protection to the written documents, including archival copies of decrees contained within her sanctuary (Din. 1.86; cf. [Dem.] 25.97), we seldom find expressions of the religious aspect of decrees in the literary testimona for them.[58] Indeed, one view is that the scarcity of reference to deities in extant symbouleutic oratory noted by Martin suggests the absence of a divine aspect from decree-making, although Mack makes a strong case for concern for them expressed through the medium of document reliefs and on the basis of the evidence for ritual practice, including prayers and sacrifices at the council and assembly.[59] It seems to be the case that the epigraphical record offers a far more theological view of decrees than does the oratorical evidence.

There are, however, other implications of epigraphical publication (some of which are echoed in the literary evidence): in cases where inscribed decrees were set up in locations other than the acropolis, Lambert identifies other motivations related alternately to specific religious interests, power dynamics and a 'message-driver' tendency consisting of the attempt to deliver a message to a particular audience (that is, to discourage or encourage particular forms of behaviour).[60] This points to an overall perspective that some, but not necessarily

---

55 Democratic accountability and inscriptional publication: D. Harris 1994; Hedrick 2000; cf. Meyer 2013, 454–7.

56 Meyer 2013, 459–60.

57 For these religious aspects, see Lambert 2018: 22–7, offering other explanations for the setting up of decrees on the acropolis; for religious underpinnings: Mack 2018.

58 Rarely do forensic speakers appear to have a claim for the divine origin of law (an exceptional case being found in the spurious (cf. Harris 2018: 195–6) *Against Demosthenes* [Dem.] 25.16); for the association of law with divinity in other genres, see Willey 2016.

59 Martin 2016; Mack 2018. For religious rituals associated with meetings of the assembly, see Rhodes 1972: 36–7, alluded to in forensic oratory: Aesch. 1.23; Dem.19.70, 23.97, 24.20.

60 Lambert 2018: 33–9. An example of an inscribed decree – set up both at the acropolis and 'the port': lines 19–20 – which aims to deliver a message to a particular group is *IG* II³ 1 399, which is aimed at those planning military operation against Euboia.

126 DECREES OF FOURTH-CENTURY ATHENS

all, decrees were written up on inscriptions with the intention that they would be read and that their details would have an impact upon readers; at the same time, their wider connotations, particularly those related to piety and honorific value, could be appreciated without necessitating close attention to their written words. Over the course of section 3.3.2 I will explore the evidence for human audiences of inscribed Athenian decrees.

3.3.2 Athenian Audiences of Inscribed Decrees

What can we say from the evidence of inscribed decrees about their audiences? We have noted already the fact that the majority of inscribed decrees were set up on the complex of shrines that was the Athenian acropolis, which suggests a desire to capitalise upon some form of religious engagement. I will consider the possibilities of non-Athenian audiences in Chapter 4 below, but for now my aim is to explore the expressions of the idea that inscribed decrees were aimed at human Athenian readers.

It is clear, at a basic level, from the statements of intention that appear on some inscribed decrees from the second half of the fourth century onwards, that they were written up with the intention that they obtain validity in the eyes of human readers:[61] a proxeny decree of the second half of fourth century states that it is to be set up on a stone *stele* at the acropolis 'so that others also may know that the people knows how to return thanks to its benefactors' (*IG* II[3] 1 516 lines 13–19);[62] a decree honouring the *prytaneis* of the Leontis tribe of c. 340–25 encourages others to show *philotimia* in speaking and acting, knowing that they will receive thanks (*IG* II[3] 1 417 lines 29–30).[63] While the majority of inscribed decrees containing expressions of hortatory intention appear on honours for non-Athenians, both citizens and non-citizens who encountered such clauses may have been encouraged to perform well on behalf of the community and to emulate the honorands if they indeed found the idea of receiving

---

61 Lambert 2011a: 202. For examples of inscribed decrees which included explicit expression of encouragement of particular behaviour by way of hortatory clauses, see *IG* II[3] 1 306, 417, 516; generally, see Henry 1996; Miller 2016. On the significance of the formulae of disclosure for expressions of honour, competitive display and encouraging emulation, see Sickinger 2009; cf. Hedrick 1999, 2000 raising the possibility of democratic undertones.

62 'ἀναγράψαι δ[ὲ] αὐτῶι τὴν προξε[ν]ί[αν τὸν γραμματ]έα <τ>ὸν κατὰ πρυτανε[ίαν εἰς στήλην] λιθίνην καὶ στῆσα[ι ἐν ἀκροπόλει], ὅπως [ἂ]ν καὶ οἱ ἄλλο[ι εἰδῶσιν, ὅτι ὁ] δῆμο[ς] ἐπίσταται χά[ριτας ἀποδιδόναι τοῖς εὐεργε]τ[. . . . . 10 . . . . .].'

63 '[ὅπως ἂν φιλοτιμῶνται] καὶ οἱ ἄλλοι λέγειν [καὶ πράττειν τὰ ἄριστα εἰδότ]ες, ὅτι χάριτας ἀξίας ἀπολήψονται παρὰ [τῆς] βο[υ]λ[ῆ]ς καὶ τοῦ [δήμου].' For a study of the implications of such hortatory intentions for an understanding of ancient Athenian competitive culture, see now Miller 2016.

LOCAL AUDIENCES FOR DECREES

honours an appealing one.[64] Perhaps, as I suggest below (section 3.3.5), it was such enhanced significance and validity to which the orators aspired when they drew attention to Athenian inscriptions. Indeed, it is worth underlining that it is clear that the role of Athenian honorific practices in encouraging civic-minded behaviour was recognised by fourth-century orators and their contemporaries (see Chapter 2.4.2 above; Isoc. 9.57; Dem. 18.120; Dem. 20.64; Lycurg. 1.102; Xen. *Poroi* 3.11).

Other inscribed decrees appear to have aimed to encourage euergetic behaviour among targeted groups of individuals,[65] such as priests of a particular cult (*IG* II³ 1 416), and also to send messages to groups, such as deterrents to those contemplating military action against Eretria (*IG* II³ 1 399) or those who were in a position to consider acquiring land in the territories of Athens' allies (RO 22 (= *IG* II² 43) lines 35–46). It is, therefore, possible, that orators and politicians might have been included among the target audiences of such decrees, but they were not specifically directed at those politically-active citizens *per se*.

3.3.3 Authority, Memory and the Inscription of Decrees

The question of why the Athenians chose to write up some – but probably not all – of their decrees on stone deserves further exploration. Setting aside the argument that they did so for reasons of democratic accountability,[66] there are two other significant schools of thought on this subject: one, espoused most recently by M.J. Osborne, is that the Athenians sought to display versions of texts that would be authoritative for reference purposes; the other, represented by Shear and others, is that the Athenians wrote up inscriptions as an act of collective memory-creation.

There is no reason to doubt the rhetorical power that inscribed versions of Athenian decrees offered to their users:[67] as we will see (Chapter 3.3.5 below), there are times when orators point to inscriptions to support their arguments (cf. Table 2 on p. 135). The view of the authority of inscribed versions of decrees has been taken to its logical conclusion by M.J. Osborne who, in a 2012 study of the publication of decrees, argued that references (in classical and Hellenistic

---

64 Miller 2016: 393. *IG* II³ 1 306 is an example of a decree for an Athenian which contains the expression of a hortatory intention: 'ὅπως ἂν [οὖν καὶ οἱ ἄλλοι ἅπαν]τες εἰδῶσι' (line 13), but hortatory clauses appear on honorific decrees for Athenians more frequently after the end of the fourth century: Miller 2016: 392.

65 Lambert 2018: 34–9.

66 See note 55 above.

67 Thomas 1989: 48: 'the epigraphic copy could be regarded as authoritative even though it was incomplete and in effect an "excerpt" from the spoken decree'; cf. Thomas 1992: 135.

inscribed decrees) to texts recorded on *stelai* suggest that inscribed versions of documents possessed a particularly high status as 'authoritative' texts.[68] There is some fourth-century evidence for the view that inscribed versions of decrees could provide texts for authoritative reference: for instance, a passage from the honorific decree for the Akarnanians of 338/7 refers to an inscribed version of the honours for the ancestors of the honorands of probably about 400 (*IG* II³ 1 316 lines 15–20), but in this case the words seem to constitute a passing reference to this inscription of the fifth century rather than implying its authority.[69] Moreover, according to *IG* II² 120, a decree which initiated the cataloguing of the contents of the *chalkotheke*, records of items were to be collected from things written up on *stelai* (line 28) though these were, surely, inscribed inventories, not decrees. Osborne supports his argument by observing that inscribed decrees sometimes order the destruction of inscriptions containing contradictory directives: both the charter of the Athenian confederacy (RO 22 (= *IG* II² 43) lines 31–5), and the alliance with the Thessalian *koinon* (RO 44 (= *IG* II² 116) lines 39–40) call upon an official (a secretary and the treasurers of the goddess, respectively) to destroy contradictory *stelai*; the same can apply in the case of laws: RO 25 (= *SEG* XXVI 72), the fourth-century law on silver coinage, contains similar provisions (lines 25–6). One view is that such orders for destruction aimed to eradicate the risk of a contradiction between authoritative inscribed texts; another is that obliteration was a symbolic act which impressed the abolition of a particular enactment into the public memory.[70]

How does Osborne's view of inscribed texts as the absolute authority for decrees of the Athenian assembly fit with the relative infrequency of references to inscriptions by fourth-century authors (Chapter 3.3.5 below)? One solution is that orators and other authors did not always feel the need to appeal to the authority of an inscription: claims about knowledge of decrees could be

---

68 Osborne 2012: 44–6. As Lambert (2018: 56–7) observes, Osborne's emphasis on the epigraphical version is undermined by the fact that there was an expectation, in the fourth century, that archival and epigraphical versions of decrees would be harmonious.

69 *IG* II³ 1 316 lines 15–20: 'since the Athenian People made Phormio the grandfather of Phormio and Karphinas an Athenian, and his descendants, and the decree by which this was enacted was inscribed on the acropolis, the grant which the People made to Phormio their grandfather shall be valid for Phormio and Karphinas and their descendants.' Sickinger 2002: 159–60 discusses other epigraphical cross-references to inscribed texts including the alliance of 378 between the Athenians and Thebans which refers to existing agreements on *stelai* (*IG* II² 40 lines 14–20).

70 On destruction as an act with explicit political significance, with a detailed survey of the practice in Athens, see Culasso Gastaldi 2014a. For the argument that normally a separate decree was required to authorise the destruction of a public text of a treaty, see Bolmarcich 2007. On the act of destruction (and also erasure and reconstruction) as a reflection of the dynamic nature of collective memory-creation, see Low forthcoming.

founded on other forms of knowledge (see Chapter 3.2 above). An alternative is that Osborne over-states the prominence of references to *stelai* in fourth-century inscriptions. Indeed, in many inscribed texts, the primary reference point for an authoritative version is not a *stele* but a *psephisma* on an unspecified medium: the proposers of inscribed directives refer to regulations 'according to the decree' (κατὰ τὸ ψήφισμα), without reference to a *stele*. For instance, in *IG* II² 111 (= RO 39) of 363/2, a decree of Aristophon made a proposal concerning the Ioulitans' payment of what they are said to owe to Athens 'in accordance with the decree of the Athenian People which Menexenos proposed' (lines 8–9). Moreover, in *IG* II³ 1 298 lines 28–9 the arrangements for the manufacture of honorific crowns are specified as 'in accordance with the decree of the People voted previously for Leukon'; no mention is made of the inscribed version which we know from lines 46–7 to have been written up on stone, probably at Piraeus (cf. Dem. 20.36): the reference point on both occasions is to a *psephisma* rather than a physically inscribed version. It is quite clear, then, that authoritative reference to a decree could be made without specific reference to an inscribed copy.

It is important to remember that the final text of a decree, and the question of whether references within it were made either to *stelai* or *psephismata*, was decided either by an individual proposer (perhaps, in the case of probouleumatic decrees, with the assistance of councillors), or by a secretary, or by the two in combination.[71] The commissioners of the texts of decrees were, therefore, essentially amateurs,[72] albeit amateurs who, through experience of political institutions, may have been well-versed in documentary language. If, when composing their decrees, they decided to make a reference to a *stele* as an authoritative text, considering that it would heighten the authority of their own text, or perhaps even lead to a symbolically or politically loaded destruction of contradictory *stelai*, they were free to do so; alternatively, they could make reference to a *psephisma* alone. It seems likely, therefore, there were indeed some Athenians who paid attention to the content of inscribed decrees; the processes both of drafting the text of a decree and of citing a decree in a persuasive context were ones in which knowledge – or at least awareness of – inscribed decrees, was potentially significant. It may have been the case, therefore, that there was a lack of clear consensus on the question of the source of the authoritative text;

---

71 On the composition process of the text of Attic decrees, see Osborne 2012: 42.

72 The secretary to the *prytaneis*, who took charge of documents and decrees, was originally elected and held office for one prytany only, but from the 360s was selected by lot and held office for a whole year: see [Arist.] *Ath. Pol.* 54.3 with Rhodes 1981: 601-2. For discussion, see above, Chapter 1.2.2.

130   DECREES OF FOURTH-CENTURY ATHENS

this absence of consensus points to a lack of a systematic notion of authority in terms of the texts of decrees.

Moreover, as Lambert has shown, Osborne is probably wrong to conclude that the Athenians inscribed all the decrees that were enacted by the assembly:[73] inscribed examples indicate that the setting up of an inscription on a *stele* required action that went beyond the provisions of the original decree and was a later add-on. An inscription of the early fourth century demonstrates that the order to write up the honorific decree for Komaios of Abdera on a *stele* was to be carried out by the secretary of the council subsequent to the passing of the original decree: the authoritative people's decree existed before any inscribed version was created; the act of inscription required this further decree of the council:

> Smikythos son of Chares of Acharnai was the secretary. The council resolved according to the decree of the people. Prytany of Hippothontid tribe; Stratios was the *epistates*; Smikythos was the secretary; Xenotimos proposed: the secretary of the council is to write up Komaios son of Theodoros of Abdera as *proxenos* and benefactor on a stone *stele* according to the decree which he succeeded in getting passed previously concerning him. (*IG* II² 77 lines 1–8)[74]

The inscription goes on to specify that at an earlier point the council had resolved, according to the decree of the people, that Komaios and his descendants were to be *proxenoi* and benefactors of the Athenians and that the council and generals were to give him protection. It is clear on this occasion that the writing up of the decree on a *stele* was carried out by order of a subsequent decree of the council.[75] Why was the order to write the decree up on stone passed at a later point? It is plausible to think Komaios may have made this request to the council himself: as we will see (Chapter 4.3.3 below), some non-Athenian honorands appear to have specifically requested that their awards be publicly inscribed. On the other hand, given that as we will see (Chapter 4.2 below),

---

73 For critiques of Osborne's claim that all decrees of the Athenians were inscribed, see Mack 2015: 13-15, Faraguna 2017: 30-1 and Lambert 2018: 47-68.

74 Σμί[κυθο]ς Χα[ρ]ίνο Ἀχαρνε[ὺς] ἐγρ[αμμάτευε. ἔδ]οξεν [τῆ]ι βουλῆι κατὰ τὸ το[ῦ] δή[μου ψήφισμα]· Ἱπποθωντὶς ἐπρυτάνε[υ]ε, Σ[τ]ράτιος [ἐπεστ]άτει, Σμίκυθος ἐγραμμάτευε, Ξε[νότι]μος εἶπε· ἀναγράψαι Κωμαῖον Θεοδώ[ρο Ἀβδηρίτη]ν τὸν γραμματέα τῆς βουλῆς εἰ[σ]τ[ήλην λιθί]νην πρόξενον καὶ εὐεργέτην [κατὰ τὸ ψήφισ]μα, ὃ ἐνίκησε περὶ αὐτοῦ πρότερ[ον το]ύ[του]' (lines 1–8).

75 Another instance of a set of honorific decrees set up not by initial decree but on the basis of later initiative is the dossier of decrees for Herakleides of Salamis of the early 320s, eventually written up by the prytany secretary of 325/4 (*IG* II³ 1 367 lines 22–5) on the initiative of the proposer Demosthenes of Lamptrai. A further example is the inscription of the honours for the Pellanians of the Peloponnese, which was inscribed only the year after the original honours were granted: *IG* II³ 1 304 lines 7–11.

LOCAL AUDIENCES FOR DECREES 131

certainly some Athenians believed that there was an audience of interested foreigners who would pay attention to their decrees, so the initiative may have been that of an Athenian.

Let us now move on to the other key interpretation of Athenian inscribing habits: the relationship between inscription and public memory. Since the late twentieth century, scholarship has, appropriately enough, tended to downplay the role of the inscription as a source of straightforward information among their contemporary audience. The works of Thomas, Lewis and Pébarthe have set out perspectives that amount to the view that Athenian inscribed decrees were designed not to communicate detailed information or reference-texts, but rather to stand as monuments to Athenian decision-making.[76] However, some recent work on social memory in ancient Athens has highlighted the role of specific inscriptions in the manufacture of social memory in particular after the restorations of democracy in 410 and 403. Shear, in her *Polis and Revolution*, emphasises the importance of inscribed decrees in the Athenian reaction to the oligarchs of 410, pointing to the example of the honours for Thrasyboulos:

> The politics of memory ... formed an important element of the dynamics of the honorific decree for Thrasyboulos and, we must imagine, his accomplice Apollodoros. In this case, to read the inscription was to remember the process which brought the text into being, the moment in the *ecclesia* when the citizens decided to honour this man ... [I]nscriptions picked out significant moments in responding to oligarchy for the Athenians to remember in the future.[77]

Shear makes a case for the role of physical structures at the Athenian agora – a number of them inscribed – in the creation of collective memories about the restoration of democracy; she argues that on this occasion, an inscribed version of a decree contributed to it being remembered at later points in history; this in turn enabled the reader to recall the 'exemplum provided by the honorand rather than the specific details of his deeds'.[78] Moreover, Steinbock's 2013 book makes claims about the role of those decrees honouring those who fought for the Athenians at Phyle 'in the formation of

---

76 Pébarthe 2006: 288: 'Nombreuses sont les inscriptions qui laissent supposer l'existence de lecteurs potentiels, les fausses comme les vraies. Mais les considérer comme de simples documents, équivalents ou non aux originaux archivés, constituerait une erreur fondamentale. Les stèles sont aussi, parfois avant tout, un monument qui communique par sa seule présence dans l'espace de la cité. Á ce titre, elles constituent un moyen privilégié de communication publique.' See also Thomas 1989: 94; Lewis 1996: 164. However, for the view that inscriptions sometimes were set out in ways designed to communicate information, see RO p. xiii.
77 Shear 2011: 161–2.
78 Shear 2011: 162.

social memory'.[79] Low offers an important advance in the understanding of the relationship between inscription and memory by observing first that the inscribed decree marks the moment where an individual proposal or an account of the past becomes a part of 'a collectively-agreed narrative' but recognising that such inscriptions were then subject to the appropriation of individual politicians.[80]

These views of inscribed decrees being read and playing an active role in bringing forth responses on particular well-documented occasions are reasonable perspectives, but we must ask how widespread such interactions between the Athenians and their inscriptions really were, and assess carefully the degree to which inscriptions can be shown to have had an impact upon public awareness of decrees. It would be misleading to presume that all inscribed decrees were treated with an equal level of attention to detail by ancient readers. Over the course of the rest of Chapter 3.3, I shall explore what the bigger picture of literary reference to decrees suggests about engagement with inscribed documents by fourth-century readers. In Chapter 3.3.4 below, I discuss those decrees for which there survive both epigraphical and literary references; in Chapter 3.3.5 below, I expand this discussion by reference to the deployment of claims about inscribed knowledge among the Attic orators.

3.3.4 Substantive Overlap in the Epigraphical and Literary Sources for Decrees

One way of assessing the extent of literary texts' engagement with inscribed media is to explore the overlap between epigraphical and literary reference to particular decrees. This in fact is a relatively scarce phenomenon: only a very small minority of decrees extant in the material record can be associated in some substantive sense with preserved references in the literary record; still fewer can be identified as making reference to the same decree (see Table 2). It seems appropriate to foreshadow analysis of the material of the period 403/2–322/1 by discussing one of the clearest cases of overlap between the epigraphical

---

79 Steinbock 2013: 243. Steinbock (2013: 243–4) observes that the fact that the inscribed version of Archinos' decree and epigram (*SEG* XXVIII 85) has been, in modern times, restored on the basis of Aeschines' text makes it hard to prove that he was drawing upon the inscription. For more discussion, see Chapter 3.3.4 below. Elsewhere, the appearance in both literary and epigraphical texts of the phrase ἀπὸ Φυλῆς κατελθεῖν in reference to the return of Thrasyboulos' foreign supporters (RO 4 line 4 with Lys. 13.77 and Aeschin. 3.195), is not a secure indication of epigraphical autopsy.

80 Low forthcoming.

LOCAL AUDIENCES FOR DECREES

and literary evidence for pre-Euclidian decrees.[81] *IG* I³ 102 = OR 182 = ML 85) is a *stele*, partially reconstructed from five fragments recovered on the Athenian acropolis, bearing a decree in honour of the assassins of the Athenian oligarch Phrynichos (Thuc. 8.92). The primary honorand was Thrasyboulos: in the inscription, an initial decree, bestowing praise and a crown upon him (lines 6–11), is followed by Diokles' amendment (lines 14–37), which is restored to state that Thrasyboulos is to be an Athenian citizen (lines 15–16: 'εἶναι δὲ Θρασύ[βολον Ἀθεναῖον]'); it says that the things the Athenians decreed are to be written up (lines 21–2). A certain Agoratos is named, alongside others, later in the same rider in association with doing good to the *demos* (lines 25–7); he was granted a number of rewards (lines 28–35), though these fall short of citizenship.[82] This man was the opponent of the speaker of Lysias' *Against Agoratos* of 399 or later; Agoratos was accused of the murder of Dionysodoros, one of the victims of the Thirty. Lysias attempted to undermine Agoratos' claims to have been made a citizen on the basis of an honorific decree: 'the truth of my statement will be shown by the decree itself', he said (13.71), pointing to the absence of an award of citizenship for Agoratos on the *stele* (13.72), and implying that he had ensured his name be inscribed as a *euergetes* through bribery .

As already noted (Chapter 2.5.1 above), Lysias uses knowledge of a decree and reference to its *stele* in his argument, demonstrating awareness of its provisions and language: we cannot prove that Lysias looked at and read the inscribed version of the decree, but what is important is that he points to the inscription as an authoritative version of it.[83] The assertions made by

---

81 The alliance between the Athenians, Argives, Mantineans and Eleians and their allies is another example of a decision preserved both in the literary record and for which there is extant a (fragmentary) inscribed version: see *IG* I³ 83 with Thuc. 5.47 and the discussion in Hornblower 2008: 109–22, suggesting that Thucydides saw the Athenian copy of the inscription at 111. Lane Fox 2010: 22–3 follows Clark's view that Thucydides' text depends upon a text of it inscribed at Olympia in summer 420; Smarczyk 2006: 506 too takes the view that it derived from an inscription rather than an Athenian archive copy. See also Müller 1997. In a later period, as Lambert (2018: 290–304) points out, there is overlap between Stratokles' decree honouring Lycurgus in 307/6, *IG* II² 45 + 3207 and [Plu.] *X Or.* 851f–852e. As Lambert (2018: 57 note 19) writes, 'the inscribed version is fragmentary, but there is enough to see that, while the text is not precisely the same, it is consistent with the literary version, which most likely derives from the archive'.

82 Agoratos was made a benefactor of the Athenians (*IG* I³ 102 line 28), was awarded *enktesis* (30) and granted protection by the *boule* (lines 32–4).

83 We might add another example of close overlap between the literary and epigraphical record for a decree of approximately the same period in the shape of the wording of Demosthenes' account in the speech *Against Leptines* of the honours for Epikerdes of Kyrene of *circa* 405, preserved also in three fragments of *IG* I³ 125: West (1995: 243) makes a case for his view that Demosthenes' reports are based on knowledge of the decree's original motivation formulae (cf. Dem. 20.42); in this case, though, Demosthenes offered no mention of an inscribed version.

Lysias appear to be to a degree compatible with the inscribed version of the text when we bear in mind both that the awards for Agoratos were bestowed only on the basis of a rider to the original proposal (lines 14–37); moreover, his claims about bribery may be related to the inscription's second rider, which mentions an investigation into allegations made against the awards for Apollodoros (lines 38–47).[84] It is, however, important that Lysias refers to other decrees, including those calling for the arrest of Agoratos and those concerning information he offered without reference to a *stele*:[85] like any other ancient Athenian user of documentary evidence, Lysias was no epigraphical purist. It seems to be the case, therefore, that the reference to a *stele* certainly bolsters this speaker's argument, but it cannot be proved that epigraphy was the primary source of his knowledge of Athenian decrees. Nevertheless, it is perhaps relevant both that a comprehensive archive of public documents at the Metroon may not have been established until the restoration of democracy in 403/2 and would probably have collected comprehensively only those documents subsequent to that date.[86] The possibility that an inscription was the text of a pre-403/2 decree that was most accessible and also authoritative may go some way to explaining Lysias' reference to it.[87] At this point we turn to probe the evidence for such engagement with the epigraphical record for decrees in the fourth century.

When we move into the post-Euclidian era, there are some 16 further occasions in which epigraphical remains appear to pertain to decrees mentioned in the literary texts: see Table 2.[88]

---

84 See Todd 2007: 515–16. The repeated mention of Apollodoros as having received citizenship alongside Thrasyboulos makes it hard to identify the decrees mentioned by Lysias with the inscribed version, but this problem may be eradicated by textual amendment or the possibility that the Lysias text makes erroneous claims about the awards (Todd 2007: 516 note 8 and above, p. 95 n. 115.). For discussion of fits- and non-fits between the texts of the inscription and Lysias, see OR p. 503.

85 Lys 13.22–3, 28–9, 33, 35, 59, with Sickinger 1999a: 165–6.

86 See Sickinger 1999a: 62–3, on the rather haphazard and unsystematic nature of the preservation of Athenian records and documents before the end of the fifth century. Cf. above, note 30, for Pritchett's view of an organised archive in the fifth century.

87 For the view that, in the fifth century, inscriptions were the 'most permanent type of document possible,' see Thomas 1989: 74–5.

88 References to honorific crowns in inscribed inventories attested also in the literary record are not collected here, but see DD 174, 190, 228, 229, 230 with *IG* II² 1496.18–54.

LOCAL AUDIENCES FOR DECREES

Table 2 Epigraphically-Attested Early Fourth-Century Decrees which are Referred to by the Literary Sources[89]

(a) **Archinos' decree rewarding the democrats from Phyle, 403/2**: D15 with *SEG* XXVIII 85 lines 73–6;

(b) **The Theozotides decrees, c. 409 and c. 403/2**: D17 with Matthaiou 2011 and OR 178;

(c) **Treaty between Boiotians and Athenians, 395**: D20 with RO 6 (= *IG* II² 14);

(d) **Awards for Satyros, before 389**: D28 with RO 64 (= *IG* II³ 1 298) lines 22–6 mentioning an alliance with Satyros;

(e) **Honours for Evagoras, 394/3**: D24 with RO 11 (cf. *IG* II² 20).

(f) **Treaties with Amadokos (Medokos) and Seuthes, 391 or 390**: DD 29–30; the kings are mentioned in fragmentary contexts in *IG* II² 21 with *SEG* XXXII 43 (Seuthes) and *IG* II² 22 with *SEG* XL 56 (Medokos);

(g) **Decree for Thasians, 389/8**: D40 with *IG* II² 33 lines 4–9;

(h) **Foundation of the Second Athenian Confederacy, 378/7**: D45 and DP 21 with *IG* II² 40 (on the ambassadors coming from Thebes) and RO 22;

(i) **Citizenship for Dionysius of Syracuse, 369/8**: [Dem.] 12.10 with RO 33 lines 30–5;

(j) **Athenian alliance with Alexander of Pherai, c. 368**: D58, with RO 44 ((= *IG* II² 116) lines 39–40 declaring that the *stele* of the alliance is to be pulled down: 'τὴ]ν δὲ στ[ή]λ[ην τὴ]ν πρὸ[ς] Ἀλ[έξα]νδ[ρ]ον [κα]θελ[εῖ]ν τὸς [ταμία]ς τῆς θεô [τὴν π]ερ[ὶ τῆ]ς [σ]υμμαχία[ς]');

(k) **Treaty between Athens and Thracian Kings, 357/6**: D83 with RO 47 (= *IG* II² 126);

(l) **Philokrates' decree on the sacred *orgas* of 352/1**: see D107 with RO 58 (= *IG* II³ 1 292);

(m) **Decree making alliance with Peloponnesian states of 343/2**: see D149 with *IG* II³ 1 308;

(n) **Decree making peace and alliance with Philip of autumn 338**: see DD 171 and 172 with RO 76 (= *IG* II³ 1 318);

(o) **Proxeny-status for Alkimachos of 337/6**: see D178 with *IG* II³ 1 319;

(p) **Statue for Astydamas of post-340**: see D222 with *IG* II² 3775.

More detailed discussions of the relation between the inscribed remains and the literary references are to be found under the individual entries in the Inventory of Decrees (See Volume 1). Unsurprisingly, the relationship

---

89 Cf. Hansen 1983: 188 note 16, counting six cases of overlap for the period 403/2–352/1.

136   DECREES OF FOURTH-CENTURY ATHENS

between the inscribed remains and the literary references is rarely a clear one and is often very problematic (for instance, see D17 on the Theozotides decree(s): Table 2(b) above). There is, however, room at this point to analyse the nature of the overlap.

On only one of these 16 occasions – the decree proposed by Archinos rewarding with olive crowns those who had returned with the democrats from Phyle (D15; Table 2(a)) – does a literary source make reference to the material existence of a decree that appears also to be epigraphically extant (albeit in a heavily restored form: see D15 T3) in the material record. This decree was one of a number of rewards proposed, upon the restoration of democracy, for those who had contributed to the democratic uprising against the rule of the Thirty.[90] Combining the literary accounts with epigraphically preserved fragments, we can surmise that the inscription appears to have consisted originally of a heading, a list of honorands ordered by tribe and an epigram, followed on the stone by a decree. In his attack of 330 on Ktesiphon's honours for Demosthenes, as a way of underlining his view of both the modesty of the historic rewards that the Athenians allocated, and the care with which they were dispensed, Aeschines paraphrased the decree (Aeschin. 3.187–8: see D15) which he said was to be seen at the Metroon ('τῷ μητρῴῳ παρὰ τὸ βουλευτήριον ... ἔστιν ἰδεῖν') and had the secretary read out the epigram ('ἀναγνώσεται ὑμῖν ὁ γραμματεὺς τὸ ἐπίγραμμα') that he said was written up ('ἐπιγέγραπται') for the honorands (3.190–1). In all extant manuscripts of Aeschines 3, the secretary appears to read much the same text;[91] this passage has been used to restore the inscribed fragments, deriving from the Athenian agora, of the epigraphical remains both of the epigram and its associated decree (*SEG* XXVIII 45; cf. *CEG* 431). Identification of the two is strongly supported by the fact that Aeschines claimed that it was possible to see the award 'in the Metroon beside the *bouleuterion*' (3.187), which is compatible with the findspot of the inscribed fragments in section E of the Athenian agora excavations. However, although it forms part of his imaginary tour of the agora,[92] it is striking that, in contrast to his discussion of the epigrams commemorating the victory at the river Strymon a little earlier in the speech – which are said to have taken the form of three inscribed stone Hermai standing in the stoa of the Hermai (3.183) – Aeschines made nothing of the details of the physical form of the award, being interested

90 On this extensively-studied document, see now Taylor 2002; Malouchou 2014. For a list of the different honours dispensed at this time by the Athenian *demos*, see Rhodes and Osborne 2003: 24-5; see Inventory DD 5, 6, 14, 15.
91 Petrovic 2013: 206 with note 28.
92 Hobden 2007: 395.

primarily in the provisions of the award, the fact of its visibility in the Metroon, and its epigram (3.190–1).[93] Aeschines' words do not reveal whether the secretary drew his text from the inscribed version or an archival record of the decree and its epigram. It is plausible that his awareness of this award – and his presumption that it was shared by his audience – was underscored by its physical existence or perhaps even memory of the epigram (D15 T2),[94] but it seems likely that the secretary read from a documentary version of it at the Metroon: there is no indication of epigraphical autopsy in the fashion of a modern scholarly reader of an ancient inscription.[95] Aeschines' interest in the physical presence of the inscription should be regarded in the context of the speech: its presence is cited to heighten the sense that the Athenians grant prestigious rewards to those – unlike Demosthenes – who are worthy of them.

There are some five cases where literary and epigraphical sources make reference to what we may reasonably identify as one and the same decree. There is clear overlap in the epigraphical and literary sources for the alliance between the Athenians and the Boiotians of 395 (Table 2(c)), known from a *stele* which preserves a subject heading and the treaty (RO 6 = *IG* II² 14). Both Xenophon (3.5.16) and Diodoros (14.82.2) talk about the Athenian decision to send help to the Thebans (or Boiotians), but only Philochoros, cited by a scholiast on Aristophanes' *Ekklesiazousai*, talks about a treaty of alliance (*to summachikon*: see D20). The absence of mention of a physically inscribed decree in our literary sources suggests that the overlap is merely coincidental and that no autopsy of the epigraphical material had taken place. The case of the citizenship decree for Dionysius of Syracuse (Table 2(i)) is similar: there is a literary reference to the Athenian grant of citizenship for him and his descendants ([Dem.] 12.10) and an extant decree which grants, among other things, this status (RO 33 lines 30–5). A comparable overlap is likely in the case of the decree for Evagoras of Salamis (Table 2(e)): literary references (D24) are to a statue, but the epigraphic evidence for the honours (RO 11) is too fragmentary to enable certain identification of the precise awards being granted.[96] The situation is the same in the case of the decree for Alkimachos (Table 2(o)), where the literary source

---

93 Orators rarely make anything of the monumentality of an inscribed decree, though for comments on the physical form and setting of the Arthmios *stele*, see Chapter 3.3.5 with Table 3 below.

94 For the view that knowledge of the epigram may have derived from a collection that was circulating in the 330s, see Petrovic 2013.

95 Similarly, the overlap in the language of the inscription rewarding Thrasyboulos' foreign supporters does not prove epigraphical autopsy. See Chapter 3.3.4 above.

96 It is possible that a statue of Evagoras is referred to in a fragmentary portion of the inscription: see discussion at D24 Commentary.

suggests a proxeny award (see D178 Commentary), but the epigraphical material is too fragmentary to allow certainty about the nature of the award (*IG* II² 1 319). In the case of the award for the playwright Astydamas (D222; Table 2(p)), the literary sources are very clear about the setting up of a statue of him; the epigraphic evidence consists of an inscribed base (*IG* II² 3775) from the theatre of Dionysos which bears the inscription ᾿Αστυ[δάμας]ʼ, and is usually associated with the episode. While it is plausible to speculate in the cases of Evagoras and Astydamas that the statue of the honorands gave rise to the literary traditions about their decrees,[97] on none of these occasions does the literary source make any reference to the inscribed version of the text.

Passing epigraphical reference to decrees sometimes overlaps with the literary record in a way that enables the identification of a decree: in the case of the rewards for Satyros (D28; Table 2(d)), it is only the reference in the inscribed decree from Piraeus for the Kings of the Kimmerian Bosporos (*IG* II³ 1 298 (= RO 64) at lines 22–6) and to the awards for Satyros and Leukon which enables us to identify Satyros – mentioned by Isocrates (*Trapezitikos* 57) – as an honorand of the Athenian *demos*. In a similar way, the literary attested decree for alliance with Alexander of Pherai (Table 2(j)) is confirmed by the declaration in an inscribed alliance with the Thessalians that its *stele* is to be pulled down (RO 44 = *IG* II² 116 lines 39–40).

At other points the overlap between the literary and inscribed record is rather less securely attested: the alliances and friendship with Thracian leaders of 391 or 390 (Table 2(f)) are well-known (DD 29–30), but in this case the fragmentary inscriptions appear to mention in passing the subjects of the decree rather than recording the enactment of the proposals (*IG* II² 21 (with Add. p. 656) and *IG* II² 22 with *SEG* XL 56). A second example is that of the inscribed treaty between Athens and the Thracian Kings (RO 47; Table 2(k)), which may well be identified as one that was developed on the basis of the *suntheke* between Chares and the kings (D83), but certain identification is impossible. William West's article of 1995 has highlighted a number of possible references to extant epigraphical texts in Demosthenes' speech *Against Leptines*, a speech that is rich in documentary evidence.[98] However, on the whole, overlap between the decrees mentioned in that speech and those which are epigraphically extant is extremely limited, consisting, for the fourth-century material, of only his reference to the *ateleia* granted to Thasians under the leadership of Ekphantos in

---

97 Another example of a statue-base related to a decree mentioned in the literary record is that associated with Chabrias: see D46 T4 with Burnett and Edmondson 1961. On the significance of statues, see Chapter 3.3.5 below.

98 West 1995.

389/88 (D40 = Dem. 20.59; Table 2(g)). In this case, therefore, there is possible overlap here with *IG* II² 33, a fragmentary decree which mentions *xenia* (4–5) and a grant of *ateleia* 'just as for the Mantineans' (lines 6–7) to Thasians exiled on the charge of Atticism. N[aumachos] and Echpha[ntos] are given the responsibility of writing up their names (lines 8–9). While in this case there are clear associations between the literary and the epigraphical evidence, it is likely that, as Osborne (*Naturalization* D9 Commentary) has argued, the inscribed decree relates not to the episode described by Demosthenes, but to an exile of pro-Athenians which followed it. Again, we have a coincidence of associated, rather than identical, developments being referred to in the two datasets.

Other occasions of apparent overlap between the literary and epigraphic record are yet more controversial. Diodorus, in his account of the establishment of the Second Athenian Confederacy (15.29.7; see D45; Table 2(h)), states that the Athenians admitted the Thebans to the *koinon sunedrion*, restored cleruchies to their former owners, and banned Athenians from cultivating lands outside Attica. This passage has clear resonances with two pieces of epigraphical evidence: on the one hand, the decree *IG* II² 40, which appears to concern an alliance with, or at least the receipt of ambassadors from, the Thebans; and the well-known prospectus of the confederacy (RO 22 = *IG* II² 43), the provisions of which against the Athenian ownership of land in allied states are at least echoed in the passage of Diodorus. In this case, the correspondences between the inscribed and the literary attestations are oblique and linguistically rather distant, but both sets of evidence share the sense of prohibiting Athenian exploitation of allied territories.[99]

So far, we have discussed a number of decrees to which there is shared reference in the epigraphical and literary sources.[100] The majority of overlaps seem to consist of coincidental reference to different aspects of the same episode. But they highlight some wider tendencies too: we might observe that the literary sources place emphasis on the motivations behind the decree, their logical and moral consequences and the processes to which they gave rise; the epigraphical accounts of them focus upon their formulaic ratification and terms. We can observe also that, given the tendencies of literary selection to emphasise decrees concerning relations between Athens and the outside world and epigraphical

---

99 The three other cases of possible overlap between the literary and epigraphical datasets (DD 17, 107 and 171/172) are all deeply controversial and are discussed in more detail in their respective Inventory entries.

100 Overlap between the award of proxeny and euergesy on Herakleides of Byzantion of Dem. 20.60 and the inscribed honours for a Herakleides of (probably Klazomenai) was decisively ruled out by Meiggs and Lewis 1998 (ML 70 with *SEG* XXXII 10, ML Addenda p. 313; cf. OR 157).

emphasis on inscribed treaties and honours for non-Athenians (see Chapter 3.4 below), the foreign-policy and outward-facing orientation of the majority of these examples is not a surprise. In terms of chronological spread it is perhaps worth noting that 10 of the 16 examples of overlap date to the period between 403/2 and the early 360s: this proportion is at odds with the growing pace of epigraphical publication of decrees in the third quarter of the fourth century (see Chapter 3.4.1 below);[101] one explanation may lie in the fact that the growth area in epigraphical publication in the second half of the fourth century was among those inscriptions which were least likely to be mentioned in the literary record, that is, honours for otherwise obscure Athenians.[102]

We should note also that, apart from the decree for the assassins of Phrynichos (*IG* I³ 102, discussed on pp. 133–4 above), the most plausible case for the significance of epigraphy to the dissemination of knowledge about decrees arises from the testimonia for the Archinos decree bestowing awards for Athenians: this may well have something to do with its exceptional place of publication, in the agora where, as already noted (Chapter 3.2 above), the Athenians, after 403/2, developed an archive into which copies of laws and decrees were deposited. At the same time, however, Aeschines makes no claim that he has seen an inscribed version of it: by talking about its visibility at the Metroon (3.187) he might be referring to an archival version. It seems to be the case, therefore, that even in cases where decrees are known, on the grounds of their physical survival, to have been inscribed in antiquity, the literary sources did not owe their knowledge of them to epigraphy. Whatever the identity of the target audience of inscribed Athenian texts, they do not seem to have attracted a great deal of attention from those ancient authors whose work is extant. But before we dismiss the significance of inscriptions to our understanding of ancient perceptions of decrees it is important to assess the claims made in the literary sources about the existence of inscriptions that are not physically known to modern scholars.

3.3.5 Claims about Inscribed Decrees

The occasional passing comments of politicians (including Aeschines, Demosthenes, Hypereides, Dinarchus and Lycurgus)[103] about the location of inscribed decrees suggest that orators were aware of their physical presence in the city and their potential relevance to their arguments. They may have

---

101 Lambert 2018: 297-8 notes that the increase accelerated after the battle of Chaironeia.
102 Lambert 2018: 187.
103 E.g. D15 TT 1–2; D19 T3; D177 with Hypereides F79 Jensen; Din. 2.24-5 (*stele* of Arthmios).

LOCAL AUDIENCES FOR DECREES 141

made reference to them on the grounds, as Richardson argues, that they expected their audience to be acquainted with some epigraphical terminology and accordingly that it would summon up a bond of shared touchstones with their speakers.[104] Such references reveal the importance of inscriptions as physical monuments to public decisions also through their expression of concern about physical damage to them: the speaker of Demosthenes 57, asserting the small-mindedness of his enemies (and revealing the limits of his own scope of argument),[105] complained that rival demesmen had chiselled out the inscription of the honorific decree granted to him. In the following sections, I offer a brief survey of engagement with inscribed provisions in rhetorical contexts with a view to assessing the significance of inscriptions to contemporary Athenian perceptions of decrees. This is not, however, the place for a full discussion of the arguments that were constructed on the basis of claims about inscribed knowledge;[106] my focus here is primarily on reference to inscriptions pertaining to decrees, and these will be discussed in turn by type.

3.3.5.1 Anti-Tyranny Provisions

One type of legislation which Attic orators cite in association with their inscribed manifestation is those laws and decrees outlawing individuals involved in office-holding over the course of a tyrannical regime. In his speech *On the Mysteries* (399) Andocides attacked his opponent Epichares by claiming that, had Solonian anti-tyranny legislation been in force, he would have been – on account of his having served in the *boule* during the regime of the Thirty – liable to lawful killing by any Athenian. He cites this law by reference to a *nomos* 'from a *stele*' which is set up 'in front of the *bouleuterion*' (Andoc.

---

104 For familiarity with epigraphic language: see Richardson 2015. For the role of inscriptions in the creation of a widely accepted narrative about the past, see Shear 2011: 11–14; for this view, with increased emphasis on the dynamism of the treatment of inscribed public documents, see Low forthcoming.

105 Dem 57.64: 'The demesmen from whom I had exacted repayment of the public moneys swore a conspiracy against me, and by a sacrilegious theft stole from the temple the shields which I had dedicated to Athena (for the truth shall be told) and chiselled out the decree which the demesmen had passed in my honour ('τὸ ψήφισμ' ἐκκολάψαντες ὃ ἐμοὶ ἐψηφίσανθ' οἱ δημόται'). And they have come to such a pitch of shamelessness that they went about saying that I had done this for the sake of my defence. Yet what man among you, men of the jury, would judge me so utterly insane as to commit an act punishable with death in order to secure a bit of evidence for my case, and then myself to destroy an inscription which brought me honour?'

106 See Richardson 2015. Diodorus, the speaker of Demosthenes 22, for instance, expressed dismay at the loss of inscriptions on dedicated crowns which was a consequence of Androtion's recasting of public dedications (Dem. 22.72).

1.95).[107] On this occasion it seems to be the case that by reminding the people of the existence of an inscribed version of this law, Andocides was able to make a stronger case for its moral significance for attitudes towards Epichares.

Given the inauthenticity of the document which appears in sections 96–8 of Andocides' *On the Mysteries*,[108] we are reliant for firm knowledge of the decree of Demophantos on tyranny (see D19) on two later testimonia: those of Lycurgus (*Against Leokrates*) and Demosthenes (*Against Leptines*). On both occasions, the orators make reference to the physical location of the text. In his speech of 331, Lycurgus deployed knowledge both of the text of the post-Euclidian decree and the Athenians' decision to set it up at the *bouleuterion* as a reminder of the severity of punishment the Athenians imposed on those who betrayed democracy (Lycurg. 1.126):

> They wrote these things, men, on the *stele*, and they set it up at the *bouleuterion*, as a memorandum for those who gather each day and deliberate on behalf of the fatherland how it is necessary to behave towards such men. And on account of this they swore to kill anyone who was perceived as even contemplating such things.

Citing it as evidence, Lycurgus had apparently decided that the provisions and reputation of the inscribed decree of Demophantos would be more rhetorically powerful than those of the more recently enacted law of Eukrates (*IG* II³ 1 320 = RO 79):[109] an old decree appeared to him to be more persuasive, as a memorandum of the jurors' duties, than a new law. Some years earlier Demosthenes, in probably 355/4,[110] had urged his audience to remember the '*stele* of Demophantos' (20.159) to underline his point that the Athenians in the past had received awards for defending democracy: in both cases, therefore, the mention of a physical manifestation makes the moral argument more enduring, but it may well be the case that discussion of such inscriptions relies not on engagement with the physical inscription but rather awareness of a tradition about an inscribed version of the document.

---

107 The interpretation of this passage presented here is not reliant upon the controversial document which purports to be a decree of Demophantos on the treatment of those implicated with tyrannical activity. See Canevaro and Harris 2012. Harris 2013–14 challenges the defence of the decree proposed by Sommerstein 2014b; its authenticity is defended also by Hansen 2015: 898–901; cf. Carawan 2017. For discussion of the document, see D19 above. For deployment in historical reconstruction of Andocides 'document' of the Demophantos decree, see, for example, Shear 2007; Teegarden 2012, 2014: 35–53.
108 See D19 Commentary.
109 For the hierarchical relationship between laws and decrees, see Chapter 1.2.2 above.
110 Kremmydas 2012: 33.

3.3.5.2 Honorific Decrees

Hypereides, in his *graphe paranomon* speech against Demades' proposal that Euthykrates of Olynthos be made *proxenos* of the Athenians, joked that the *stele* for this honorand would be more justly set up among the rubbish dumps (*oxythymia*) than among the temples (Hypereides F79 Jensen; cf. D177).[111] At this point in the speech, it seems that Hypereides was attacking the decree by focussing upon the provision to set up an inscribed version of the award, perhaps on the acropolis. As Demosthenes does elsewhere (Dem. 20.149; see below), he suggests that it was normal for honorific decrees to be set up in sanctuaries. Yet the fragmentary preservation (Harpokration, s.v. ʿὀξυθύμιαʾ) and rhetorical context of this testimonium means that it is impossible to be certain about whether the decision to write up an honorific award on stone is exceptional or not. The fact that, of the 80 honorific decrees for Athenians and non-Athenians discussed in the literary sources (some of them – such as Ktesiphon's decree for Demosthenes (D179) – in detail), only four others made reference to an inscribed version (see D15: for democrats; D23: for Konon; D39: for Iphikrates; D54: for Leukon), makes it seem unlikely that the Athenians automatically inscribed all copies of honorific decrees.[112] We should follow the view taken by Aristotle, that a written memorial constituted a reward in its own right just as did a spectrum of other awards: sacrifices, monuments without words, privileges, grants of land, front seats, public burial, state maintenance (*Rh.* 1361a34–6).

The occasions when honorific decrees were cited by reference to their inscribed manifestations merit some analysis: in the *Against Leptines* Demosthenes, in support of the view that his opponent's law would unjus-tifiably annul rewards granted to both Athenians and non-Athenians, cited an inscribed honorific *stele* for Konon and introduced it with the moti-vation formulae 'since [Konon] … liberated the allies of the Athenians' (ʿἐπειδὴ [Κόνων] … ἠλευθέρωσε τοὺς Ἀθηναίων συμμάχουςʾ: Dem. 20.69): Demosthenes envisages that this statement would, to an Athenian reader, rep-resent the *philotimia* of Konon, while showcasing, to a Panhellenic audience, the *philotimia* of the Athenian community.[113] Such a statement represents

---

111 For an alternative interpretation of the term *oxythymia*, see Chapter 5 note 110 below.

112 The limited overlap between inscribed and literary testimonia for honorific decrees supports this assertion: see Table 2 on p. 135.

113 20.69: 'These words represent, jurors, his ambition to win respect among you, and your ambi-tion to win the same among the Greeks' (ʿἔστιν δὲ τοῦτο τὸ γράμμ', ὦ ἄνδρες δικασταί, ἐκείνῳ μὲν φιλοτιμία πρὸς ὑμᾶς αὐτούς, ὑμῖν δὲ πρὸς πάντας τοὺς Ἕλληναςʾ). For discussion of Athenian decrees outside Athens, see Chapter 4.2–3 below.

clearly the way that an inscribed honorific decree might be perceived as speaking to its honorand while also setting out the ambition of the awarding body. Demosthenes elsewhere in the speech drew significance from inscribed versions of honorific decrees, claiming the durability of *stelai* as enduring memorials of the city's character (20.64). Furthermore, when he talked in detail about the decrees for Leukon at section 36 he maintained that the *stelai* themselves were held to symbolise the agreements into which the Athenians had entered for the sake of reciprocal benefit, but that, if the Athenians upheld Leptines' abolition of *ateleia*, they would stand 'forever as proof (*tekmerion*) that those who want to slander our city are telling the truth' (36–7). Later in the speech he argued that Leptines' law would remove the awards which 'had been written up in sanctuaries' (ἐν τοῖς ἱεροῖς ἀναγράψας) and which 'everyone knows' (πάντες συνίσασιν: Dem. 20.149). The *stelai* of decrees are held by Demosthenes, therefore, as significant in their creation of a legacy of Athenian character, which Leptines' law threatened to undermine. He makes a case for the view that inscribed *stelai* have implications for the relationship between the Athenians and their benefactors and for the image of Athens throughout Greece. At the same time, the places of publication of the stone listed by Demosthenes himself – Bosporos, Piraeus and Hieron – suggest that he was drawing not directly upon autopsy of the *stelai* but rather was exploiting his and his audience's shared view of the implications of these places of publication.[114]

When we move beyond the *stelai*, we find that the decrees dispensing the most prestigious honours – in particular a statue – win more attention in the literary sources: those who received statues, for instance, Konon (D23), Evagoras (D24), Timotheos (D47), Chabrias (D46) and Iphikrates (D54),[115] were more prominent than those who did not. The Athenian decision to honour Evagoras of Salamis in 394/3 is known from some fragments of a decree (RO 11) in which it is said that '[something]' (the inscribed text is lost) is to be placed or done '[in fron]t of the stat[ue]' ('[ἔμπροσθ]εν τοῦ ἀγάλμα[τος]'): that is, in front of the statue, probably of a deity: lines 21–22): we can reasonably assert that this '[something]' was a reference either to the statue of Evagoras reported by Isocrates and Pausanias (D24) or to the stele of the inscription. It is relevant, on this occasion, that while the literary sources refer to a statue, the inscribed copy of the decree is never deemed

---

114 The inscribed decree for Leukon's sons, with its mention of the *stele* for Leukon and Satyros, stands as another testimonium of the award for Leukon: RO 64 lines 46–7.

115 See Oliver 2007: 184.

important enough for a mention:[116] in this case, and surely in others too, a statue attracted more attention than a *stele*. An honorific *stele* was clearly not enough to secure fame in fourth-century Athens but a statue would offer a firmer guarantee of it. We may observe, finally, that while honorific documents appear to have been among the type of decree that was most frequently cited by orators – primarily for their moral implications – it is striking that the examples cited by reference to inscriptions are mostly exceptional and high-profile rather than run-of-the-mill examples of minor officials being honoured for good conduct.

3.3.5.3 Treaties

As already noted (Table 1 on pp. 12–13), the treaty is one of the most frequently attested forms of fourth-century Athenian decree in literature. The inscribed version of the Peace of Philokrates attracted occasional passing reference among its contemporaries.[117] The probably spurious Andocides' *On the Peace* cited a *stele* bearing terms according to which the Athenians made peace with the Spartans at the end of the Peloponnesian War, comparing them unfavourably with the proposals of 392 (D25).[118] The terms of the settlement to which Andocides refers here are uncontroversial, but the testimony to the existence of a *stele* bearing such terms is unique; this peculiarity may be explained by the fact that the terms of the settlement were embarrassing to the Athenians, and not the type of thing to discuss in a public context even had they been inscribed on the acropolis. Andocides' style of reference, as Sickinger argues,

---

116 In addition to this, we might also take note of *IG* I³ 113 (= Osborne 1981–3 D3), which is a very heavily restored award of citizenship for Evagoras of probably early 407; the grant of citizenship to him is mentioned in Philip's *Letter* (= [Dem.] 12.10) and Isocrates' *Evagoras* 54, but neither of these sources mentions an inscribed version.

117 For passing references to the *stele* of the Peace of Philokrates, see D130 Commentary. Philochoros (T13) says that the people voted to destroy the stele which was set up regarding the peace and alliance with Philip; [Dem.] 12.8 (on which see D204) talks also of the names of Teres and Kersobleptes being left off the *stelai* of the Peace. Aeschin. 3.70 also mentions a *stele* of the Peace, to which, according to a resolution of the allies of the Athenians, any Greek state could add its name.

118 Andocides, *On the Peace*, 12: 'Look at the provisions of the two as they are written down ('ἐξ αὐτῶν τῶν γραμμάτων'); contrast the conditions of the truce inscribed upon the stone ('ἐν τῇ στήλῃ γέγραπται') with the conditions on which you can make peace today. In the inscription there, we have to demolish our walls: in these terms we can rebuild them. There, we are to keep 12 ships: now, as many ships as we like. Then, Lemnos, Imbros and Skyros are to be kept by those who held them at the time: now, they are to be ours. Now, we are not required to let any of the exiles return: then, we were required to, with the result that the democracy was subverted.' For discussion see Sickinger 2002: 157–8.

'all but prove that he had studied the inscription itself'.[119] Yet given the probable inauthenticity of the speech,[120] we cannot rule out that the *stele* was the fantasy of the speech's later fabricator. At the same time, however, we cannot necessarily dismiss the existence of unfavourable *stelai* on Athenian soil: Isocrates, for instance, refers to *stelai* which bring shame upon the Athenians (4.176, 180), and those that the Great King forced them to set up, in which case it is clear that he was talking about the terms of the Peace of Antalkidas.[121]

3.3.5.4 *Other Inscribed Public Documents*

To our observation that reference to inscribed versions of fourth-century Athenian decrees was occasional among literary sources, we can add the point that such references appear to be concentrated among those lawcourt speeches (including Demosthenes' *Against Leptines* and Lycurgus' *Against Leokrates*) in which the speaker construed the case as being of public concern. Unsurprisingly, while inscriptions could be drawn upon as a source of persuasive capital, there is nothing that we have seen so far to suggest that they represented the primary authoritative source of information about decrees. As points of evidence in argumentation, therefore, inscriptions offer an enhancement of an argument, rather than its defining point, and rather than being essential to an overall line of argument they strengthen it. But orators did not consistently take advantage of this opportunity: even Lycurgus, when he read out the text of documents that had been inscribed probably in the years immediately before his speech of 331,[122] did not mention a physical version of either the ephebic oath or the oath of Plataea (Lycurg. 1.76, 80–1).

What we have seen, so far, is that the citation of inscribed versions of documents is a practice related to the underlining of specific rhetorical points, but

---

119 Sickinger 2002: 157.
120 For the view that the speech is spurious, see Harris 2000a; Rhodes 2016a remains unconvinced of the speech's inauthenticity.
121 Isoc. *Panegyrikos* 180: 'Yes, and he has compelled us to engrave this treaty on pillars of stone and place it in our public temples ('ταύτας ἡμᾶς ἠνάγκασεν ἐν στήλαις λιθίναις ἀναγράψαντας ἐν τοῖς κοινοῖς τῶν ἱερῶν καταθεῖναι') – a trophy far more glorious for him than those which are set up on the fields of battle ('πολὺ κάλλιον τρόπαιον τῶν ἐν ταῖς μάχαις γιγνομένων'); for the latter are for minor deeds and a single success, but this treaty stands as a memorial of the entire war and of the humiliation of the whole of Greece.' Compare also Isoc. 4 *Panegyrikos* 176 on agreements allowing the cities and islands to be autonomous as 'μάτην ἐν ταῖς στήλαις': presumably a reference to the Peace of Callias.
122 An inscription bearing texts of both was set up in the middle of the fourth century, and probably antedates the reform of the ephebic organisation of the 330s (RO 88 with Commentary).

it demonstrates little by way of straightforward documentary consultation of public inscriptions: the contemporary sources are rarely interested in the run-of-the-mill type inscribed decrees (such as proxeny-awards or honours for officials) that dominate corpora of extant inscribed decrees. On one occasion, an orator appears to make reference to a relatively mundane epigraphical form, an inscribed list of naval debtors, in which Demochares and Theophemos appear, as he urges them to pay up what they owed by reference to the inscribed version (Dem. 47.22–3).[123] But among the extant speeches of Attic orators, there appears to be some emphasis upon those public inscriptions that are extraordinary or pertain to exceptional circumstances, as the following list of references to extraordinary inscriptions in oratory in Table 3 suggests.

Table 3 References to Extraordinary Inscriptions in Oratory

(a) **Historic honorific inscriptions:** enfranchised Plataeans ([Dem.] 59.104); inscribed Hermai (Aeschin. 3.183–5); *ateleia* for descendants of Harmodios and Aristogeiton (Dem. 20.128); epigram for those who died at Chaironeia (Dem. 18.289);

(b) **Historic laws:** Lysias 1.30 (from the Areopagos), 1.47; Dem. 47.71; sacred regulations for the Basilinna: [Dem.] 59.76; the *patrios nomos* on Eleusinian mysteries: And. 1.115–16;

(c) **Lists of traitors:** Lycurg. 1.117–19; And. 1.51; Ar. *Rhet.* 1400a32–6; cf. Schol. Ar. *Lys.* 243, Stroud 1978: 31–2;

(d) ***Stele* of Arthmios:** Dem. 9.41–3, 19.271–2; Aesch. 3.258; Din. 2.24, 25; Plu. *Them.* 6.4; Aristides ii, p. 392 (= Krateros F14); Isocr. 16 *Team of Horses* 9;

(e) **Verdict and curses against Alkibiades:** D.S. 13.69; Isocr. 16 *Team of Horses* 9);

(f) **Material from outside Athens:** altar at boundary: [Dem.] 7.41; inscribed dedications of Athens at Delphi: Aeschin. 3.116; Chaironeia epigram: Dem. 18.239.

Table 3 outlines the more extraordinary inscribed public documents that attracted citation by Attic orators and emphasises how far removed this audience's attention was from what are today the extant remains of Athenian state inscriptions. The material is dominated by oddities: the inscribed honorific decrees cited consisted of exceptional and famous cases (Table 3(a)). Orators

---

123 As Davies 1994a: 211 notes, records of this trierarchy survive in the published accounts of naval *epimeletai* (*IG* II² 1612 line 314; 1622 line 615).

were ready also to make claims on the basis of inscriptions from extra-Athenian contexts (Table 3(f)). Moreover, a significant proportion of the interest shown in inscribed laws consists of reference to legislation whose physical creation lies deep in the Athenian past (Table 3(b)):[124] claims were made sometimes about famous historical inscriptions, such as those related to the legislation of Draco and Solon.

The most frequently cited inscription occurring in the texts of the Attic orators was that of the bronze *stele* about the traitor Arthmios (Table 3(c)), the likes of which there is no physically attested parallel. One apparent attraction of this document was the prominence of its physical manifestation on a bronze *stele* close to the statue of Athena *Promachos* (Dem. 19.272) on the acropolis: accordingly, both its setting and monumentality were available to those who wanted to harness it as an example of the way that the morally upstanding Athenians of the era of the Persian wars and their aftermath treated traitors. Demosthenes quoted it verbatim in his *Third Philippic* (9.42) to create a contrast between the freedom-loving Greeks of the past (Dem. 9.36) whose power was feared by the 'barbarians' (Dem. 9.45) and his fallen contemporaries. Demosthenes makes a point about the intention (*dianoia*: 9.43) of the Athenians: to ensure the safety of Greece (Dem. 9.45). Arthmios was not the only 'inscribed' traitor whose treatment was held up as paradigmatic: Lycurgus had read out loud in the court of 331 the Athenian decree to create an inscribed list of traitors on the acropolis out of the melted bronze statue of Hipparchos the son of Charmos in order to assert that the Athenians were creating an example of how to treat traitors (Lycurg. 1.117–19). It is significant that the profile of decrees against traitors and inscriptions related to them (Table 3(c) and (e)) is not matched in the epigraphical record; what is becoming very clear is that the oratorical presentation of inscribed decisions is not a balanced reflection of the inscribed output of the fourth-century Athenians.

It is important to remember that the orators used claims about inscribed decrees to make rhetorical points to the Athenian *demos* at the assembly and the jurors: orators, therefore, expose them to traditions about those inscriptions which evoke historical or pseudo-historical situations which support their view of the present, with the intention of evoking a deep-seated moral of political consciousness in a way that will support their case. And celebrity, myth–historic inscriptions do this more effectively than run-of-the-mill contemporary inscribed decrees. It seems highly likely that there did really exist inscribed versions of decrees like that against Arthmios on the Athenian acropolis, but it is

---

124 See also Hansen 1990; Thomas 1994.

also likely that orators would have felt able to develop or elaborate traditions – within bounds set by their consciousness of the knowledge of the people – about their content to suit the rhetoric of their argument:[125] in such cases the shared consciousness of the physical inscription gave authority to the claims made by the orator.[126] This notion that inscribed versions offer supplementary value to decrees is reflected, as we shall see shortly (Chapter 3.4.1 below), in the publishing habits of the Athenians.

The actual overlap between the epigraphical and literary evidence for decrees, therefore, is limited, and represents a very slim proportion of the literary testimonia for decrees. We can draw the conclusion that the epigraphical publication of a decree served as no guarantee of fame, at least among orators and ancient Greek literary authors (who, of course, did not necessarily constitute the primary audience of inscribed decrees). Even in cases where inscribed versions of decrees were available, this does not seem to have led to close engagement with them by ancient writers. Inscriptions were deployed by orators for a number of purposes, but the examples outlined at Table 3 are, in terms of substance, very different from the types of decree that the Athenians were regularly inscribing in the fourth century. The next step in this analysis is to set side-by-side the epigraphical and literary records for fourth-century Athenian decrees (Chapter 3.4 below).

3.4 Inscribed and Literary Evidence Set Side-by-Side

3.4.1 Comparing the Range of Decrees in the Literary and Epigraphical Evidence

The current organisation of epigraphical publications of fourth-century Athenian decrees means that analysis of inscribed decrees is best divided between two periods, 403/2–353/2 and 352/1–322/1. Table 1 (pp. 12–13) sets side-by-side the quantitative data from the epigraphic and literary evidence on decrees. For the earlier period, there are published some 223 extant inscribed decrees of the Athenian *demos*.[127] Of these, 50 are too fragmentary for certainty about their content to be possible; of the other 173 of whose content we can

---

125 On the negotiation of collective memory, see Olick 2007: 37–54.
126 On the role that reference to material objects play in unleashing the capital of cultural identity, see Assman 1995: 132.
127 The fact that the most recent publication of these decrees dates to 1913 (*IG* II² 1–203) means that these numbers are approximate. A revised publication of these decrees is currently being undertaken. The total figure, including fragmentary decrees, is likely to be higher than 223.

be certain, there are some 47 alliances or decrees concerning external relations; the majority of them, however, that is 113, are honorific awards granted to non-Athenians, of which 61 bestow the award of proxeny-status and nine bestow citizenship. There is a very small group of decrees, three of them, which honour groups of Athenian citizens in some way; there are ten regulations, of which half concern sacred matters. Accordingly, the epigraphical evidence for this period very strongly suggests an emphasis in this period on the inscribing of decrees with honorific intention – initially those for non-Athenians – and, to a lesser extent, treaties.

Lambert offers a breakdown of the inscribed laws and decrees of 352/1–322/1 whose subject matter can be identified as follows: of the 199 decrees of discernible content there are 180 honorific decrees of which 29 can be firmly identified as honours for Athenians, one is for a deity, 116 contain honours for foreigners, while certainty is impossible about the honorands of the other 34; there are 11 treaties, and five religious regulations.[128] As Lambert notes, the tendency of the Athenians to publish honours for Athenians on freestanding stone *stelai* is something that appears to commence in the second half of the fourth century probably as a way of promoting competitive civic performance and *philotimia* in the face of Athens' changing geopolitical profile: the earliest inscribed decree honouring Athenians in what might be thought of as a regular series of publication is *IG* II³ 1 301 of 346/5; yet it is certain that the Athenians honoured their officials before this date.[129] The increasing proliferation of inscribed honorific decrees in the aftermath of the Athenian defeat at Chaironeia in 338 reflects an attempt to make more use of Athens' connections with private individuals in a world where whole communities were less interested in formulating formal relations (in the shape of treaties) with the Athenians.[130] At the same time, the decline in the frequency of bilateral alliances and treaties in the inscribed record of the post-338 period is indicative of Athens' declining geopolitical standing.[131]

---

128 Lambert 2018: 62–4.
129 Lambert 2011a: 197. As Lambert points out in the online commentary on *IG* II³ 4 57 (https://www.atticinscriptions.com), a dedication (of Euktemonides, perhaps a *hieropoios* at Eleusis) of 357/6 is 'the earliest datable dedication by an Athenian official in which it is stated explicitly that he had been crowned by the Council and People' though, as Lambert points out, 'crowns dedicated by boards of officials are recorded in inventories of the treasurers of Athena earlier than this': for the *syllogeis tou demou* of 370/69 and 368/7 dedicating crowns to Athena, see *IG* II² 1425 lines 126 and 225; cf. *IG* II³ 4 72 of 351/0. See now Lambert, *AIO Papers* 9, emphasizing the year 357/6 as that during which the Athenians began to fund publicly the inscribing of dedications commemorating the award of honours on the successful fulfilment of an official's term of office.
130 Lambert 2018: 96–9.
131 Lambert 2012a: 377–86.

It is reasonable to accept that these figures – notwithstanding the vagaries of preservation – are likely to be a reasonable reflection of Athenian epigraphical practice: they show a clear emphasis on publishing honorific decrees. At the same time, it is plausible to take the view that the large proportion of extant honorific decrees for non-Athenians is related to the possibility that the enduring significance of these honours as examples both of good individual behaviour and of Athenian gratitude meant that the Athenians were less likely to destroy this type of decree than those which set out alliances and regulations which, once obsolete, were liable to alteration.[132]

How do the patterns of publication suggested by the inscribed record compare with those of the literary evidence? I set out the range of genres of decree preserved or referred to in the literary evidence in the third column of Table 1 on p. 12–13. There are some clear differences in the patterns of preservation. The literary dataset is smaller, consisting of 245 decrees for the whole period 403/2–322/1, for most of which (235) we can be reasonably certain of their content. Literature gives also evidence for decrees that appear to have been rejected, or were challenged and over-ruled through the process of *graphe paranomon* in the courts.[133] The focus of many of the literary sources for this period of history upon military aspects of Athenian foreign policy goes some way to explaining the percentage (14.3) of decrees concerning military dispatches and mobilisation in the literary record, which are virtually unknown in the epigraphical record.[134] Moreover, the number of decrees pertaining to domestic appointments, financial matters and regulations initiating legislative developments is strikingly small in the epigraphic evidence when we compare it to the large number (51 out of 245 literary-attested decrees, that is 20.8 per cent)[135] in

---

132 Bolmarcich 2007 argues that the norm was to allow obsolete treaties to remain on inscriptions, although they were sometimes dismantled under the orders of the *demos*. The destruction of an honorific *stele*, when it was undertaken, was a significant political statement: see, for instance, the account of the destruction of the *stele* for Euphron of Sikyon in the restored version: *IG* II² 448 lines 58–67.

133 On decrees attested to have been challenged in the courts by the process of *graphe paranomon*, see the comprehensive study of Hansen 1974. Decrees over-ruled by *graphe paranomon*: DD 5, 66, 109, 110, 115, 164, 209, 210, 211, 224-5, 237, 238; decrees rejected: DD 4, 6, 26, 108, 132, 167a, 192.

134 For the single inscribed decree of this period relating to the dispatch of an ambassador, see *IG* II³ 1 370, a decree organising a colonising expedition to the Adriatic, which was inscribed not on a dedicated *stele* but within the slab recording the accounts of the naval *epimeletai*.

135 This includes decrees for the reorganisation of legislation after the restoration of democracy, the impeachment of individuals; there are procedural decrees arranging for the initiation of *nomothesia* and meetings of the assembly, decrees concerning qualifications for citizenship, the repayment of loans, taxation, coinage, the reform of the alphabet, etc.

the literary evidence.[136] The Athenian literary references offer us a great deal of information about the contribution of Athenian decrees to the legislative reconstruction of democracy during the archonship of Eukleides (DD 1, 2, 7, 8, 9), about which there is little in the extant epigraphical record.[137] The literary sources, therefore, place more emphasis on decrees relating to domestic arrangements, including appointments, constitutional changes and other procedural matters.

However, there are some areas of apparent compatibility between the impressions given by the literary and inscriptional evidence for decrees: when we view them from the perspective of the entire period 403/2–322/1 the proportion of alliances in the literary record is in line with the figures for the inscribed material, representing 15.9 per cent of the literary decrees and 11.8 per cent of the epigraphic material;[138] both records confirm that treaties with other communities were seldom undertaken in the period after Chaironeia, as the Athenians tended to use honorific transactions as a lever to fulfil their foreign-policy aspirations in this era.[139] Just as the epigraphical dataset does,[140] the literary testimonia also assert the prominence of honorific transactions, concern with foreign policy and negotiation with external communities in the decree-making activity of the Athenians. Both datasets suggest that fewer than 5 per cent of the decrees of the Athenian assembly concerned religious regulations; religion, of course, was regulated also by law as well as decree, and so the evidence for decrees may well underplay the profile of religion in Athenian public institutions (or it may be the case that on the whole, new religious regulations were exceptional). But the implications of this comparison point to the likelihood that a great deal of the Athenian assembly's business was concerned with the formulation of foreign policy through the making of alliances, military expeditions, the dispatch of ambassadors and the passing of honorific decrees for non-Athenians.

---

136 I do not take into consideration the inscribed evidence for fourth-century laws, for which see Stroud 1998: 15–16 and Canevaro 2016b section 8, counting 11 fourth-century laws on stone.

137 However, for the intention to inscribe laws (now lost) in front of the stoa after the re-organisation of democracy in 403/2, see Andocides 1.82 and (in 409/8 BC) *IG* I³ 104 lines 5–8; cf. also Robertson 1990; Rhodes 1991: 100; Canevaro and Esu 2018.

138 11.8 per cent is the figure produced when combining the epigraphic material for the whole period 403/2–322/1.

139 It is clear also that the number of epigraphically attested alliances goes into steep decline after the Athenian defeat at Chaironeia: see Lambert 2012a: 377–87, suggesting (at 385) 'a marked shift of emphasis from the interstate level of operation to a focus on achieving those objectives through relations with individual foreigners'.

140 For discussion of religious regulations of the period, see Lambert 2012a: 48–92.

LOCAL AUDIENCES FOR DECREES

Both the epigraphical and literary data make reference to decrees relevant to a wide range of types of honour, especially citizenship, often in combination with other awards, and including also the award of both olive and gold crowns, bronze statues, exemption, *sitesis* at the *prytaneion*, and other awards.[141] Both datasets suggest that awards could be granted in combination: citizenship would often be combined with a crown (DD 43, 84, 180),[142] and proxeny could be combined with *ateleia* (DD 31, 32).[143] However, further differences emerge from the two datasets when we look in detail at the patterns of preservation of honorific decrees. On the one hand, the epigraphic evidence for honours for non-Athenians places emphasis on the grant of awards of proxeny and the proclamation of individuals as *euergetai*;[144] on the other hand, the literary evidence is far less interested than the epigraphical evidence in awards of proxeny-status.[145] On the whole, the epigraphical sources offer far more specific details of the honours dispensed and, in the case of crowns, their value. The literary sources demonstrate that honours for Athenians were passed at the assembly far earlier in the fourth century than the epigraphic record suggests.[146] And throughout the fourth century the literary sources place emphasis on prominent, wealthy, benefactors, whereas the epigraphical record of the second half of that century attests to a far lower proportion of named honorands who derived from the propertied classes.[147] The literary dataset emphasises that honours for Athenians were frequently dispensed for the sake of military (particularly before the defeat at Chaironeia in 338) and financial contributions and ambassadorial activity,[148] but these activities are less visible in the inscribed record. Whereas the inscribed record of honours for Athenians shows Athenian recognition of the value of small-scale political activity and the holding of cult office, the literary record points up the career-spanning contributions of prominent men like Demosthenes and Demades.[149] It might be reasonable to draw the inference that the literary sources' focus on big political debates leads to an

---

141 For a breakdown of the honorific decrees in the literary sources see Volume 1 Appendix 2; for those in the epigraphical record, see Lambert 2012a: 3–48, 93–183.

142 On epigraphically inscribed citizenship awards, see Osborne 1981–3 DD 5–25; for detailed discussion of those of the later period, see now Lambert 2012a: 93–113.

143 For the range of epigraphically-preserved awards for non-Athenians of the later period, see Lambert 2012a: 138–83.

144 Liddel 2016: 344-5; for awards of proxeny and euergesy, see Lambert 2012a: 113–37,

145 See Table 1 note 5, counting 6 proxeny awards in the literary record but 27 citizenship awards; cf. Liddel 2016: 344–5.

146 Liddel 2016: 237. See also Volume 1 Appendix 2.

147 Liddel 2016: 339.

148 Liddel 2016: 339–42.

149 Liddel 2016: 342-3.

exaggeration of the proliferation of honours among the elite throughout the fourth century and in particular those awards whose controversy was held to have public significance.

3.4.2 Interpreting the Comparison

The available sources, therefore, offer us two accounts of the Athenian decree. The literary evidence places emphasis not only on honorific decrees but also those related to alliances and the sending of expeditions, and this emphasis is more pronounced when we take into consideration those less firmly attested 'probable decrees' (testimonia identified as 'DP': see Volume 1 Inventory B).[150] Generally speaking, the epigraphical record accentuates the growing proliferation of honorific decrees and suggests that the Athenians were inscribing decrees in the hope that their physical manifestation – combined with expressions of hortatory intention which often appeared within their texts – would spur on others to emulate the standards of civic benefaction set by the honorands.[151] The literary record for Athenian decrees shows that honours for high-profile Athenians (as well as non-Athenians) were passed throughout the whole period: this is a consequence of the interest of our literary sources both in political conflicts concerning honorific rewards and in drawing upon the moral connotations for honours for prominent Athenians.[152] Yet despite these foci, the literary record does itself show a shift in the honorific record from decrees honouring military leaders in the first half of the fourth century to honouring financial donors and ambassadors in the second half.[153] Still, it is clear that there is an inclination of the literary sources to take an interest in far-reaching, politically controversial, and sometimes exceptional, decrees rather than the relatively low-key epigraphical record (see Chapter 3.3.2 above).

What is more, the comparison affirms that the Athenians passed a far wider range of decrees than those which they published on stone.[154] It is clear that, as Hansen observed in 1987, the Athenians very rarely inscribed decrees whose

---

150 The vast majority of such 'probable decrees' (DP) amount to the dispatch of military expeditions, instructions and ambassadors.
151 Lambert 2011a.
152 On the importance of honour in Athenian politics in the era of Demosthenes, see Brüggenbrock 2006: 265–308.
153 Liddel 2016.
154 See discussion in Chapter 3.3.3 above.

LOCAL AUDIENCES FOR DECREES

task was primarily to initiate an act of hostility or military activity;[155] and there is also certainly a tendency to inscribe those decrees which have a long-term significance in terms of encouragement of euergetic behaviour but not those with only ephemeral impact (such as decrees arranging for the dispatch of embassies or organising meetings of the assembly).[156] As Lambert notes, there is a notable group of inscribed honorific decrees for Athenians from the 340s.[157] However, the fact that the publication of decrees on stone appears to be geared heavily towards the honouring of foreigners and the setting up of alliances suggests, therefore, that the act of inscribing aimed in particular to address issues relating to the Athenians' negotiation with the rest of the world (an area that will be explored in Chapter 4 below), and also, perhaps, at ensuring public accountability with respect to the contributions of Athenian citizens – as proposers of decrees – to the formation of such policy.

3.5 Conclusion

Over the course of this chapter, we have built up an impression of the ways in which awareness and knowledge of decrees were disseminated among Athenian citizens. Dissemination appears to have taken place through a range of processes, including engagement in public decision-making and legal institutions, through the agency of those magistrates and private citizens enforcing them, and through hearsay (3.2.1). The creation of an archive of public documents at the end of the fifth century offered a potential source of authoritative knowledge, but only on rare occasions is it clear that speakers drew purposefully on archivally stored details (3.2.2). Orators deploying decrees within narrative frameworks made claims about collective awareness; such claims were sometimes backed by requests to a secretary to read a decree out loud to the

---

155 Hansen 1997: 110–13; Osborne 1999: 342. As Lambert (2018: 52) points out 'there is, in fact, only one inscribed decree of this period which provides for a military expedition: the decree of 325/4 providing for a naval expedition to found a colony in the Adriatic, *IG* II³ 1 370; but significantly it is not a self-standing decree, erected at the initiative of the Council or Assembly, but embedded in a naval inventory. It is an exception which proves the rule that decrees making provisions for military expeditions were not generally inscribed on *stelai*.'

156 The lack of inscribing of decrees concerned with ephemeral matters is observed by Woodhead, in his commentary on *Ag.* XVI 48. But note that some extant inscribed decrees contained clauses requiring immediate action (*autika mala*): see Rhodes, 1972: 280; see also Chapter 2.5.2 above. As Lambert (2018: 52) points out, 'In our corpus *IG* II³ 1 292, 18 requires that the sacred *orgas* and the other sacred precincts be cared for "for all time" (εἰς τὸν ἀεὶ χρόνον); at 447, 33 arrangements are made for the Little Panathenaia festival to be finely celebrated "for all time" (εἰς τὸν ἀεὶ χρόνον).'

157 Lambert 2018: 76.

judges (3.2.3). Awareness of, and ideas about, decrees appears to have been disseminated through socialisation, both inside and outside institutional settings. Archival research into decrees appears to have had rather limited significance for purposes of political persuasion, but may have been carried out by those who wished to know more detail about a particular decree of which they were already aware. Orators made claims about the content of decrees as they believed their audiences would find them authoritative and persuasive; these claims were occasionally magnified by making claims about archival reference or the existence of inscribed versions of them.

The setting up of decrees on inscribed stones was undertaken for reasons relating to religion, the encouragement of euergetic behaviour, and the intention to disseminate messages (3.3.1–2). They constituted one, but not the only, authoritative source of information about decrees (3.3.3). A number of factors cast doubt on the extent to which orators and politicians paid attention to the inscribed record of decrees: one is the relative lack of substantive overlap in the epigraphical and literary datasets for decrees (3.3.4); another is the fact that when orators make claims about inscribed decrees, they do so primarily by reference to famous and extraordinary documents which are very different in substance and tone from the extant inscribed record (3.3.5). Orators, in their deployment of decrees in the fourth-century lawcourts, were not reliant on inscriptions for information about decrees, nevertheless they did at points draw upon the additional persuasive capital offered by inscribed monuments (3.3.5), as Demosthenes did in the speech *Against Leptines*. However, the depth of epigraphically informed knowledge of decrees displayed in Demosthenes 20, despite its high reputation in antiquity,[158] was never repeated in any extant speech. Epigraphical publication, therefore, did not guarantee a high profile for a decree among Athenians. When we compare the epigraphical and literary evidence for decrees (3.4) we find a number of fits- and non-fits between the evidence: both datasets suggest a concern with the recognition of euergetism and the formulation of foreign policy; distinctions that can be observed at a closer level of analysis support the view that epigraphical publication of decrees was not comprehensive over the course of this period of Athenian history.

In the light of this analysis, therefore, we can offer a distinction between two distinct types of epigraphical knowledge: that which was formulaic and perhaps mundane (which was of interest primarily to some of those who drafted the texts of decrees and which is preserved in the extant epigraphical record);

---

158 West 1995; Kremmydas 2012: 62–4; for its high reputation, see Kremmydas 2007b and Dionysius of Halicarnassos, *ad Amm.* 1.4, calling it 'most elegant and accurately-written of speeches' (χαριέστατος ἁπάντων τῶν λόγων καὶ γραφικώτατος).

LOCAL AUDIENCES FOR DECREES

and the famous and spectacular, prevalent among the citizens who manned the juries, which is the material that was cited in the lawcourt for the sake of its moral implications (see 3.3.5 above), and knowledge of which was disseminated by their existence in the public memory. Yet the awareness of decrees which is suggested in the literary record is, for the most part, distinct from these two forms of knowledge: Athenians got to know stories about decrees by way of political participation and word-of-mouth, processes which, for obvious reasons, would not nurture exact knowledge about decrees. The fact that most orators and historians were vague about their sources of information for decrees points, on the one hand, to the likelihood that they drew upon hearsay, with knowledge about decrees wrapped up in stories about events, or actual experience in the courts or assembly: a sense emerges of messy familiarity with decrees.

We might try to explain in practical terms the relative lack of engagement with the inscribed record among those fourth-century Athenians interested in decrees: was there perhaps a lack of confidence about locating the right decree among the mass of inscriptions that had built up on the acropolis by the middle of the fourth century? Had the Metroon simply become a more comprehensive and better-organised archive, and accordingly an easier-to-access resource, and had the epigraphic record become, with the proliferation of epigraphical publication, far harder to master? We might, therefore, envisage a maze of inscriptions standing upon the fourth-century Athenian acropolis, apparently competing for conspicuousness, but not entirely succeeding in captivating close attention of those who saw them.[159] But the inaccessibility of inscribed texts of contemporary decrees is not the whole explanation: as Klaffenbach pointed out, ancient audiences of inscriptions were less obsessed with producing verbatim-accurate transcripts than were their modern counterparts;[160] they were much more interested in unleashing their moral and political capital without close attention to substantive detail.

It is possible at this stage to draw some conclusions about the nature of dissemination of knowledge of decrees. In Chapter 4 of his 2008 book, *Democracy and Knowledge*, Ober insightfully outlines a view of the ways in which Athenian political institutions gave rise to the 'aggregation' of knowledge about political processes and contributed to policy-making decisions. Ober talks in terms of

---

159 For an inscribed decree that appears to have been lost, see *IG* II² 172, ordering it to be re-inscribed because it had disappeared: lines 9–11: [ἐπειδὴ] ἠφάνισται αὐτῶ[ι ἡ στήλη].

160 Klaffenbach 1960: 34–6.

'informational cascades'.[161] How far should we think in terms of a cascade of information about decrees? What needs to be emphasised is that the rhetorical and political context of the activity in Athenian institutions means that we should not expect discussions of decrees to have been objective or straightforward.[162] While speakers talking about particular decrees in formal institutional contexts would have avoided – for fear of facing criticism – making factually false claims (see Chapter 3.2.3 above), we should emphasise that speakers cite decrees for the most part to support arguments, to justify policy, or to attack the policy of another. Accounts of them were, nevertheless, open also to distortion or exaggeration.[163] Instead of thinking in terms of the cascade of information, therefore, we should envisage the dissemination of impressions of decrees among audiences both within formal institutional space and beyond. The citation of a decree in one particular context would have given rise to its deployment in other ways too: in the speech *Against Leptines*, Demosthenes set out Chabrias as a model recipient of honours (D46 TT 1–2), and some years later Aeschines followed this view of the honorand (D46 T4), setting out his praiseworthiness (and that also of Timotheos and Iphikrates) as a way of questioning Demosthenes' worthiness of honours. In this case, it is clear that we are dealing not just with the dissemination of straightforward knowledge of decrees, but that of perspectives on how they can be deployed rhetorically.

The Athenian democracy was an organisation in which knowledge was a vital tool in political engagement among aspirational citizens:[164] awareness of decrees was an important commodity in the assembly, council and lawcourts. Its accrual and circulation happened by way of wide range of public and private transactions, some of them invisible to us today. Even, therefore, within a culture in which documents and writing had attained new-found status, socially based knowledge of decrees was the chief factor behind their deployment. In the final chapters of this book, I will explore the possibility of audiences beyond those of Athenian politicians, discussing both the evidence for a non-Athenian audience of their decrees (Chapter 4 below), and also the wider reception of Athenian decrees in literary texts (Chapter 5 below) where, as we shall see, the emergence of traditions about Athenian decrees is an important medium through which information about them circulated in the *longue durée*.

---

161 Ober 2008: 180. For a view of human exchanges as providing a background to political education, see Livingstone 2016, acknowledging the potential for challenges to democratic ideals (Livingstone 2016: 86–8).
162 Indeed, Ober does allow for the possibility that aggregated knowledge might sometimes produce bad policy: Ober 2008: 167.
163 See the discussion of Aeschines' citation of decrees in Chapter 2.5.1 above.
164 Kallet-Marx 1994.

4

The Audiences of Decrees Beyond
Athenian Citizens

4.1 Introduction

Thus far, this exploration of the deployment, dissemination and reception of Athenian decrees has focussed on their local audience: one which was primarily Athenian, consisting both of politically engaged citizens and also the broader group of those upon whose lives decrees had an impact (Chapter 3 above). On one level, focus upon a primary audience of Athenians is entirely appropriate: decrees were enacted at Athens by the Athenian people, a body whose sovereignty extended only as far as the borders of Attica. In fourth-century Athens, political activity – including the discussion and proposal of decrees, and voting on their enactment – was the perquisite exclusively of male Athenian citizens. However, *poleis* were not narrowly inward-looking communities and interaction with external political units was inevitable and necessary for the functioning of the city: regardless of whether they were either hegemonic or insignificant, their decisions had consequences for communities of non-citizens; more often than not, these took the shape of decrees. In the case of the Athenian *demos*, a community with interests and aspirations that went beyond its borders, the decrees of the assembly – in particular those which dispatched expeditions or embassies or honoured foreigners – had significance well beyond the borders of the *polis*.[1] Moreover, the proposal of honorific decrees offered those ambitious Athenian politicians who possessed private connections beyond their community the opportunity to secure links and networks overseas and to manage and nurture mutually interested relations with outsiders. Accordingly, even as Athens' geopolitical influence waned over the course of the fourth century (cf. Chapter 1.4 above), the *demos* continued to pass decrees which either appealed

---

1 On the proportion of Athenian decrees that concerned the *demos'* interaction with other communities (in the form of expeditions, alliances, and honorific transactions), see Table 1 on pp. 12–13 with discussion in Chapter 3.4.1.

159

to, or had implications for groups of non-Athenians, even if their scope and effectiveness became more compromised than ever before.[2]

There has been a tendency in recent work on Greek history to challenge the long-established primacy of the *polis* as the prism for understanding ancient social and cultural phenomena;[3] this tendency has underlined the significance of inter-*polis* political institutions, exchanges and phenomena.[4] Yet there has been relatively little consideration of the reception of Athenian political acts and values outside that city. Indeed, assessments of Athenian political activity have tended to focus very much upon what Athenian politicians did and how they behaved when they were inside Athens, without much attention to their associations with, or appeals to, the outside world.[5] The study of Athenian decrees, I suggest, offers a perspective on the extent to which there was a sense among Athenians of the broader relevance of the political activity that went on within the *polis*: in this section I shall assess the degree to which the Athenians envisaged that there existed non-Athenian audiences of their decrees (Chapter 4.2 below), and then shall explore the possibility that such audiences were real by considering their likely identity and the modes through which news about Athenian decrees was disseminated (Chapter 4.3 below). By 'non-Athenian audiences' I refer both to individuals and groups of non-Athenians inside the *polis* of Athens and to those who resided outside Attica. In Chapter 5 below I shall explore a rather different aspect of the reception of Athenian decrees, focussing on the indications that ancient literary authors were interested in portraying Athenian decrees and the activities that were related to them.

2 See on the shift of emphasis away from decrees that made alliances towards those which honoured foreigners, Lambert 2018: 93–113; Chapter 3.4.1 above.

3 Vlassopoulos 2007a. For cross-community studies of Greek political activity, see e.g. Murray 1990; Welwei 1998. The general consensus in the modern scholarly literature is that the political systems of the classical Greek world were dominated by *polis* institutions, and that individual communities managed their own independently developed political institutions and structures. While these shared in common some key features, such as a bouleutic body, and mechanisms for making decrees – the significance of which has been demonstrated by Rhodes with Lewis 1997 (cf. Robinson 2011, s.v. *probouleusis*) – they were, as Mitchell (2006) shows for the classical period and Robinson (1997) for the archaic, very diverse. On the diversity of political institutions see also Jones 1987. Indeed, the Aristotelian project which gave rise to the publication of 158 monographic descriptions of the *politeiai* of Greek states in the late fourth century suggests that Aristotelians valued the *polis*-by-*polis* approach to the history of political institutions. An analysis of inter-community political activity is offered in Liddel 2018.

4 Emphasising inter-community interaction, see, for instance, Herman 1987; Mitchell 1997; Low 2007; Hunt 2010, esp. 201–10; Mack 2015. Finley's 1966 article (= Finley 1975) initiated a discussion of the 'unity' of Greek law; On shared and diverse aspects of epigraphical practices, see, for instance, Massar 2006 and Hagamajer Allen 2003.

5 For political activity in Athens (a selection): Rhodes 1986; Bleicken 1987; Ober 1989; Yunis 1996; Allen 2006.

The first dimension of the inter-community relevance of Athenian decrees to be explored, therefore, is the Athenians' belief that representatives of other communities (both *poleis* and non-*poleis*) were interested in, or profoundly affected by, their constitutional form and their decrees.

4.2. Athenian Perception of Non-Athenian Interest in Athenian Politics and Decrees

Pericles' statement on the *politeia* of Athens – viewing it as a model for others – suggests that some Athenians took the view that their way of life was potentially a model for other communities:

> We make use of a constitution that does not imitate the laws of our neighbours (πολιτείᾳ οὐ ζηλούσῃ τοὺς τῶν πέλας νόμους). It is more the case of our being a model (παράδειγμα) to others, than of our imitating anyone else. (Thuc. 2.37.1)

The degree to which Thucydides' account of the funeral speech is a reflection of the words spoken by Pericles is much debated,[6] but the fact that a similar claim about the innovative nature of the Athenian constitution is made also in the *epitaphios logos* of Lysias (Lys. 2.18) supports the conclusion that this type of assertion would have been received favourably by its listeners and that it was an appropriate thing for Pericles to have said in this context. His audience consisted primarily of Athenians mourning the passing of those in their community who had fallen in battle, and so the claims made in front of them appealed to their beliefs about Athenian political superiority. A similar ideal, that the Athenian way of politics was inherently superior, surfaces also in fourth-century lawcourt oratory, with speakers in political cases at points making boasts about Athenian excellence in deliberation (Dem. 23.109) or claiming that the Athenians made better laws than did other communities (Aeschin. 1.178); orators at points compared Athenian legislative habits favourably with those of other communities, or attacked the idea that one might look to others' legislation in the formation of legal argumentation.[7] Lycurgus in his *Against Leokrates*, urging his audience not to be misled by the digressions of speakers, claimed that they should look to the Areopagus court which offered 'the finest example of the Greeks' (Lycurg. 1.12). In making these claims, it seems that

---

6 See Thuc. 1.22.1 for Thucydides' statement that the speeches in his work combine statements of 'what was appropriate' (*ta deonta*) with the actual things spoken. For the view that the speech is 'a potent distillation of the speech Pericles actually delivered', see Bosworth 2000: 16.

7 Dem. 20.110-11 offers the argument that it was wrong to cite Lacedaimonian or Theban laws; Dem. 23.212-4 offers an attack on the Aeginetans', Oreitans' and Megarians' meanness with honours.

they were attempting to align their audiences' views with their own and appealing to them as judges to have the confidence of casting ballots in their favour. Notwithstanding these perspectives, however, there were still points at which Athenian orators in the lawcourts saw it as politically worthwhile to cite the laws of other communities, usually as moral paradigms.[8] The rectitude of constructing arguments on the basis of non-Athenian values and legislation was, however, contested, and less widespread than the idea that Athenian political ideas and acts had relevance beyond Athens.

A view was also put forward at both the assembly and the lawcourts that non-Athenians were interested specifically in decrees of the Athenian *demos*. We have noted already (Chapter 2.5.2 above) that, as Mader points out, Demosthenes in his symbouleutic speeches sometimes attempted to rouse his audience into action by criticising their failure to fulfil the promises of their decrees (e.g. Dem. 3.4–6):[9] on one level this would suggest a degree of insecurity among the Athenians about their political system, and we will return to discuss this phenomenon later on in this chapter. But at the same time we must acknowledge the existence of a discourse that said that their decrees had a wide audience, one which reached beyond that of Athenians. Even in the second half of the fourth century, when the Athenians' interstate clout was much reduced, Athenian orators appealed to their audiences and attempted to draw them into particular lines of argument by claiming that their political decisions were much heeded by non-Athenians: in his account of the Second Embassy, for instance, Aeschines focuses his listeners' attention on the negotiation of the Peace of Philokrates by imagining that, as the Athenian ambassadors at Pella arrived with an Athenian decree, all of the Greeks were watching their negotiations with Philip:[10]

> For ambassadors from Thebes are here, ambassadors from Lakedaimon have arrived, and here we are with a decree of the people in which it stands written, 'The ambassadors shall also negotiate concerning any other good thing that may

---

8 Examples of non-Athenian legislation as moral paradigms to the Athenians: Lycurg. 1.95–6 (Sicilian values), 103 (Hektor exhorting the Trojans), 106–7 (quotation of Tyrtaios, here claimed to be an Athenian), 128–30 (Spartan law condemning to death all those who refused to fight for their *patris*); Dem. 24.139–42 (Locrian legislative conservativism); Aeschin. 1.180–1: Spartan attitude towards shameful men; cf. also Fisher 1994, 2007. Aeschines (3.122–4) discusses a decree of the Delphic Amphictyony as part of his case against Demosthenes. See also note 69 below.

9 Mader 2006.

10 Cf. Hunt 2010: 209, noting the importance that Greek communities attached to publicising interstate commitments. On the rhetoric of the claim that foreigners had come to Athens to hear a case or that the Athenians would face the judgement of the Greeks as a whole, see Lewis 1996: 46.

be within their power.' All the Greeks are watching to see what is going to happen ('ἅπαντες δὲ οἱ Ἕλληνες πρὸς τὸ μέλλον ἔσεσθαι βλέπουσιν'). (Aeschin. 2.104)

The rhetorical strategy of emphasising the significance of Athenian decrees by reference to the breadth of their audience was not limited to lawcourt oratory: in his *On the Chersonese* Demosthenes, speaking to the assembly, invites his audience to imagine the Greeks calling the Athenians to account for the opportunities missed in resisting Philip (Dem. 8.34–5). This was a vision designed to persuade an audience of Athenians at the assembly to support their general Diopeithes' actions against Philip in Thrace. Indeed, the idea that other Greeks were watching was noted by Aristotle, perhaps on the basis of hearsay:[11] he claimed that, in the fifth century, the orator Kydias, haranguing the people about the allotment of territory at Samos, implored the Athenians to picture that the Greeks were standing around them and would not only hear but would also see what they were going to decree (*Rh.* 1384b32–5).[12] But such claims were ones made in front of predominantly Athenian audiences: they were set out for rhetorical purposes – as a way of heightening the sense of responsibility of the Athenian listeners – and should not, therefore, be taken as straightforward indications that other Greek communities were interested in Athenian decrees.

Yet the theme that non-Athenians were interested in the decrees of Athenians received extended treatment in two high-profile cases in the fourth-century courts, that against the decree of Aristokrates (Dem. 23; cf. D94) and that against Leptines' law abolishing *ateleia* (Dem. 20): in both cases, the speaker's argument hinged on the idea that other Greeks were paying attention to Athenian decrees. In the speech *Against Aristokrates*, which argues against the proposal to grant protection to Charidemos, a Euboian mercenary who fought on behalf of the Thracian king Kersobleptes (see D94), Demosthenes reveals a number of distinct Athenian assumptions about the wider significance of their decrees. On the one hand, he appeals to the *polis*-patriotism of the audience and their concerns for Athens' status abroad when he claims that the standard of legislation he is challenging is lower than that of the people of Aigina, Megara and Oreos (23.211–12): the assumption he makes is that the Athenians care about how their decrees measure up to those of other states.[13] Other elements of his case are dependent upon the idea that Athenian decrees were

---

11 This is the view of Trevett 1996a of the sources of the historical references in Aristotle's *Rhetoric.*
12 For discussion of this as a rhetorical trope, see Serafim 2017: 55–6; cf. Hunt 2010: 212.
13 For a similar criticism, that the Athenians are currently passing decrees of an equivalent quality to those of the Corinthians or Megarians, see Hypereides, *Against Diondas* 20 Horváth.

indeed taken seriously by leaders of other Greek states. This is the implication at the point when he talks about the effect of an Athenian decree upon the rebellious Thracian aristocrat Miltokythes (D71):

> And so that you may not be quite surprised to hear that decrees made in Athens have such great power (τὰ παρ' ὑμῖν ψηφίσματα τηλικαύτην ἔχει δύναμιν), I shall remind you of something that happened in the past that you all know. After the revolt of Miltokythes against Kotys, when the war had already lasted a considerable time, when Ergophilos had been superseded, and Autokles was on the point of sailing to take command, a decree was proposed here in such terms (ἐγράφη τι παρ' ὑμῶν ψήφισμα τοιοῦτον) that Miltokythes withdrew in alarm, supposing that you were not well disposed towards him, and Kotys gained possession of the Sacred Mountain and its treasures. (Dem. 23.104)

The example he picks here, that of Miltokythes stepping down from his revolt at the prospect of an Athenian decree, suggests the assumption that Athenian decrees possess so much clout that they will deter a foreign potentiate from behaving against the interests of the Athenians. Demosthenes makes arguments also on the grounds of the far-reaching consequences of the decree of Aristokrates that he is challenging: he suggests at 23.123 that if the award to Charidemos is maintained, then other leaders in the area, like Bianor or Athenodoros, would expect the same treatment; further on in the same speech he suggests that the immunity bestowed on Charidemos would essentially put the world at the mercy of his patron Kersobleptes, claiming that this is 'precisely the effect of that decree' (23.140).

Demosthenes proposes another line of reasoning which envisages the reaction of an external audience: this is the suggestion, at 23.105, that if the Athenians do not annul Aristokrates' decree, 'the kings and their commanders will be immensely discouraged, viewing themselves as slighted and will imagine that your favour is inclining towards Kersobleptes', and they might at a later date refuse help when the Athenians ask for it. This argument suggests not that other leaders care about Athenian decrees because they threaten them but rather because they value Athenian favour. Elsewhere, Demosthenes contrasted those honorands who he claimed desired Athenian citizenship for the personal advantages rather than out of an admiration for Athenian character and customs (Dem. 23.126), arguing that the Athenians ought to be on guard against the former category (23.127–8).

Honorific awards are the type of decrees that most frequently arise in discussions of non-Athenian audiences in the decree-intensive rhetoric of Demosthenes speeches 20 and 23. The Athenians in particular appear to have used the system of granting by decree honorific rewards as a way of securing and extending the goodwill of those communities, leaders and traders who had access to raw materials, in particular grain.[14] Indeed, institutional praise of virtuous behaviour, a common political transaction among fourth-century Greek states, was a practice that clearly exuded inter-*polis* transferable value.[15] As Hagemajer Allen argues with reference to the publication and physical form of honorific decrees, cultural and political differences between the Athenian community and non-Greeks did not, for the most part, have a significant impact upon the values of honorific exchange that went on between them;[16] accordingly, it follows that the honorific values by the Athenians would have, in all likelihood, been esteemed also by non-Athenian Greeks.

Expressions of the idea that there is an overseas audience of Athenian honorific decrees loom large in Demosthenes' speech attacking Leptines' law abolishing awards of *ateleia* to foreign benefactors. Demosthenes challenged the proposal on the basis of a claim that this legislation would effectively annul honorific decrees that the Athenians had passed for their benefactors. One of the scenarios he offered was that, by upholding Leptines' legislation, the Athenians would incur shame on the grounds that, whereas the Chians let their rewards for Chabrias stand despite the fact that he attacked them as an enemy, the Athenians would have revoked rewards for such an honorand even though he had done nothing against them (20.81).[17] Underscoring his argument was the view that Athenian honorific decrees illustrate the generosity of their people, pointing to those for Leukon set up at Piraeus, in the Bosporos and at Hieron (Dem. 20.36–7 (= D39 T2); cf. 42, 54, 86); inscribed Athenian decrees have the effect, he argued, of ensuring that Athenian honorands suffered no harm when they were alive and also stood as evidence 'to those who wish to do us good' of how many *euergetai* the Athenians had given returns to (Dem. 20.64). Demosthenes, therefore, points to awards which had been set up specifically at those places where those individuals whose involvement in the grain-trade might have been encouraged to be generous to the Athenians;[18] as Lambert suggests, it is plausible that the Athenians were advertising not only the trading

---

14 Engen 2010; Moreno 2007.

15 This is already well established for the Hellenistic world: see Hellenistic period, see Massar 2006; Ma 2003.

16 Hagemajer Allen 2003.

17 Moreover, in the speech *Against Aristokrates* Demosthenes claims that a decree for Charidemos, a brutal mercenary commander employed by a Thracian autocrat, would give the Athenians a bad reputation (23.138)

18 Cf. the suggestion of RO p. 324, that the setting up of *IG* II³ 1 298 (= RO 64), the inscribed honours for Spartokos and his brothers, was set up at the Piraeus 'to impress men arriving from the Bosporos'.

privileges that they had granted to the kings of the Bosporos but also those which had been granted to them by the Bosporan kingdom.[19]

In the speech *Against Leptines*, Demosthenes offers an interesting thought-experiment by envisaging what would happen were Leptines' law to be upheld and the exemptions bestowed upon Athens' benefactors were withdrawn: it would lead them to reverse the favours that they bestow on the Athenians (Dem. 20.34). Moreover, given that any honours that the Athenians might award in the future would be rendered untrustworthy (Dem. 20.120, 124), the city would appear to deceive its benefactors (134–5), and its system of established reciprocal trust would be destroyed. Accordingly, Leptines' law would leave behind it a shameful legacy of illegality, and would cause the Athenians to lose the goodwill of foreigners who act with *philotimia* towards the Athenians (20.155). Central, therefore, to Demosthenes' argument against Leptines is the assumption that Athenian awards of exemption matter to Athens' benefactors, and they are the motivation for their acts of euergetism.

The arguments reviewed so far suggest that Athenian speakers supposed their Athenian audiences would share the view that other Greeks would react in some way to their decrees both because they feared Athenian military power and because they valued Athenian honorific capital.[20] There exist also epigraphical indications of the Athenians aspiring to a non-Athenian audience for their decrees: relevant here are the statements of hortatory intention which emerge in Athenian decrees, as Lambert has observed, from the middle of the fourth century. In 330/29, for instance, the Athenians praised the grain-merchant Herakleides of Salamis with a crown, 'so that others may also show love of honour, knowing that the Council honours and crowns those who show love of honour'(IG II³ 1 367 lines 64–6): in this case and others, the epigraphically expressed aim was to encourage not only Herakleides, but also other grain-merchants to behave in a way which would earn them honours;[21] what lay behind this sentiment was an assumption that there was an audience of these decrees which included foreign grain-dealers hungry for honours.

Epigraphical expression of related sentiments can be found in rather different circumstances too: a citizenship decree for Peisitheides of Delos, probably

---

19 Lambert 2018: 36.

20 Other speeches indicating the centrality of the decree-system to Greek diplomacy include the diplomatic exchanges recorded in the letters and decrees between Philip and the Athenians referred to in Demosthenes 18.163–8.

21 See Lambert 2011a: 194 and 2011b: 181–2. For a detailed study of hortatory clauses and their implications, see now Miller (2016: 393), suggesting a primarily Athenian audience for such claims, arguing that they aimed to encourage Athenians to emulate the deeds of both other Athenians and non-Athenians.

a long-standing partisan of Athenian interests who had come to Athens (*IG* II³ 1 452 lines 35-7) in the 340s to flee anti-Athenian sentiment on Delos,[22] contains the statement that the award was made 'so that everyone might see that the Athenian people repays great favours to those who are its benefactors and maintain their good will towards the people' ('ὅ]π[ως ἃ]ν εἰδῶσιν ἅπαντες ὅτι ὁ δῆμος [ὁ Ἀ]θηναίων ἀποδίδωσιν χάριτας με[γ]άλας τοῖς εὐεργετοῦσιν ἑαυτὸ[ν] καὶ διαμένουσιν ἐπὶ τῆς εὐνοία[ς] τοῦ δήμου': *IG* II³ 1 452 lines 11–16);[23] in this case, the subject of the verb εἰδῶσιν, the anticipated audience – ἅπαντες – would surely suggest that it was aimed at an audience including non-Athenians. The Athenians expressed the belief that other communities would pay attention to the honours granted by the people, and that they had the potential to inspire a reaction from those communities in terms of euergetic behaviour. Viewed in this way, the decree seems to encourage a wide audience to maintain long-standing pro-Athenian policies. But the fact that the decree for Peisitheides was to be set up at Athens on the acropolis (lines 28–9) and nowhere else suggests that the potential audience of this decree did not consist of the Delian's countrymen back in their home community, some of whom were hostile to his and Athenian interests at the time. A clue to its intended audience lies in the fact that the decree contains clauses threatening anyone who kills Peisitheides or any city which harbours his killers (lines 31–5) and grants him a subsistence allowance of one drachma per day while he is unable to return to Delos; such clauses, it is possible, were written up for the benefit and reassurance of the honorand. Other Athenian honorands, especially *proxenoi*, may well have taken reassurance from pledges made in Athenian decrees about protecting them from injustice.[24]

Before we turn to assessing the degree to which the audiences that the Athenians envisaged were real, it is worth raising two final points. The first is to observe that Athenian decrees were discussed as if they were a transaction through which the image specifically of the Athenian *demos* was projected; the reputation of individual politicians beyond Athens was a consideration not enunciated in Athenian decrees;[25] it is highly likely, however,

---

22 Osborne 1974: 175–84 places it in the 330s. See also Tuplin 2005 on its implications for anti-Athenian sentiment in Delos in the 340s.

23 cf. *IG* II³ 1 306 A lines 13–15; cf. 400 lines 7–10, 378 lines 17–20. For further comparable clauses see Hedrick 1999: 414–15 and Sickinger 2009; for discussion of their significance, see Lambert 2011a.

24 For other examples of honorands granted protection against injustice, see Henry 1983: 171–6.

25 Other speeches offer the possibility of prospective admiration, with, for instance, the appeal that a particular verdict will raise the moral rating of Athens among its allies (Lys. 14.12–13; Lycurg. 1.14; cf. And. 1.140).

that some ambitious politicians like Demosthenes (with interests in Thebes (D162) and the Cimmerian Bosporos (D227), Androtion (with interests in the Cimmerian Bosporos: *IG* II³ 1 297), Aristophon (with interests in the island of Keos: see D66); and Demades (with interests in the Hellespont–Black Sea area and Euboia) would have deployed the proposal of decrees as a way of securing private political and/or commercial links with communities and prominent individuals beyond Attica.[26] Naturally, such links were presented by their opponents as if they endangered the interest of the city (e.g. Aeschin, 2.141; Din. 1.41–3). The second point is one already made, which is the possibility that, over time, politicians felt gradually less confident of the high prominence of contemporary Athenian decrees among non-Athenians.[27] In the aftermath of the Peace of Philokrates, the Second Athenian Confederacy was in terminal decline.[28] By the 340s, therefore, it was no longer the case that every state was in thrall to the decrees of the Athenians: the absence of evidence for inscribed bilateral alliances between Athens and other communities in the aftermath of the battle at Chaironeia is indicative of the Athenians' falling stock.[29]

The feeling of insecurity of the Athenians in the late fourth century about their interstate profile is reflected in expressions of concern that decrees of the *demos* are doing damage to the image of the Athenians. Both Demosthenes and Aeschines suggest that the other has managed to lower the interstate reputation of Athens in their contributions to disreputable decrees: Demosthenes claimed at 19.291 that, owing to Aeschines' machinations, the Peace of Philokrates turned out as shameful to, rather than equitable for, the Athenians; moreover, at Aeschines 3.76, he says that a decree of Demosthenes (= BD 5; cf. D126), in its flattery, makes the city look ridiculous (*katagelaston*).[30] A more direct indication of at least the perception of an interstate audience of Athenian decrees can

---

26 For Demosthenes' links with Thebes, see Trevett 1999 and Mack 2015: 114-15, cf. Harris 1995: 199 note 15; for his links with the Bosporan kings, see Moreno 2007: 166-7, 220-2, 252-6. Moreno (2007: 175-7, 269-75) suggests close ties between Androtion and Polyeuktos, proposers of a decree for the Bosporan kings (*IG* II³ 1 297), and the honorands, On Demades' associations, see Gabrielsen 2015; cf. Mitchell 1997: 212-13. For other close ties between proposers and non-Athenian honorands, see Lambert 2018: 197-9. Mitchell (1997: 90-110) offers an overview of classical-period Athenian magisterial appointments of individuals with links to other communities.

27 See Chapter 1.4 and 2.5.2 on [Dem.] 12.9 above.

28 Dreher 1995: 287-92.

29 Lambert 2012a: 377-86; for the view (against Lambert) that the inscribed version of the league of Corinth constituted a bilateral alliance between the Athenians and Macedonians (*IG* II³ 1 318 (= RO 76)), see Worthington 2009.

30 The claim that a decision might make a city look ridiculous (*katagelaston*) is also deployed in by Socrates in his defence: Pl. *Ap.* 35a–b.

be found in a speech of Aeschines, who suggests in his *Against Ktesiphon* (3.227) that by seeking rewards in the shape of honours, Demosthenes was making Athens an object of ridicule in all the cities in Greece, and this is what led him to launch his *graphe paranomon* against Ktesiphon's decree.

As the power of Philip emerged over the course of the late 350s and 340s, the Athenians expressed concern that the changing balance of power was having an impact on the prominence of their decrees. One feeling enunciated was that Philip was able to remain aloof from the decisions of the Athenians, so much so that he denied knowledge of a proposed amendment to the Peace of Philokrates (Dem. 7.18–19 = D140). It is well established that one of the important themes in the *First Philippic* – and in Demosthenes' symbouleutic oratory generally – was the idea that Athens' decrees were empty and that Athens' military behaviour failed to live up to the expectations of its decrees:[31] indeed, Demosthenes (4.45) in the *First Philippic* went as far as warning the people that when they send out a general with an empty decree (*psephisma kenon*), they were mocked by their enemies while their allies were frightened. There was also a feeling that decrees of the assembly were doing the Athenians themselves damage, as Demosthenes claims that they actually provoked Philip to march out to Elateia (18.168). Hegesippos claimed that the Peace of Philokrates undermined Athenian interests at Amphipolis, which were themselves based upon past decrees ([Dem.] 7.25 = D140 T2). A different kind of reaction was that of Hypereides (*Against Diondas* 6 Horváth), who joked that Philip pressured the Athenians to grant proxeny-awards to those who launched attacks against them on his behalf:[32] we get the sense that the Athenians have a growing feeling that their powerlessness was being increasingly reflected in their decree-making tendencies.

At a time of political instability, it is, therefore, possible to detect Athenian insecurity about the potential reaction to their decrees. Athenian orators, it seems, cared particularly about what Philip thought about their decrees because he was such a political and military threat to their own position in the Greek world. What seems to be emerging is that the level and type of interest of prospective non-Athenian audiences of Athenian decrees was deeply contingent on the inter-community power dynamics of the era. Indeed, as already noted (Chapter 1.4 above), the increasingly compromised position of Athenian foreign policy over the course of the fourth century meant that by the period after Chaironeia, the Athenians scarcely appeared to have made alliances with other

---

31 Mader 2006.
32 The same insecurity emerges in the spurious letter of Philip to the Athenian council and *demos*, preserved as number 12 in the corpus of Demosthenic speeches: see Chapter 2.4.2 above.

communities, and instead used honorific transactions mostly for individual foreigners as the most important lever of foreign policy (Chapter 3.4.1 above).[33]

So far, I have brought together evidence that the Athenians made claims that their decrees were of interest to non-Athenian audiences. At this point I turn from the perceptions to the practicalities. Which groups of non-Athenians were interested in Athenian decrees? How, if at all, were Athenian political decisions and in particular the activities of the Athenian assembly disseminated across the Greek world? What resistance was there to the provisions sent out in decrees?

4.3 Non-Athenian Audiences of Athenian Decrees

4.3.1 Non-Athenians with Interests in Athenian Decrees

While non-Athenians were largely excluded from the decision-making process at the Athenian assembly (cf. Lys. 13.73), in a city where decisions were made by the people assembled in the open air, it is likely that news of Athenian decrees would have spread quickly among Athenians and non-Athenians concerned with them.[34] In informal contexts, individual Athenians would have spoken about Athenian decrees in different forms of social interaction, just as Theophrastos describes his Boorish man talking to his hired labourers about matters that had arisen at the assembly (*Characters*, 4.3).[35]

The physical proximity of non-Athenians to Athenian institutional activity would have led to the dissemination of information about Athenian decrees. Apollodoros' citation of a law requiring the *prytaneis* to set out ballot boxes and allocate ballots to the people when citizenship awards were being decided 'before the foreigners (*xenoi*) come in and the barriers have been removed' ([Dem.] 59.90) suggests that the presence of non-Athenians around the edges of the assembly was presumed normal. One might envisage that non-Athenian bystanders took interest also in judicial disputes taking place in the Athenian agora: Aeschines, for instance, reminded his audience that gathered at the courts were individuals (those 'standing around': *periestekotes*) from other Greek communities who had come to find out about whether the Athenians know how to make good laws, to judge between the good and the not good, if

---

33 Lambert 2018: 93-13.
34 For the view that it was impossible for the assembly to entrust top-secret discussions to the council or to ambassadors: Ste Croix 1963: 116-17, but this is no longer widely-accepted: see the discussion at D79 Commentary.
35 For interaction and social circulation of knowledge between Athenians and non-Athenians in the agora at Athens, see now Sobak 2015.

they know how to honour good men, and if they are able to punish those who put the city to shame (Aeschin. 1.117–18).[36] Aeschines' claim is one that chimes with the familiar rhetoric of Athenian superiority in deliberation (see Chapter 4.2 above); other allusions, such as his claim at the trial about the crowning of Demosthenes that there were more foreigners present than for any trial in living memory (3.56), suggest the plausibility of the claim that foreigners took an interest in the outcome of Athenian public debates about decrees.[37] But once again we must remember that these claims about the presence of non-Athenians are politically loaded ones which were brought out with a view to impressing upon the audience the wider significance of the cases under discussion.

Knowledge of Athenian decrees would have disseminated among non-Athenians who were the recipients of Athenian honours, those involved in treaties with the Athenians, or those on the receiving end of acts of hostility delivered by the decrees of the Athenian assembly. Non-citizens, including metics and other visitors to Athens, were frequently involved in litigation in the Athenian courts, and on such occasions they would have been exposed to arguments about Athenian decrees: the metic Athenogenes, defendant in a private lawsuit about a contract concerning the purchase of three slaves and a perfume business, would have heard his opponent talk about the Athenian assembly's decree making the Troizenians citizens (Hyp. *Athenog.* 31–3 = D175 T1).[38]

One assumes that members of other communities would have taken an interest in Athenian decrees for self-interested reasons. Sensitive military decisions would have been of interest to Athens' enemies: Aineias Tacticus, in his advice to communities about how to survive under a siege (*Poliorketika*), takes it almost for granted that, at a time of crisis, decisions of an assembly would be leaked to an enemy (9.2–3), perhaps owing to the presence of foreigners in the city (10.9). There are literary testimonia which suggest that information was disseminated in this way in Athens:[39] Xenophon reports, for instance, that

---

36 *Periestekotes*: see Lanni 1997.

37 For further claims about the significance to non-Athenian audiences of the jury's verdict in public trials, see Pl. *Ap.* 35a–b, Hyp. *Dem.* col. 22; Lys 12.35). In such contexts foreigners would have heard the decrees and other political transactions of Athens discussed. Foreigners were probably in the audience of the *epitaphioi logoi*: Thuc. 2.36.4.

38 At the same time it is worth observing that decrees do not appear normally to have been used as evidence in speeches relevant to maritime suits, probably because they were viewed largely as irrelevant to the litigants and the disputes between traders. On the significance of ideas about relevance to such speeches, see Lanni 2006: 149–74.

39 In the fifth century, Thucydides' account suggests that the generals were cautious of putting a crucial decision to the vote lest its result were communicated to enemy forces (Thuc. 7.48, 50–1). On political intelligence, see Starr 1974; on the role of *proxenoi* in passing on information, see Gerolymatos 1986.

Demotion's advice in the assembly for the Athenians to check the power of Corinth was disclosed to the Corinthians with the consequence that 'they sent at once sufficiently strong forces of their own men to all places garrisoned by the Athenians and told them they could go away, as they had no further need of garrisons' (*Hell.* 7.4.4). [40]

Present at Athens were groups of non-Athenians at particular points who felt, for reasons of personal or community self-interest, a serious interest in Athenian decrees, and this feeling must have been particularly strong among groups of non-Athenian residents in Attica. Exiles or refugees – such as those Boiotians or Phokians who were present in Athens in 343 (Aeschin. 2.142–3) or the Olynthians who had been granted the right to stay in Athens in 348/7 (D120) – would have made up interested audiences of decrees, as would those individuals who aspired towards receiving refuge at Athens. Astykrates, an exile from Delphi, is known to have successfully appealed to the council for its help (*IG* II² 109 of 363/2 lines 8–10).[41] The award of granting priority access to non-Athenian honorands to the Athenian assembly after the treatment of sacred business, known, for instance, in the honours written up for loyal Samians in 403/2 (RO 2 lines 72–3; cf. *IG* II² 107 lines 15–16; 212 lines 55–7) strongly suggests that some non-Athenians would have valued highly the possibility of access to the Athenian decree-making body in times of political necessity.

Those who had settled and been accepted as metics in Athens, often for the purposes of pursuing business interests, would also have had an interest in Athenian decrees. This is demonstrated in the text of a decree which in 333/2 granted the Kitian merchants at Athens the right to acquire land for the foundation of a temple of Aphrodite (RO 91 = *IG* II³ 1 337). This thought-provoking document was found at Piraeus, but the fact that it lacks a publication clause leads Lambert to suggest that the inscribed version of the decree was written up by the Kitians as a way of demonstrating to passers-by that they had legitimate permission to establish this sanctuary.[42] One audience of the decree, therefore, consisted of those Kitians at Athens who were granted this privilege; if Lambert is right about the Kitians being the creators of the inscribed version, it seems that they envisaged a further interested audience in the decree: they had the

---

40 [Plu.] *X Or.* 845d suggests that there were individuals who would report to Philip the public speeches of Demosthenes.

41 On those who sought refuge at Athens in the fourth century, and aid to deserving refugees as an Athenian characteristic, see Gray 2015: 297–8. For other appeals by resident exiles to the Athenian council and assembly for privileges, see Gray 2015: 316 with note 144; for their participation in multilateral alliances of the Athenians, see Gray 2015: 217–18.

42 Lambert 2018: 39.

document written up in order to justify their establishment of a sanctuary in front of a yet wider group of Athenians and non-Athenians who saw the inscription.

4.3.2 Foreign Ambassadors

Another audience interested in prospective Athenian decrees – and in persuading the Athenian *demos* to enact them – were those foreign ambassadors who made appeals to the council or who were present at the assembly at the time of the enactment of decrees: Xenophon, for instance, describes a meeting of the assembly at Athens in 369 with the Spartans at which were present Spartan and Phleiasian ambassadors (Xen. *Hell.* 7.1.1–14) and which resulted in the assembly decreeing an alliance with the Spartans (D56). Aeschines (2.58) says that embassies from other communities were awarded the right of addressing the assembly by a decision of the council.[43] A clue to the interest that such visitors to Athens had in the decrees of the *demos* lies in the references within inscribed texts to requests for alliances and honours reportedly made by visiting ambassadors; these references crop up in a range of decrees across the fourth century, several of which are relevant to the entrance of members to the Second Athenian Confederacy.[44] Two such inscriptions (*IG* II² 42 (= RO 23) of 378/7 and *IG* II² 96 (= RO 24) of 375/4) record decrees which enrol communities into the alliance: they make respective reference to what was said by 'the Methymnaians' and what was said by the envoys of Kerkyra, Akarnania and Kephellenia in front of the Athenian council (lines 3–4; lines 5–6, respectively): in this context, it is generally assumed that these envoys had appealed to the Athenians to enrol their communities in the new alliance. But an example from 362/1 gives pause for thought. In that year, Thessalian envoys appear to have offered an alliance to the Athenians, though the text of the inscription suggests that the Athenians had actually approached the Thessalians previously (*IG* II² 116 (= RO 44) lines 8–9, 34–6): this is a useful reminder of the fact that, sometimes, on occasions when alliances appear to have been initiated by the appeal

---

43 On the rhetoric of ambassadors, see Rubinstein 2016, emphasising their stress on the collective ethos of the communities they represented. Another group of non-Athenians given access to the assembly consists of those who made supplications: see Gottesman 2014: 102–10: on one occasion in 346/5 Dioskourides of Abdera was taken under the protection of the Athenian generals and archons and was honoured with food at the *prytaneion*: *IG* II³ 1 302 lines 18–22. One may suppose that their rhetoric would have placed more emphasis on self-representing the character and situation of the suppliants themselves.

44 *IG* II² 17, 42, 44, 109, 116, 118, 141 (= RO 21); *IG* II³ 1 295, 298, 299, 302, 304, 313, 316.

of foreign ambassadors to the Athenians, there may have in fact been a longer series of prior negotiations in the background.[45]

On a number of occasions, the Athenians granted honours by decree in response to things said by the envoys of other communities: the two decrees for Mytilene of 369/8 and 368/7, inscribed on the same *stele* (*IG* II² 107 = RO 31), form a good example. The chronologically earlier of the two decrees consists of Kallistratos' proposal answering a question posed by some envoys from Mytilene ('ἀποκρίνασ]θαι δὲ τοῖς πρέσβεσι[ν τοῖς ἥκουσιν ...]': lines 40–1) with an account of Athenian foreign policy; the later decree praises the Mytileneans and grants them access to the Athenian assembly with priority, and responds to 'the things about which the ambassadors from Lesbos say on coming here' ('[π]ερὶ ὧν οἱ πρέσβεις οἱ ἐκ Λέσβου ἥκοντ[ες] λέ[γο]υσιν': lines 8–9). The inscribed honours for Spartokos and his brothers (*IG* II³ 1 298 (= RO 64) lines 9–11) recount both a letter which the Kings sent to the Athenians and the report of their ambassadors. Other mid fourth-century honorific decrees passed for those who are recorded as having made statements to the Athenians include that for the satrap Orontes (*IG* II³ 1 295 of 349/8 lines 2–3); the honours for Dioskourides of Abydos and his brothers of 346/5 (who had made supplication to the council so that they would hear him: *IG* II³ 1 302 lines 7–9, 23–4), those for the Tenedians of 340/39 (*IG* II³ 1 313 line 6) and for the Akarnanians of 338/7 (*IG* II³ 1 316 line 6).

4.3.3 Appeals for Inscriptions?

Accordingly, it seems that some Athenian decrees were made either as a result of ongoing discussions between Athens and other states or at the specific request of outsiders. We can introduce a further refinement to this impression: on at least one occasion, the inscribed texts of an honorific decree appears to have been set up on stone up in response to a request of non-Athenians:[46] the inscription, bearing two decrees of the 340s, honouring the Pellanians of the Peloponnese (*IG* II³ 1 304) is restored to this effect:

> [... concerning what the] envoys of th[e Pellanians have report]ed, be it resolv[ed by [the People: as regards the dec]ree which Aristo- ... [proposed about the] Pellanians [last year? = 345/4], [the secretary of the C]ouncil shall inscribe on a [stone *stele* and sta]nd it on the acr[opolis]. (lines 5–11)

---

45 In the same era, an alliance was made with the Chalkidians on the basis of 'the things that the Chalkidians say' (*IG* II² 44 lines 7–8 of 378/7). Other treaties made in response to an appeal from foreign envoys include that with the Mytileneans of 347/6 (*IG* II³ 1 299 lines 6–7).

46 For another possible example, see *IG* II² 77, discussed in Chapter 3.3.3 above.

AUDIENCES BEYOND ATHENIAN CITIZENS

What we can ascertain here is that the decrees (both the original honorific decree of 345/4 honouring them and that of 344/3 setting out the decision to write up the honours on stone and to praise the ambassadors) were written up on stone in response to the Pellanians' appeal.[47] But what precisely the Pellanians were asking for is unknowable: it could be that they were asking for something more than honours; accordingly, it might be right to think of this writing up of the decree as, in Lambert's words, 'a consolation prize, in effect the outcome of a failed negotiation' (cf. lines 9–20).[48] But, as Lambert points out, the fact that the act of inscription appears to have been endowed with a hortatory intention '[so that the city of the] Pellan[ians shall continue always to be friendly] and we[ll-disposed to the Athen]ian [people]' (lines 16–18) suggests that the setting up of an inscription was something that the honorands found desirable (or at least that the Athenians thought they would find inspiring).

Another instance where the text of a decree might suggest that a foreigner was particularly interested in having a decree written up on stone was that for Sthorys of Thasos (probably a seer, who was rewarded for his services before the battle of Knidos)[49] of 394/3. This is a difficult but interesting text consisting of 8 fragments,[50] containing two decrees: a main decree (lines 24–40) describing the honours granted and specifying that the decree is to be written up on his own account is preceded by a supplementary decree (lines 6–12), perhaps a clarification,[51] of the Council which specifies that the *stele* is to be set up in two locations:

> Supplementary decree, lines 6–12:
> Since his ancestors were [*proxenoi* and] benefactors of the city of the Athenians, and the Athenians made [him] a citizen, the secretary of the Council [shall inscribe] ... what the People have voted [about Sthorys on two stone *stelai*] on the acropolis and in the Python; and to invite Sthorys also to dinner tomorrow in the city hall.

> Main decree, lines 33–6:
> ... and the secretary of the Council shall inscribe this decree at the expense of Sthorys, on a stone *stele* where the previous decrees for him have been inscribed.

The supplementary decree, therefore, clarified the two places of publication of the citizenship decree for Sthorys – at both the Python (probably that in

---

47 Osborne 2012: 47 note 85 makes the rather unconvincing claim that this demonstrates that all decrees were normally inscribed.
48 Lambert 2011a: 199 = Lambert 2018: 78.
49 See Osborne, 1981–3 D8
50 I have used the text of *Agora* 16.36, and the translation of Attic Inscriptions Online.
51 The view that this is a clarification is a view taken by Osborne, 1981–3 D8 Commentary, but this is a view rejected by Gauthier, *BE* 1996, no. 126 and *REG* 99 (1986) 123.

Athens) and the acropolis: Osborne's suggestion was that the earlier decree granting citizenship did not make this clear, 'since it spoke of only one stele'.[52] The style of the *stele*, with a sunken surface, is reckoned to have been made in a characteristically Thasian shape.[53] It has been suggested that this clarification about the place of publication of the inscription was introduced as a result of Sthorys' own appeal, though this cannot be proven.[54] But the fact that he was asked to pay for his own *stele* may well support the hypothesis that he had a say in where it was set up:[55] perhaps Sthorys was very keen on having his decrees set at a specific location, made in a style familiar to his native community, and was even ready to pay for them.[56]

The evidence, therefore, for non-Athenians making appeals about the setting up of inscriptions is rather thin on the ground. We cannot produce, on the basis of Sthorys' inscription and the Pellanians' appeal, a general hypothesis about the audiences of Athenian decrees: the Thasian's case was exceptional and, moreover, his work as a seer may have given him occasion to have been a regular resident of Athens. The fact that he appears to have borne the responsibility for paying for the inscription of his award (*Ag.* XVI 36 lines 34–5) also makes him exceptional: the provision that an honorand was to pay for the inscription of honours is rare in fourth-century decrees,[57] and better attested in the fifth century, probably when the Athenians reckoned on their ability to force subject-states to fund the imposition of such monuments.[58] The prob-

52 Osborne, 1981–3 D8 p. 46, but noting the objections of Gauthier. For another interpretation, see Mack 2015: 97 note 27, suggesting that the double place of publication was intended to assert the finality of a controversial award.

53 As Osborne, 1981–3, II, p. 48 note 147.

54 Such a hypothesis is reliant on the restoration in a lost section of line 5 of the words 'περὶ δὲ ὧν λέγει Σθόρυς' ('concerning what Sthorys says'), presumably in an appeal to the Athenian council. As Polly Low suggests to me, it is plausible to think that *IG* II² 6, a restoration of a proxeny-decree for some Thasians, was also set up on the initiative of the honorands or their offspring, especially given that the honorand was asked to pay for the inscription.

55 The fact that the honorand of *IG* II² 6, Eurypylos, was asked to provide the expenses of his own re-inscribed proxeny decree in 403/2 (lines 14–16), suggests that he may have requested that it be set up after the restoration of democracy.

56 On occasion, it seems to have been the case that non-Athenian honorands might make a request about the wording of a decree: one interpretation of the rider to the award for Oiniades, which changed his ethnic from 'Skiathos' to 'Palaioskiathos' was that it was proposed at the assembly by a political ally upon his request (*IG* I³ 110 lines 26–31): see ML p. 277, suggesting that 'Oiniades is perhaps a little touchy; he wants to make it clear on the stone that he comes from the old town'; cf. OR p. 517.

57 See, however, *IG* II² 54 lines 4–5 and 130 line 18, where honorands are to pay for the *stele*, and also the treaty *IG* II² 98 line 26 to be funded by the Kephallenians.

58 *IG* I³ 156 line 28; cf. payment for *stelai* by allies who appear to have revolted: on Kolophon: *IG* I³ 37; Chalkis: *IG* I³ 40; Mytilene: *IG* I³ 66; Low 2005: 100–1.

lem we are faced with, however, when hypothesising about the appeals that lay behind these awards, is that the decrees never say anything about what exactly the envoys who had communicated with the Athenians were requesting: that is left to deduction. Once again, therefore, it is important to note that the testimonia that we have looked at are purely Athenian perceptions of non-Athenian audiences.

So far we have discussed a good amount of evidence which demonstrates a range of contexts in which non-Athenians took an interest in Athenian decrees. In the next sections I shall assess the efforts the Athenians made to disseminate information about their decrees among non-Athenians by proclamation (4.3.4) and epigraphical publication (4.3.5).

4.3.4 Proclamation

Already in Chapter 3 above we have discussed the importance of the proclamation of honours in their dissemination among Athenian audiences. On those occasions where proclamation was undertaken at the theatre of Dionysos, we might reasonably accept Demosthenes' view that the aim of such proclamations was to introduce the whole audience – including Athenians and non-Athenians – to emulate the service towards the city undertaken by the honorand (Dem. 18.120–1)[59]. But proclamation was important in the dissemination of news outside the civic institutions of the Athenians.

Other than the informal spreading of information by word of mouth, the primary mode of dissemination of decrees to non-Athenian audiences consisted probably of oral proclamation to a targeted group of non-Athenian magistrates, a council, or an assembly: as Lalonde notes, on the basis of non-Attic evidence, diplomatic decrees or declarations of war would usually be copied down on papyrus or other lightweight material and would have been physically carried to the affected city and read out by heralds, ambassadors or even generals.[60]

---

59 On the legality of this proclamation at the theatre, see the discussion in Chapter 2.2.2.1 and 3.2.1 above.

60 Lalonde, 1971: 77-84. Decrees which contained threats or warnings (Plu. *Per.* 30) would have been taken to the hostile state and proclaimed by herald; treaties were made by an exchange of oaths undertaken by ambassadors: accordingly, envoys would have read the decrees under which they were acting at the community they were visiting (Aeschin. 2.101, 104 = D133 TT 2, 3); generals might also read out decrees, as Paches, the general of 428/7, was required to do to the Mytileneans (Thuc 3.36.3). For the role of heralds in the communication of news beyond the *polis*, see Lewis 1996: 63–8. The use of interstate festivals as centres for the dissemination of news emerges, however, only at the very end of the fourth century: Lewis 1996: 71, 73. On the reading aloud of decrees by ambassadors in the Hellenistic period, see Chaniotis 2013, 2016 and Rubinstein 2013; on the rhetoric of envoys in the classical period, see Rubinstein 2016.

Decrees of the Athenian imperial era that bore implications for other cities appear on occasion to have been disseminated also through oral announcement. In 425/4 the decree re-organising tribute assessments directs that heralds be sent around the regions of the Athenian empire to announce the prescriptions of the decree (OR 153 = ML 69 lines 5–6, 41–2; Kleinias' decree on tribute collection contains comparable provisions (OR 154 = ML 46 lines 26–7)). A similar mode of dissemination is suggested in Aristophanes' parody of Athenian imperial administration which introduces a decree-seller who announces to Peisthetairos the Athenian decree imposing Athenian weights, measures and decrees on the people of Cloud-Cuckoo Land. His mention also of a *stele* – vandalised by Peisthetairos – upon which Athenian decrees were written up (Aristophanes *Birds*, 1037–56) suggests that epigraphic and oral modes of dissemination coincided with one another.[61] It is likely, therefore, that whereas some Athenian decrees of the imperial period might have received a sympathetic audience among pro-Athenian groups (such as the Eteokarpathians recognised as benefactors in *IG* I³ 1454 lines 5–8), others might have given rise to resistance or indifference: the latter response is suggested in Plutarch's account of the Greek states' refusal to toe the line of Pericles' Congress Decree, which arranged for the dispatch of 20 Athenian citizens to the cities of Greece to call upon communities to send representatives to Athens to discuss destroyed Greek sanctuaries, sacrifices owed to the gods, and the questions concerning sea power (Plu. *Per.* 17).[62] In the fifth century, therefore, it is possible to find evidence for Athenian attempts to disseminate their decrees, but the response of the projected audience to them is still hard to discern.

As we have already noted (Chapter 3.2.1 above), in the fourth century too Athenian magistrates could be charged with the job of disseminating news about Athenian decrees beyond Athens: the decree of Philokrates concerning the sacred *orgas* of 352/1 (D107) gave rise to guidelines about delineating the consecrated area on the borderlands between Eleusis and Megarian territory; according to the literary sources (D107 TT 1, 2) the Eleusinian magistrates Lakrateides the hierophant and Hierokleides the *daidouchos* were to mark out the boundary; accordingly, they were effectively charged with the diffusion of the impact of the decree among Athenians and Megarians alike. But on this occasion the nature of the dispute – combined perhaps with the resistance of the Megarians and the reduced clout of the Athenians – meant that the Athenians

---

61 On this passage, see Chapter 5.3.2 below.

62 On this controversial decree, see Meiggs 1972: 512–15; Stadter 1989: 201–4, suggesting that it was genuine.

found it useful to consult the Delphic oracle by means of lottery about the best way forward (*IG* II³ 1 292 lines 23–54).

Epigraphical evidence gives us clear indication that Athenian ambassadors could be sent out with the explicit charge of imposing Athenian decrees on weaker states in this era. An inscribed Athenian decree of the mid fourth century, RO 40, preserves Koresian and Ioulietan responses to an Athenian decree concerning the Athenian regulation of Kean ruddle export. It contains a passage (lines 37–8) which makes it very clear that the decree of the Ioulietans acquiescing with the demands of the Athenians' decree was to be inscribed at the harbour at Ioulis; moreover, that same inscription demonstrates that the Athenians had sent envoys to the cities of Keos to disseminate the Athenian assembly's decree (lines 9–10, 25–6, 39–40). Another inscribed decree of fourth-century Athens that includes arrangements for its own proclamation is RO 35 (= *Ag.* XVI 48), an inscription containing a decree of Kephisodotos of 367/6, declaring that a herald was to go to the Aetolians to demand the release of those that the Trichonians (of south-west Aetolia) had unlawfully imprisoned (lines 14–18). It may well give us insight into a practice of oral information that was widespread, in particular for those decrees which were of ephemeral nature and would not have usually have been set up on stone.[63] Moreover, the inscribed dossier of decrees honouring Herakleides of Salamis (*IG* II³ 1 367) states that the Athenians were to select an envoy to travel to Herakleia to request the return of the honorands' sails and to ask them to refrain from such behaviour in the future (lines 37–41).

In the fourth century, members of the Athenian naval confederacy affected by directives of Athenian decrees would presumably have been the recipients of information about them: to take one example, Moirokles' decree (D207 = Dem. 58.53) of the mid fourth century stated that Athens' allies were to be persuaded to organise a stronghold against the pirates, presumably through a *dogma* of their *synedrion*.[64] It is plausible that the Athenian decree would have been communicated to the organisers of the meeting of the *synedrion* and disseminated

---

63 Rhodes and Osborne suggest, for epigraphical reasons, that the decision to write up the inscription may have been taken by officials of the Eleusinion rather than the Athenian state: RO p. 173.

64 Cf. also the Peace of Philokrates (= DD 130, 131), which required ratification by the members of the confederation; for exchanges between the *synedrion* of the League and the Athenian council, see Rhodes 1972: 60–1. On the other hand, the allies could introduce proposals to the Athenian council: see, for instance, *IG* II² 112, an inscribed alliance with some Peloponnesian communities, which the allies introduced to the Athenian council on the grounds of things that the Peloponnesians had promised (lines 12–16); cf. *IG* II² 97, specifying that aspects of an Athenian alliance should be carried out according to the *dogma* of the allies (lines 14–15).

on that occasion. At the time of the Peace of Philokrates, an amendment to the agreement said that *synedroi* were to give oaths to Philip's ambassadors which ensured that member-states of the Confederacy were party to the terms of the peace (D131 T1 = Aeschin. 3.73–5). Again, we can reasonably take the view that the *synedrion* of allies was the mechanism that communicated the decisions of the Athenian confederacy to Athens' allies.

Interestingly, however, there is rarely any provision for honorific decrees to be announced at an honorand's home, and it is unclear from Diodorus' description of the honours announced for Philip at Olympias' wedding whether the announcement was made by a herald of Macedonia or of an individual Greek state:

> Not only did individual notables crown him with golden crowns but most of the important cities as well, and among them Athens. As this award was being announced by the herald, he said finally that if anyone plotting against Philip were to flee to Athens for refuge, he would be handed over. (D.S. 16.92.1–2 = D180 T2).

Perhaps it was the case that provision for the announcement of honours to foreigners was left up to the initiative of the honorands themselves: in 403/2 when the Athenians granted proxeny-status to Poses of Samos they inscribed the decree at Athens and the secretary was ordered to give him a document (*biblion*) with the text of the decree (RO 2 lines 61–2); perhaps Poses would have had the decree inscribed back at home on Samos.[65] The literary evidence for announcement of the peoples' decrees outside Athens is rather limited; just occasionally, however, the pronouncement of a decree to other communities was an important part of its substance: the decree of Diophantos (D105 = Dem. 19.86) appears to make arrangements for the announcement abroad of praise and thanksgiving after the defence of Thermopylai; in many senses this was a decree designed to display Athenian piety and to celebrate an act of resistance: announcement would have reinforced the fulfilment of such intentions.

On the occasions when they passed a decree of general significance, the intended non-Athenian audience of a decree may well have been made up of many separate communities, and the Athenians arranged for wide distribution. The limited literary evidence for such dissemination suggests the importance of oral proclamation: according to Diodorus, in 323 the Athenians issued a decree sent round to various cities which said that they should organise in support of *koine eleutheria* for Greece (D.S. 18.10.2–5). Earlier, in 378/7, as Diodorus reports, the Athenians had appealed to cities subject to the Lakedaimonians,

---

65 Lewis 1996: 134.

presumably after they had decided to establish an anti-Spartan alliance which would form the basis of the second Athenian confederacy (DP 20 = D.S. 15.28.2). But as Athenian power dwindled in the second half of the fourth century, and it was increasingly the case that decrees of the Athenian state required negotiation with another party, we see that a decree could sometimes only reach its final form once it had been ratified by another party: one view of this process is offered by Plutarch (*Phoc.* 17.4) who states that the Athenian decree responding to Alexander's request that they hand over certain important politicians was at first cast away in disgust by Alexander, but that he was willing to give it more thought when it was brought by Phokion in person.

There is little, therefore, to suggest that there was any system in place to ensure that decrees of the Athenian *ecclesia* were comprehensively disseminated: the spread of news about decrees was introduced when the Athenians decided that it needed to be done. Past decrees were re-announced to a secondary audience when they were relevant to ambassadorial missions: the significance to diplomatic exchanges of past decrees could be re-iterated in speeches made by Athenian ambassadors: Aeschines (2.109–10) says that Demosthenes, when he was serving as an ambassador at Pella, read out several decrees: Philokrates' decree that Philip be allowed to send ambassadors (D121), his own proposal for safe conduct to the herald and ambassadors (D126), the motion that restricted the people's discussion of peace to certain days (D127 T1), the decree which provided that the people should discuss an alliance (D127 T3), and the motion about assigning the front seats at the Dionysia to Philip's ambassadors (probably a council decree: see D126 and BD 5). From this passage, we might surmise that Demosthenes went to Pella armed with dossiers of decrees for the sake of persuasion or perhaps, if we follow Aeschines' view, appealing to the Macedonians, and it is quite plausible to think that ambassadors on other occasions would have been similarly well equipped.

4.3.5 Epigraphical Dissemination

How far was the epigraphical publication of decrees aimed at audiences of both Athenians and non-Athenians? It may be relevant that there was a tendency for the Athenians to set up decrees at the potentially cosmopolitan spaces of the acropolis and agora: these were locations which might have been visited by non-Athenians without restriction;[66] furthermore, there is no evidence to say

---

66 For the agora as a 'cosmopolitan' place, see Vlassopoulos 2007b and Sobak 2015; most visits to the acropolis would have been during times of festivals; for non-Athenians on the acropolis see Liddel 2003: 80–1 and Lambert 2018: 27–9.

that inscribed decrees were set up on the Pnyx Hill, the seat of the Athenian assembly which, with the exception of supplicants and foreign ambassadors granted permission to visit it, appears to have excluded foreign visitors.[67] At the same time we cannot assume that the publication of decrees at such locations is an indication that they were aimed specifically at an audience of non-Athenians. There is, however, a sub-set of decrees whose places of epigraphical publication suggests that they were indeed aimed at an audience of non-Athenians: the epigraphical evidence attests to 27 Athenian decrees set up outside Athens in the classical and Hellenistic period; of these, eight are fifth-century, and seven are dated to the fourth century.[68] It is perhaps revealing, moreover, that there is, in the classical period, much more evidence for decrees of the Athenian *demos* being set up outside Attica than there is for non-Athenian decrees being set up in Attica: only a handful of non-Athenian decrees are attested to have been set up inside Athens.[69]

On such occasions, the Athenians appear to have ordered that their decrees be set up in locations of cities affected directly by the provisions contained within them, and there appears to have been a variety of motivations for such a decision. When the Athenian *demos* enacted regulations about the imposition of Athenian standards on its imperial subjects, probably in the period 425–415,[70] it appears to have supported the dissemination of information about this decision by ordering that the decree should be set up in front of the mint in the cities of the empire 'for anyone who wishes to scrutinise' (*IG* I^3 1453 section 12). The discovery of fragments of this document (*IG* I^3 1453) of the late fifth century in 9 locations across the Athenian empire suggests that wide physical publication of the decree aimed to support the dissemination of knowledge about it. While certainty about the effectiveness of this intention is impossible,

---

67 Hansen 1987: 87.

68 Liddel 2003: 93 collects the evidence. To this figure we should add RO 17, which appears to be an Athenian decree set up at Erythrai, though one which does not preserve an extant clause relating to its place of publication; see discussion in Chapter 4.3.6 below. See also, on decrees of the Athenians set up in allied states, Low 2005: 100–1.

69 Non-Athenian legislation in Athens: *IG* II^2 1126–37 including decisions of Panhellenic congresses, on which see Sickinger 1999a: 119–21; note in particular *CID* I 10 and RO 40 (an Athenian decree recording the dispatch of ambassadors to Keos, which incorporates parts of three related Kean decrees; see discussion in Chapter 4.3.4 above); Lalonde 1977; for the Chabrias monument from the Athenian agora, bearing records of honours of Greek communities for Chabrias, see *SEG* XIX 204 = *Hesperia* 30 (1961) 74–91. For non-Athenian legislation cited in the lawcourts, see Lys. 1.2; Dem. 20.71 (awards for other states for Konon); Dem. 18.93–4; Aeschin. 2.32, 3.48, 103–5, 123–5; Din. 1.25–8; Hyp. *Ath.* 32–4, and note 8 above.

70 On the dating of the Standards decree probably to the mid 420s at the earliest, see Papazarkadas 2009: 72; OR 155 suggests c. 425–415.

it suggests that the Athenians at least attempted to disseminate news of this imposition to allied states with a view to enforcing the regulation. And it is likely that some allies would have had little choice other than to face up to the implications of Athenian decisions promulgated by decrees of the assembly.[71]

There are other indications that the Athenians in their era of imperial power attempted to disseminate their decrees through epigraphical publication:[72] an Athenian decree praising the Eteokarpathians of the third quarter of the fifth century as euergetists was to be set up both on the Athenian acropolis and at Karpathos in the sanctuary of Apollo (*IG* I³ 1454 lines 34–6); as Low notes,[73] the fact that this relationship is recorded only in an Athenian decree means that the only view we have of this episode is that projected by the Athenians; but the decision to set up the decree on the island of Karpathos at least suggests that this was an account that the Athenians projected at a local audience.

It seems to be the case that in the fourth century too there was some deliberate Athenian dissemination of inscribed versions of their decrees into non-Athenian space. In a context already discussed (Chapter 4.2 above), Demosthenes claimed that both the Athenians and Leukon set up copies of the honorific decree for him (at Bosporos, Hieron and Piraeus: Dem. 20.36), and that this practice would have disseminated awareness of them among non-Athenians with the effect of encouraging foreign benefactors.[74]

Just as the fifth century saw the Athenians imposing their decrees (or bestowing honours) upon their allies as they pleased, so too the strength and influence of the Athenian *polis* in the first half of the fourth century meant that its state decisions had a fundamental impact on other Greek states: on occasion, Athenian legislation potentially affected the political configuration of small communities beyond Attica.[75] We have already seen (Chapter 4.3.4 above) the Ioulietans of Keos acquiescing with the demands of the Athenians that a decree was to be inscribed at the harbour at Ioulis (RO 40). Another indication that the Athenians were still ready to impose their will upon this small community – and did so by way of epigraphical publication – emerges in the

---

71 Cf. Low 2007: 242.

72 For Athenian decrees inscribed outside Athens as an imperialist 'message-driver', see Lambert 2018: 39–41.

73 Low 2007: 249–50.

74 For detailed discussion of Athenian decrees for the Bosporan kings, see Lambert 2018: 34–9, suggesting that the three locations were 'part of a deliberate policy by Athens and the Bosporan rulers to advertise and secure the unusual trading privileges enjoyed by the latter, perhaps with reciprocal advertisement of privileges in the Bosporan kingdom enjoyed by Athens'.

75 Hagermajer Allen 2003: 234–9; Engen 2010.

inscription of 363/2 which sets out Athenian arrangements for the same city of Ioulis: the decree sets out details of the Athenian settlement after a revolt against the Athenians on the island (*IG* II² 111 = RO 39 lines 27–46). It gives an account of the return of some Ioulietan exiles who had returned to the city, made war against the Athenians, and overturned *stelai* upon which details of an earlier reconciliation with the Athenians had been written (lines 27–46). Not only does the inscription provide us with a clear indication of an Athenian decree which made the Kean cities swear an oath of allegiance to the Athenians (lines 69–73), but it also informs us that earlier Athenian inscribed arrangements were an object of the wrath of the rebels. The Athenian motivation for having the inscriptions set up at the sanctuary of Pythian Apollo in Ioulis was presumably to act as a reminder for the Ioulietans to repay what the Athenians were demanding (*IG* II² 111 (= RO 39) lines 19–22). The Kean example is something of an exception: evidence for the Athenians imposing political arrangements through inscriptions on their fourth-century allies is fairly limited.[76]

On one occasion, it seems to be the case that the epigraphical publication of an honorific decree had a practical function. A *stele* of white marble (*IDélos* 88) discovered close to the old Artemision in Delos contains two decrees of Athens of 369/8 and 363/2:[77] one of them honours Pythodoros of Delos, making him *proxenos* for having carried out certain services concerning the finances of the God and the people of Athens; the other decree extends the award to his nephew. A rider to the first decree states that the Athenian council and the generals and the Amphictyons are to make sure that no one harms him (lines 15–20), that the secretary of the (Athenian) council is to have it set up on the (Athenian) acropolis (lines 20–22), that the secretary of the Amphictyons is to write up a copy of the decree at the sanctuary of Apollo at Delos which they (the Amphictyons) are to fund 'from the money taken from those who have been condemned' (lines 22–5): these were probably those enemies of Pythodoros who opposed Athenian interests, perhaps during an outbreak of anti-Athenian sentiment in the mid 370s.[78] It seems likely that the Athenians specified its dual publication to the Delians as a way of asserting the duties of protection for Pythodoros that were implied for both the Athenians and Amphictyons. On this occasion, therefore,

---

76 On Athenian intervention in the affairs of the allied states of the fourth century, see Cargill 1981: 146–88, arguing that it was restrained. For decrees concerning Athenian settlements overseas of the fourth century, see DD 65, 150, 208; *IG* II² 114 = *IG* II² 1613 lines 297–8; *IG* II² 1629 lines 17–21; DPP 52, 63. An inscribed decision of the Second Athenian Confederacy of probably 372 mentions a 'reconciliation' between the Athenian allies and the Parians: RO 29 lines 7–8.

77 Discussion: see Osborne 1974: 170–4.

78 As Plassart 1950: 43 and Osborne 1974: 171; cf. Tuplin 2005: 55.

AUDIENCES BEYOND ATHENIAN CITIZENS

the Athenians appear to have attempted to ensure, through epigraphical publication, that the man who championed their interests was protected even at Delos: while the decree was certainly projected at Delians, it is likely that its setting up at the sanctuary of Apollo was an Athenian, rather than Delian, initiative.

At other points the motivation for the Athenians to set up decrees outside Athens appears to be the aim to ensure that allied communities had access to the details of the obligations implied by bilateral treaties (e.g. *IG* II² 44, a treaty with Chalkis of 378/87; *IG* II² 55 concerning Athens and Aphytis of the second quarter of the fourth century); indeed, we would expect treaties to have been published in each of the participating states on their own initiative (cf. Thuc. 5.47.11). Relevant decrees were set up in new Athenian cleruchies perhaps either to assert the rights or to praise the activity of new settlers[79] or, in the case of the cleruchy on Lemnos, perhaps to assert the piety of the Athenians towards divine matters.[80] Whereas the act of setting up the proxeny-decree at Delos might have been an attempt to prevent the abuse of Pythodoros in his Delian home, and the agreements between Athens and Chalkis and concerning Aphytis might have been of interest to those communities with whom the Athenians were making agreements. It was generally the case that the setting up of Athenian decrees outside Athens was carried out on the initiative of the Athenian assembly and was motivated by Athenian interests. The exception to this pattern dates from a period of relative Athenian weakness: the setting up of an inscribed version of the treaty between the Athenians and Alexander of probably 336 at both Athens and at Pydna in the sanctuary of Athena (*IG* II³ 1 443 line 13) can be explained probably by the strategic significance of that city for relations between the Greeks and Macedonians.[81] Given that this was probably the inscribed Athenian version of a multilateral treaty between Alexander and the Greek cities, it is likely that its erection at Pydna was the choice of Alexander.

4.3.6 Resistance to Athenian Decrees

The Athenians declared wars and launched military expeditions against their enemies by way of decree. We have noted already (Chapter 4.2 above) that one Athenian insecurity about their decrees was the fear that Philip could remain

---

79 *IG* II³ 1 387 is a decree concerning the cleruchy at Sestos, which was set up both at Athens on the acropolis and at Sestos, perhaps in its *agora* (lines 7–8).

80 *IG* II² 1222 (cf. *SEG* XLV 126) lines 5–7, set up at Hephaistia: 'so that it might be clear to everyone [that the Athenian *demos* at Hephaistia] is pious with respect to divine matters' ('ὅπως ἂν ἅπασιν φανερὸ[ς ἦι ὁ δῆμος ὁ Ἀθηναίων τῶν ἐν Ἡφαιστίαι] εὐσεβῶν τὰ πρὸς τοὺς [θεούς]').

81 Voutiras 1998: 115–16.

aloof from their decisions. Among some communities, therefore, news of Athenian decrees might have been received with indifference; in others with outright hostility (as they were among the revolting Ioulietans of Keos: RO 39: see Chapter 4.3.5 above); yet in other cases with trepidation.[82] Moreover, within many Greek communities, there was probably considerable debate about the extent to which adherence to the decrees and politics of the Athenians mattered, and such debates would have surfaced in full relief in situations of civil strife. Such a situation of conflict is one that emerges in an inscription from Erythrai containing an Athenian decree concerning the Erythraians, dated to the period before the King's Peace, which was published in 1976 (RO 17). This decree of the Athenian assembly (lines 2–3) prohibits reconciliation of outsiders with 'those within the city' without the consent of the Athenian people (lines 5–7); exiles were not to be restored, meanwhile, without the consent of the Erythraian people (lines 7–11). It appears from the decree that a group of Erythraians had appealed to the Athenians to prevent their city being handed over 'to the barbarians' (as it was after the King's Peace), and the inscribed document represents the reply of the Athenians (lines 11–16) which the pro-Athenians may well have had set up at a part of Erythrai which was friendly to them; this decision is one which foreshadows the Hellenistic practice of smaller cities inscribing edicts of more powerful political entities as a way of securing their own position (e.g. *IK Erythrai* 30 and 31).[83] One envisages, though, that the Erythraian exiles would have been of a faction who opposed Athenian intervention and the imposition of their decrees.[84]

Even among those city factions which drew upon Athenian support, there is evidence for uneasiness about reliance upon, or adherence to, the provisions of the Athenian people's decrees. This much is suggested in the rhetoric of Pelopidas, according to Plutarch's account (*Pel.* 7.1–2), during the Theban resistance to the Spartan occupation of the Kadmeia after winter 382: Pelopidas incited fervour among the Theban exiles in Athens by berating them for 'hanging upon the decrees of the Athenians' ('ἐκκρέμασθαι τῶν Ἀθήνησι ψηφισμάτων'). Ironically, however, he also is reported to have persuaded them – by pointing to the Athenian example of Thrasyboulos (on the basis that he returned

---

82 One anticipates such a reaction of the Megarians or Phleiasians to the Athenian decrees launching expeditions against them: see DD 111, 112.

83 I am grateful to Polly Low for this suggestion. For inscribed letters of Hellenistic kings set up by small communities, see Welles 1934.

84 On this decree see now Matthaiou 2017, taking the view that those locked outside the city were oligarchs and that the opposing democrats supported by the Athenians held the city; for the alternative view, that those 'within the city' (in lines 5–7) are dissidents with whom the Athenians are refusing to reconcile, see RO p. 77.

from Thebes to liberate Athenians) – they should return from Athens to liberate Thebes. Accordingly, Pelopidas appears to have resented the power of the Athenians' decrees but still acknowledged that their political history provided examples worthy of emulation.

4.4 Conclusion

The Athenian orators (Chapter 4.2 above) were probably right in claiming that there was a significant audience of non-Athenians interested in the decrees of the Athenians; however, it appears to have been the case that this audience consisted of specific self-interested groups rather than – as some Athenians liked to imagine – a general audience of those who were enthusiastic about Athenian *charis* for its own sake: attractions such as partisan political alliance and protection appear to have been key factors in the generation of interest in decrees. Those non-Athenians with an interest in Athenian decrees would have consisted of non-Athenians at Athens (Chapter 4.3.1 above), ambassadors visiting the city (Chapter 4.3.2 above) and those who perceived that an honorific decree, sometimes even in an inscribed version (Chapter 4.3.3 above), was a desideratum. Beyond those factions who advocated Athenian intervention on their behalf or who were directed by the provisions of Athenian decrees we have, so far, come across little by way of straightforward evidence that there was a general, broad, audience of non-Athenians hanging on the words of decrees. Athenian perceptions, however, can be revealing: the claim that Athenian decrees were of profound interest to other political communities suggests that the Athenian *demos* and its politicians sometimes possessed an inflated view of the significance of their own enactments, a belief that at times appears out of balance with the declining inter-community significance of the decisions of the fourth-century Athenians.

It is clear that there were many situations in which we can conceive of non-Athenian communities, or sub-sections of those communities, caring about Athenian decrees, but these were essentially contingent on numerous factors, most prominently that group's political and economic relationship to Athens, and the extent of their reliance upon the political favours of the Athenians. The fact that it is possible to observe some Athenian influence in inscribed documentary style from the classical period supports the idea that there were non-Athenians who paid close attention to the language of Athenian decrees.[85] However, dissemination of knowledge about Athenian decrees was uneven and

---

85 The study of Athenian influence on non-Athenian documentary styles is under-developed, but see Rhodes with Lewis 1997: 550–60; Liddel 2010.

unsystematic and reliant in part upon social interaction: while there is a fair amount of evidence to suggest that the Athenians did make some attempts to disseminate their decrees to other communities by way of proclamation and the dispatch of ambassadors (4.3.4), their reception would have been unpredictable. Again we note (as we did in Chapter 3 above) that epigraphical publication was not the primary means of dissemination of Athenian decrees, but the act of inscription either coincided with oral proclamation or was something that added extra value to the power of the decree and its representation of Athenian interests (4.3.5). It was argued at the end of this chapter that not all news of Athenian decrees would have been welcome: some non-Athenians would have been hostile to the content of Athenian decrees (4.3.6).

At this point, it is time to extend our exploration into further audiences of Athenian decrees over time as we consider the reception and representation of Athenian decrees in extant literary texts more broadly (Chapter 5 below) and the implications for our understanding of the circulation of perceptions about decrees of the Athenian *demos*.

5

Literary Representations of Athenian Decrees

5.1 Introduction

Beyond epigraphical publication, the chief indication of the esteem in which decrees were held – among a different but sometimes overlapping audience – is their profile in literary texts. The theme of this volume so far, drawing heavily upon the Attic orators, has been the representation of decrees of the fourth-century assembly among Athenian and non-Athenian contemporaries. But at this point we turn to explore the engagement of other literary authors with Athenian decrees and the ideas associated with them. In this chapter, I will investigate the deployment, representation and fabrication of decrees in Greek literature more broadly, raising the possibility that, while the processes of decree-making and of discussing decrees were institutional practices with political and social significance, they had also a wider cultural presence that can be detected in literary references to them.

Before we begin assessing the ways in which decrees surface in different genres, it may be worth recalling three critiques of the democratic system that surfaced in the fourth century. First, there is the argument familiar to Demosthenes' symbouleutic oratory, that Athenian power is undermined by the gap between the ambitiousness and hostile intent of the decrees of the people and the Athenians' inability to live up to them in terms of military activity (Dem. 3.4–6).[1] This is a view that suggests the potential inanity and even vanity of Athenian decrees. A related criticism was that decrees were the tool of self-interested politicians (Dem. 23.201). The other critique was associated with Greek worries about it as a tool of an extreme, unbridled democracy.[2] As we observed earlier (Chapter 1.3 above), Aristotle expressed, at points, misgivings about the role of the decree in democracy, suggesting that the situation in which a decree can over-ride the law was symptomatic of mob-rule and equivalent to anarchy. Aristotle's views reflect a wider anxiety about the assembly making critical and uncensored decisions and imposing

---

1 A phenomenon identified and discussed by Mader 2006; see Chapter 2.5.2 above.
2 For discussion of criticisms of Athenian democratic procedure – which never extended to criticism of the system as a whole – see Harris 2006b; Saxonhouse 1996: 128, 131.

189

its unbridled will on the wider community. His fear about the power of the decree as a tool of a rampant assembly is a criticism largely unattested in fourth-century oratory. At this point, I turn to assess the degree to which such views about the decree surface in other writings, and aim to establish a clearer sense of the themes that recur in the wider representation of the decree in Greek literature. My analysis takes a genre-based approach, beginning with writing about the past (historiography and biography: 5.2), proceeding into classical drama (5.3), the work of antiquarians and travel-writers (5.4), later rhetorical treatises (5.5), and ending with the representation of decrees in post-Hellenistic satirical literature (5.6). The reception of fourth-century decrees in later texts was determined by broader attitudes towards both documents and political activity.

As a way of engaging with classical attitudes to decrees more broadly, it seems appropriate over the course of this final chapter not to restrict discussion to those decrees that constitute the core of fourth-century material, but to introduce also some consideration of decrees of earlier periods, in particular those of the fifth century.

5.2 Historiography

5.2.1 Histories of the Greek World

At the most general level, historians of the classical era made reference to decrees in their description of historical narrative. At points, they were conceptualised simply as decisions of a sovereign body: even though he made some use of inscriptions as a way of elaborating his narrative,[3] Herodotus had little reason to discuss decrees of the Athenians in any depth. However, in his account of the result of Aristagoras of Miletos' appeal for support in 499, he says that the Athenians were persuaded (ἀναπεισθέντες) by him and voted (ἐψηφίσαντο) to send twenty ships to assist the Ionians (5.97.3): these twenty ships, famously, turned out to be the beginning of misfortunes for Greeks and non-Greeks; the author's reference to the Athenian voting process, therefore, underlines the Athenians' responsibility for the decision. At other points Herodotus represents the Athenians as being persuaded by prominent individuals to take certain decisions, but nothing is made of their institutional details: the Athenian resolution to abandon Attica was presented as the initiative of Themistocles (Hdt. 7.143.1–2; cf. 7.144.1–3). In this case, though, Herodotus had little interest in the intricacies of Athenian decree-making institutions.

---

3 West 1985.

LITERARY REPRESENTATIONS OF DECREES

Another Athenian decision that he discusses was the *bouleutes* Lykidas' proposal (*gnome*) at the council that the Athenians should put to vote at the assembly Mardonios' appeal that they surrender: in Herodotus' account this angered a mob which proceeded to stone to death the proposer, his wife, and children (Hdt. 9.5.2–3). As Gottesman observes, Herodotus described how a proposal at the council might be presented as giving rise to an expression of public anger;[4] Lycurgus' account of the same episode, on the other hand, offers an account of a public lynching of the proposer undertaken by order of a decree of the council and appears to have been supported by his reading of a documentary version of the decree (Lycurg. 1.122). Lycurgus' version of the events reveals the orator's own interests both in the formal role of the council as a punitive body and also the importance of the decree as the catalyst of all forms of public action. Herodotus, on the other hand, expressed less interest in Athenian political institutions or the formally imposed details of Athenian decrees and closer engagement with the public reaction to them.[5]

Compared to Herodotus, Thucydides paid more attention to Athenian decision-making institutions, though accurate constitutional description is rarely a priority in his account. His truest explanation (*alethestate prophasis*) of the origins of the Peloponnesian War underplayed the significance of the Athenian decrees concerning the Megarians.[6] However, his report of diplomatic exchanges in the build-up to war, recounting the Athenian refusal to accede to the Spartan demand that they revoke the Megarian decree (Thuc. 1.139.1–2), highlights the role of the decisions of the Athenian assembly in the outbreak of hostilities. Elsewhere, Thucydides drew extensively upon documentary material pertaining to decrees in his history, in particular at the end of book 4 and in book 5, where he shows familiarity with, and quoted verbatim, a number of treaties (Thuc. 4.118; 5.18–19, 47, 77, 79). Describing the year's truce of 424/3, Thucydides cited words which, to an Athenian, may have resembled the enactment formula of a decree of the Spartans and their allies (4.118.4)[7] and a fuller version of that of the Athenians (4.118.11)[8]; in doing so, he was perhaps the first historian to record such close attention to the language of a decree: this

---

4 Gottesman 2014: 64–5.
5 For another occasion in which a fourth-century source describes a decree relating to an incident known from Herodotus' work, see Introduction note 7 above.
6 Ste Croix 1972: 225–89. As Pelling (2000: 103-11) notes, he may have underplayed the significance of Athenian decrees against the Megarians as a way of contradicting the belief that the war was Pericles' making.
7 'τάδε δὲ ἔδοξε Λακεδαιμονίοις καὶ τοῖς ἄλλοις ξυμμάχοις …'
8 'ἔδοξεν τῷ δήμῳ. Ἀκαμαντὶς ἐπρυτάνευε, Φαίνιππος ἐγραμμάτευε, Νικιάδης ἐπεστάτει. Λάχης εἶπε, τύχῃ ἀγαθῇ τῇ Ἀθηναίων …'

underlined one aspect of the accuracy of reference to which he was aspiring in the writing of his history; at the same time the familiarity and immediacy of decree-style language contributed to the authority of his account. There is, however, modern scholarly debate about whether he drew upon documentary Peloponnesian versions of these agreements, or somehow had access, even as an exile, to documents kept at Athens.[9] It is highly unlikely that he carried out autopsy of inscribed versions.[10] Yet as recent scholarship has suggested, the appearance of documents in his text might be seen as underlining the high status of the written word in Thucydides' text,[11] his high regard for the inscribed text in his view of history,[12] and also in his attempt to reconstruct the historical past with accuracy.[13] Thucydides drew upon and presented documentary evidence for interstate treaties for the narrative of his history: he had a high regard for their status as sources of historical detail and as records of political decisions and even statements of political intent.

But the decree, as a political transaction, played another important role in Thucydides' account of Athenian history. In those documentary citations already mentioned, Thucydides was interested primarily in their status as treaties rather than as decrees of the Athenians; yet his language at 4.118.11–14, where he cites verbatim the Athenian decree by which it was enacted that the Athenians would accept the truce and would deliberate on the peace, is striking. In his account of this decision, Thucydides appears to omit the role of the Athenian council: he uses the enactment formula 'the *demos* decided' (ἔδοξεν τῷ δήμῳ) rather than the usual 'the council and *demos* decided' (ἔδοξεν τῇ βουλῇ καὶ τῷ δήμῳ).[14] Hornblower has argued that, here and elsewhere, Thucydides has purposefully under-reported the role of the Athenian council in his history; this was tantamount to depicting the Athenians as impulsively

---

9 Athenian sources: Hornblower 2008: 110–11; Peloponnesian sources: Lane Fox 2010. For discussion of the treaty documents and possible explanations for Thucydides' inclusion of them, see Hornblower 1996: 113–19. For the view that Thucydides made use of the inscribed versions of the Thirty Years Peace at 5.18 (where he does not record enactment formulae), see Wallace 2003. For the view (not widely accepted), however, that the documents are editorial insertions, see Müller 1997.

10 Even on an occasion where there is explicit reference to an inscription, Thucydides says nothing about autopsy of a stone inscription, and may have followed others' accounts: Thuc. 5.47.11; 6.54.7

11 Steiner 1994: 65–7; Smarzyk 2006.

12 Moles 1999.

13 For the view that Thucydides' inclusion of documents is important to historical narrative, see Bearzot 2003.

14 Gomme (1956: 602–3), however, thought that the text of Thucydides was defective at this point.

LITERARY REPRESENTATIONS OF DECREES

making decisions on the basis of discussion only at the assembly.[15] An alternative view would be that here and elsewhere Thucydides is focusing upon the decisions of the assembly as the body that held the final vote on what was to be undertaken by way of decree; in that sense, he was simply reflecting the reality of the fifth-century situation. Yet one might detect that Thucydides – as part of his wider scepticism about democracy – takes a view of decrees as the pernicious manifestation of the whims of an irrational but powerful *demos*,[16] not least in his account of the decrees that led to the Sicilian expedition:

> The Athenians called an assembly and listened to the further reports of the Egestans and their own ambassadors. The reports, which were untrue, were encouraging on the subject of money which was said to be ready in large quantities in the common treasury and in the temples. Accordingly, they voted (ἐψηφίσαντο) to send 60 ships to Sicily and appointed as commanders with full powers Alcibiades son of Cleinias, Nicias the son of Nikeratos and Lamachos the son of Xenophanes. (Thuc. 6.8.2)

According to Thucydides, the Egestan ambassadors were given an audience at the assembly, which in response made a decree to send out the expedition with Alcibiades: there was in Thucydides' account no place for the council to hear the ambassadors, as it undoubtedly would have done, nor for it to make preparations for the agenda of the assembly or preliminary decrees (*probouleumata*) for it to discuss.[17] Thucydides' view is clearly that the people ought to take responsibility for their impetuosity in sending out the expedition, even if this is a blame that – once the expedition had ended in disaster for them – they place on the shoulders of their politicians 'as though they themselves had not voted for the expedition' (Thuc. 8.1.1: ὥσπερ οὐκ αὐτοὶ ψηφισάμενοι). In the Mytilenean debate, on the other hand, Cleon introduced a criticism of the impermanency of the Athenian decision-making process: 'worst of all is if nothing is established as secure concerning the things about which we have resolved' (Thuc. 3.37.3: πάντων δὲ δεινότατον εἰ βέβαιον ἡμῖν μηδὲν καθεστήξει ὧν ἂν δόξῃ πέρι); he then dismisses politics as a performance in which politicians are *agonistai* (competitors: 3.37.4).[18] In this way Thucydides identifies

---

15 See Hornblower 2008: 133–7 and Hornblower 2009.

16 See Foster 2017: 117 for the observation that 'Thucydides frequently shows the assembly's policies were emotional rather than reasonable (as at 2.59.2, 2.65.3–4, 4.27–29.1)'.

17 The immediacy of the Athenians' vote to send the expedition is re-iterated at Thuc. 6.26.1, where the assembly immediately voted full powers to the generals after hearing Alcibiades' speech.

18 On the debate about liability for Athenian decrees in Thucydides' account of the Mytilenean debate, see Chapter 1.6 above. For Diodorus' account of the debate in terms of his account of Athenian democratic characteristics, see Holton 2018: 17884.

194   DECREES OF FOURTH-CENTURY ATHENS

a problem with democracy that manifests itself in the way that decrees were formed.

The implication that the decree was a tool of the impulsive *demos* prone to abuse by self-interested politicians is one which surfaces also in Xenophon's *Hellenika*, despite the fact that he made comparatively less use of documents than did Thucydides.[19] In particular, it is a view which appears during the course of his detailed account of the debate about the treatment of the generals after the battle of Arginusae in 406: according to Xenophon, Kallixenos was persuaded by Theramenes to propose an extraordinary decree (referred to as a *gnome*, but which amounts to a *probouleuma* of the council) against the generals; it was cited verbatim:

> They (sc. Theramenes and his men) persuaded Kallixenos to make an accusation against the generals in the council. At that point they called a meeting of the assembly, in which the council brought in the following proposal of Kallixenos (ἡ βουλὴ εἰσήνεγκε τὴν ἑαυτῆς γνώμην Καλλιξένου): 'That, since in the previous assembly the speeches in accusation of the generals and the speeches of the generals in their own defence have been heard, the Athenians shall now vote by tribes; each tribe shall place votes in two urns; that in each tribe a herald shall proclaim that whoever judges the generals guilty for not picking up the men who won the victory in the sea battle shall cast his vote in the first urn, and whoever judges them not guilty shall cast his vote in the second urn; and, if they are adjudged guilty, they shall be punished with death and handed over to the Eleven, and their property shall be confiscated to the state and the tenth part of it shall belong to the goddess.' (Xen. *Hell.* 1.7.8–10)

This proposal, which gave rise to the decree of the assembly on the treatment of the generals, is quoted at a crucial point in Xenophon's account of the story: its substance was integral to the unfolding of the drama and judgement on its nature was offered in his account of the reaction of those who opposed it. Not only was the proposal to try the generals by a single vote considered controversial (1.7.26, 34) and its effect damaging for the Athenians, but it was probably also, as its opponent at the assembly Euryptolemos maintained, illegal (1.7.12, 16–33, esp. 25).[20] Kallixenos rallied the people against those councillors who objected to it (1.7.12–14). Xenophon's account of those who thought that

19 Bearzot, exploring Xenophon's use of documents, counts 34 decrees (of which 19 are Athenian) mentioned in the *Hellenika*: see Bearzot 2014: 97–9. On Xenophon's use of the language of Athenian decrees in describing decisions reached by groups of soldiers, see Hornblower 2004 and Papazarkadas 2014: 236 note 69.

20 One possibility is that Kallixenos' proposal contradicted a law that no one should be put to death without trial: Harris 2013a: 342; for the view that it violated not a prescribed law, but a 'deeper constraint', see Carawan 2015: 176; for the perspective that it violated not a law but the principle that a fair trial should precede a verdict, see Ostwald 1986: 431–45.

LITERARY REPRESENTATIONS OF DECREES

it was a terrible thing to prevent the people from doing as they pleased (1.7.12) implies that he judged democratic power to have spiralled out of control at this point.[21] In Xenophon's account, Euryptolemos' speech against the proposal, in which he appealed to the decree of Kannonos[22] against those who wrong the Athenian people (1.7.20), initially won favour, but was subject to an objection under oath by Menekles (1.7.34); a second vote upheld Kallixenos' original proposal, and the generals were condemned and executed. This irreversible decision was, famously, greatly regretted by the Athenians (Pl. *Ap.* 32b and D.S. 13.103.1); their capriciousness was expressed in another decree presented by Xenophon:

> And not much later the Athenians changed their mind and voted (ἐψηφίσαντο) that whoever had deceived the people should have complaints lodged against them, and they should provide sureties until they came up for judgement, and one of these to be Kallixenos. (Xen. *Hell.* 1.7.35)

Xenophon's story of the aftermath of Arginusae, therefore, might be read as another damning indictment of the capricious way that the Athenian people wielded power by way of the decree. The theme was captured by later writers too: the rhetorician Aelius Aristides, writing in the second century AD, appears to have fabricated a story about an indictment of a proposal of Kallixenos – not preserved in the accounts of Xenophon or Diodorus – that the generals not be buried within Attica:[23] this account offers an example of the way in which Athenian debates about decrees caught the imagination of later rhetorical writers who wished to illustrate rhetorical themes with pseudo-historical decrees, to which I shall return (see Chapter 5.5 below).

Xenophon's account of the Arginusae debate is the part of his history which offers closest engagement with the process of a debate about a decree. If viewed as part of the author's characterisation of the behaviour of the Athenian *demos* at the end of the Peloponnesian War, it perhaps also owes something to the historiographical theme that associated Athenian decrees of the fifth century with their readiness to impose extreme punishments on those opposed to them: the punishments of the Skionians and Melians were made famous by Thucydides

---

21 Flaig (2013) assesses the debate as an example of a clash between the constitutional powers of the *boule* and those of the assembly. For analysis as an indication of Xenophon's attitude towards the effectiveness of democratic leadership, see Ferrario 2017: 69.

22 On the decree of Kannonos (date unknown), see Chapter 5.4 below and Develin 1989: 114. The phrase ἔγραψε γνώμην at 1.6.34 arguably suggests that Euryptolemos' speech constituted a proposed decree.

23 Stephens 1983, discussing Aelius Aristides IV.736.5–20 Walz = Behr 1981–6 volume 1 Appendix 1 fragment 111. On Aelius' interest in decrees, see Chapter 5.4.1 with note 119 below. Not burying the generals did, however, appear in a counter-proposal of Euryptolemos: Xen. *Hell.* 1.7.22.

(Thuc. 5.32.1, 116.4); less well known, however, is the decree – opposed by one man, Adeimantos – to cut off the hands of captives (Xen. *Hell.* 2.1.31–2);[24] and the view of a later historian was that the Athenians had utterly destroyed subject cities by their decrees (D.S. 13.30.7). While these constitute individual examples of critical accounts of disastrous decree-making and enforcement, rather than general reflections on the decree as a transaction, it seems reasonable to say that these classical historians, at the end of the fifth century, illustrated reservations about both the power of the people through its decrees and their deployment in the hands of demagogues.

When we look at Xenophon's narrative of the post-Euclidian period, decrees do not seem to be deployed to illustrate the capriciousness of the *demos*, and they are outlined in less negative contexts: we might point, for instance, to his mention of the decree concerning alliance with the Thebans (D20 T2, where Thrasyboulos makes reference to a decree as an answer to the envoys), the one recalling the Athenians from Aegina (D37), or that recalling Timotheos (D48 T1). His account of the Athenian decision to send armed assistance to the Spartans (D55 T1) and make an alliance (D55 TT 1–3) in 369/8 is one which features a reference to debate and decree-making at the assembly. In these instances, Xenophon – as did Herodotus – made mention of decrees as a way of informing the reader how the Athenians initiated developments significant to elements of his narrative. But it is worth commenting that there are key moments in his work where Xenophon describes a decision elsewhere attested as a decree without explicit reference to it as a *psephisma*: the ratification of the reconciliation and amnesty in 403/2 is one such example (D1 T4), as are the honours for Evagoras (D33 T1).[25] On such occasions Xenophon is not interested in making anything of the institutional basis of such developments. We might note also some oddities of Xenophon's description of decrees: at *Hellenika* 6.5.33, he describes a decision of the Athenian council according to which they decided to hold an assembly to discuss the activity of the Spartans (Xen. *Hell.* 6.5.33: 'ἐκκλησίαν ἐποίησαν κατὰ δόγμα βουλῆς'). Oddly, this decree of the council is described as a 'decision' (*dogma*), a term which was reserved usually for descriptions of decisions of the Athenian Confederacy (Aeschin. 2.32–3)[26] or of the Spartan allies (Xen. *Hell.* 5.4.37) or the Theban allies (Xen. *Hell.* 7.3.11), though it is rarely used by other authors to refer to decrees of the Athenians (e.g. Harpokration, s.v.

---

24 For discussion, and the suggestion that it was a proposal of Philokles, see Papazarkadas 2014: 236–7. See also Suda, s.v. Λειπόναυτα' (Adler *lambda*, 384).

25 For further possible examples, see DPP 2, 4, 8, 12, 13, 14, 15, 16, 17, 26, 28, 30, 33, 37, 38.

26 Dreher 1995: 117–18.

"Ἑρμῆς ὁ πρὸς τῆι πυλίδι' (= *FGrH* 328 F40a = D22)).[27] Such technical inaccuracy appears probably in contexts where precise detail was less important than it was in, for instance, the crucial narrative about the decree concerning the generals at Arginusae.

In the fourth-century sections of his work, it seems, therefore, that while decisions made by the Athenians – usually in the form of decrees – do have bearing upon his history, Xenophon has little interest in exploring the rhetorical potential of attestations about decrees. His focus on military and diplomatic detail means that he has no reason to make mention of those honorific decrees for generals which loom large in oratory: moreover, the military successes of Chabrias and Timotheos gain a lesser profile in the work of Xenophon than they do in the orators; Iphikrates has a much higher profile, but not always a positive reputation.[28] Otherwise, in the fourth-century sections of his work, there does not seem to be any significant patterning to his deployment of decrees, nor were they used to blacken the image of Athenian democracy.

Historians of the Hellenistic period were often critical of the workings of Athenian democracy: the narrative that said that the Athenians descended into ochlocracy in the period after that of virtuous leaders such as Themistocles is a familiar one from Polybius and others (Plyb. 6.57.1–9 with Champion 2018). Diodorus' account of the mobilisation decree proposing war against Macedon of summer 323, echoing the sentiments of his source Hieronymos of Kardia, is presented by the author as carried through by irresponsible orators embodying the impulse (*horme*) of the people against their own interests, having failed to learn lessons from the past (D.S. 18.10.2–4 = D199); the passages prepare the reader for the defeat of the Athenians in the Lamian war (D.S. 18.18.6). On occasion, however, decrees could be held up by Hellenistic historians as examples of the virtues of the Athenian *demos*: Diodorus, for instance, represented the Athenian decision to return land taken up by cleruchs to its former owners as an act of kindness (*philanthropia*) which won them goodwill (*eunoia*) among the Greeks (D.S. 15.29.7–8 = D45 T1); he characterised the Athenian *demos* as magnanimous (*megalopsychos*) and humane (*philanthropos*) on the basis of its decision to assist the Spartans in their hour of need in 369/8 (D.S. 15.63.2 = D55 T3); it was driven by *sympatheia* for the fate of its politicians when they were demanded by Alexander in 335/4 (D.S. 17.5.3 = D186 T1): these three passages

---

27 *Dogma* is not normally used to describe a decree of the Athenian *ecclesia*: on another occasion it is used to describe an enactment of a meeting of delegates making the peace of 370: Xen. *Hell.* 6.5.2. On the use of the term, see Hansen 1983: 277 note 32, suggesting that it could be used in a rather vaguer sense to apply to a decision made by the Athenians.

28 See, for instance, Xenophon's criticisms of Iphikrates at *Hell.* 6.5.51.

contribute to his wider portrayal of Athenian *philanthropia* (cf. Gray 2013 and Holton 2018); elsewhere he presented the Athenian decision to send forces to Thebes when the Spartans had occupied the Kadmeia in 379/8 as a repayment of the Theban *euergesia* (presumably the hosting of Athenian democratic refugees during the civil war of 404/3: D.S.15.26.1 = D44 T2); the decision to end the Social War was described as a manifestation of cautiousness (D.S. 16.22.2 = D90 T1).

5.2.2 Local Histories

It seems that in classical histories, which take as their subject the interstate affairs of the Greeks, there was awareness of, and even concern about, the power of the decree as a tool of the unrestrained *demos* in the fifth century; at least in the work of Xenophon there is a certain ambivalence about the Athenian decrees of the fourth century. As we now turn to the evidence of local histories which concern Attica, are these patterns repeated?

A good starting point is a not a history of the Athenians or their *polis*, but a work which combines a history of their constitution (*politieia*) with an account of its workings. This is the work attributed to Aristotle, bearing the title *Athenaion Politeia* (*Constitution of the Athenians*). Among the earliest 'decrees' attested in Athenian literary sources is the mention by the author of this work of a decree granting a bodyguard to Pisistratus before his first seizure of power in 561/0, a proposal described, perhaps anachronistically,[29] as the proposal of a certain Aristion (Ἀριστίωνος γράψαντος τὴν γνώμην: *Ath. Pol* 14.1). The citation illustrated Pisistratus' popularity and persuasive abilities, but emphasises the relevance of proposals of individual citizens to his accrual of power.

As Rhodes has observed, however, the author of the *Athenaion Politeia* can reasonably be said to have drawn mostly on earlier narrative accounts (such as historians of Attica) or on accounts of Athenian *nomoi* or even the *nomoi* themselves,[30] but not *psephismata*. This is certainly the case for the bulk of this work, which consists of a history of constitutional development and the description of political arrangements; but there are times, when describing

---

29 Rhodes 1981: 200. It is possible that the account of the appointment of a bodyguard by decree was an innovation of [Aristotle]: cf. Hdt. 1.59.4 with discussion in the Introduction note 7.

30 Rhodes 1981: 20–5, 35–7, 516; Rhodes 2014: 25–32; on the laws in the *Ath. Pol*, see Rhodes 2004b. For the Aristotelian works on constitutions, see Aristotle fragments. 381-603 Rose; for Theophrastos' work on laws, see Szegedy-Maszak 1981, Keaney 1993; Diogenes Laertius 5.80.1 refers to a work of Demetrios of Phaleron with the title *On Laws* and another *On Lawmaking at Athens*: see *BNJ* 228 T1 and FF 4–7.

historical developments with significance for political change, that he mentions, or even quotes, documentary decrees: the decree (which, according to Rhodes' interpretation of the text, was proposed at the assembly by Melobios but was authored by Pythodoros in the council)[31] to reform the constitution in 412/1 is quoted verbatim, and the author also introduces details about Kleitophon's amendment (*Ath. Pol.* 29.1–3); the abolition of democracy in 404 was itself associated with a decree proposed by Drakontides of Aphidna (*Ath. Pol.* 34.3; cf. D.S. 14.3; *Lys.* 12.73). Moving into the period of the aftermath of the restoration of democracy, [Aristotle] mentions the indictment of Thrasyboulos' decree which proposed to offer citizenship to those who had joined in with the citizens' return from Piraeus, adding that 'some of whom [the honorands] were manifestly slaves' (D5 T1), and describes Archinos' indictment of the decree as unconstitutional as an example of his exemplary political behaviour ('καὶ δοκεῖ τοῦτό τε πολιτεύσασθαι καλῶς Ἀρχῖνος'). What is apparent here from such a selection is the role played by decrees in some of the ultimately traumatic constitutional changes experienced by the Athenians: the author of this work appears to hold a largely negative view of the *demos*' deployment of them and their impact upon Athenian history. The fact that the decrees described in the *Athenaion Politeia* are high-profile ones which tend to surface within broader narratives suggests that the author of this work encountered them within the pre-existing accounts – preserved orally or in written form – that he drew upon in his research.

Other historians of Attica (authors of *Atthides* – the Atthidographers – fragments of whose works are quoted by later writers) do seem to have reported decrees in their texts, and appear to have done so as part of their accounts of events in which they were interested; their accounts of Athenian decrees, in contrast to those of the Attic orators, appear not to have assumed that their audience would have prior familiarity with the developments they described.[32] The fourth-century Philochoros' mention of names of the eponymous archon (*FGrH*328 F155 = D107 T1 and D111 T2; *FGrH*328 F56a = D164) and exact details of forces dispatched by decree (*FGrH*328 FF 49–51 = D113 T2) suggests that documentary sources – perhaps an archival version – may have been the ultimate source of information for Philochoros

---

31 Rhodes 1981: 370, 375.

32 See D27 T1, D107 TT 1–2, D111 T2, D113 T2, D159 T3, D164 T1. For discussion of the nature of the Atthidographers and their (diverse) interests, see Rhodes 1990. For the observation that local historians framed their discussions of Athenian decrees through third-person narratives, see Tober 2017: 470–1 referring to DD 27 and 107. On the other hand, orators sometimes referred to decrees in the second person as the resolutions of their audience: see, for instance D23 T2, D41 T1, D46 T2 and Chapter 1.5.1 above.

(and other Atthidographers, including Androtion). However, it is clear that their accounts of how decrees were put into action, such as those concerning the dispute with the Megarians over the sacred *orgas*, drew upon non-documentary narratives (*FGrH*328 F155 = D107 T1 and D111 T2; *FGrH*324 F30 = D107 T2).[33] The appearance of decrees in these fragments enables only limited insight into the Atthidographers' deployment of decrees,[34] and the most we can say is that they contributed factual elements to their information about narrative history and succoured their interest in it.

Thus far, we can conclude that accounts of decrees were used to illustrate the ways in which the Athenian *demos* initiated or at least attempted to initiate political developments; in Thucydides' and Xenophon's accounts of fifth-century developments there is some representation of them as the manifestations of a capricious *demos*, but this view does not extend into their analysis of post-Euclidian decrees. At this point we turn to analysing the deployment of decrees in the other main non-fictional genre that dealt with the past: biography.

5.2.3 Biography

The value of the decree in the reconstruction of accounts of human lives is one that comes across very clearly in Attic oratory. This is demonstrated, as we have already noted (Chapter 2.3 above), by Demosthenes in his speech in defence of Ktesiphon's crown, where he points not only to the decrees honouring him, but also those that he had proposed, in the account of his political performance. In biography, decrees that are elsewhere represented as illustrations of the wider policies of the Athenian *demos* can be re-framed as part of the character-portrayal of their proposer.[35] The Cisalpine biographer Cornelius Nepos (*Thrasybulus* 3.2 = D1 T7), for instance, represents the decree of the amnesty and reconciliation of 403/2 as an example of a noble (*praeclarus*) deed of Thrasyboulos whereas the Greek sources (see D1, T2) present it as an indication of the Athenian people's moderation towards their enemies.[36]

---

33 For the possibility of Philochoros and Androtion's drawing upon documents for dates, and information like troop numbers or names of commanders, see Harding 1994: 36–7, 44 with *FGrH* 328 F49–51; *FGrH* 324 F30. For the view that the Atthidographers drew upon documentary sources but supplemented details from other accounts, see Rhodes 2006: 23.

34 Even the Oxyrhynchos Historian's account of the dispatch of a message to Milon: *Hell. Oxy.* 6.1–3 (= DP 4) after a trireme had been sent out without the permission of the people seems relatively free of value judgement.

35 On the development of biographical detail in Greek epigraphy and decrees, see Rosen 1987; Low 2016.

36 On the presentation of the amnesty decree as exemplifying Athenian attitudes, see discussion in Chapter 1.5.1 above.

Haake has illustrated in great detail some of the ways in which Hellenistic biographers were ready to deploy decrees, but also to modify their terms or even fabricate them. Versions of honorific decrees or substantive proposals were employed by biographers writing in apologetic modes to refute criticism of individuals. Of particular relevance to our understanding of Athenian decrees of the period 403/2–323/2 is what purports to be an Athenian honorific decree for Aristotle, transmitted in the work of the Arabic scholar Ibn Abī Usaybiʿa, the text of which suggests that it was granted to the honorand as a return for the benefits that he had bestowed upon the Athenians and in particular his entreaties to Philip on their behalf. Haake has demonstrated, however, that this decree is a forgery, created probably by a Greek Hellenistic tradition upon which the Arabic scholar drew: it was fabricated originally probably as part of a biographical defence of Aristotle.[37] Moreover, as Haake shows, not only did the Hellenistic-era scholar fabricate a decree for Aristotle, but he also developed a story about it, which aimed to blacken the reputation of Aristotle's opponents.[38] The forger claimed that one of them, Himeraios, physically destroyed the decree, before it was restored by one of his allies. Accordingly, it was not just the content of the decree but the story about it that underscored the likely apologetic contribution of the decree in its original context.

Aristotle was not the only philosopher whose character was defended through the fabrication of a decree: Diogenes Laertius in his *Lives of the Eminent Philosophers* (7.10–12) quoted what purported to be a third-century Athenian honorific decree for Zeno at length. The quotation not only reinforced Diogenes' assertion that the Athenians held him in high honour (7.6), but its content also contributes to the biographical description of Zeno. The biographer uses an honorific decree to make a terse and accurate statement about the life and character of an individual while also giving insight into his reception by a community. As Haake has argued, it is likely that this decree was drawn upon by the Stoic Apollonios of Tyre, a Hellenistic apologist for Zeno, who aimed to defend his character by demonstrating that his reputation was high among his contemporaries.[39] In this case, Haake acknowledges the possibility that Apollonios drew upon the evidence of an original Athenian decree for Zeno, but elaborated its content imaginatively.[40]

---

37 Haake 2006: 332–6, 348–50; cf. 2007: 55–60.
38 Haake 2013: 94–6.
39 Haake 2013: 98–100.
40 Haake 2004. For fabricated decrees which emerged in biographical accounts, see Chapter 5.4.2 below with Appendix 2 X1, 2, 8, 9, 11.

As an author who was well versed in both antiquities and the work of some Hellenistic biographers, Plutarch was well aware of the potential that decrees offered, noting in the introduction to his *Life of Nicias* that both decrees and dedications offered certain facts which had eluded most writers altogether and would contribute to the understanding of the character and nature of those he was studying (Plu. *Nic.* 1.5).[41] There are times where Plutarch's narrative clearly appears to be informed by knowledge – even if second hand rather than documentary – of decrees: his account of Themistocles' dispatch of military men to the triremes and evacuation of children and wives to Troizen before the battle of Salamis presents these acts as enacted by decree of the people (Plu. *Them.* 10.4–5). In this case there is nothing to indicate that his knowledge was based upon the documentary version of the decree that had been in circulation probably since the late fourth century (see discussion in 5.4.1 below), and his knowledge of it was gleaned probably from narrative accounts of Athenian preparation before the battle. There are times when one wonders whether later authors tended simply to presume (probably correctly) without firm evidence that developments were undertaken on the basis of decrees proposed by prominent politicians: this might be the case in the association of Themistocles with a proposal allowing exiles to return before Salamis (11.1).

Plutarch's *Pericles* is another text which draws heavily upon accounts of its subject's decrees, some of which implicitly contribute to the portrayal of Pericles' character: his decree recalling his rival Cimon is recalled (*Per.* 10.4) as an example of his readiness to go along with the whims of the masses (οὐκ ὤκνησε χαρίσασθαι τοῖς πολλοῖς) at an early stage of his career. Among Pericles' later achievements Plutarch enumerates his proposal concerning the Long Walls (13.7) and that which set out that a musical festival be held as part of the Panathenaic festival (13.11), which he proposed because of his love of honour (φιλοτιμούμενος). Pericles' decree, which said that all Greeks were to be invited to send delegates to Athens to discuss the destroyed Greek sanctuaries, sacrifices owed to the gods, and the control of the sea (17.1), is cited to demonstrate Pericles' ambition and the loftiness of his thoughts (17.4: ἐνδεικνύμενος αὐτοῦ τὸ φρόνημα καὶ τὴν μεγαλοφροσύνην).[42] His decree dispatching a herald to go to the Megarians complaining about their uses of sacred land at Eleusis (30.2: εὐγνώμονος καὶ φιλανθρώπου δικαιολογίας ἐχόμενον) is described as 'reasonable and humane'

---

41 For discussion of Plutarch's use of inscribed documents and decrees, see Liddel 2008 (though Plutarch does not mention any inscribed fourth-century decrees); for the view that Plutarch's interest in the moral implications of decrees reflected a wider epigraphical tendency, see Low 2016.

42 On this controversial decree, widely known as the 'Congress Decree', see Meiggs 1972: 512–15; Stadter 1989: 201–4, arguing that there was indeed an authentic decree on this subject.

in juxtaposition to the hostility of Charinos' decree which said there should be continuous and implacable enmity towards the Megarians (30.3). At Chapter 32, in his illustration of the opposition Pericles faced, he recites decrees which were hostile to him, namely Diopeithes' decree against those who did not believe in gods, a decree of Drakontides requiring Pericles to submit his accounts to the *prytaneis*, along with Hagnon's procedural emendation (32.32.2–4).[43] Accounts of decrees, in the examples of these fifth-century lives, are deployed by Plutarch to illustrate points about his subjects' contributions to political processes and also the opposition that they faced. [44]

Plutarch's *Demosthenes* was also informed very much by awareness of decrees: Plutarch mentions Demosthenes' proposal to invade Euboia (Plu. *Dem.* 17.1 = D152 T4) as an example of his resistance to Philip, and his decree that the Areopagos should investigate the Harpalos affair (26.1 = D195 T8) as an example of his political resilience. Moreover, his knowledge of Demosthenes' career reveals also knowledge of lore concerning decrees relating to Demosthenes: he tells us that Philip celebrated over the bodies of the dead at Chaironeia by parodying a Demosthenic decree in verse (20.3), and Philip's arrogance is contrasted not only with his later realisation – in the cold, sober, light of day – of Demosthenes' ability and power (δεινότης καὶ δύναμις), but also Demosthenes' reluctance, after the battle, to propose decrees in his own name, avoiding it as 'inauspicious and unfortunate' (21.3). Their respective style of engagement with the culture of the decree, therefore, serves to contrast Demosthenes' nobility and superstition with the arrogance of Philip. Plutarch also shows he is aware that Demosthenes' recall from exile was proposed by his cousin Demon (27.3 = D200): this is important to his assessment of his reputation because it substantiates his claim that Demosthenes returned from exile more honourably than Alcibiades did, given that he had persuaded, rather than forced, the citizens to accept him. Plutarch's association of decrees with their individual proposers was an expression of his view that the Athenian assembly tended to become an instrument of individual political power and ambition:[45] the proposal and enforcement of decrees was a convenient depiction of this.

---

43 The decree of Diopeithes is generally agreed to be ahistorical: for linguistic, cultural and chronological arguments against its authenticity, see Dover 1976: 39–41; Wallace 1994: 137–8; Filonik 2016: 128.

44 For the view that the biography was informed by Krateros' collection of decrees, see Stadter 1989: lxix–lxx, 202.

45 For this perspective on Plutarch's view of Athenian politics, see Schmitt Pantel 2014: 102; on his interest in ancient *philotimia*, with reference to that in his Greek lives, see Nikolaidis 2012. On Plutarch's attitude towards the behaviour of the Athenian *demos*, which distinguished between good and bad democratic practice, arguing that his subjects' interaction with the *demos* was one way of assessing their character, see Erskine 2018: 239–45.

DECREES OF FOURTH-CENTURY ATHENS

The prosaic engagement of Plutarch's *Lives* with decrees, as noted above, can be contrasted with the largely descriptive treatment of such material that we encounter in the author (or authors)[46] of the *Lives of the Orators*, a text preserved among Plutarch's works.[47] This set of biographical essays makes numerous references to decrees of relevance to the lives of its subjects,[48] or ones which were proposed by them,[49] as part of its account of its subjects' deeds. The *Life of Antiphon* draws to a close with a quotation of the decree concerning the trial of Aristophon (833e–f, citing as a source the first-century BC Sicilian orator and critic Caecilius of Caleacte), and the condemnation communicated in this text is an appropriate way of ending the chapter dedicated to Antiphon. Appended to the end of the work are three documents, purporting to constitute texts of the request for the grant of posthumous honours for Demosthenes (of 280/79: [Plu.] *X Or.* 850f–1c), the honours for Demochares (of 271/70: 851d–f) and the extension of benefits to Lykophron the descendant of Lycurgus (of 307/6: 851f–2e). The closing section of the third of these documents contains what appears to be the enacted version of this decree for Lycurgus' descendants:

> For good fortune, the people have decided that Lycurgus of Boutadae, the son of Lycophron, is to be commended for his goodness and justice; that a bronze statue of him is to be erected in the Agora (excluding those places where it is illegal for statues to stand); that dining rights in the Prytaneum are to be granted in perpetuity to the eldest of the descendants of Lycurgus in each generation; that the State Secretary is to set up all copies of his decrees, which are to remain valid, on stone *stelai* and place them on the Acropolis in the area given over to such dedications; and that for the inscription of the *stelai* the State treasurer is to draw 50 *drachmas* from the funds reserved by the people for matters relating to decrees. ([Plu.] *X Or.* 852e, trans. Waterfield in Roisman and Worthington 2015).

Differences between the text of this decree as it appears here and the fragmentary inscriptions which preserve parts of it may be explained by reference to the possibility that the literary version stems from a different archival or even

---

46 Martin (2014: 324, 334) argues that the incoherence of the work's structure and its contradictions and factual errors might be explained by the possibility that different authors contributed to it over time, suggesting that it was an 'unstable text, in which material was replicated and put to use'; for a view of it as a stylistic pastiche, see Pitcher 2005; for the view that there was a single author, see Roisman and Worthington 2015: 11–12.

47 On this text, see now Roisman and Worthington 2015.

48 [Plu.] *X Or.* 835f–6a (= D6 T1); 843c (posthumous honours for Lycurgus, granted in 307/6); 846a (D166a T2); 846d (D200 T2),

49 The decrees of Lycurgus and Hypereides: [Plu.] *X Or.* 842c, 848f–9a (= D166b).

privately owned version of the decree.[50] The general sense of the decree is reasonable enough for Faraguna to make a strong case about the reliability of the document,[51] though the arrangements for the setting up of Lycurgus' decrees (presumably those he proposed) as a memorial to the man (852e) are strikingly unique.[52] Yet what is relevant to our current purposes is the question of why this dossier of requests for honours is appended to the work: the author of this piece sees fit to, apparently uncritically, reproduce documentary material. Roisman and Worthington have suggested that the author was interested in them 'not for their evidentiary but for their antiquarian value, in the hope that they would add something new and authentic to his sources'.[53] But decrees to that author appear to represent evidence which is perhaps less immediately impressive or informative: whereas he offers a substantial account of the laws proposed by Lycurgus (841f–842b), he gives only the briefest notice that he introduced decrees, observing that he drafted them, allegedly, with the help of an Olynthian (842c).[54]

As we have already noted, some of the decree-material which is drawn upon in the biographical tradition is very problematic: this is the case also in the Pseudo-Plutarchian text where there is a claim that Hypereides proposed a decree to honour Iolas, the son of Antipater, because he had given poison to Alexander the Great ([Plu.] *X Or.* 849f = Appendix X3). Iolas, the son of Antipater, is otherwise attested as Alexander's chief cupbearer (Plu. *Alex.* 74.1); his father was indeed honoured by the Athenians (see D173). But it is hard to accept the decree as genuine: even if it were the case that Alexander had been poisoned by his cupbearer (and other accounts are not incompatible with this possibility),[55] it is incredible that the Athenian *demos* would have openly praised the assassin. One can only guess that this is the invention of either a

---

50 On the epigraphically extant version of the decree for Lycurgus, *IG* II² 457, see Martin 2014: 331–2 and Lambert 2018: 290–304, associating also *IG* II² 3207 with the decree. See also Oikonomides 1986.

51 Faraguna 2003 and Domingo Gygax 2016: 209 take the view that the documents are reliably authentic. Shear 2012: 276–7, 285–6, 290–2 discusses the implications and politics of Laches' proposal for the honours of Demochares, noting similarities to other inscribed documents. Roisman and Worthington 2015: 18, 22, 23–4 suggest that the author of the work himself saw inscribed versions of the decrees. An alternative view is that of Frost 1961, suggesting that the decrees were composed by Caecilius of Caleacte.

52 Cf. Low 2016: 161, emphasising the oddity of [Plutarch]'s claim (*X Or.* 843f) that a record of Lycurgus' achievements was to be written up on a *stele*. For the view of the posthumous writing up of Lycurgus' decrees as a dedicatory practice, see Lambert 2015: 305.

53 Roisman and Worthington 2015: 24.

54 For discussion of this passage, see Roisman and Worthington 2015: 200.

55 Arrian 7.27–8, mentioning a grudge of Iolas; D.S. 17.117.1–2; Plu. *Alex.* 75.3–4.

rhetorician or a biographer offering a perspective on the character and activities of Hypereides.[56]

What we have seen from Plutarch's and [Plutarch]'s work is that decrees were deployed to represent the contribution of individuals to political developments as well to characterise their style of activity. It is highly likely that biographers often drew these vignettes of decree-related activity from earlier sources which characterised the behaviour of individuals by reference to their decrees (see, for instance, Appendix 2 X1 below); such characterisations surface also in writers of other genres too: for instance, Diodorus' remark on the artfully composed (φιλοτέχνως) Demades' decree which responded to Alexander's demands for the surrender of anti-Macedonian politicians (D.S. 17.5.3 = D186 T1) likely reflected an earlier critique of Demades' political style. But Plutarch's interest in decrees should also be seen as representative of the intellectual interests of writers of the second sophistic period in what they saw as an intriguing classical phenomenon; this is a theme to which we shall return when we look at their appearance in the work of Athenaios and Lucian (see Chapters 5.4 and 5.6 below).

Thus far, we have been assessing the role of decrees in essentially factual accounts. As we shall now see, the representation of decrees in literature is one that has a background extending into the development of fictional narratives about decrees in the fifth century, as we turn to look at the appearance of decrees on the tragic and comic stage of Athens.

5.3 Drama

5.3.1 Tragedy

Modern scholars have long debated the nature of fifth-century Athenian tragedy's engagement with contemporary political themes; what is clear, though, is that it dealt with important questions about the nature of the *polis*.[57] *Polis*-institutions loom large in some plays, and questions about justice, law and legal argumentation play an important role in debates and plots in tragedy.[58]

---

56 On this highly suspect decree, followed by Photios too, see Roisman and Worthington 2015: 258.

57 For the debate about the engagement of tragic drama with ideas about democracy, see Goldhill 1987, 2000; Euben 1990; Rhodes 2003b (emphasising the engagement with questions about the *polis*); Carter 2007, 2011; Burian 2011. On the relations between drama and democracy generally, see Henderson 2007; on the resemblances between rhetoric in the courts and on the dramatic stage, see Hall 1995.

58 On the complex interplay of law and drama, see Ostwald 1986: 148-61; Allen 2005 (discussing in particular the relationship between 'public' and 'private' law); Harris, Leão and Rhodes 2010. On the rational aspects of appeals to pity, see Konstan 2000; on justice in tragedy, see Euben 1990: 67–95. On the depiction of assembly-scenes in tragedy, see Carter 2013.

LITERARY REPRESENTATIONS OF DECREES

In Euripides' *Suppliant Women*, a play which is particularly closely interested in democratic themes, Theseus claims that by liberating the city 'on terms of an equal vote' (*isopsephos*: 353) he put the people in charge of Athens.[59] Yet allusions to decrees – real or fictional – and decree-making are infrequent in extant Athenian tragedy.[60] There is an important exception to this general rule, which occurs in Aeschylus' *Suppliants*, performed at Athens for the first time in the late 460s.[61] This is the episode in which the Egyptian Danaos, on arriving from the Argive assembly, informs his fugitive daughters, the Danaids, that the Argives – guided to do so by their ruler, Pelasgos[62] – have granted them, by way of decree, the asylum which they were seeking by supplication:

> Danaos: Rejoice, children; things go well with respect to the affairs of the inhabitants of the land; decrees with full authority of the people have been resolved ('δήμου δέδοκται παντελῆ ψηφίσματα').

> Chorus of Danaids: Greetings envoy, bringer of precious news. But please tell us, with what effect has the decision been settled, and in what way did the authoritative hand of the people ('δήμου κρατοῦσα χείρ') win its majority?

> Danaos: A decree was resolved by the Argives ('ἔδοξεν Ἀργείοισιν') with no objection, such as to make my old heart young again. For the air bristled with right hands when, unanimously, they ratified the following decision: 'That we live as metics (μετοικεῖν) in this country, free, subject to no seizure and inviolable

---

59 Later in the same play, Theseus describes Athens as a city featuring common and written laws (lines 430–41) where Athenians are equal (408, 432, 434, 441); freedom is said to consist of making a spoken proposal at the assembly (438–41): this follows a theme which presents Theseus as a democratic king: see Morwood 2007: 9; cf. Carter 2013: 11.

60 On the rarity of language related to decrees and decree-making in verse outside comedy, see Friis Johansen and Whittle 1980: II. 488, 493, acknowledging that the terminology of decree-resolution was known elsewhere, pointing to E. *Hec.* 22 ('the Achaians resolved': ἔδοξ' Ἀχαιοῖς) and *Or.* 46 ('the Argives resolved': ἔδοξε δ' Ἄργει). It should also be noted that the Argive herald in Euripides' *Herakleidai* refers to those who have been 'sentenced to die by the laws in place' ('νόμοισι τοῖς ἐκεῖθεν ἐψηφισμένους θανεῖν'), but this seems to refer not to a decree but to the imposition, by vote, of a penalty set out in law: Eur. *Herakl*, 141–2. I have not discussed Antigone's challenge to Kreon's edict (*kerugma*: lines 7–8, 26–34, 450–5) on the grounds that his decree is the proclamation of a single ruler rather than the product of a democratic vote. Accordingly, while it addresses issues relating to authority and claims about legality, it does not give rise to the same kind of debates about the responsibility of the people and instead emphasises the opposition between established laws and the will of a single ruler; see further Harris 2006b: 41–80.

61 On the date of the play, see Bowen 2013: 10–21, suggesting 463.

62 For Pelasgos' use of manipulation to get the decree for the protection of the suppliants passed, see Sommerstein 1997: 75–6; compare Pelasgos' enigmatic statement that 'I will not do this without the people, though I have the power [or, as Garvie 2006: xvi: 'even if I had the power'], in case they say some day, if the outcome were somehow not good, "You gave respect to immigrants and destroyed our city"' (Aesch. *Suppl*. 398–401).

("ξύν τ' ἀσυλίᾳ") by any mortal; that no one, either among natives or among aliens, may carry us off as captives; and that if any one uses violence against us, he out of the landholders here who does not succour us shall lose his civic rights and be exiled by order of the people.' (Aeschylus, *Suppliant Women*, lines 600–14, trans. Friis Johansen 1980, adapted)

In terms of language, Danaos' description of the Argives' voting procedure and their decree bears some resemblance to practices associated with Athenian decree-making and ideas about democracy.[63] The term associated with the decree's enactment, δέδοκται (line 601), resembles but is not identical to the common Athenian enactment formula 'ἔδοξεν τῶι δήμωι' or the motion formula 'δεδόχθαι τῆι βουλῆι'; the phrase 'ἔδοξεν Ἀργείοισιν' (line 605) is what an Athenian might, by way of analogy with Athenian decree-language, have expected Argive resolution formulae to look like. Danaos announces that the Argives had resolved decrees (600–1) without objection (605: 'οὐ διχορρόπως') by voting (607–8: 'χερσὶ δεξιωνύμοις') and had granted that his daughters be allowed to live among the Argives as metics (609).[64] The idea that the decrees are authoritative (παντελῆ: 601) and that the vote of the people is all powerful (δήμου κρατοῦσα χείρ: 604; cf. πανδημίᾳ γὰρ χερσί: 607) might be viewed as representing an early manifestation of a democratic ideal of popular sovereignty [65] – even if it was framed in language which resembles, rather than reproduces, that of Athenian democratic documents. Danaos' report that his daughters had been granted protection against seizure and reprisals (610) ends with a clause which threatens those who fail to assist them in the face of threats to their sanctuary (612–14): this is reminiscent of some Athenian awards of the fourth century which offer security to honorands by guaranteeing seizure of those who assault them (D94; cf. D58 T1; *IG* II^2 286), but in this case it goes further in specifying a penalty for those who fail to rescue the Danaids.

---

63 On the decrees in the play, see Petre 1986. On the resemblance of the language to that of Athenian democratic institutions, see Ehrenberg 1950: 517–22 and Easterling 1985: 2; Carter 2013: 31 and Harris 2010: 3 offer useful summaries of the passage in which this decree is announced; Friis Johansen and Whittle 1980: lines 487–503 for a line-by-line commentary with some epigraphical parallels. On the oddity of this scene, see Podlecki 1966: 45–52.

64 On metic status in this play see Bakewell 1997, suggesting that it was a recently introduced status-group at the time of the play's performance in 463. However, it is far from certain that the status existed formally among the Athenians at this time: as Whitehead (1977: 7) notes, the word *metoikos* appears in extant documents from the second quarter of the fifth century, and Watson (2010: 271) suggests it was introduced as a formal status-group at the time of the citizenship law of 451/0 BC.

65 This is the view of Ehrenberg 1950: 522–4; on the idea of democracy in this play, see Lotze 1981. On fifth-century popular sovereignty, see Ostwald 1986: 77–83. For the possibility that the scene represents a critique of democracy, see Carter 2013.

Accordingly, one view is that some of the documentary language introduced by Aeschylus may have served to make the purported Argive decision-making processes look familiar to an audience in democratic Athens. Some scholars have taken the view that this might be intended to evoke Athenian popular sympathy for the depiction of the Argive democratic decision-making: indeed, as Zeitlin suggests, Argos often occupies something of a middle-ground between Athens and Thebes in Greek tragedy, as a place that is tortured by conflict but at the same time can be depicted as democratic and led by a wise king, Pelasgos.[66] The cautiousness of Pelasgos who acts not as an absolute monarch but sponsors a popular decree is strikingly pragmatic: by acting as if he were a democratic politician he attempts to deflect responsibility from himself while also acknowledging the democratic legitimacy of the decree.[67] Yet as Carter points out, Aeschylus' depiction of a single ruler in the Argive system (one who plays the role of persuading the people to support a decree: lines 616–24) would have made it look rather undemocratic to an Athenian audience, as would the absence of opposition to the proposal (605): Argos is presented not a democracy in the Athenian style but rather a monarchy where the king has the option of consulting the people.[68] The use of language which resembled, but was not identical to, that of Athenian decree-making, may have led the audience not to empathise with the situation in Argos, but rather to stimulate their interest and invite debate about the nature of Argive politics as it was represented on the stage.

An alternative perspective on the role of the decree in this play is put forward by Gottesman, proposing that these passages constitute a 'critique of extra-institutional politics' on the basis that 'this decree is a jarring

---

66 On the idea of Argos in this play, see Zeitlin 1986: 118, 145; Said 1993: 168–9, 174–6; cf. Podlecki 1966: 50. On Argos in tragedy more generally, see Said 1993 and Rosenbloom 2004, suggesting that Argos is represented in many different forms, often inconsistent, in tragedy. For the representation of Argos as a democratic state 'very like Athens itself, deceived with "tricks of oratory"', see Sommerstein 1997: 76; cf. Rosenbloom 2012 and Pattoni 2017. Carter 2013: 29–31 points out that, given the role of Pelasgos as ruler, the representation of Argos is not straightforwardly as a democracy. It is also surely relevant that while the Argives deployed democratic institutions in the fifth century, the language of their decrees was rather different from that of Athenian inscriptions: see Rhodes with Lewis 1997: 67–71. On Argos' democratic political system and civic identity, see Piérart 2000, 2004; Leppin 1999; Robinson 2011: 6–21.

67 Podlecki 1993: 82–6; 1994: 72–3, juxtaposing the authority of Pelasgos referred to elsewhere in the play with his deployment of the democratic system in this context. For the view that it supports a view of Pelasgos as a 'democratic king' in the shape of Theseus, see Papadopoulou 2011: 71

68 Carter 2013: 31–2; cf. Easterling 1985: 2, emphasising that Aeschylus in these passages mixes the language of democracy with that of monarchy.

anachronism that serves to underscore how the extra-institutional machinations of Danaus, the Danaids, and Pelasgus have translated into an official pronouncement': the people of Argos were persuaded to accept – and approve by decree – the supplication on the basis of appeals and supplications put forward by Pelasgos, Danaos and his daughters (398–502).[69] Whatever one makes of Gotteman's distinction between the rather slippery concepts of institutional and extra-institutional politics,[70] the fact is that the decision of the decree is one which is challenged by the suitors who pursue the Danaids and the Egyptian herald who demands their surrender; accordingly, the clash between their acts and the provisions of the decree brings war upon the Argives (950–1, 1044) and ultimately ends Pelasgos' leadership of the city. The decree, therefore, is of pivotal significance for the plot of the play.[71] One gets the sense not so much of the author encouraging Athenian sympathy for the Argive decree or highlighting Danaos' manipulation of the system but rather deploying the enactment of the decree as a crucial element in the narrative.

At the same time, Aeschylus makes reference to debates about the nature of decrees: in the speech of Danaos he raises the question about the balance of responsibility between the Argive *demos* and the decree's sponsor, Pelasgos.[72] While it is clear that the Argive *demos* had made this resolution unanimously, Pelasgos' sponsorship of the decree is emphasised, given that he is said to have made the speech that persuaded the people to grant asylum to the Danaids (615–24). This passage is an important one in that it points up Pelasgos' role in enacting the decree: his attempt to deflect responsibility away from himself was unsuccessful. Accordingly, Aeschylus referred his audience to the perennial debate about responsibility for the acts of a democratic assembly.[73] The play offers also a perspective on the source of the authority of the decree:[74] at a later point, when the herald of the Egyptians tries to take away Danaos' daughters, Pelasgos protests against them on the basis of the people's vote (ψῆφος: 943); its

---

69 Gottesman 2014: 88–91 at 88; for the inventive use by tragedians of anachronism, see Easterling 1985.

70 For a critique of Gottesman's account of this distinction, see Harris 2012–13. On the co-existence of both formal and informal institutional norms, see Introduction above. Burian (2007: 201–8) challenges the view of the constitutional activity as deliberately anachronistic and reflects instead Pelasgos' reluctance to accept responsibility for the decision.

71 Burian 2007: 206: 'the dramatic function of the Argive assembly's decision is surely primary, and whatever praise it implies of democracy, Argive or Athenian, is only subsidiary.'

72 Carter 2013: 26 makes the point that tragedy provides commentary on the balance of responsibility between leaders and led.

73 See Chapter 1.1 and 1.6 and Chapter 2.3 and 2.4.2 above.

74 For the question about the decree's source of authority, see Chapter 3.3.3 above.

authority, he adds, is based not upon a written version either in a *biblion* or a *pinax*, but instead upon its announcement.[75]

5.3.2 Comedy

Aristophanic comedy was deeply political in many senses. Its characters and themes mocked politicians, their acts and aspirations, and parodied also the political administration of the Athenian *demos*. Political themes were confronted on different levels,[76] and mockery of political institutions played a significant role in the construction of humour.[77] Wohl, in an investigation of the place of law in Athenian comedy, has argued convincingly that in the *Wasps*, Aristophanes demonstrates that the 'city needs its laws'; accordingly, 'comic justice works together with civic justice and its institutions, reaffirming them in a form improved by comic critique'.[78] In the following discussion I argue that Aristophanes demonstrates how decrees provide yet further scope to combine political and comic critique.[79]

In contrast to tragedy, surviving Old Comedy engages extensively with both real and imaginary *psephismata*. On the one hand, Aristophanic comedy gives rise to some parody of normative values about decrees. This is expressed

---

75 946–9: 'ταῦτ᾽ οὐ πίναξίν ἐστιν ἐγγεγραμμένα οὐδ᾽ ἐν πτυχαῖς βίβλων κατεσφραγισμένα, σαφῆ δ᾽ ἀκούεις ἐξ ἐλευθεροστόμου γλώσσης' ('it is not a text scratched on tablets, nor has it been sealed in rolls of papyrus; you hear it clearly uttered by a tongue that speaks freely' trans. Bowen 2013). Here I have advocated the interpretation of Friis Johansen and Whittle 1980, lines 250–2. For a view of lines 944–5 underlining not the contrast between publicly displayed texts and those which are sealed and not visible, see Faraguna 2015.

76 For examples of the mid twentieth-century attempts to assess the political views of Aristophanes, see Gomme 1938 and Forrest 1963, both of which challenged the idea that Aristophanes expressed partisan views; Ste Croix, on the other hand, argued that he enunciated a conservative political perspective (Ste Croix 1972: 355–76). Sommerstein 2014a and Olson 2010 provide a useful overview of scholarship as well as different perspectives. For a collection highlighting the different ways in which Aristophanic comedy can be said to engage with political theory, see Mhire and Frost 2014. One assessment suggests that the political content of his work points to the possibility that it refers to a primary audience of politically sophisticated intellectuals: see Sidwell 2014; for the view that Aristophanes' comedy was philosophical but yet aspired to mobilise the author's 'tacit commensal knowledge to evocative ends', see Clements 2014: 194.

77 Workings of the assembly: Rhodes 2004a, 2010; inscriptions: Lougovaya 2013: 255–64; official language: Harris 2006b: 425–30 and Willi 2003: 72, both arguing against the idea that the details of legal language would have been too technical for the average male citizen; law: MacDowell 2010, emphasising that the evidence of Aristophanes might be used as evidence in the reconstruction of Athenian legal procedures.

78 Wohl 2014: 333.

79 The discussion of Lougovaya 2013: 262–4 concentrates specifically upon inscribed documents.

in an idea about their wider civilising role: Pheidippides joked in Aristophanes *Clouds* that what distinguishes men from the roosters and other animals is that they pass decrees (*Clouds* 1428–9); in this way he parodied the idea that decrees are central to human justice.[80] The association of decrees with the conceited political activity of particular types of politician also emerges in comedy: in the *Clouds*, it was implied that under the influence of the Weaker Argument, Pheidippides will acquire – as a surprise addition to a number of unappealing bodily features – a long decree (1016–19). It is, therefore, expected that after this training he will become an orator and propose long-winded decrees,[81] which of course was a criticism levelled at Demosthenes by Aeschines (Aeschin. 3.100).[82] In the *Acharnians*, Aristophanes' emphasis on Pericles' responsibility for the Megarian decree, while offering a short-cut comedic explanation of the outbreak of war, reflects the tendency to identify decrees with their proposers, envisaging the Megarian decree as a small spark set off by Pericles which set the city on fire (*Peace* 608–9; cf. *Acharnians* 530–7).[83]

In the *Wasps*, a mockery of religious authority is invoked through a humorous deployment of a decree: the Chorus urges Philokleon to escape from home, telling him that if his son tries to destroy him, 'I'll make him bite his heart and struggle for dear life, so he'll know not to step on the decrees of the Two Goddesses ('ἵν' εἰδῇ μὴ πατεῖν τὰ ταῖν θεαῖν ψηφίσματα': 374–8, trans. Sommerstein 1983, adapted). In this passage, the term *psephismata* is used as a surprise substitute for the *mysteria* with which the goddesses are associated,[84] suggesting the overblown claim that 'the legal underpinnings of jury service are as inviolable as mystic rites',[85] but another view might be that the 'Two Goddesses' constitute an allegoric reference to the *boule* and *demos* of the Athenians, a breach of whose decrees would be taken very seriously.

---

80 This idea, that there was a complication in the relationship between decrees and justice, was developed later by Aristotle who expressed the view that the essence of the decree (τὰ ψηφισματώδη) was justice of a conventional but not natural sort (Arist. *NE* 1134b 24): see Chapter 1.2.2 above.

81 For discussion of the language of political administration in this play, see Harris 2006b: 425–30.

82 We might also compare the idea that busybodies propose petty decrees: in Alkiphron 2 *Letters of Farmers* 2, a slave about to run away from his master disparages him as proposing decree-lets and resolution-lets at the assembly.

83 For Aristophanes' manipulation of the audience's knowledge of the Megarian decrees, see Pelling 2000: 151–8.

84 Sommerstein 1983: 179.

85 Biles and Olson 2015: 208.

Decrees were parodied more extensively in four extant comedies: *Birds* (414), *Lysistrata* (411), *Thesmophoriazousai* (411) and *Ekklesiazousai* (391).[86] In the *Birds*, the premise of the establishment of the alternative state Cloud-Cuckoo Land is motivated by the protagonist's disenchantment with Athenian fondness of litigation (40–1). Over the course of the play we encounter an expression of mild irritation about them as tools of imperial politics: on arriving at Cloud-Cuckoo Land, the Athenian inspector (*episkopos*), responding to Pisthetairos' enquiry as to who had sent him there, responds that he was dispatched there by 'some wretched note (φαῦλον βιβλίον τι) of Teleas' (line 1024). The βιβλίον is presumably a reference to a copy of the decree, perhaps in the form of a scroll, which ordered him to go there.[87] A little later, Aristophanes introduces an Athenian decree-seller to Cloud-Cuckoo Land (1035–45),[88] who arrives bearing a clutch of imperialist documents, including a decree threatening those subjects of Athens who carry out an offence against an Athenian (1035–6).[89] He brings also a parodic version of the Athenian standards decree (1040–1), one which claims that the citizens of Cloud-Cuckoo Land 'shall use [Athenian] measures, weights and decrees' ('χρῆσθαι Νεφελοκοκκυγιᾶς τοῖς αὐτοῖς μέτροισι καὶ σταθμοῖσι καὶ ψηφίσμασι καθάπερ Ὀλοφύξοι'), the term ψηφίσμασι replacing the νομίσμασι of the inscribed version (*IG* I³ 1453 (= OR 155) composite text section 10): as well as parodying specifically the standards' decree, a joke is made about the Athenian rule of decree and the allies' frustration with it.[90] The official is driven away after reading this decree, but a little while later he returns, reminding the subjects, by reference to a third decree, both of the threat against those who expel Athenian officials and those who do not admit them 'according to the *stele*' (1049–50); on this occasion, he goes further, reminding the subjects of their past acts of subversion by claiming that

---

86 There is of course humorous use of mock political language in other plays too: on the metaphorical assembly in the *Knights*, see Rhodes 2010; generally, on Aristophanic fun at the assembly in *Acharnians*, *Thesmophoriazousai*, *Lysistrata* and *Ekklesiazousai*, see Rhodes 2004a.

87 For βιβλίον as a reference to a documentary copy of a decree, perhaps one on papyrus, see RO 2 line 61, where the secretary of the council is to hand over the '*biblion* of the decree' with Osborne 2012: 43. See Chapter 3.2.2 above. For the suggestion that the *Birds* suggests a private trade in copies of Athenian decrees, see Slater 1996: 100.

88 For the view of a 'decree-seller' as a parody of a new style of 'professional' politician, see Jackson 1919. The notion of the 'decree-seller' as a profession was, of course, a parodic one: Dunbar 1995: 567.

89 Dunbar 1995: 568–9, substantiating the view that this clause 'closely resembled the sanction clauses in decrees prescribing penalties originally imposed for killing an Athenian citizen anywhere in the empire'.

90 For discussion of this passage, see Dunbar 1995: 569–72. The passage is sometimes used to date the decree to c. 414: see the commentary on OR 150.

the birds used to deposit their droppings on the *stele* (1054).[91] As Lougovaya argues, the citation of a *stele*, and perhaps the introduction onto the stage of such an object – and the emphasis on its abuse – not only heightens the comedic effect of Athenian decree, but also represents the decree-seller's third and final attempt to impose his authority;[92] nevertheless, regardless of his inscription, he is forced to flee and does not appear again in the play. As the leadership of the new community is increasingly concentrated in the hands of Pisthetairos, he receives a golden honorific crown from a herald of the Athenians (1274–5),[93] who had by this time metamorphosed into bird-men, and whose mark of civilisation was that they spend time foraging among the laws and browsing among the decrees (1287–9). Accordingly, although Pisthetairos' community became a place worthy of praise (1277–1307), those who metamorphosed into birds were unable to escape the culture of the decree; Pisthetairos accepts the decree (1276) but persists with his resistance to Athenian hegemony. Overall, therefore, the effect of decrees in the *Birds* is both to parody the futility of Athenian attempts to impose their authority through decrees while stressing the inevitability of Pisthetairos' new community falling into line with the normative expectations of the decree-culture.

Similarly, the *Lysistrata* is pervaded by a theme of disillusionment with the decrees of male Athenian politicians: the magistrate (*proboulos*) sent to clamp down on the women's revolt launches into a tirade about the proposals that he heard Demostratos make (that an expedition be launched to Sicily and that the Athenians recruit Zakynthian mercenaries) while his wife yelled from the roof of his house (*Lysis.* 387–98). As Henderson observes,[94] the thesis of this passage is that 'failure to control wives brings disaster to husbands', but also Demostratos' readiness to propose controversial decrees is being criticised. Elsewhere in that play, the leader of the women's chorus expresses defiance in the face of the male-dominated medium of Athenian decrees, claiming that the Athenians will never be able to do anything about the power of the women, not even if they decree seven times (698). But at the same time she expresses frustration at the nature, frequency and number of Athenian decrees: not only are they petty, but they are also frequent and persistent:

> Why, just yesterday I threw a party for the girls in honour of Hekate, and I invited my friend from next door, a fine girl who's very special to me: an eel from Boiotia.

---

91 This is a passage which inspired Meiggs 1972: 587 to speculate 'there must have been a strong temptation to oligarchs as well as dogs to deface or foul decree stones'.
92 Lougovaya 2013: 263.
93 Dunbar 1995: 634–5, noting that a gold crown for conspicuous service would probably have been rare at the time.
94 Henderson 1987: 120.

But they said they wouldn't let her come because of your decrees. And you will never, ever stop passing these decrees until someone grabs you by the leg, throws you away, and breaks your neck. (700–705, trans. Henderson 2000)

Sommerstein's view of these lines is that they refer to Athenian decrees restricting trade with Athenian enemies,[95] a view which points to the passage as an expression of frustration at such measures.

Aristophanes' *Thesmophoriazousai* was set at an irregular meeting of women at the Thesmophorion in Athens, where they discuss how they will take revenge on Euripides for his abusive portrayal of the female gender. This play too makes comedy by criticising Athenian decree practice. At 361–2, the speech of the Chorus of women attacks those who, as well as carrying out other inversions of normality, seek 'to change decrees and law to their opposites' ('ψηφίσματα καὶ νόμους ζητοῦσ᾿ ἀντιμεθιστάναι'): such a phrase could be reasonably viewed as an allusion either to Euripides' poetic deception, or a reference to the oligarchs' proposal that the assembly pass decrees which would transform the democratic constitution (Thuc. 8.67.1).[96] But in this play we witness the protagonists of the play making use of the template of the Athenian decree to enact their decisions: when the council of the women enacts a decision to hold an assembly, they announce their resolution in the language of a decree of the council, and also place deliberation about the punishment of Euripides on the agenda of their assembly:

Listen everyone. The Council of Women resolves as follows ('ἔδοξε τῇ βουλῇ τάδε τῇ τῶν γυναικῶν'). Timokleia presiding ('Τιμόκλει᾿ ἐπεστάτει'), Lysilla was the secretary ('Λύσιλλ᾿ ἐγραμμάτευεν'); Zostrate proposed ('εἶπε Ζωστράτη'): to convene an assembly at dawn in the middle of the Thesmophoria, at which point we have some leisure-time, and to do business in the first place about what Euripides should suffer for he seems to all of us to be a criminal. Who wishes to speak ('τίς ἀγορεύειν βούλεται;')? (lines 372–9)

The passage makes, with its resolution clause, mention of the *epistates* (presiding officer of the council), the secretary, and proposer, an excellent parody of an open *probouleuma*.[97] It largely follows the patterns of the prescript of an inscribed decree,[98] though the omission of the prytanic tribe – if we make

---

95 Sommerstein 1990: 193.

96 Austin and Olson 2004: 170. See the insightful discussion at Clements 2014: 190 note 99.

97 Rhodes 1972: 59 note 3. See also *Eccl.* 397–8, in answer to the question of what brought the people to the assembly so early in the morning: 'why, what else than the *prytaneis* deciding to make a proposal about saving the city?' (τί δ᾿ ἄλλο γ᾿ ἢ ἔδοξε τοῖς πρυτάνεσι περὶ σωτηρίας γνώμας καθεῖναι τῆς πόλεως;).

98 As Rhodes 2004a: 225 observes.

anything of it – may be read as a deliberate distancing from the usual documentary pattern;[99] accordingly, it sets the scene for a discussion at the assembly on Euripides. Adherence to normal bouleutic procedure perhaps indicates that the women have fully taken on normal decree-making practice.

The *Thesmophoriazousai* makes its humour in this case by portraying the women as behaving like men, but in the *Ekklesiazousai*, the whole plot hinges upon on a gendered transformation of politics by putting the women in charge of the city,[100] and by assessing through experiment whether women could become rulers of the city by decree of the assembly.[101] The play emphasises Praxagora's regime's reliance on *psephismata* – rather than *nomoi* – to turn power over to the women (lines 649, 812–13), and in doing so disputes the legitimacy of the women's reform[102] whilst asking probing questions about the authority of the decrees of the assembly. The background of the women's plans was formulated by resolutions (*bouleumata*) which had evidently been resolved – as enunciated in Praxagora's documentary-style language[103] – at the women's festival of the Skira: according to these decisions, the women decided that they would assume actions to take over the running of the community, but would also put to an end the shaving of body-hair (lines 17–18; 59).[104]

The eventual turning over of power to the women is done by a decree of the assembly in which the women, disguised as men, were able to infiltrate (383–5); the decree was reported in a discussion between Blepyros (husband of the heroine, Praxagora) and his neighbour Chremes (429–70); their barbed comment is that it is sometimes the fact that the maddest decrees do the most good (474–5). From this point, the women assume control of what is usually the male-controlled territory of the decree. However, the men in the play undermine the permanency of the women's legislation,[105] with the Dissident criticising Chremes' obedience to the women's government by labelling their laws 'δεδογμένοι' (762–4: 'enacted', that is, rather than long-established, laws); this joke about the transience of legislation is reinforced by an account of

---

99 Austin and Olson 2004: 172.

100 See Zeitlin 2000; Ober 1998: 122–55; Shepherd 2016, emphasising the role of Praxagora in enunciating a call for strong leadership of the democratic Athenians.

101 Ober 1998: 135.

102 Cf. Shepherd 2016: 473.

103 As Shepherd 2016: 465 notes, the formula 'Σκίροις ἔδοξε ταῖς ἐμαῖς φίλαις' (line 18: 'it was resolved by my friends at the Skira') is reminiscent of documentary language and 'immediately establishes the register of assembly-style speech'.

104 This is a resolution through which, as Ober (1998: 136) suggests, Aristophanes emphasises that the appearance of femininity is a consequence of human action: 'if women are naturally hairy and brown like men, might they also be naturally political, like men?'

105 For this point, see Rothwell 1990: 62–3.

Athenian decrees which have turned out to be particularly fickle or never acted upon (797–8; 812–29; see DD 95, 96, 97). Such mockery of probably-real decrees of the Athenian assembly sets the stage for the realisation, by decree, of Praxagora's version of communism, which says that men who want to have sex with a girl first have to do so with an older woman (596–648, 706). Later on in the play the new regulations are implemented: when a youth, Epigenes, attempts to resist the advances of an old woman, she attempts to persuade him by announcing that she bears the decree with her (1010–13) and then reading it out:

> Old Woman: A decree says that you've got to come to my house.
> Epigenes: Read out what it actually says.
> Old Woman: All right, I shall: 'The women have decreed (ἔδοξε ταῖς γυναιξίν): if a young man desires a young woman he may not hump her until he bangs an old woman first. Should he in his desire for the young woman refuse to do this preliminary banging, the older woman shall be entitled with impunity to drag the young man off by his pecker.' (1013–20, trans. Henderson 2002)

The over-reaching powers of this decree of the women's assembly, which lacks any indication of preliminary consideration by a council,[106] makes it seem a perversion of the normal, democratic law-making procedure. The confusion between laws and decrees emphasises this: a young girl then attempts to rescue the young man, but her efforts are thwarted also by the entrance of a second old woman, who cites the document, referring to it as a νόμος (1050), before he is dragged off with violence. There is one last decree-themed joke: dragged off by the old women, he found the energy to parody the decree of Kannonos, which made those found guilty of harming the Athenian people be bound in chains and face the people (cf. Xen. *Hell.* 1.7.20):

> Epigenes: This is obviously Kannonos' decree put into practice: I've got to appear in irons and fuck my accusers! (1089–90, trans. Henderson 2002)

Not only does this play experiment with the decree as the key to disrupting customary gendered and political restrictions, its frequent blurring of the distinction between laws and decrees (e.g. 1050, 1089–90) may well underline the possibility, even in the 390s, the distinction between laws and decrees may have been less than clear.[107]

---

106 As observed by Rothwell 1990: 69.
107 As Ober, 1998: 145–6. For the view that Aristophanes is poking fun by confusing *nomos* and *psephisma*, see Shepherd 2016: 272–5; on the distinction between laws and decrees in the *Thesmophoriazousai*, see also Canevaro (Chapter 1.2.1 note 23 above).

Aristophanes' comedy contains other references to decrees and their proposers,[108] and this is surely what lies behind the phrase attributed to him, preserved in Athenaios: 'bearing fish-baskets full of decrees' (Ath. 4d: γυργάθους ψηφισμάτων φέροντες); given that most of his decrees reflect fifth-century developments, this is not the place for a full comprehensive exploration of them. For now, it is enough to say that the Aristophanic deployment of decrees drew both upon their normative implications, critiqued them as the rash products of a capricious people and suggests some disillusionment with their impositions and general effect. The success of this humour was underpinned by the fact that while responsibility for a decree lay with its proposer, it could also be deployed to mildly berate the *demos* for enacting it. It is also clear that the idea of the decree is also at the centre of the subversive plots of the gynaecocratic *Ekklesiazousai* and *Thesmophoriazousai*, in which Aristophanes allows women to make use of them as transactions with a level of, but not unassailable, authority. Whereas the most intensive engagement with the decree occurs in the *Ekklesiazousai*, it is in the *Thesmophoriazousai* that Aristophanes undertakes the creation of a document that closely resembles a *probouleuma* of the Athenian council.

Aristophanes' fabrication of decrees was one which appears to have been followed by the Middle Comedian Alexis, as we see in a fragment of his *Dorkis or The Girl Who Popped Her Lips*, to which Athenaios was drawn in his discussion of crayfish:

> It is voted by the fish-sellers ('τοῖς ἰχθυοπώλαις ἐστὶ ἐψηφισμένον'), so the people say, to erect a bronze statue of Kallimedon in the fish market, during the Panathenaia, holding a roasted crayfish in his right hand, since he is the sole saviour of their trade and everyone else is against them. (Athenaios 3.104d–e = Alexis fr 57 Arnott)

On this occasion, it is impossible to be certain whether a real decree for a statue of an individual called Kallimedon lay behind the humour, but it is quite

---

108 In *Ekklesiazousai* 22, Praxagora makes reference to a certain Phyromachos, who is connected with a proposal which meant that 'we wenchmen must grab our seats' (trans. Henderson). A later scholiast appears to have rationalised this by reference to a decree: Suda, s.v. 'Σφυρόμαχος' Adler *sigma*,1764 (= Schol, Ar. *Ekkles*. 22) says that a certain Sphyramachos introduced a decree that men and women could not sit together ('Σφυρόμαχος· οὗτος ψήφισμα εἰσηγήσατο, ὥστε τὰς γυναῖκας καὶ τοὺς ἄνδρας χωρὶς καθέζεσθαι'). Given that women could not attend the assembly, the decree is likely to be false. 'Sphyromachos' is probably a parody of Aristophanes' Phyromachos. For other explanations of this passage of *Ekklesiazousai*, see Sommerstein 1998: 140 and Appendix 2 X10 below.

plausible to think that one did.[109] The same poet, in his play *Epidaurios*, made fun of the award of citizenship for the sons of the fish-importer Chairephilos, though in that case a genuine decree may be at the background of the humour: see D235 T2. The fragmentary nature of our knowledge of Alexis (just as for other authors of Middle Comedy) means that we will always be guessing about the precise nature of his mockery of decrees; the fact that the examples we have share a piscine-theme may be down to the preferences of our source, Athenaios. For now, all we can do is suggest that his use of decrees to mock Athenian honorands may well have been inspired by the ridicule mockery of decrees in the plays of Aristophanes, and that others in the Middle period of Greek comedy may well have done the same.

Decrees, then, were deployed on the dramatic stage for a number of different ends: represented in the mouths of speakers and, on occasion, physically represented on stage, reports of them could act as a turning point in tragic narrative, and humour could be drawn from their wider connotations. Comic poets reached for the language of decrees and a collective comprehension of how they functioned, reassured that their predominantly Athenian audiences would be familiar with it, and hoped that audiences would be engaged by their parody of it. The deployment of decrees on the stage is a reflection of the familiarity of their language to an Athenian audience and the high cultural profile of the decree.

Parody of decrees, of course, was not limited to comedy, and its possibilities may well have been exploited in the courts, if we follow the reports of later authorities: Hypereides, in his speech *Against Demades* in support of a *graphe paranomon* against making Euthykrates a *proxenos* of the Athenians (see D177), is said to have parodied Demades' justification of the decree, claiming that he could be honoured only 'because he speaks and acts in the interests of Philip; because, as cavalry commander, he betrayed the Olynthian cavalry to Philip and through this act was responsible for the destruction of the Chalcidians; because, on the capture of Olynthos, he assessed the prices of prisoners; because he opposed the city's interests concerning the temple at Delos ...': he even appears to have drawn up a mock decree: 'Demades, son of Demeas of the deme Paiania, proposed that, whereas Euthykrates betrayed his own city, Olynthos, to Philip, and was responsible for the destruction of the forty cities

---

109 The politician named here was an orator and politician of the 320s whose wealth depended partly on mining interests (*IG* II² 158 line 12; *APF* 8157 III); indeed. Arnott (1996: 179) raises the possibility that the poet was mocking the speech or decree in which he was designated 'saviour of the city': in this case, the joke appears to be that he was fond of eating fish (it is parodied elsewhere: Ath. 340b–d; Alexis fr. 249 Arnott); the idea is that he ate so much fish that he was the saviour of the fishmonger's business.

of the Chalkidians, etc.' (Hypereides F76 Jensen), and suggested that such a *stele* would be more suitably raised at the crossroads, that is to say at the rubbish-dump (ὀξυθύμια), than in our sanctuaries' (F79 Jensen = Harpokration s.v. 'ὀξυθύμια').[110]

We will return to the parody of decrees when we come to look at Lucian's deployment of them (see Chapter 5.6 below). Having now shown that the literary representation of the decree has a heritage which stretches back into the fifth century, I turn to explore other fabrications of Athenian decrees in later prose works, in order to assess the other uses to which knowledge of decrees were put.

5.4 The Deployment of Elaborated and Fabricated Documents

For the most part, the Inventory of classical Athenian decrees (see Volume 1) takes the view that the Athenian orators' references to, and deployments of, decrees provide potentially reliable testimonia for their content: I have suggested the view that the dangers of being shown up as a liar would have dissuaded orators from outright falsification of the content of contemporary decrees in a public context (see Volume 1 Introduction).[111] Accordingly, fourth-century orators, while they were ready to construe the motivation and intention of Athenian decrees in different ways, tend not to falsify the content of contemporary decrees or invent them outright.[112] That is a rule which, generally, applies to decrees of current times and the recent past. Our literary sources' perspectives into decrees of earlier eras, however, tend to be prone much more to distortion than are contemporary documents. In Chapters 5.4 and 5.5 below I suggest four different contexts for the elaboration or even fabrication of decrees in literary texts: the fabrication of such documents in the fourth century for

---

110 Suda, s.v. 'ὀξυθύμια' offers alternative interpretations of this term: 'Hyperides in the [speech] *Against Demades* [says]: "Concerning which, the stele would have been far more justly set up amongst the gallows-refuse than amongst our shrines." Some, including Aristarchus, maintain that *oxythymia* is the term applied to the wooden [gallows] from which certain people are hanged, [the term deriving] from being quick [*oxys*] to anger [*thymos*]; these [gallows] they cut down and root out and burn. But Didymus asserts that *oxythymia* is the name for refuse and filth; for [he says that] this is taken out to crossroads whenever they purify houses.' (trans. Suda on Line)

111 For a general view of assessing the credibility of the claims made by orators, see Harris 1995: 15–16; Carawan 2013: 13.

112 Though there are exceptions: see D128 Commentary for discussion of the debate about the proposal to honour the ambassadors returning from the Second Embassy to Pella and Aeschines' disingenuous presentation of proposals as decrees.

patriotic reasons, their development in biographical contexts, their deployment by antiquarians and their use by rhetoricians.

5.4.1 The Invention of Decrees in *Demos*-Oriented Narratives

Both epigraphical and literary evidence points to a movement, perhaps born of the existential threat to Athens of the rising power of the Macedonians from the 350s onwards, to revive, or perhaps to fabricate documentary versions of patriotic, Persian War-era, decrees.[113] It is likely that these documentary decrees were fabricated on the basis of already existing accounts of Athenian decisions in the Persian Wars. Probably in the late fourth century, some examples, such as the decree of Themistocles, the Ephebic oath, the Oath of Plataea, and the Peace of Callias (ML 23, RO 88 i, ii;[114] Harpokration, s.v. Ἀττικοῖς γράμμασιν'), and the decree against the traitor Arthmios were even written up on *stelai*.[115] There may have been a tacit acknowledgement that these documents were not straightforward records of enactments made at the assembly, but rather that they reflected stories told about the decisions that the Athenians had made and emphasised the unity of purpose of the *demos* in the face of external aggressors and the threat of Greek traitors; they were held up usually as paradigms of appropriate behaviour.

There was, in the fourth century, awareness of the possibility of outright forgery: famously, Theopompos denied the authenticity of the Peace of Callias on the basis of the version of the letter-forms on the version that he had seen

---

113 The documents outlined as such inventions are outlined by Habicht 1961: 17–19 as the following: the decree of Miltiades of 490 to engage the Persians at Marathon (Dem. 19.303; Ar. *Rhet.* 1411a10: see D82 T2); Themistocles' decree of 480 evacuating Athens (Dem. 19.303 with ML 23); the decree of the Troizenians granting support to Athenian refugees (Hyp. *Athenog.* 32–3; see D175 Commentary); the decree of the Athenian council against the man executed at Salamis (Lycurg. 1.122, with discussion in Chapter 5.2.1 above); the Oath of Plataea (Lycurg. 1.80; D.S. 11.29.3 with RO 88 ii; cf. Krentz 2007); the decree destroying the statue of Hipparchos (Lycurg. 1.117); the decree against Arthmios of Zeleia (Dem. 19.271, 9.41–2; Din. 2.24–5; Aeschin.3.258–9); the Peace of Callias (Dem. 19.273; Lycurg. 1.73; *BNJ* 342 F13); the Ephebic Oath (Dem. 19.303, 311–12; Lycurg. 1.76–7 with RO 88i). To this list we might also add the Athenian decision to restore exiles and reinstate disenfranchised citizens before Marathon: see And. 1.107 with MacDowell 1962: 140. See also, on invented documents, Davies 1996. Other candidates include those decrees mentioned by Plutarch: see Chapter 5.2.3 above. The fact that reference to the terms of the Peace of Callias makes its first appearance in c. 380 (Isoc. *Panegyrikos* 118–20) suggests that such documents had their origins in earlier accounts.
114 For the view that RO 88 ii represents the Oath of Marathon, not Plataea, see Krentz 2007.
115 It is not clear which body authorised the setting up of such inscriptions: the Themistocles decree, set up in Troizen; RO 88, was dedicated by the priest of Ares and Athena Areia in the deme of Acharnai.

(*FGrH* 115 F154 cited by Harpokration, s. v. Ἀττικοῖς γράμμασιν').[116] But accuracy about the substance of decrees of past eras or qualms about their authenticity would have mattered little in the forensic contexts upon which they were cited: of these documents, the decision (described as a decree by Dinarchus 2.24–5 and Harpokration, s.v. 'ἄτιμος') which condemned a Persian war traitor, Arthmios, to death,[117] was cited occasionally, often by reference to an inscribed version on the acropolis. In such cases, orators deployed them as a way of sketching moral standards in a way that made them publicly indisputable.[118] The best approach to such documents is to treat them not as windows onto a fifth-century reality, but rather to think of them as perspectives, lodged in the public memory of the fourth century, onto that past. We cannot be certain about the identity of the producers of the documentary versions of these decrees, but orators' references to them in the lawcourts and assembly demonstrate that they captivated listeners in fourth-century Athens who wanted to hear stories about Athenian resolution against the Persians. Yet accounts of these decrees had a wider captive audience also during the period of the Second Sophistic. In his *To Plato: in Defence of the Four*, the second-century rhetorician Aelius Aristides launched into a eulogy of the decree of Themistocles evacuating Attica, praising its proposer and the Athenian resolve in carrying it out, concluding 'this decree is the fairest, most glorious, most perfect evidence of all under the sun in regard to virtue' (III *To Plato* 249 trans. Behr 1981–6).[119] Aristides' view gives us a sense of the reception of one strand of the fourth-century Athenians' ideas about decrees: that which projected a rose-tinted view of a unified purpose of the Athenian *demos* in the face of Persian aggression. At this point we turn to exploring Hellenistic and later representations of Athenian decrees.

116 But of course, the authenticity of the peace has been defended: Grote, for instance, suggested that Theopompos had seen either a later version or one inscribed with Ionic style letters for an audience used to them: Grote 1849: 547 note 1; Hartmann 2013: 37, 52; Pownall 2008; Higbie 2017: 170–1. Bosworth (1990) highlights the role of fourth-century traditions in influencing the claims made by later sources; for more recent bibliography on the Peace of Callias, see Hartmann 2013: 37 note 28. Theopompos *FGrH* 115 F153 has sometimes been associated with the Peace of Callias, but this is uncertain: see Krentz 2009, associating it with an earlier Athenian treaty with Dareios (Hdt. 5.73).

117 Habicht 1961; Meiggs 1972: 508–12 offers a useful comparison of what different sources say about the 'Arthmios decree', while maintaining a positive view of its authenticity. On its use by the orators, see Nouhaud 1982: 239–42.

118 Cf. Petrovic 2010.

119 Aelius Aristides also demonstrated an interest in the patriotic documents connected by fourth-century sources with Athenian activity of the Persian Wars: see Habicht 1961: 17–19. For his praise of Athens in the *Panathenaika*, see Day 1980; for his discussion of the Peace of Callias, see Day 1980: 140–71.

5.4.2 Biographical Creations

The survey, in Appendix 2 below, of fabricated fourth-century decrees, points to other, not-patriotic reasons for the fabrication of decrees. We have already noted (Chapter 5.2.3 above) that decrees were extensively deployed in biographical literature and were sometimes fabricated by those who were interested in the lives of, and in particular in creating apologetic accounts of, prominent statesmen.[120] Discussion of the biographical deployment of such decrees has already been undertaken (Chapter 5.2.3 above), where we emphasised their role in the construction of narratives about individuals and their role in Athenian politics.

5.4.3 Decrees in Antiquarian Literature

There are some references in ancient sub-literary texts to probably fabricated decrees whose origins are all but impossible to decipher (see, e.g. Appendix 2 X10). But it seems to be the case that the antiquarian writer of antiquity who took an interest in Athenian decrees to its furthest extent was Krateros of Macedonia, born in the late fourth century. [121] Accordingly, it is appropriate to commence discussion of the appearance of decrees in antiquarian literature with an assessment of Krateros' use of them. He is said to have authored a work entitled *Synagoge Psephismaton* (*Collection of Decrees*) which one later reporter, implausibly, claimed to have collected all the decrees in the Greek world.[122] Recent scholarship has been divided between the views of, on the one hand, Higbie and Carawan,[123] that he relied primarily upon material inscribed on stone and the view of Erdas,[124] that he drew primarily upon archival material. In all likelihood, he made use of both, though neither comprehensively.[125]

---

120 See also Appendix 2 X1, 2, 8, 10, 11 below.

121 For a definition of the notion of the antiquarian, as someone who collects artefacts which are informative on the practices of antiquity, see Momigliano 1950; cf. Payen 2014, emphasising the antiquarian aspects of Plutarch's erudition. For the possibility that his material was among the sources used by later editors to reconstruct the documents in Andocides' *On the Mysteries*, see Carawan 2017.

122 *BNJ* 342 T1c (Scholiast, Aristides Πρὸς Πλάτωνα ὑπέρ τῶν τεττάρων (*To Plato, on the Four*) 46, 217–18): Ἀρατερός τις ἐγένετο, ὃς συνῆξε πάντα τὰ ψηφίσματα τὰ γραφέντα ἐν τῆι Ἑλλάδι' ('There was a certain Krateros who collected all the decrees written in Greece.' (trans. Carawan, *BNJ*)); and collected not only decrees but also legal indictments (e.g. Plu. *Arist.* 26.4 = *BNJ* 342 F12) and information from the Athenian Tribute Lists (e.g. Suda, s.v. Νύμφαιον' = *BNJ* 342 F10).

123 Carawan in *BNJ* 342 Biographical Essay; see Higbie 1999.

124 Erdas 2002; the view of Jacoby was that he used archival material: Jacoby *FGrH* III b I96 with ii 64 note 26 and 33; cf. Ste Croix 2004: 309–10.

125 This is the view of Faraguna 2006.

It is highly likely that he would also have taken an interest in those decrees that he encountered in narratives preserved in oral and written form. The fact that he remarked on decrees that were specifically inscribed (*BNJ* 342 FF 5b, 17), far from being a proof of epigraphical autopsy, reflects probably his awareness of traditions about these inscriptions. These are the references to Athenian decrees:

BNJ 342 F5b, the bronze *stele* setting out the punishment of Antiphon and Archeptolemos of 411 ([Plu.] *X Or.* 833d–4b);

BNJ 342 F13, the Peace of Callias (Plu. *Cim.* 13.4);

BNJ 342 F14, the decree against Arthmios (Schol. Aristides Πρὸς Πλάτωνα ὑπέρ τῶν τεττάρων (*For Plato, on the Four*) II 287 Dindorf);

BNJ 342 F15, the decree of Kannonos (Schol. ad Aristophanem *Ekklesiazusae* 1089; cf. Xen. *Hell.* 1.7.20 and Develin 1989: 114);

BNJ 342 F17, the bronze *stele* setting out the punishment of Phrynichos (Schol. ad Aristophanem *Lysistrata* 313; to be distinguished from a second decree which honoured his killers, *IG* 1³ 102; see above, p. 95.).

When we look at the Athenian material attributed to his collection, we note that it is dominated by celebrity decrees of the fifth century,[126] and there is little evidence of interest in run-of-the-mill fourth-century decrees. A significant proportion of the testimonia pertains to the punishment of traitors including the bronze *stelai* setting out the punishment of Antiphon, Archeptolemos and Phrynichos (FF 5b, 17), the decree against Arthmios (F14) and the decree of Kannonos (F15), which – according to Xenophon's version – provided for the throwing into a pit of those found guilty of doing harm to the Athenians.[127] The fragmentary remains reflect not only Krateros' own interests but also those of his audience of later writers who were, after all, responsible for the fragments that survive of his work: they were more interested in the deployment of such material to make moral points. Once again (cf. Chapter 3.3.5.4 above), we note a gap between the type of decree-material that antiquarians were interested in and that which provides the bulk of our evidence for decrees in fourth-century Athens. There is little to suggest, however, that Krateros had any reason to fabricate decrees, though he may have taken seriously decrees, such as that against Arthmios, which modern scholars have found reason to treat with scepticism. It is clear that Krateros collected information about decrees, but it is a work

---

126 For the view that his work concentrated on fifth-century material see Erdas 2002: 27–8; Carawan *BNJ* 342 Biographical Essay; Jacoby *FGrH* 342 *Kommentar* 97.

127 Krentz 1989: 166, suggesting that it was an archaic law revived when the Athenians were re-codifying their laws after the fall of the Four Hundred; cf. Lavelle 1988.

LITERARY REPRESENTATIONS OF DECREES

that went beyond simple antiquarianism: a reference to Krateros' discussion of the prosecution of those not born of two Athenian parents who had attempted to enrol into a phratry by Harpokration (s.v. 'ναυτοδίκαι' (= Krateros *BNJ* 342 F4a)) suggests that the interest of his work extended into the implementation of decrees as well as their substance (cf. D14).

The fragmentary preservation of the antiquarian literature like that of Krateros in the works of later scholars leads us next into some discussion of the interests of one such inventive polymath of the late second century, Athenaios of Naukratis (see Appendix 2 X12–15 below). Much of the evidence for interest in Athenian decrees among Hellenistic writers derives from his *Deipnosophistai*, a lengthy work presented in the form of conversations on matters of wide cultural and literary interest. The authenticity of many of the authors and works referred to by Athenaios is far from clear: at points he seems to invent the names of authors and their works; at other times he draws upon plausible-sounding scholarly traditions;[128] accordingly, each reference must be assessed on its own merits. His references to decrees suggest a considerable Hellenistic interest in decrees which would otherwise be largely unknown to modern scholarship.[129] Early on in this work, Athenaios launches into praise of a Larensios, the host of the discussion,[130] who, he claims, gained his knowledge from a study of *psephismata* and *dogmata* (Ath. 2d). It appears, therefore, that the status of the decree, as a source of antiquarian knowledge, is asserted from the outset of his work. Athenaios' alertness to decrees and interest in lore about them emerges elsewhere: his long account of the tyranny of the Peripatetic Athenaion in the early 80s BC is generally accepted as an accurate account of the longest historical narrative connected with Poseidonios (*Deipnosophistai* 211d-15b).[131] According to this account, the Athenians were reported to have sent a force against the revolting Delians under the command of a certain Apellikon of Teos, a naturalised citizen; the expedition turned out to be a failure owing to Roman intervention. What is relevant here is his claim – as an illustration of Apellikon's 'colourful and diverse life' – that Apellikon collected, in addition to the works of Aristotle, copies of old decrees from the Metroon ('τά τ' ἐκ τοῦ Μητρώιου

---

128 On the difficulty of distinguishing between allusion and invention in the work of Athenaios, see Ceccarelli, Biographical Essay on *BNJ* 166 Athenaios. Jacob (2013) places more emphasis on Athenaios' deployment of the Hellenistic intellectual tradition to provide a complex and reflective work.

129 For the view of Athenaios' work as a reflection on lost Greek culture, see Jacob 2013: 113–20.

130 On the figure of Larensios, see Braund 2000; on his 'circle', see Jacob 2013: 19–23.

131 See e.g. Dowden, Commentary on *BNJ* 87 F36. Habicht 1997: 304–5, draws upon the account for historical narrative purposes.

τῶν παλαιῶν αὐτόγραφα ψηφίσματα'): he had been caught doing this surreptitiously and had fled from Athens (214e). While there are aspects of Athenaios' account which may be later fabrications, the story may reflect the interest of Hellenistic collectors in the documentary heritage of the Athenians; moreover, it is possible to detect some disparaging irony or even ridicule in the praise offered to this collector of decrees.

Among such Hellenistic writers preserved in fragmentary form, some – like Krateros – appear to have been interested more broadly in physically inscribed documents or inscriptions.[132] One of the most frequently cited of the documentary antiquarians was Polemon of Ilion, a writer of the second century, of whose work Preller and Müller collected 102 fragments.[133] Polemon was a favourite of later writers, especially Athenaios, who cites his works 45 times. Some 34 book titles are attributed to Polemon, of which several suggest significant epigraphical content.

Polemon was interested in laws and decrees too, as is made clear in a fragment cited by Harpokration (s.v. 'Νεμέας' = Polemon F3 Preller): in this passage, which purports to derive from his work *About the Akropolis*, he describes as a decree (*psephisma*) a regulation according to which the Athenians forbade the naming of certain categories of individual (a slave, a liberated woman, a prostitute, or a flute-player) after the penteteric festivals. Davies takes the view that this citation is an example of a vintage of invented documents restricting behaviour of, or with respect to, women,[134] and it is therefore likely to be a forgery of a Hellenistic antiquarian or Athenaios himself. It is, anyway, highly unlikely that such a restriction would have, in the fourth century, been introduced on the basis of a decree: its content is much more likely to reflect that of a law in the post-403/2 era.[135]

---

132 In the second century, Heliodoros of Athens, who wrote about the Athenian acropolis, is reported to have described Athenian dedications, tripods and monuments (*BNJ* 373 T2, F6–7): among these would have been inscriptions. For other ancient collectors of documents, see Larfeld 1902–7: 1.16–25. Note also: Diodorus the Periegete (*BNJ* 372), author of *Peri Mnemata* (F34); cf. F35 on Hypereides' burial place and the tomb of Themistocles; Heliodorus, *BNJ* 373 (with Roisman and Worthington 2015: 25–7), author of *On the Akropolis* (FF 1, 4), On the *Tripods at Athens* (F6); Menetor, *On Dedications* (Ath. 594c = *FHG* iv.452); Neoptolemos of Parion, *Peri epigrammaton* (Ath. 454f); Philochoros of Athens, *Epigrammata Attika* (*FGrH* 328 T1); cf. Alketas, *On the dedications at Delphi* (*FGrH* 405 F1 = Ath. 591c).

133 Polemon of Ilion: see Preller 1838; Müller 1853: 108–48.

134 Davies 2000: 217. Another example is the decree alleged to have been passed by the Athenians permitting bigamy towards the end of the Peloponnesian war: see Aulus Gellius 15.20.6; Diogenes Laertius 2.26; Suda s.v. 'λειπανδρεῖν', though taken seriously by Patterson 1981: 142–3.

135 The regulation is mentioned also by Athenaios, though as a law: 13.587c.

Yet more striking is Athenaios' discussion of Polemon's report of epigraphical material, including a decree concerning *parasitoi*:[136]

> Polemon – the *stele*-glutton (*stelokopas*) – says the following when he writes about *parasitoi*: 'Parasite is today a disreputable term, but among the ancients I find that the parasite was sacred and resembled an invited guest at a meal. **In the precinct of Herakles in Kynosarges is a *stele* inscribed with a decree moved by Alcibiades when Stephanos son of Thoukydides was secretary in which the following is said concerning the title: "let the priest, accompanied by the *parasitoi*, make the monthly offerings. Let the *parasitoi* be drawn from the bastards and their children, in accord with ancestral practice. If anyone is unwilling to serve as a parasite, let him be indicted in the law-court, in connection with these matters." The following is inscribed on the *kurbeis* concerned with the sacred ambassadors to Delos: "And the two heralds from the Kerykes clan associated with the Eleusinian Mysteries. These men are to serve as *parasitoi* in the precinct of Delian Apollo for a year." The following is inscribed on the dedications at Pallene: "The Archons and *parasitoi* in the year when Pythodoros was an eponymous archon made this dedication after being crowned with a gold garland. In the year of the priestess Diphile the *parasitoi* were Epilykos son of … -stratos of the deme Gargettos, Pericles son of Perikleitos of the deme Pithos, and Charines son of Demochares of the deme Gargettos." And among the laws relating to the archon *basileus* is written: "The Acharnians' *parasitoi* are to sacrifice to Apollo."' (Athenaios 234d–f (= Preller/Mueller F78): trans, Olson 2008 adapted) [137]

The passage, as it is preserved, suggests that Polemon was, at this point in his work,[138] interested in citing inscriptions (he appears to make reference to four of them in this passage) primarily for what they tell us about the meaning of the word '*parasitos*'; he may have organised them according to their relevance for the subjects in which he was interested. He presents some of this as an inscribed decree (emboldened in the above quotation). The mentions of a plausibly named distinguished proposer (Alcibiades: *PAA* 121630; for his proposals see *IG* I³ 117, 118, 119, 120, 227bis) and a secretary (Stephanos son of Thucydides: *PAA* 834135), a place of publication (albeit a unique one), and some reasonable directives concerning the selection of *parasitoi* has led this passage to have become accepted as evidence for a fifth-century decree of the

---

136 For Athenaios' interest in the term *parasitos* and its wider use, see Bouyssou 2013 and Constantakopoulou: 2017: 2, 238 (especially on the characterisation of the Delians as parasites).

137 The parts of the text related to the purported decree are emboldened.

138 Moreover, as Athenaios claims, they derive probably from a work called *The Letter Concerning Obscure Names* (ἐν τῇ Περὶ ὀνομάτων ἀδόξων ἐπιστολῇ: Müller F77).

Athenians on the subject.[139] Indeed, the physical existence of an inscribed list of magistrates and *parasitoi* of Athena from the chapel of Agia Triada at the intersection of the roads from Athens to Marathon and Athens to Sounion (*SEG* XXXIV 157) is rather reminiscent of the types of dedication that Polemon identified at Pallene, and could be cited in supportive of the authenticity of the epigraphical claims made in this passage. Notwithstanding this question, it is a firm indication of the fact that decrees – real or fabricated – could be used by Hellenistic writers, alongside other documents, as proofs of religious directives. We should recognise that while Polemon had some interest in Athenian decrees, epigraphy was not his sole preoccupation: the spectrum of titles attributed to him suggest that places, objects, and associated stories were his primary interest.[140] Had, therefore, his work survived, it might resemble that of a traveller or *periegetes*, like Pausanias (see below), rather than an epigrapher or someone primarily interested in documentary decrees.

At this point it is appropriate to note that Athenaios, the principal reporter of Polemon, has particular agendas related to the interests of his work: he makes other references to decrees which have reasonable credentials but concern exotic topics; this example crops up in his discussion of *protenthai* (perhaps best glossed as 'food inspectors'):

> I also find a decree ('εὑρίσκω δὲ καὶ ψήφισμα') which came about during the archonship of Kephisodoros at Athens ('ἐπὶ Κηφισοδώρου ἄρχοντος Ἀθήνησι γενόμενον'), in which the *protenthai* are something like a board of men, just as those called the *parasitoi* are. The decree is as follows: 'Phokos proposed ("Φῶκος εἶπεν"), so that the council may celebrate the Apatouria with all the other Athenians in the traditional manner ("ὅπως ἂν ἡ βουλὴ ἄγῃ τὰ Ἀπατούρια μετὰ τῶν ἄλλων Ἀθηναίων κατὰ τὰ πάτρια"), that it should be decreed by the council ("ἐψηφίσθαι τῇ βουλῇ") that the councillors are to be released from duties on the days when the other councils ("αἱ ἄλλαι βουλαί"[141]), who also receive such release, for five days starting on that day when the *protenthai* start to celebrate the festival.' (Ath. 171d–e)

---

139 See, for instance, Murray 1995: 236; Parker 2005: 438. Develin 1989: 195 places it in the period 431/0–404/3.

140 Other works of Polemon, e.g. *On the Sacred Road* (Preller/Müller FF 11–13) or *On the Poikile Stoa at Sikyon* (Preller/Müller FF 14–15) or *On the Treasuries at Delphi* (Preller/Müller FF 27–9).

141 Lambert (1998: 156 note 76) prefers MSS βουλαί to Wilamowitz's ἀρχαί: 'such legislation may represent a decision of the Athenian *boule* giving itself a holiday as long as that enjoyed by *boulai* on other Ionian states and, possibly, the Areopagos at Athens.'

The content of this passage does not rule out the possibility that this is a report of a genuine decree of the council, proposed by a certain Phokos,[142] and dated to the archonship of Kephisodotos (a plausible archon-dating, which could refer to the archon either of 366/5 or 323/2: see BD 8);[143] indeed, it is reasonable to accept the possibility that the council may well have been empowered to pass decrees which concerned its own organisation. The motion formula for a decree of the council, 'be it decreed by the Council' ('ἐψηφίσθαι τῇ βουλῇ') is well-attested in inscribed Attic decrees,[144] and so it is quite plausible that the author is either drawing upon documentary material (or is well informed). Accordingly, the content of this decree, which appears to enable all councillors to take part in the Apatouria, a festival celebrated throughout Attica and also among phratries,[145] is generally taken very seriously by scholars: for instance, Rhodes cites it as evidence that the council gave itself five days' holiday for the Apatouria.[146] Parker cites the passage as evidence for a festival of the *protenthai* (foretasters) on the day before the *dorpia* (the first day of the Apatouria).[147] Moreover, Lambert's suggestion is that they 'were responsible in some way for the organisation of phratry dinners on the *dorpia* [the first day of the Apatouria] and in consequence had their own a day early'.[148] The *protenthai*, however, are extremely obscure: while Athenaios appears to have collected information on them, they are not mentioned in the epigraphical sources, and the only classical reference to them crops up in Aristophanes' *Clouds* (1198). Davies, however, casts doubt on the authenticity of this decree, chiefly on the basis that it was not the kind of thing that would have been written up on stone and 'it is hard to identify any other route by which the text could have been preserved to reach Athenaios'.[149] Its authenticity, therefore, must remain uncertain; however, one must acknowledge the possibility at least that Athenaios drew upon a source

---

142 A certain Phokos is mentioned by Plutarch (*Phoc.* 20, 30, 28) as the son of Phokion, and the same son is mentioned a little earlier in Athenaios (4.168e–9a). But the identification is uncertain, and there are other occurrences of the name (*LGPN* II, s.v. 'Phokos'). The invention of a decree, and indeed a proposer, is hardly beyond the imagination of Athenaios. However, as Lambert (1998: 156) points out, the hedonistic nature of this festival would seem to match the allegedly profligate character of Phokion's son. Yet such a connection would suit Athenaios' literary intentions well, and does not therefore necessarily support the authenticity of this decree.

143 As Lambert points out (1998: 156 note 75), its relevance to festivals and phratries is much more characteristic of a later date.

144 See Rhodes with Lewis 1997: 5. See for example *IG* II² 128 line 10 of 356/5.

145 Parker 1996: 105.

146 Rhodes 1972: 30.

147 Parker 2005: 458.

148 Lambert 1998: 155.

149 Davies 2000: 213.

which itself had drawn upon Athenian decrees in the archive or knew of an orally preserved tradition about such a decree.

Davies is rightly cautious about the authenticity of other decrees that crop up in Athenaios' work. Athenaios (590d–f) claims that, according to the biographer Hermippos of Smyrna (author of the *Life of Hypereides* of c. 200 BC; *FGrH* 1026 F46a), the Athenians made a decree (*psephisma*) after the trial of Phryne (fr. 178 Jensen) forbidding both speakers from lamenting on the behalf of others and the putting on display of men or women while their case was being decided. Davies suggests that this was another 'product of the decree-manufacturing industry' which coincided with the theme of book 13 (women, prostitutes and their lovers) and Athenaios' widely-expressed interest in the regulation of human, particularly female, behaviour and the role of the *gynaikonomoi* (6.245b–c).[150] Yet it is quite possible that this decree was the fabrication of the Hellenistic biographer, Hermippos, to whom Athenaios attributes the story.[151] Athenaios' claim about bigamy being permitted by decree at a time of scarcity (556a) falls into the same category: Diogenes Laertius 2.26 (attributing knowledge of it to Satyros and Hieronymos of Rhodes) mentions a comparable decree, according to which men were allowed to have children by one woman while being married to another: as Haake suggests,[152] it was probably a Hellenistic composition fabricated in a pseudo-biographical apology to defend Socrates on charges of bigamy.

Other than the examples discussed, as Davies concluded,[153] among the material pertinent to decrees that we find in Athenaios' work, there is little genuine documentary material, though there are traces of material which may have derived from manufactured decrees. Perhaps it is worth, however, observing that by valuing the testimonia of – most of them extraordinary – decrees and connecting them with learned people, he drew on decrees which he had encountered in his own source-material to illustrate points and expand discussion of words, food and individuals (especially women). Decrees, real or fabricated, are there to show off knowledge and even to entertain. For Athenaios, it should be added, there is little by way of moral assessment of the decrees under discussion: knowledge of them is there for his speakers to impress their collocutors with their knowledge of classical culture. This was one expression of the

---

150 Davies 2000: 213; Filonik 2016: 132–3 also takes the view that the decree was a forgery.
151 Bollansée 1999: 388 suggests that the account of the trial and its aftermath was the invention of Hermippos; on the different versions of Phryne's trial, see Eidinow 2016: 23–30 and, emphasising the role of Hermippos and his source Idomeneus of Lampsakos, see Cooper 1995.
152 Haake 2013: 104 note 169, 107-8.
153 Davies 2000: 217.

wider phenomenon of the Second Sophistic of admiring things classical: the decree-culture of classical Athens, so richly attested in the works of comedians, orators and Hellenistic antiquarians, was to Athenaios and others an important aspect of classical culture; they presumed that their audience of readers were familiar enough to appreciate their exploration of it. Yet as we will see from the next author to be briefly discussed, not every Second Sophistic writer was fascinated by decrees.

The most detailed extant physical description of Athens extant from antiquity is that of Pausanias book 1; Pausanias was deeply interested in inscriptions, dedications and honorific statues,[154] and while he is usually thought of as a travel writer (*periegetes*), in this sense he might be viewed as an antiquarian collector of inscribed information. But his eye was rarely caught by decrees and he did not fabricate information about them: one of the rare references to a decree in his work is that to Oinobios' decree, probably of 404/3 (Develin 1989: 186), which permitted the return of the historian Thucydides to Athens (Paus. 1.23.9: ψήφισμα γὰρ ἐνίκησεν Οἰνόβιος κατελθεῖν ἐς Ἀθήνας Θουκυδίδην). On this occasion, Pausanias was led into mentioning the decree as he was reporting a statue of the proposer close to the Athenian acropolis. Later on, in his fifth book, his description of the terms of the 30-year peace of 446/5 crops up owing to the fact that the bronze *stele* containing its terms stood in front of Olympian Zeus (5.23.4). While they contribute an element of detail to his description, there is, therefore, little to suggest that Pausanias was interested in Athenian decrees for their own sake: they seem to have had little significance for someone whose interests were primarily in the material aspects of the Greek world. Only on one occasion, his mention of the Athenian decree associated with Miltiades before the battle of Marathon – granting their slaves who died in battle a public burial and allowing the inscription of their names on stone (Paus. 1.29.7; cf. 7.15.7) – did he use a decree to contribute to his portrayal of Athenian character.[155]

5.4.4 The Fabrication of Documentary Decrees by Rhetoricians

The later fabrication of decrees in literature is not restricted to antiquarian or biographical works. Certain manuscripts of Andocides and Demosthenes

---

154 On Pausanias' use of inscriptions, see Habicht 1984; Whittaker 1991; Zizza 2006; Tzifopoulos 2013.

155 A version of this decree is offered in Andocides 1.107, who says that it restored exiles and reinstated disenfranchised citizens; see also [Arist.] *Ath. Pol.* 22.8; Plu. *Them.* 11.1; Plu. *Arist.* 8.1 and MacDowell 1962: 140.

contain passages which appear to represent documentary versions of decrees, such as that of Kallisthenes ordering the evacuation of Attica in Skirophorion 346 (Dem. 18.37–8: see D135), or that of the decree of Ktesiphon for Demosthenes (Dem. 18.118: see D179). The inauthenticity of such decrees has been confirmed by Canevaro's landmark study of them.[156] But it is important to note that their creation is a phenomenon quite separate from that of the development of historic documents with patriotic intent. There appears to have been little political motivation behind their fabrication. The wide range of standards and subjects of forged documents leads Canevaro to envisage different contexts in which the texts of decrees, especially those which were referred to in Demosthenes' speeches, were fabricated, including engagement with the system of rhetorical education of the era before the second century AD in which 'it was standard practice to compose fictitious laws and decrees to form the subject of oratorical exercises'.[157] As Canevaro notes, 'one of the preliminary exercises (*progymnasmata*) for students of rhetoric, according to our sources, was called *nomos* and involved arguing for and against a law or decree, which had been invented by the teacher for the purpose of the exercise. This was one of the most advanced exercises in the rhetorical curriculum, directly connected with the preparation for composing and delivering a proper *declamatio* (μελέτη), a fictitious speech which was the centre of the production of professional rhetoricians from the Hellenistic age on.'[158] The 'Art of Rhetoric', a work of the third-century AD Greek rhetorician Apsines of Gadara – which will be discussed in Chapter 5.5 below – is perhaps the clearest indication of the continuation of such practice; Canevaro points also to Hellenistic scholarly and antiquarian interest in the history of Athens as the likely origin of such documents.[159] He suggests that such documents – invented by knowledgeable teachers – came to be inserted into the manuscripts of speeches by editors who were troubled by the lack of authentic documents that appeared in the texts; their fictitious nature was soon forgotten by users of their texts and accordingly they found their way into the historical tradition. The process by which such texts came to be incorporated in certain manuscripts of the orators has already been discussed extensively by Canevaro, but there is more

156 For a list of documentary versions of decrees: see Appendix 2 note 1 below.
157 Canevaro, 2013: 333; cf. Canevaro forthcoming. Carawan 2017 argues that whereas the documents that appear in Demosthenes' *On the Crown* are the creations of rhetorical schools, those in Andocides' *On the Mysteries* are more likely to have been reconstructed by over-zealous editors with historical interests working on the basis of sources such as Krateros' work on decrees.
158 Canevaro forthcoming; on these fictitious classicisng speeches, see Cribiore 2001: 231–8.
159 Canevaro 2013: 338; cf. Canevaro forthcoming.

LITERARY REPRESENTATIONS OF DECREES

to say on the advice given by rhetoricians on the deployment of decrees in the construction of arguments.

5.5 Decrees and Argumentation in Later Rhetorical Works

It was argued in Chapter 2 above that Athenian political activity of the fourth century demonstrates the existence of a 'decree-minded' sentiment among politicians, which is to say that not only were they involved in the proposal and challenge of decrees, but also that they deployed knowledge of decrees as an important and pliable tool in invective and in the formulation of arguments. Epigraphical evidence indicates that the decree played a prominent rhetorical role in interstate negotiations in the Hellenistic period,[160] and the public announcement of decrees was an important aspect of honorific transactions in that era.[161] From the fourth century onwards, there was some explicit recognition of the role of the decree in persuasion: Aristotle in the *Rhetoric*, on occasion, offers examples of decrees drawn upon in argumentation; most of these examples, as Trevett points out, drew upon oral tradition, or even collections of sayings attributed to famous men.[162]

Equally pertinent to our exploration of the representation of fourth-century Athenian decrees is the fact that post-classical rhetoricians recognised their potential as sources of 'non-artistic' proof. They drew, in all likelihood, upon Hellenistic and Roman-era rhetorical handbooks.[163] The *Anonymous Seguerianus*, author of a work with the title *The Art of Political Speech*, wrote as follows:

> Non-artistic proofs (*atechnoi pisteis*) are, for example, witnesses, decrees, contracts, such things, as many are written down. They are called 'non-artistic' since nothing comes from the thought of the speaker but is what any ordinary person might discover. The task of the orator in non-artistic proofs is to amplify and confirm those that aid his case and to diminish and attack those against us as not credible. (3.145)

According to this author, therefore, decrees were one of a number of instruments that were accessible and could be deployed effectively without specialist knowledge; in doing so the author went a step further than Aristotle by

---

160 On the performance of decrees in the Hellenistic period, see Massar 2006; Rubinstein 2013.

161 Ceccarelli 2010: 106–38 (announcement of honours at tragic contests); Chaniotis 2013.

162 Trevett 1996a. See Arist. *Rh.* 1411b6–10 (= D46 T6); 1384b32 (= D65 T1), 1411a6–10 (= D82 T2), 1399b 1 ff (= D100 T2).

163 Dilts and Kennedy 1997: ix.

classifying decrees as *atechnoi pisteis* in their own right.[164] Further on in his work, he advised that the refutation of arguments formulated on the basis of decrees be carried out by means of alternative interpretation, or in making points about the intention (*dianoia*) of the proposer (3.188). The seriousness which later writers attached to decrees is reflected by the popularity in the Hellenistic and Roman periods of a number of speeches that were pertinent to the proposal or the indictment of decrees, among them Demosthenes' *On the Crown* and *Against Leptines*.[165] This legacy is apparent in the work of the fourth-century AD rhetorician Apsines of Gadara who, in his handbook on political rhetoric, drew upon texts of the Attic orators and offered advice on the ways in which to use decrees in order to make key points of argumentation (for his decrees, see Appendix 2 X3–7 below). He made reference to the decree that was the subject of Demosthenes *Against Aristokrates* (on Charidemos' inviolability: D94) in his discussion of how to deal in a speech with things spoken or written (1.46–7); his suggestion was to raise the subject of the consequences of the decree (1.57). He gave advice about the refutation of arguments based on decrees, suggesting the 'scrutiny of intent (*dianoia*)' (3.10–11). He advised orators to prepare judges for a verdict by reminding them of the defendant's services, which could take the form of the proposal of laws and decrees (10.18). He recommended that speakers should, after persuading an audience on some matter, go on to introduce another theme: he offered several (some of them imaginary) proposals to illustrate this point:

> Whenever, after persuading the hearers of something, we introduce some different second thing; for in these cases it will be fitting to praise the hearers for having been persuaded on the previous matter. For example, you might say: 'First, it is right to praise you, gentlemen, in that you have recently paid attention to those of us speaking the best advice to you and have disregarded those speaking the opposite and deceiving you; but then let us think to add also what follows from this (from your earlier decision)', as in those problems for declamation where Pericles, after persuading the people to remain within the walls, then seeks to persuade them to lay waste Attica. Or again: Themistocles, after persuading them to abandon the city, introduces a motion for them to burn the citadel. Or again: some individuals have destroyed a city. The exiles bring the destroyers to trial before the Greeks and are successful in their prosecution, after which, when a speech is made concerning punishment, they propose for them to suffer the same

164 For Aristotle's view of laws as *atechnoi pisteis*, see *Rh.* 1375a22–b25 with discussion at Chapter 2.2.1 above.

165 See, for instance Kremmydas 2007b, discussing a third-century declamation steeped in knowledge of Attic oratory; Kremmydas 2012: 62–4; Wankel 1976: I. 63–82; generally, on the ancient reception of Demosthenes' speeches, see Drerup 1923; Canevaro 2013: 329–42.

things. Or again: after successfully prosecuting Timarchos, Aeschines introduces a motion to abolish the trierarchic law. As you see, he has already persuaded the judges to condemn Timarchos and he will praise them for this. Or again: after Hypereides successfully introduced a motion that when Philip was in Elateia Demosthenes alone should be the adviser to the city, then he proposes to give Demosthenes a bodyguard as well. Apsines, *Art of Rhetoric*, 1.4–9 (trans. Dilts and Kennedy 1997)

In cases where a proposer's initial suggestion was rejected, Apsines recommended the use of *barytes* ('heaviness'), that is, claiming that one was forced to speak because of circumstances. When Demades' motion that Philip be made a Thirteenth God was rejected, instead he proposed that a temple be dedicated to Philip (1.19). Apsines cited blatantly fabricated decrees to support his arguments about the refutation of reputations (1.27: Isocrates' decree about refraining from naval operations) and to advise about the argumentation from the benefit of the city (1.72 and 3.16: Demosthenes' proposal about digging a canal through the isthmus of Corinth). He also refers at several points to a parody of a decree, allegedly attributed to the Athenian politician Aristogeiton at a time of scarcity, to turn a blind eye to bribery (2.13, 19; 3.11).[166] The texts of the anonymous rhetorician and of Apsines suggest that they were directly imitating the classical tendency to use decrees as rhetorical proofs which we have discussed at length (see Chapter 2.6 above). But they also indicate the emergence of a readiness to fabricate or expand on stories about decrees with a view to persuading an audience.

Overall, while offering advice about creating arguments pertaining to decrees and showing knowledge of episodes containing debates about historical decrees, Apsines also shows a readiness to fabricate historically implausible decrees. While, therefore, Apsines' use of the decree as a rhetorical yardstick demonstrates an interest in their fourth-century deployment, his readiness to invent decrees also underlines the existence of a more imaginative approach to the decree – one which had an earlier manifestation in the comic parody of Old Comedy.

5.6 Parody Beyond Comedy

We have already established that decrees of the Athenian *demos* – even though they could sometimes be represented as manifestations of unity of purpose – could also be parodied in comedy and other genres (Chapter 5.3.2 above). The

---

166 For the view that 'none of Apsines' quotations are reliable sources for the texts of authors he cites' see Dilts and Kennedy 1997: xvii.

second-century AD satirist Lucian, inspired perhaps by the classical parody of decrees, was able to create humour out of them. The language of Athenian documents was, for instance, deployed in his portrayal of Timon the misanthrope. Not only did Timon declare his misanthropy by way of a speech set out as a mock law (*Timon*, 42–4),[167] but he was mocked by the imaginary orator Demeas, who praised him with a long and ridiculous parody of an honorific decree 'resolved by the council, assembly, the jurors, the tribes and demes, both individually and in common' to set up a golden statue of Timon beside Athena on the acropolis with a thunderbolt in his hand and a halo above his head, justified on the basis that he continuously did his best for the city' (50–2).[168] In the *Menippos* (19–20), the satire against wealth and power was heightened by way of a verbatim citation of a motion of the demagogues against the rich, which led to a parody both of content of decree and its reception:

> Be it resolved by the council and the people ('δεδόχθω τῆι βουλῆι καὶ τῷ δήμῳ'), that when they die their bodies be punished like those of the other malefactors, but their souls be sent back up into life and enter into donkeys until they shall have passed 250,000 years in the said condition, transmigrating from donkey to donkey, bearing burdens, and being driven by the poor; and that thereafter it be permitted them to die. On the motion of ('εἶπε τὴν γνώμην …') Scully Fitzbones of Corpsebury, Cadavershire.
>
> 'After this motion had been read, the officials put it to the vote ("ἐπεψήφισαν αἱ ἀρχαί"), the majority indicated assent ("ἐπεχειροτόνησε τὸ πλῆθος") by the usual sign, Brimo brayed and Cerberus howled. That is the way in which their motions are enacted and ratified.' (trans. Harmon adapted)

In his *Parliament of the Gods* (14–18) the Gods passed decrees of their own too, and an enactment was fabricated which arranged for a meeting of the Gods and allocated duties to each one individually. Besides these examples, Lucian, famously, in his *True History* (1.20) introduced a peace-treaty to put an end to the war between the Moon-ites and Sun-ites, which was to be set up on an electrum *stele* in space. As Ní Mheallaigh observes, the use of such documents illustrates one of Lucian's classicising interests,[169] and may be viewed

---

167 For discussion of the language of the 'Misanthrope's Charter', which Hopkinson (2008: 188, 193) suggests echoes the Athenian decrees like those quoted in Demosthenes' *On the Crown*, see Householder 1940, Delz 1950: 134–50.

168 Hopkinson 2008: 193 suggests that the decree praising Demeas was 'couched in the conventional language of such proposals', pointing to the phrase 'he continues doing the best things for the city' ('διατελεῖ τὰ ἄριστα πράττων τῆι πόλει': section 50; cf. Dem. 18.118).

169 Ní Mheallaigh 2008. For a useful survey of Lucian's knowledge of the Athenian assembly, see Delz 1950: 115–50. On his 'inscription-fiction' see Ní Mheallaigh 2014: 254–8. For his criticism of Hypereides and Lycurgus for framing 'little proposals and *probouleumata*' when Philip threatened Athens, see *Parasit.* 42.

as part of his wider attempt to appreciate – occasionally through accounts of the Athenians' decrees – the past glories of classical Greek culture,[170] a phenomenon which surfaced also in the work of Plutarch, Aelius Aristides and Athenaios (see, Chapters 5.2 and 5.4 above). As with those authors, Lucian's parody of Greek decree-activity shows his desire to demonstrate the depth of his immersion in Greek culture[171] and his anticipation that his audience of readers would be familiar enough to appreciate the parody of the decree. But the satirical aspect of them demonstrates that Lucian's perspective on the classical period went beyond straightforward nostalgia,[172] and might be read as a critique of the democratic Athenian culture of accomplishing things and granting rewards by decree. Moreover, these passages must be seen within the wider context of the literary deployment of decrees: Lucian's fabrications demonstrate engagement not only with classicising documentary habits, but also the tradition – the first manifestation of which appears in Old Comedy – of fabricating and parodying them.[173]

5.7 Conclusion

The idea, enunciated by Aristotle, that the decree was the political tool of an unreflective mob and a transaction that undermined the wellbeing of political communities was an image that appealed not only to those who described the history of fifth-century Athens but to later writers too. It remained an important model of analysis to those who bought into an anti-democratic tradition: Cicero, in defence of Flaccus, dismissed the *psephismata* read out in court by his opponent Laelius as the products of intimidation, claiming that 'they are not based upon considered votes or affidavits nor safeguarded by an oath, but produced by a show of hands and the undisciplined shouting of an inflamed mob' (15); this argument was extended with the claim that such a tendency was responsible for the decline of the Greek world: 'that Greece of ancient times, once so flourishing in its wealth, dominion and glory, fell through this single evil, the excessive liberty and licence of its meetings' (16). Accordingly, Cicero

---

170 Cf. Hopkinson 2007: 7; generally on the revival of Greek culture in the era of the Second Sophistic see Bowie (1970).
171 We might compare this with his complex engagement with the Greek idea of *philotimia*, as worked out by Mossman (2012).
172 Cf. Hopkinson 2007: 8.
173 Hopkinson 2007: 8: '*Timon* is set in Classical Athens; but the existence there already of spongers, charlatans and ingratiating hangers-on gives the lie to idealising views of that time. The language of Attic Greece is turned against its own origins, and a new Old Comedy arises, burlesquing the gods and treating self-important citizens with irreverence.'

dismissed the arguments of Flaccus' opponents claiming that 'what you call Greek resolutions (*psephismata*) are not evidence at all, but the clamour of the impoverished and some reckless impulse of a meeting of Greeklings' (23).[174]

The image that Cicero offers of the decree could not be further from the calm serenity of the *stele* inscribed on white stone. Cicero's vision, that of the decree as a reckless measure, born of political desperation and popular whim, and put to irresponsible use by a self-seeking politician, had its origins in hostile literary traditions about Athenian decrees. I began this chapter by asking how widespread such a negative characterisation of Athenian decrees – as a tool of an out-of-control mob with excessive political power – was in Greek writers. Some fifth- and fourth-century writers, such as Thucydides, in his account of the Mytilenean debate and Xenophon in his account of the controversy on the treatment of the generals after the battle of Arginusae certainly make this association (5.2.1). And the pivotal role of decrees in the *Ath. Pol.*'s account of the anti-democratic revolutions at the end of the fifth century certainly represents the view of their capacity for committing acts of institutional self-harm (5.2.2). Moreover, Aristophanes' parody of decrees certainly also plays on a wider disillusionment in decrees as a tool of self-seeking politicians and a product of the short-sighted *demos* (5.3.2). But as we have seen, this portrayal of decree-making in a critique of democratic activity represents only one of a number of representations of the decree which occur in the literary sources. They reflect the poet's belief that his audience would be sensitive enough to the language of decrees for it to engage them. The other perspective with which we opened discussion in this chapter – that of Athenian decrees as unfulfilled and inane – does not appear to have taken root in the literary traditions about decrees.

When we move into the fourth-century parts of Xenophon's *Hellenika* and the works of fourth-century Atthidographers, we find accounts of decrees playing a role in the unfolding of narrative accounts of the past, with little to suggest they support a critique of democratic activity (5.1.2). In the *Suppliants* of Aeschylus too we see the enactment of the decree of the Argive assembly as a pivotal development in the plot as well as a reflection on the responsibility of Pelasgos for its enactment (Chapter 5.3.1 above). When we turn to Plutarch, we find decrees deployed extensively in biographical narration, as a way of characterising the political activity of individuals (5.2.3; cf. 5.4.2).[175] We see that authors working on a range of genres were sensitive to engaging with the debate about the balance of responsibility between proposer and *demos*. The potential

---

174 Translations of Cicero are those of MacDonald 1977.
175 For the deployment of the form and language of the Greek decree as an empowering narrative tool in Luke's *Preface*, see Moles 2011.

that decrees offered in the construction of arguments (deployed extensively by Attic orators in political and litigious contexts; see Chapters 1 and 2 above) may have been influential upon the tendency among biographers to draw upon the evidence of decrees in apologetic works and literary characterisation. It may have informed also later rhetorical writers who fabricated decrees as a way of showing how they might be used in persuasion (Chapters 5.4.4 and 5.5 above)

We can observe how certain antiquarians, such as Krateros and later Athenaios (Chapter 5.4.3 above), developed a taste for exotic decrees and inscriptions, an interest stimulated perhaps by the fourth-century Athenians' own fabrication of patriotic documents relating to the Persian war era (5.4.1). Athenaios' interest in obscure and extraordinary Athenian decrees might be viewed as an expression of interest in idiosyncratic things from the classical period and of the view that an audience of intellectuals would have been sufficiently interested in the history of decrees to be entertained by them. But this survey of the occurrence of decrees in literature suggests also a distinct tradition, which had its origins in the fabrication of mock-decrees of Old Comedy: Aristophanes appears to have drawn a great deal of humour from the assumption that his audience would have been familiar with the language of decrees. And this presentation of decrees may have been among the forces that gave rise to the classicising enthusiasm of Aelius Aristides, Athenaios and Lucian (Chapters 5.4 and 5.6 above) for decrees. What we see, therefore, is that the representation of decrees in post-classical literature builds upon several tendencies of the classical period: the deployment of decrees in logical argumentation, in accounts of historical narratives, and their critique and parody. Decrees, therefore, in the classical period and beyond, were a rich source of literary engagement for a wide range of writers; moreover, we have seen clear evidence for a fertile tradition in elaborating and fabricating stories about decrees. These provide a clear indication of the broad cultural significance of the ancient Athenian decree and its legacy. What was originally a political institution was transformed, over the course of antiquity, into a theme of great cultural significance.

Conclusion

> Are there any decrees or any laws which have not brought him money? ... Would you tell me, men of the jury, do you believe that he proposed that there should be upkeep at the *prytaneion* and a statue set up in the agora for Diphilos as a present? Or that he made Chairephilos, Pheidon, Pamphilos, Pheidippos, and even Epigenes and Konon the bankers citizens as a present? Or to set up bronze statues in the agora of Pairisades, Satyros, and Gorgippos, the tyrants from the Bosporos, from whom he receives a thousand *medimnoi* of wheat per year, this man who will straightaway allege that there is nowhere for him to flee? (Din. 1.43; cf. DD 227, 234, 235, 236)

Thus, Dinarchus, in his speech against Demosthenes attacking his involvement in the scandal arising out of the receipt of the fugitive Macedonian treasurer Harpalos and his monies, alleged that his opponent took bribes in return for proposing honorific decrees, and implied that he put his own interests above those of the Athenians. This is a rich passage for what it says about several decrees apparently proposed by Demosthenes the orator over the course of his political career; moreover, it demonstrates also how allegations about the motivations of decrees might be used in an attack on an individual. It is, however, a piece of evidence that evokes two methodological challenges: that concerning the 'hard' data for the content of Athenian decrees and that concerning the 'soft' data concerning the political interpretations of decree-proposers' intentions.

The first of these methodological challenges is treated over the course of the Inventory of Decrees (Volume 1 Inventory A). It concerns the question of how to move from the literary sources' claims about the content of decrees to the reconstruction of the likely substance of decrees as they were resolved by the assembly at a point in the fourth century (the 'hard' data). The literary evidence suggests that there was a certain degree of attention paid by those with political interests to the substance and language of decrees, but that argumentation was based not always on close familiarity with their texts but rather on awareness of their approximate content. This means that, with some exceptions, it is rarely possible to confidently reconstruct the precise wording of decrees; on many occasions it is hard to be certain that the testimonia amount to secure evidence for a decree (see Volume 1 Inventory B). Yet our problems are mitigated by the fact that orators were aware that their audiences had some – perhaps sketchy – awareness of the substance of specific decrees: this meant that they generally avoided making false claims about the content of decrees. Moreover,

240

the fact that our literary sources (chiefly oratory) were very much interested in offering 'soft' data in the form of accounts of the intentions behind decrees and their consequences is what enables us to ask the questions pursued in Volume 2 about the deployment and reception of decrees in fourth-century Athens.

The second methodological challenge is confronted in Volume 2 and concerns the interpretation of this 'soft' data just identified. To put it crudely, our sources claim that the proposal of individual decrees was either aligned with the interests of the community (in other words, it followed the informal constraints of decree-making), or alternatively, that a decree was proposed for self-interested reasons which were against the interests of the city-community. While it has been possible to identify individuals such as Demosthenes (and others, including Androtion, Aristophon and Demades) who proposed decrees that would have obliged their associates in other communities, such self-interested explanations of decrees were never acknowledged by proposers, even if some politicians, like Demosthenes, were visibly eager to draw symbolic capital from accounts of their own proposals. The subjectivity of accounts of decrees is what stands in the way of achieving secure knowledge of the balances of interests that were at stake in the proposals behind them. But yet the variegated nature of the soft data is what allows us to write a history of the decrees of the fourth-century Athenians which uncovers the cultural status of this institution and its legacy and enriches the picture of decrees that can be drawn out on the basis of the epigraphical record.

Over the course of this volume I have drawn upon epigraphical and literary texts to develop a set of interrelated perspectives on Athenian decrees of the fourth century. I have made a case for both their practical and symbolic significance to ancient Athenian politics and have argued that their profile in epigraphical and literary contexts indicates their cultural significance to the ancient Athenians in the fourth century and to Greek writers in the classical period and beyond. The foundation of the decree's status, in ancient Athens, was the collective acknowledgement (which had its roots in formal rules but which was enunciated in literary contexts and epigraphical formulae) that they were authoritative decisions of the Athenian *demos*; yet responsibility for them could be placed alternatively upon the shoulders of their proposers. The trusted status of decrees as accurate records of past decisions, sometimes underscored by monumental presence, meant that they offered value as proofs in the Athenian courts and elsewhere. This was an element of the 'decree-minded' mentality among the politically active in fourth-century Athens. Accordingly, decrees and stories about them were available for manifold uses in the context of arguments made in the Athenian lawcourts and other institutional contexts. Decrees – both contemporary and historic – could be used to support paradigmatic narratives about civic unity and accounts of the actions of the Athenian people in the face of crisis; decrees were drawn on to support defences of, or attacks upon, individual political records. But in a number of speeches – especially those related to challenges to laws or decrees – orators focussed closely upon decrees in the construction of their arguments.

In contrast to the established laws (in particular those associated with ancient lawgivers), contemporary decrees were frequently prone to criticism and hostility: their status was therefore potentially unstable and they were generally viewed as subordinate to laws. However, decrees that were associated with bygone eras, preserved in collective memory and then instantiated in inscribed versions (or accounts of inscribed versions), such as the decree against Arthmios or that associated with Demophantos, appear to have acquired a more resilient status by being deployed as paradigms of the moral standards put in front of Athenian audiences at the assembly and lawcourts. Orators made claims which implied the perception of a timeless relevance of decrees to their arguments; such a perception of institutional continuity and stability with respect to the system of decree-enactment assured their sustained high status in setting moral standards. Arguments built on decrees, therefore, went well beyond the ideology of them as pertinent to only short-term and specific matters: they demonstrate one way in which decrees could be used to posit informal rules.

Accounts of activities related to decrees were extensively used as evidence in the character evaluation of their proposers and challengers. These assessments consisted alternatively of praise or criticism; they were formulated sometimes in terms of the relationship of decrees to established values such as honour, shame and reciprocal exchange but also in terms of their benefit to the community. While we have encountered expressions of a consensus that decrees which had been carefully enacted using the appropriate channels possessed a high level of authority, new decrees were prone to attack by way of the *graphe paranomon* process, and the value of other past decrees enacted within living memory too was prone to criticism. The readiness to attack and criticise decrees, then, was an aspect of decree-minded political activity: whereas Athenian citizens conformed with it by proposing decrees and boasting about them, they could also object to others' associations with decrees.

Another aspect of the decree-minded mentality we have identified among the fourth-century Athenians consisted of the readiness of a broad spectrum of citizens to undertake the proposal of decrees; this activity appears not to have required any great degree of expertise beyond that which would be gleaned through civic activity or discussions with other Athenians. If it is appropriate to talk about an expertise in decree-related activity, we should think of it as

CONCLUSION   243

a specialism which was within reach of the broad spectrum of Athenian citizens who were involved in some capacity in civic institutions. As argued in Chapter 5 above, the fact that Aristophanes frequently reached to the language of decrees in the production of humour strongly suggests that he presumed his audience was familiar enough with such language to find it funny. The relative accessibility, therefore, of activity relating to the proposal of decrees was an important expression of the positive liberty of the Athenian citizen.

While we have found much evidence in the literary texts for broad engagement with knowledge about decrees, it has not always been clear how far that engagement was founded upon detailed accounts of their texts. With some exceptions, orators and historians appear to cite decrees in the hope of making general or moral points rather than building detailed arguments on the basis of close readings of their texts. Accordingly, debates about Athenian decrees that occur in literary texts tend to focus on the broad interpretation of their relevance to a case rather than arguments about close detail (though, as we have seen, there are a number of disputes that took place in the fourth century which concerned the legality of specific provisions within a decree). This phenomenon leads us back to a point already made: that knowledge of, and ideas about, decrees, was something that circulated socially rather than being based on autopsy of documentary authority. Knowledge about decrees circulated through both institutional and non-institutional routes, more often than not through human interaction in the form of socialisation or official activity carried out by magistrates. A small number of decrees (those leading to the award of statues in recognition of outstanding service to the Athenians) gained a reputation for offering persuasive value in the courts; this sustained a general awareness, rather than detailed knowledge, of them. The archive in the agora offered a source of authoritative texts; it is likely that it provided a resource for those litigants who wanted to have the texts of decrees read aloud in the lawcourts, but we should not pretend that it was a starting-point for awareness of decrees: those who used the archive in this way probably knew what they were looking for. It is evident also that the Athenians passed many more decrees than those which they inscribed, and that the epigraphical habit was about monumentalising those Athenian decree-making activities which had enduring significance rather than providing a comprehensive archive of them. References to inscribed versions of decrees in the literary sources were made on those occasions when orators wished to exploit the persuasive capital offered by knowledge of a physical version of a text. When it comes to inscriptions, ancient authors appear to have been attracted very much to celebrity inscriptions of bygone eras: relatively little attention was paid to the more everyday types of decree that we encounter in the epigraphical record.

The emphasis among decrees preserved in both the literary and epigraphical records on interactions with individuals and communities beyond Athens (in the shape of alliances and honorific decrees) is indicative of the importance of decrees for Athenian engagement with the world beyond Attica. Both literary sources and epigraphical testimonia suggest the view that some Athenians believed that there was a significant audience of non-Athenians who were interested in their decrees; the size and makeup of these audiences in reality was, however, heavily contingent on the nature of the decree and also Athens' geopolitical standing at the time. Dissemination of knowledge of Athenian decrees beyond Attica was undertaken through a range of means. It is clear that the epigraphical publication of decrees concerning non-Athenians had monumental significance and was important for Athenian expressions of hope that future benefactors might pay attention to their honorands. Moreover, the inscription of honours was prized by some non-Athenians, but it is clear that it was not the primary medium for the spreading of news about decrees.

The richness of the decree as a social practice is demonstrated when we consider in combination the political and literary contexts in which they loom large. Our literary sources indicate a much wider context for the deployment of knowledge about decrees: they could be drawn upon in the manufacture of (real and hypothetical) arguments in rhetorical contexts, in the construction of historical narrative or biographical apology, in the recreation of particular scenarios, and in discourses about, and critiques and parodies of, political behaviour and morality. Literary authors elaborate, imagine, or even fabricate decrees, emphasising their rhetorical and political, or even their comic significance, but not always their physically inscribed presence. Their widespread presence in performative genres suggests that authors would have presumed the Athenian audience's familiarity with the language of decrees and the process of decree-making.

How can such a legacy be accounted for? In historical terms, despite the preoccupation of Athenian decrees with the pursuit of interstate relations, the decree-making activity of the fourth-century democratic Athenians evidently failed to restore the geopolitical standing of the fifth-century city-state. But the assembly's perseverance with decree-making as a primary instrument of diplomacy (in terms of alliances, acts of aggression, and honorific transactions) assured them a prominent place in narratives about Athenian politics and democracy. Moreover, the symbolic value of decrees to individual political legacies meant that they became lodged not only in narratives of Athenian politics but also biographical accounts of individuals. We can explain the perseverance of the decree as an institution by reference to the fact that it provided for the Athenians a way of making decisions and reacting to particular scenarios while also opening up routes of political self-promotion for those who sought them. At this point it is appropriate to recall the 'path-dependence' dynamic of Historical Institutionalist thought which was explored in the Introduction above: the institution of the decree appears to be one that has considerable influence on guiding the behaviour of self-interested political actors. Aware of the significance of the decree in Athenian history and incentivised by the potential rewards that decree-making offered, politicians and orators themselves participated in the decree-minded mentality by engaging in the proposal of, and attacks on, decrees and by telling stories about them. And in turn their legacy precipitated the emergence of a wider cultural interest in decrees.

Finally, it remains to consider the broader implications of a decree-centred approach to ancient Athens. Its conclusions are relevant to understanding the nature of epigraphical publication: we have confirmed that it was not the case that all Athenian decrees were automatically inscribed and that the decision to write up particular decrees on stone was one which was supplementary to the original decree. Some Athenians took an interest in inscribed decrees, but their attention was drawn primarily to 'celebrity' inscriptions. This investigation has emphasised important distinctions between the inscribed and literary views of decrees: the default setting for the erection of those Athenian decrees of the fourth century which were written up on stone *stelai* was their acropolis, a cluster of sanctuaries and the spiritual home of their city. In an important sense, the setting up of an inscription on the acropolis was a practice saturated with religious significance: decisions of the Athenian *demos* were accordingly granted supernatural protection, and its decisions were set out in front of the eyes of the deities. The literary sources, however, offer us a very different insight: the act of making a decree is one that offers to bestow upon its proposer a type of fame. But this fame does not follow automatically as the result of the processes of decree-making: it was a kind of capital that was available for extraction in contexts of political persuasion and invective; moreover, association with a decree was at times turned against those associated with a particular measure. As already noted, the status of the decree was potentially unstable and was open to debate.

In terms of democratic activity, our investigation demonstrates the centrality of foreign policy and honorific transactions to decree-making activity at the Athenian assembly; accordingly, such subjects must have taken up a considerable portion of the time dedicated to discussion undertaken at the council and the assembly. In terms of the rules of politics, the decree-making system is evidently one which created an informally regulated system of accountability: both proposer and the *demos* were liable to be called to account for any decree and its consequences. But it was also a system which allowed individuals a route of political self-promotion by way either of advocating decrees or by attacking them. This form of self-promotion was evidently extensively deployed by some orators, but the breadth of attested proposers indicates that less prominent citizens were able to partake in the decree-making system. Moreover, we have argued that the type of expertise involved in engagement with the rhetoric of decrees was one which could be built up through engagement with civic institutions.

We have detected a tendency in the literary sources to associate the process of decree-making and other activities relating to decrees with the problems of democracy, including the capriciousness of the *demos* and its failure to act on decrees that it had enacted. But we can note also that according to most critics, decrees and the decree-making system appear not to be the cause of democracy's problems but an expression of the wider issue of being ruled by the people who could change their mind and were swayed by proposers who could be guided by selfish interests. Indeed, decrees of the Athenian assembly amounted to an institution which permitted the Athenians to address crises with decisions agreed by the people; in the medium term, even if the system did not allow them to restore their former supremacy over the Aegean, it enabled them to adapt to the emergence of new and different forms of geopolitical situation at the dawn of the Hellenistic period. Yet within the period of this study, only in the first year of the restored democracy do the Athenian people appear to have deployed decrees as a way of initiating far-reaching institutional change; perhaps this goes some way to explaining the stability of the democratic decision-making system of fourth-century Athens.

Appendix 1
Proposers of Decrees at the Athenian Assembly
403/2–322/1[1]

This inventory lists named proposers of decrees at the assembly in the period 403/2–322/1. It updates that of Hansen 1989: 34–72; epigraphical references are based on those of Lambert 2018: 205–23. Cases in which attribution to a particular proposer is uncertain are marked with an asterisk (*). Where there is uncertainty about the authenticity of a particular example as a decree, or other serious problems with its identification, this is indicated with a dagger (†). Literary attestations are followed by epigraphical attestations.

Aleximachos Charinou Pelekes *PA* 545, *PAA* 120375
(1 literary decree)

D132 Decree that an envoy coming from Kersobleptes should partake in the oaths for the Peace of Philokrates; date: 25th Elaphebolion 347/6; Aeschin. 2.83–5.

Alkimachos eg Myrrinouttes *PA* 622, *PAA* 121995
(1 epigraphical decree)

IG II³ 1 **331** Honours for Nikostratos; date: 335/4.

Andokides Leogorou Kydathenaieus *PA* 828, *PAA* 127290, *APF*
(1 literary decree)

D26† Proposal of peace with Spartans (rejected; authenticity doubtful); date: 392/1; *Hypothesis* to Andocides 3 *On the Peace* (= *FGrH*328 F149b).

Androtion Andronos Gargettios *PA* 913 + 915, *PAA* 129125, *APF*
(3 literary decrees; 2 epigraphical decrees)

D57 The repair of processional vessels; date: 368/7 or later; Dem. 22.69–70.

---

1 Note: this list does not include decrees of the council, which are included in Hansen 1989: 34–72. See Volume 1 Appendix 1.

248 APPENDIX 1

D88 Decree arranging the recovery of arrears of *eisphora*; date: 356/5; Dem. 24.160.

D89 Decree for honours for council of 356/5; date: 355/4; Dem. 22.5.

IG II² **216-17** Concerning temple treasures; date: before 365/4.

IG II³ **1 298** Honorific decree for Bosporan rulers; date: 347/6.

Antimedon *PA* 1134, *PAA* 134485 (1 literary decree)

D212 Decree for the people of Tenedos; date: before 340; Dem. 58.35.

Apollodoros Pasionos Acharneus *PA* 1411, *PAA* 142545, *APF* (1 literary decree)

D115 Decree (probouleumatic) concerning the theoric fund; date: spring 348; [Dem.] 59.4.

Archedemos Archiou Paionides *PA* 2325, *PAA* 209125 (1 epigraphical decree)

IG II³ **1 296** Treaty with, or honours for, the Echinaioi; date: 349/8.

Archedikos Naukritou Lamptreus *PA* 2336, *PAA* 209325 (1 epigraphical decree)

IG II³ **1 484** Honours for friends of the King and Antipater; date: 324–322/1.

Archinos ek Koiles *PA* 2526, *PAA* 213880 (2 literary decrees)

D15 Decree honouring those who returned from Phyle; date: 403/2 or 401/0; Aeschin. 3.187.

D16 Decree concerning the Ionian alphabet; date: 403/2; Scholiast to Dionysius Thrax (Hilgard *Grammatici Graeci*, vol. 1.3. Leipzig: Teubner, 1901, 183) lines 16–20.

Aristion *PA* 1734, *PAA* 166265 (1 epigraphical decree)

IG II² **72** Honorary decree; date: 378/7.

Aristogeiton Kydimachou *PA* 1775, *PAA* 168145 (1 literary decree)

D237 Decree concerning the punishment of those stealing sacred garments; date: 335–330; [Dem.] 25.87.

APPENDIX 1

Aristokrates *PA* 1897, *PAA* 170830 (1 literary decree)

D94 Decree of protection for Charidemos; date: 353/2 or 352/1; Dem. 23.16.

Aristonikos Aristotelous Marathonios *PA* 202 + 2028, *PAA* 174070 (1 literary decree; 1 epigraphical decree)

D156 Decree honouring Demosthenes; date: late 341/early 340; Dem. 18.83.
IG II² **1623 line 282** Decree on pirates; date: 335/4.

Note: The decree on pirates is presented in the accounts of the naval *epime-letai* as proposed jointly by 'Lykourgos Bouta(des)' and Aristonikos: *IG* II² 1623 line 280–3.

Aristophon Aristophanous Azenieus *PA* 2108, *PAA* 176170, *APF* (7 literary decrees; 5 epigraphical decrees)

D9 Decree to re-enact a Solonian law concerning the *xenikon*; date: 403/2; Dem. 57.32.
D12 Proposal concerning the repayment of debt to Gelarchos; date: 403/2; Dem. 20.149.
D66 Proposal relating to Keos; date: late 360s; Schol. Aeschin 1.64 Dilts 145.
D67 Decree concerning the mobilization of triremes; date: 24th Metageitnion, 362/1; [Dem.] 50.3–7.
D91 Decree appointing commission of inquiry; date: before 353/2; Dem. 24.11.
D215–216 Two decrees formulating policy towards Philip; date: 346–338; Dem. 18.75.
IG II² **111** Relations with Ioulis; date: 363/2.
IG II² **118** Concerning Poteidaia; date: 361/0.
IG II² **121** Unknown content; date: 357/6.
IG II² **130** Proxeny for Lachares; date: 355/4.
IG II³ **1 307** Honours for Kephallenians; date: 343/2.

Note: Aristophon is said to have been acquitted 75 times for making illegal proposals (Aeschin. 3.194), which suggests that Aeschines was able to make a credible claim about him as an extremely prolific proposer of decrees. Two fragments of Hypereides' speech against Aristophon for making an illegal proposal survive: Jensen FF. 41, 44.

Aristoteles Marathonios *PA* 2065, *PAA* 174985 (1 epigraphical decree)

IG II² **43** Decree on Second Athenian Confederacy; date: 378/7.

Aristoxenos Kephisodotou *PA* 2044, *PAA* 174440
(1 epigraphical decree)

IG II³ 1 347 Honours for Amphis of Andros; date: 332/1.

Astyphilos Philagrou Halaieus *PA* 2662 + 266 + 2664, *PAA* 223310
(2 epigraphical decrees)

IG II² 42 Alliance with Methymna; date: 378/7.
Agora 16.42 Unknown content; date: 378/7.

Athenodoros *PA* 259, *PAA* 110940 (1 epigraphical decree)

IG II² 26 Decree concerning honours for Iphitos; date: 394–387.

Athenodoros *PA* 260, *PAA* 110945 (1 epigraphical decree)

IG II² 47 Concerning the Asklepieion; date: early fourth century.

Autolykos P--- *PA* 2746, *PAA* 239810 (1 epigraphical decree in the
form of an amendment)

IG II² 107 Amendment concerning Mytilene; date: 368/7.

Blepyros Peithandrou Paionides *PA* 2881, *PAA* 267030
(1 epigraphical decree)

IG II² 189 Amendment: subject unknown; date: c. 353/2.

Brachyllos Bathyllou Erchieus *PA* 2928, *PAA* 268840 (1 epigraphical
decree)

IG II³ 1 306 Honorific decree; date: 343/2.

Chairedemos *PA* 15112 + 15113, *PAA* 971980 (1 literary decree)

D85 Decree concerning collection of naval equipment; date: 357/6; Dem. 47.19.

Charikleides *PA* 15396, *PAA* 982760 (1 epigraphical decree)

IG II² 1673 **line 9** Decree of unknown content; date: 333/2.

APPENDIX 1

Chairionides Lysaniou Phlyeus *PA* 15269, *PAA* 978120 (1 epigraphical decree)

IG II³ 1 **338** Honours for Pytheas; date: 333/2.

Demades Demeou Paianieus *PA* 3263, *PAA* 306085, *APF* (9 (or more) literary decrees; 14 epigraphical decrees[2])

D171 Proposal of peace and alliance with Philip; date: late 338; Demades; [Demades'] *On the Twelve Years* 9.

D172 Decree relating to common peace and Athenian membership in the League of Corinth; date: late 338; Pl. *Phoc.* 16.4–5.

***D173** Award of proxeny-status and citizenship for Antipater; date: autumn 338; Harpokration, s.v. '*Alkimachos*'.

D177 Decree awarding proxeny-status to Euthykrates of Olynthos; date: 338–336; Hypereides F76 Jensen.

***D178** Award of proxeny-status to Alkimachos; date: Gamelion 337/6; Harpokration, s.v. '*Alkimachos*'.

D180 Decree granting honours (statue, citizenship, and crown) for Philip of Macedon; date: summer 337 and 336; Demades [Demades'] *On the Twelve Years* 9.

D185 Decree for the election of ten ambassadors to be sent to Alexander; date: 335/4; Arrian *Anab.* 1.10.2–3.

D186 Decree responding to Alexander's demands for statesmen; date: 335/4; D.S. 17.15.3.

D188 Proposal of peace with Alexander; date: 335/4; [Demades'], *On the Twelve Years* 14.

D197 Decree to deify and set up a statue of Alexander; date: autumn 324; Aelian *Hist. Misc.* 5.12.

D201 Decree sending envoys to Antipater; date: after Metageitnion 322; Plu. *Phoc.* 26.3–5.

***D202** Decree imposing death or exile on anti-Macedonian politicians; date: Metageitnion–Boedromion 322; Plu. *Dem.* 28.2.

IG II³ 1 **321** Content unknown; date: 337/6.

IG II³ 1 **322** Honours for a courtier of Philip II; date: 337/6.

IG II³ 1 **326** Concerning Lemnos; date: 337/6.

IG II³ 1 **330** Honorific decree; date: 335/4.

IG II³ 1 **334** Content unknown; date: 334/3.

IG II³ 1 **335** Honours for Amyntor son of Demetrios; date: 334/3.

IG II³ 1 **346** Honours for Aristeides; date: 332/1.

---

2 Brun 2000: 176-7 lists also those decrees of the post 322/1 period.

IG II³ 1 **356** Honours for a Larisan; date: 329/8.

IG II³ 1 **358** Honours for Eurylochos of Kydonia; date: 328/7.

IG II² **1629 lines 859–69** (cf. 1628 339–49) Concerning *sitonika*; date: 326/5.

IG II² **1627 lines 246–65** Multiple decrees concerning activity and support of triremes; date: 326/5.

IG II² **1629 lines 516–43** Concerning vessels bringing produce from Chalkis; date: 325/4.

IG II³ 1 **929 lines 9–16** Honours for a (Theban?) flute-player; date: c. 325.

IG II³ 1 **384** Honours for a foreigner; date: 322/1.

Demeas Demadou Paianieus *PA* 3322, *PAA* 306870, *APF* (1 epigraphical decree)

IG II³ 1 **480** Honours for a Plataean; date: c. 325–322/1.

Demetrios Euktemonos Aphidnaios *PA* 3392, *PAA* 310410 (1 epigraphical decree)

IG II³ 1 **348** Honours for Phanodemos; date: 332/1.

Demomeles Demonos Paianieus *PA* 3554, *PAA* 317410, *APF* (1 literary decree)

D166a Decree of honours for Demosthenes; date: 339/8; Dem. 18.223.

Demon Demomelous Paianeus *PA* 3736; *PAA* 322730, *APF* (1 literary decree)

D200a–b Decree recalling Demosthenes; date: 323/2; Plu. *Dem.* 27.6.

Demophantos *PA* 3659, *PAA* 320600 (1 literary decree)

D19 Decree protecting democracy; date: 403/2 or later; Lycurg. 1.127.

Demophilos *PA* 3664, *PAA* 320855 (1 literary decree)

D137 Scrutiny of the citizen body (introduced probably by decree); date: 346/5; Scholiast to Aeschin 1.77 Dilts 169b.

Demophilos Demophilou Acharneus *PA* 3675, *PAA* 321330, *APF* (1 epigraphical decree)

IG II³ 1 **419** Honours for an Amphipolitan; date: c. 340–320.

APPENDIX 1

253

Demosthenes Demokleous Lamptreus *PA* 3593, *PAA* 318530 (2 epigraphical decrees)

IG II³ 1 355 Honours for managers of Amphiaraia; date: 329/8.
IG II³ 1 367 Honours for Herakleides of Salamis; date: 325/4.

Demosthenes Demosthenous Paianieus *PA* 3597, *PAA* 318625, *APF* (39 or 40 literary decrees; 1 epigraphical decree)

D108 Proposal on mobilisation against Philip; date 352/1 or 350; Dem. 4.33.

D124 Decree praising Aristodemos; date: 347/6; Aeschin. 2.17.

D126 Decree calling for truce for Philip's envoys; date: late Anthesterion/ Elaphebolion 1–4 347/6; Aeschin. 2.53.

D127 Decree organising meetings of the assembly; date: Anthesterion/ Elaphebolion 1–4 347/6; Aeschin. 2.67.

D128 Decree honouring Athenian envoys; date: Anthesterion/Elaphebolion 1–4 347/6; Aeschin. 2.45–6.

D139 Decree proposing an embassy to be dispatched to the Peloponnese; date: 344; Dem. 18.79.

D145 Decree to execute Anaxinos of Oreos; date: 343; Aeschin. 3.223–4.

D146 Crowning of an embassy; date: 343/2; Aeschin. 3.83: στεφανώσας τοὺς μετὰ Ἀριστοδήμου εἰς Θετταλίαν καὶ Μαγνησίαν παρὰ τὰς τῆς εἰρήνης συνθήκας πρεσβεύσαντας.

D147 Decree of alliance with Chalkis; date: 344/3 or 343/2; Aeschin. 3.92–3.

D148a Proposal for ambassadors to go to Euboia; date: 343/2; Dem. 18.79.

D148b (= 148a?) Decree for ambassadors to go to Eretria and Oreos; date: 343/2 or summer 341; Aeschin. 3.100–102.

D149 Alliance with Achaians and others; date: 343/2; Dem. 18.237.

D151 Alliance with Byzantines; date: spring 341; Dem. 18.302.

D152 Alliance with the Abydians; date: spring 341; Dem. 18.302.

D154 Proposal for expedition to Oreos; date: summer 341; Dem. 18.79.

D155 Decree dispatching expedition to Euboia; date: summer 341; Dem. 18.79.

D158 Proposal to dispatch forces to Byzantion, Chersonese, and other places; date: summer 340; Dem. 18.88.

D159 Decree of mobilisation against Philip; date: 340/39; Dion. Hal. *ad Amm.* 1.11.741 (= *FGrH* 328 F55a).

D160 Decree establishing *nomothetai*; date: 340; Dem. 18.105.

D161 Decree concerning the attendance of the Athenian representatives at the meetings of the Delphian Amphictyony; date: autumn 340/spring 339; Aeschin. 3.125–8.

D162 Decree about marching to Eleusis and sending envoys to Thebes; date: 339/8; Dem. 18.179.

D163 Decree of alliance with the Thebans; date: spring–late 339; Aeschin. 3.142–3.

D164 Decree for transfer of funds to the stratiotic fund; date 339/8; Dion. Hal. *To Ammaeus* 1.11.741f (= *FGrH* 328 F56a).

D169 Decree(s) for military improvements; date: autumn 338; Dem. 18.248.

D170 Decree for dispatch of embassies and organisation of citizens; date: August 338; Din. 1.78.

D176 Decree prescribing meetings of the tribes for the repair of the walls; date: 29th Thargelion 338/7; Aeschin. 3.27.

D182 Honours for Pausanias; date: late 337/6 or early 336/5; Plu. *Dem.* 22.1.

D184 Alliance with Thebans and preparations for war; date: 335/4; Aeschin. 3.239.

D193 Decree detaining Harpalos; date: early summer 324; Din. 1.68.

D195 Decree ordering the Areopagus to investigate politicians involved in the Harpalos affair; date: summer 324; Din. 1.4

D198 Proposal that only established deities be worshipped; date: 324/3; Din. 1.94.

*D203 Award of citizenship for Antiphanes; date: between 388 and 330; *Anon de Com.* 12 p. 9 (Kaibel).

D206 Decree of unknown content; date: 353–340; Dem. 58.36.

D214 Decree empowering the Areopagos; date: 340s or later; Din. 1.62–3.

D227 Bronze statues in the agora of Pairisades, Satyros and Gorgippos, the tyrants from the Bosporos, and possible alliance; date: 330s or earlier; Din. 1.43.

D231 Proposal of citizenship for Taurosthenes and Kallias of Chalkis; date: c. 341/0 or early 330s; Aeschin. 3.85.

D234 Decree of *sitesis* and statue for Diphilos; date: c. 334–324; Din. 1.43.

D235 Decree(s) making Chairephilos and his sons citizens; date: 330s; Din. 1.43.

D236 Decree(s) making the bankers Konon and Epigenes citizens; date: 330s–320s; Din. 1.43.

D242 Proposal of unknown content; date: 340s–320s; Dionysius of Halicarnassus *On Dinarchus* 11 p. 317 2 R.

IG II³ 1 **312** Honours for a Megarian; date: 340/39.

Demotion *PA* 3646, *PAA* 320127 (1 literary decree)

*D63 Alliance with Arcadians; date: 366/5; Xen. *Hell.* 7.4.2.

Diogeiton *PA* 3790, *PAA* 325585 (1 epigraphical decree)

IG II² **152** Honours for Timaphenides; date: c. 370.

Diopeithes Diopeithous Sphettios *PA* 4328, *PAA* 363695, *APF* (1 literary decree; 1 epigraphical decree)

D217 Decree formulating policy towards Philip; date: 346–338; Dem. 18.69–70.
IG II³ **1 302** Honours for Abderites; date: 346/5.

Diophantos Phrasikleidou Myrrinousios *PA* 4435, *PAA* 367500, *APF* (3 epigraphical decrees)

IG II³ **1 324** Honours for Euenor of Akarnania; date: 337/6.
IG II³ **1 324** Honours for Euenor of Akarnania; date: 322/1.
IG II³ **1 325** Honours for an Athenian; date: 337/6.

Diophantos Thrasymedous Sphettios *PA* 4438, *PAA* 367640 (1 literary decree; 2 epigraphical decrees)

D105 Decree celebrating a military victory; date: late summer 352; Dem. 19.86.
IG II² **106** Honours for Koroibos; date: 368/7.
IG II² **107** Honours for envoys from Mytilene; date: 368/7.

Emmenides *PA* 4687, *PAA* 387540 (1 epigraphical decree)

IG II² **1544 line 30** Relating to Eleusinion; date: 332/1 or earlier.

[Father of] Epichares Cholleides *APF* pp. 58–9 (1 literary decree):

D209 Decree awarding *sitesis* to Charidemos; date: 357–340; Dem. 58.30.

Epichares *PA* 4976, *PAA* 399220 (1 epigraphical decree in the form of an amendment)

IG II² **188** Amendment to a proxeny decree; date: 353/2.

Epikrates Menestratou Palleneus *PA* 4909, *PAA* 394105, *APF* (1 epigraphical decree)

IDélos I **88 line 15** Amendment to an honorary decree for Pythodoros; date: 369/8.

Epikrates ---otetou Palleneus *PA* 4863, *PAA* 393525, *APF*
(1 literary decree)

D93 Decree concerning establishment of *nomothetai*; date: 11th of Hekatombaion of 353/2; Dem. 24.26–9.

Epiteles Soinautou Pergasethen *PA* 4963, *PAA* 398510
(1 epigraphical decree

IG II³ 1 375 Honours for Lapyris of Kleonai; date: 323/2.

Euboulides Antiphilou Halimousios *PA* 5323, *PAA* 427825
(1 epigraphical decree)

IG II³ 1 302 Honours for Abderites; date: 346/5.

Euboulos Spintharou Probalisios *PA* 5369, *PAA* 428495
(3 or 4 literary decrees)

D98 Decree exiling Xenophon; date: 399–394/3; Diogenes Laertius 2.59 (= Istros *FGrH* 334 F32). Proposer Euboulos or Euboulides.
D101 Decree recalling Xenophon; date: 386 or 371–362; Diogenes Laertius 2.59 (= Istros *FGrH* 334 F32).
D116 Decree dispatching envoys across Greece; date: 348/7; Dem. 19.303–4: ὁ μὲν γράφων τὸ ψήφισμ᾽ Εὔβουλος ἦν.
D218 Decree formulating policy towards Philip; date 346–338; Dem. 18.69–70.

Euetion Autokleidou Sphettios *PA* 5463, *PAA* 430885, *APF*
(1 epigraphical decree)

IG II³ 1 359 Honours for priest of Asklepios; date: 328/7.

Euktemon *PA* 5784, *PAA* 438085 (1 literary decree)

D92 Decree ordering the collection of money; date: before Skirophorion 354/3; Dem. 24.11–14.

Euphiletos Euphiletou Kephiseus *PA* 6054, *PAA* 450035, *APF*
(1 epigraphical decree)

IG II³ 1 378 Honours for Euphron of Sikyon; date: 323/2.

Eurippides or Heurippides Adeimantou Myrrinousios *PA* 5949 + 5955 + 5956, *PAA* 444540, *APF* (1 literary decree; 1 epigraphical decree)

D97 Decree concerning the *eisphora* tax; date: before 393; Scholiast on Ar. *Eccl.* 825.
IG II² **145** Honours for Eukles; date: 403/2.

Euthymachos *PA* 5624, *PAA* 433505 (1 epigraphical decree)

IG II² **138** Honours for Xennias; date: 353/2.

Euxitheos *PA* 5901, *PAA* 441185 (1 epigraphical decree)

IG II² **60** Honours for Xanthippos; date: before 378/7.

Exekestides *PA* 4710, *PAA* 388085 (2 epigraphical decrees)

IG II² **116** Alliance with Thessaly; date: 361/0.
SEG LIX **107** Concerning Thessalians; date: 361/0.

Glaukon *PA* 3011, *PAA* 276730 (1 literary decree)

D81 Decree sending embassy to Kersobleptes; date 358/7; Dem. 23.172.

Gnathon Lakiades *PAA* 279215 (1 epigraphical decree)

Agora XVI **38** Unknown content; date: early 4th century.

Hagnonides Nikoxenou Pergasethen *PA* 176, *PAA* 107455 (1 epigraphical decree)

IG II² **1629 lines 13–15** Concerning naval equipment; date: 325/4.

Hegemon *PAA* 480755 (1 epigraphical decree)

IG II³ 1 **385** Honorific decree; date: 322/1.

Hegesandros Hegesiou Sounieus *PA* 6307, *PAA* 480930, *APF* (1 epigraphical decree)

IG II² **123** Concerning Andros; date: 357/6.

APPENDIX 1

Hegesippos Hegesiou Sounieus *PA* 6351, *PAA* 481555, *APF*
(4 literary decrees; 2 epigraphical decrees)

D87 Decree of alliance with the Phokians; date: 356/5 or 355/4; Aeschin. 3.118.

D140 Decree in response to Philip's ambassador concerning amendments to the peace; date: 344/3; [Dem.] 7.18–19.

D144 Proposal to respond to Philip's letter; date: late 344/3; [Dem.] 7.46.

D219 Decree formulating policy towards Philip; date: 346-338; Dem. 18.75.

IG II³ 1 **399** Treaty with Eretria; date: 348 or 343.

IG II³ 1 **316** Honours for Akarnanians; date: 338/7.

Hierokleides Timostratou Alopekethen *PA* 7463, *PAA* 531940
(2 epigraphical decrees)

IG II³ 1 **294** Honours for Theogenes of Naukratis; date: 349/8.

IG II³ 1 **297** Concerning Eleusis; date: 349/8.

Hieronymos Oikophelous Rhamnousios *PA* 7570, *PAA* 534235
(1 epigraphical decree)

IG II³ 1 **469** Honours for Kallikratides; date: c. 330.

Hippochares Alopekethen *PA* 7670, *PAA* 539220
(1 epigraphical decree)

IG II³ 1 **327** Honours for Phyleus; date: 336/5.

Hippostratos Etearchidou Palleneus *PA* 7669, *PAA* 539190
(1 epigraphical decree)

IG II³ 1 **309** Concerning people of Elaious; date: 341/0.

Hypereides Glaukippou Kollyteus *PA* 13912, *PAA* 902110, *APF*
(2, 3 or 4 literary decrees)

D166b Modification of honours for Demosthenes; date: 339/8; [Plu.] *X Or.* 846a: ἐστεφανώθη.

D167a Decree proposing that slaves, aliens and disenfranchised slaves be enfranchised; date: summer 338; Lycurg. 1.41.

APPENDIX 1

D167b Decree to evacuate women and children from the countryside to within the walls and that the generals should appoint any Athenians or other residents to defence duties as they saw fit; date: summer 338; Lycurg. 1.16.

D167c Decree providing that the *boule* of 500 should go to the Piraeus armed to meet for the protection of that harbour and that it should be ready to do whatever seemed to be in the people's interests; date: summer 338; Lycurg. 1.36–7.

Kallias Hipponikou Alopekethen *PA* 7826, *PAA* 554500, *APF* (1 literary decree)

D52 Proposal for peace put to the vote; date: 371; *Did.* in *D.* Col 7.71–4.

Kallikrates Charopodou Lamptreus *PA* 794 + 797 + 8213, *PAA* 556845 (2 epigraphical decrees)

IG II³ 1 301 Honours for Kephisodotos; date: 346/5.
IG II³ 1 313 Concerning Tenedians; date: 340/39.

Kallippos Paianieus *PA* 8078, *PAA* 559430 (1 literary decree)

D208 Decree concerning property in Kardia; date: 357–340; Dem. 7.42–3.

Kallisthenes *PA* 8090, *PAA* 559815 (1 literary decree; 1 epigraphical decree)

D135 Decree ordering the evacuation of Attica; date: 27th Skirophorion 346; Dem. 19.86.
IG II² 127 Alliance with Ketriporis, Lyppeios and Grabos; date: 356/5.

Kallistratos Kallikratous Aphidnaios *PA* 815 + 812 + 8130, *PAA* 561575, *APF* (2 literary decrees; 2 epigraphical decrees)

D27 Decree impeaching ambassadors who negotiated with the Spartans; date 392/1 or 387/6; Dem. 19. 276–9.
D55 Decree for armed assistance to the Lakedaimonians; date: 369/8; Xen. *Hell.* 6.5.49; [Dem.] 59.27.
IG II² 84 Rider to honours for Polychartides and Alkibiades; date: 378–376.
IG II² 107 Response to Mytilenean ambassadors; date: 369/8.

APPENDIX 1

Kephalos Kollyteus *PA* 8277, *PAA* 566650
(1 literary decree; 1 epigraphical decree)

D44 Decree for armed intervention in Thebes; date: winter 379/8; Din. 1.39.
IG II² **29** Rider to honours for Phanokritos; date: 387/6.

Kephalos, according to Aeschines, boasted that he was the author of more decrees than any other Athenian, but had never been once indicted for making an illegal motion (Aeschin. 3.194).

Kephisodotos ek Kerameon *PA* 8331, *PAA* 567790
(2 literary decrees; 2 epigraphical decrees)

D56 Decree concerning the command of the forces in the alliance; date: 369/8; Xen. *Hell.* 7.1.14.
***D82** Dispatch of force to Euboia (apparently by decree: Ar. *Rhet.* 1411a6–10); date 358/7; Dem. 8.74–5.
Hesperia **8 (1939: 5–12) no. 3** Concerning Aetolian League; date: 367/6.
IG II² **141** Honours for Straton of Sidon; date: c. 364.

Kephisodotos (not in *PA*, *PAA* 576485) (1 literary decree)

D187 Decree granting statue and *sitesis* to Demades; date: 335/4; Din. 1.101.

Kephisophon Kallibiou Paianieus *PA* 8417, *PAA* 569315, *APF*
(2 literary decrees; 2 epigraphical decrees)

D129 Decree dispatching Antiochos to an Athenian general; date: Anthesterion or Elaphebolion 1–4 347/6; Aeschin. 2.73.
D220 Decree formulating policy towards Philip; date 346–338; Dem. 18.75.
IG II³ 1 **306** Honours for *boule*; date: 343/2.
IG II³ 1 **418** Rider to honours for Asklepiodoros; date: c. 340–320.

Kephisophon Lysiphontos Cholargeus *PA* 8419, *PAA* 569375
(1 epigraphical decree)

IG II³ 1 **370** Dispatch to Adriatic; date: 325/4.

Kratinos *PA* 8752, *PAA* 584320 (3 epigraphical decrees)

IG II² **109** Honours for Astykrates; date: 363/2.
IG II² **134** Honorific decree; date: 354/3.

APPENDIX 1

261

IG II² 172 Honours for Demochares; date: before 353/2.

Kritios *PA* 8798, *PAA* 585380 (1 epigraphical decree)

IG II² 96 Alliance with Kerkyrians; date: 375/4.

Ktesiphon *PA* 8894, *PAA* 587570 (1 literary decree)

D179 Decree of honorific award for Demosthenes; date: winter 337/6; Aeschin. 3.49.

Kydias *PA* 8924, PAA 588215 (1 literary decree)

* D65 Decree sending cleruchs to Samos; date: 366/5; Arist. *Rh.* 1384b32–5.

Lykourgos Lykophronos Boutades *PA* 925 + 9247, *PAA* 611335, *APF* (up to 5 literary decrees; 7 epigraphical decrees)

D190 Decree honouring Diotimos; date; 338/7 or 334/3; [Plu.] *X Or.* 844a.
D230 Decree of honours for Neoptolemos; date: c. 338/7 or later; Dem. 18.114; [Plu.] *X Or.* 843f.
D233 Proposal of unknown content; date: before 330; Hyp. *Against Diondas*, p. 3 line 19.
*D240 Decree concerning piety; date: before 331; Lycurg. 1.146.
*D241 Decree on the behaviour of priestesses; 330s–320s; Lycurg. Fr 51 ap. Suda s. v. 'συσσημαίνεσθαι'.
IG II³ 1 329 Honorific decree; date: 336/5 or 335/4.
IG II³ 1 336 Honours for Diotimos; date: 334/3.
IG II³ 1 337 Concerning Kitian temple; date: 333/2.
IG II³ 1 345 Honours for a Plataean; date: 332/1.
IG II³ 1 352 Honours for Eudemos of Plataea; date: 330/29.
IG II³ 1 357 Honorific decree; date: 328/7.
IG II³ 1 432 Honours for Sopatros of Akragas; date: 337–325.
The decree on pirates is presented in the accounts of the naval *epimeletai* as proposed jointly by 'Lykourgos Bouta(des)' and Aristonikos: *IG* II² 1623 lines 280–3.

Lysanias. Identity uncertain (1 epigraphical decree)

SEG LXIII 74 Concerning Corcyra; date: 373/2?

Meidias Meidiou Anagyrasios *PA* 9720, *PAA* 637275, *APF* (1 literary decree)

D136 Decree honouring Phokion; date: 24th Gamelion 346/5; [Plu.], *X Or.* 850b.

Melanopos Lachetos Aixoneus *PA* 9788, *PAA* 638765 (1 epigraphical decree)

IG II² **145** Appointment of a herald; date: 366/5.

Menexenos *PA* 9972, *PAA* 644845 (2 epigraphical decrees, 1 in the form of an amendment)

IG II² **141** Amendment to decree for Straton of Sidon; date: 364/3.
IG II² **111** Arrangements for Ioulis on Keos; date: 363/2.

Moirokles Eleusinios *PA* 1040 + 10401, *PAA* 658480 (1 literary decree)

D207 Decree against those who threaten merchants; date: 357–340; Dem. 58.56.

Monippides *PA* 10414, *PAA* 658780 (1 epigraphical decree)

IG II² **7** Honours for Kleonymides; date: 403/2.

Nausikles Klearchou Oethen *PA* 10552, *PAA* 701680, *APF* (1 literary decree; 1 epigraphical decee)

*****D223** Decree of unknown content; interpretation of the passage is uncertain; date: after 338; Aeschin. 3.159.
IG II² **1623 line 313** Decree concerning naval equipment; date: 334/3.

Nikomenes *PA* 10968, *PAA* 716940 (1 literary decree

D14 Decree concerning citizenship; date: 403/2 or later; Schol in Aeschin, 1.39.

Nothippos Lysiou Diomeieus *PA* 11131, *PAA* 720955 (1 epigraphical decree)

IG II³ **1 351** Honours for Rheboulas; date: 331/0.

APPENDIX 1

------, son of Oinobios of Rhamnous *PAA* 741140
(1 epigraphical decree)

IG II³ 1 204 Honours for Pellanians; date: 344/3.

Pandios *PA* 11575, *PAA* 763635 (2 epigraphical decrees)

IG II² 103 Honours for Dionysios; date: 369/8.
IG II² 105 Alliance with Dionysios; date: 368/7.

Periandros Polyaratou Cholargeus *PA* 11800, *PAA* 772185, *APF*
(1 epigraphical decree)

IG II² 112 Alliance with Peloponnesian cities; date: 362/1.

Phanias *PA* 14010, *PAA* 915070
(1 literary decree)

D99 Decree of unknown content; date: c. 400-380.

Phanodemos Diyllou Thymaitades *PA* 14033, *PAA* 915640
(1 epigraphical decree)

IG II³ 1 349 Crowning of Amphiaraos; date: 332/1.

Philagros *PA* 14203, *PAA* 921960
(1 epigraphical decree)

IG II² 2 Honorific decree; date: 382/1.

Philippides *PA* 14351, *PAA* 928850 (3 literary decrees)

D181 Decree of honours for *proedroi*; date: 336/5; Hyp. *Phil.* 4.
D224–225 Proposals of unknown content; date: before 336: Hyp. 4 *Phil.* 11.

Philodemos Autokleous Eroiades *PA* 14488, *PAA* 933905,
APF (1 epigraphical decree in the form of an
amendment)

IG II³ 1 401 Amendment to an honorific decree for Aratos; date: 345–338.

APPENDIX 1

Philokles Phormionos Eroiades *PA* 1452 + 14541, *PAA* 935990, *APF*
(1 literary decree)

D196 Decree concerning Harpalos' money; date: summer 324; Din. 3.2.

Philokrates Ephialtous PA 14586; PAA 937130
(1 literary decree; 1 epigraphical decree)

D107 Decree concerning the sacred *orgas*; date: 352/1; Didymos col. 13.42-58 = Philochoros *FGrH* 328 F155.

IG II³ **292 lines 54-3** Concerning the sacred *orgas* (perhaps = D107); date: 352/1.

Philokrates Pythodorou Hagnousios *PA* 1459 + 14576, *PAA* 937530
(6 literary decrees; 2 epigraphical decrees)

D121 Decree allowing Philip to send herald and ambassadors; date: 348/7; Aeschin. 2.13: δίδωσι ψήφισμα Φιλοκράτης ὁ Ἁγνούσιος.

D125 Decree dispatching ambassadors to Philip (the 'First Embassy'; date: 347/6; Aeschin. 2.18.

D130 Decree for peace and alliance with Philip: the 'Peace of Philokrates'; date: 19th Elaphebolion 347/6; Aeschin. 3.54.

D131 Decree on the swearing of oaths of the 'Peace of Philokrates'; date: 25th Elaphebolion 347/6; Aeschin. 3.73-5.

D134 Decree honouring Philip, extending the peace to posterity, inserting a clause against the Phokians; date: 16th Skirophorion 347/6; Dem. 19.47-9.

D213 Decree formulating policy towards Philip; date: 346-343; Dem 18.75.

IG II² **182** Honorific decree; date: before 353/2.

IG II² **182** Amendment to honours for Apollodoros.

Philotades Philostratou Palleneus *PA* 14927, *PAA* 958025
(1 epigraphical decree)

IG II² **136** Honours for Apollonides; date: 354/3.

Phokion Phokou Potamios *PA* 15076, *PAA* 967590 *APF*
(up to 3 literary decrees)

*D143 Decree concerning intervention at Megara; date: 344/3; Plu. *Phoc.* 15.1–2.

*D157 Dispatching forces to Hellespont (probably by decree); date: 340/39; Pl. *Phoc.* 14.3.

APPENDIX 1

265

*D202 Decree imposing death or exile on anti-Macedonian politicians; date: 322/1; Arrian *FGrH* 156 F9.13.

Phormisios *PA* 14945, *PAA* 962695 (1 literary decree)

D4 Proposal concerning restriction of the franchise; date: 403/2; D.H. *Lys.* 32.

Phoxias *PA* 14942, *PAA* 962590 (1 epigraphical decree)

I Délos I **88** Honours for Pythodoros; date: 369/8.

Phrynon Diognetou Rhamnousios *PA* 15032, *PAA* 966010 (1 literary decree)

D117 Decision to send envoys to Philip; date: summer–late summer 348; Aeschin. 2.12.

Poliagros *PA* 11893, *PAA* 776850 (1 epigraphical decree)

IG II² **28** Concerning Klazomenai; date: 387/6.

Polyeuktos Kydantides *PA* 1194 + 1192 + 11927, *PAA* 778230 (1 literary decree; 1 epigraphical decree)

D238 Decree concerning the apportionment of land at Oropos; date: after 338/7–336/5; Hyp. *Eux.* 14–18.
IG II² **1628 lines 38–9** Decree concerning triremes; date: 326/5.

Polyeuktos Sostratou Sphettios *PA* 1192 + 1193 + 11950, *PAA* 778285 (4 epigraphical decrees)

IG II² **128** Concerning Neapolis; date: 356/5.
IG II³ 1 **342** Honours for Theophantos; date: 332/1.
IG II³ 1 **343** Honours for Theophantos; date: 332/1.
IG II³ 1 **439** Honours for Dionysios; date: 337–322.

Polyeuktos Timokratous Krioeus *PA* 11946, *PAA*; *APF* (1 epigraphical decree)

IG II³ 1 **298** Honours for Bosporan rulers; date: 347/6.

Polykrates Polykratous *PA* 12027, *PAA* 779315 (see also seangb.org, s.v. 'Polykrates') (1 literary decree; 1 epigraphical decree)

*D150 Decree on settlers at Chersonese; date: 343/2 or later; [Dem.] 12.16.
IG II³ 1 295 Honours for Orontes; date: 349/8(?).

Prokleides Pantaleontos ek Kerameon *PA* 12200, *PAA* 788752 (1 epigraphical decree)

IG II³ 359 Honours for priest of Asklepios; date: 328/7.

Pyrrandros Anaphlystios *PA* 12496, *PAA* 796155 (1 epigraphical decree)

IG II² 44 Alliance with Chalkidians; date: 378/7.

Satyros *PA* 12575, *PAA* 812970 (1 epigraphical decree)

IG II² 110 Honours for Menelaos; date: 363/2.

Skiton (*PAA* 824360, LGPN, s.v., cf. *APF* 12728) (1 literary decree)

D210 Decree of unknown content; date: before 347; Dem. 21.182–3.

Smikros *PAA* 825720 (1 literary decree):

D211 Decree of unknown content; date: before 347; Dem. 21.182-3.

Sophilos *PA* 13414, *PAA* 870920 (2 epigraphical decrees)

IG II² 19 Honorific decree for Phil---; date: 394/3.
IG II² 20 Honours for Evagoras; date: 394/3.

Stephanos *PA* 12879, *PAA* 833430 (2 literary decrees)

D226 Proposal, perhaps on water-pipes; date: before 335; Dionys. Halic. *De Din.* 10, p. 312, 1 R.
D239 Decree(s) of unknown content; date: before 360s; [Dem.] 59.43.

APPENDIX 1

Stephanos Antidoridou Eroiades *PA* 12887, *PAA* 834250
(1 epigraphical decree)

IG II³ 1 **299** Alliance with Mytilene; date: 347/6.

Teisamenos Mechanionos *PA* 13443, *PAA* 877610
(possibly 1 literary decree)

*D7 Decree concerning the revision of laws; date 403/2; And. 1.82.

Telemachos Theaggelou Acharneus *PA* 13562, *PAA* 881430
(3 epigraphical decrees)

IG II³ 1 **315** Unknown content; date: 339/8.
IG II³ 1 **36** Honours (two decrees) for Herakleides of Salamis; date: 330/29–328/7.

Theomenes Oethen *PA* 6957, *PAA* 508585 (1 epigraphical decree)

IG II² **3207** (with Lambert *AIO Paper* 6: 10) Honours for Lycurgus; date: before 324.

Theozotides *PA* 6913 + 6914, *PAA* 507785, *APF*
(1 literary decree; 1 epigraphical decree)

D17 Decree concerning war-orphans; date: 403/2 (?); Lys. F130 Carey lines 72–82.
IG II² **5** Honorific decree; c. 400.

Thoukydides *PA* 7265, *PAA* 515410 (1 literary decree)

D205 Decree concerning the contribution of the Ainians to the naval confederacy; date 357–342; Dem. 58.37–8.

Thrasyboulos Lykou Steirieus *PA* 7310, *PAA* 517010, *APF*
(2 or 3 literary decrees; 1 epigraphical decree)

D5 Decree extending citizenship to those who had taken part in the return; date 403/2; *Ath. Pol.* 40.2.
D6† Proposal of citizenship for Lysias (authenticity uncertain); date: 403/2; [Plu.] *X Or.* 835f–6a.

D20 Decree concerning alliance with Boiotians; date: 395/4; Xen. *Hell.* 3.5.16.

IG II² 10 Second grant of citizenship to democrats; date: 401/0.

Timarchos Arizelou Sphettios *PA* 13636, *PAA* 884310 (2 literary decrees)

D122 Decree concerning the export of weapons to Philip; date: 347/6; Dem. 19.285–7.

D138 Decree concerned with public works on the Pnyx Hill; date 346/5; Aeschin. 1.81.

Timarchos is said to have proposed more than one hundred decrees (Aeschin. 1 *hypoth.*).

Timonides *PA* 13855, *PAA* 891020 (1 epigraphical decree)

IG II² 139 Decree of unknown content; date: 353/2.

Appendix 2
Literary Inventions

The biggest source of fabricated versions of documentary of decrees is the corpus of Attic orators. These documents have been discussed and analysed in detail in the work of Canevaro and Harris,[1] which has shown that they were fabricated by Hellenistic or later rhetoricians for the sake of creating literary exempla and were inserted into manuscripts by later editors. This appendix, however, focuses on accounts – which arose in a range of circumstances – of further fabricated decrees associated with the fourth-century Athenians. They emerge in a number of different biographical, antiquarian and rhetorical contexts.

X1 Decrees brought by the Athenians to Alexander

Plutarch (*Phoc.* 17.5-6: see D186 T2), after reporting Phokion's advice to the Athenians about responding to Alexander's demand of Athenian

---

1 Decrees are to be found in some versions of the Demosthenes MSS at the following references: Dem. 18.29 (= BD 5, decree of Demosthenes concerning the envoys: Canevaro 2013: 239–43); Dem. 18.37-8 (= D135, decree of Kallisthenes: Canevaro 2013: 243–8); Dem. 18.73-4 (= D218, the decree of Euboulos and the twenty ships: Canevaro 2013: 249–53); Dem. 18.75 (= D215/D216, decree of Aristophon: Canevaro 2013: 253–5); Dem. 18.84 (= D156, decree of Aristonikos in honour of Demosthenes: Canevaro 2013: 255–60); Dem. 18.90-1, 92 (Byzantine, Perinthian and Chersonitan decrees for Demosthenes: Canevaro 2013: 261–7); Dem. 18.105 (= D160, decree about Demosthenes' trierarchic law: Canevaro 2013, 267–71); Dem. 18.115 (= D190, honours to Nausikles: Canevaro 2013: 275–9); Dem. 18.116 (= DD 190, 228 decrees for Diotimos and Charidemos: Canevaro 2013: 279–83); Dem. 18.118 (= D179, decree of Ktesiphon: Canevaro 2013: 283–90); Dem. 18.154-5 (Amphictyonic decrees: Canevaro 2013: 295–304); Dem. 18.164-5 (decrees about Philip's approach towards Attica: Canevaro 2013: 304-10); Dem. 18.181-7 (= D162, decree of Demosthenes: Canevaro 2013: 310-18); Dem. 24.27 (= D191, decree of Epikrates: Canevaro 2013: 104-13); [Dem.] 59.104 (fifth-century decree of naturalisation for Plataeans: Canevaro 2013: 196–208). On the decrees in Andocides' *On the Mysteries*: And. 1.77-9 (decree of Patrokleides: Canevaro and Harris 2012: 100-10; Harris 2013-14; Hansen 2015; Canevaro and Harris 2016: 10-33; Carawan 2017: 404-7); And. 1.83-4 (= D7, decree of Teisamenos: Canevaro and Harris 2012: 110-16; Hansen 2016; Canevaro and Harris 2016: 33-47; Carawan 2017: 404-11); And. 1.87 (law about laws: Canevaro and Harris 2012: 116-19; Hansen 2017); And. 1.96 (= D19, decree of Demophantos: Canevaro and Harris 2012: 119-25; Sommerstein 2014b; Harris 2013-14; Carawan 2017: 411-17).

269

politicians, omits discussion of Demades' proposals (cf. D186), and moves from Phokion's (probably rejected) proposals to surrender the statesmen, to an account of Alexander's reception of Athenian decrees. He says that when Alexander received the first decree that the Athenians passed, he cast it down, but accepted the second because it was brought by Phokion. This represents a rival account to that preserved in Diodorus, in which Demades does the persuading on the embassy (D17.15.2 = D186 T1). There is no reason to believe that the content of the decree envisaged by Plutarch was anything other than that proposed by Demades, to resist Alexander's demands. It is likely, then, that Plutarch's account of a decree of Phokion was based on stories he had encountered about Phokion's political activity. Date: 335/4, after the fall of Thebes.

X2 Honours for Iolas

According to [Plutarch], Hypereides proposed honours for Iolas the son of Antipater, who was supposed to have poisoned Alexander ([Plu.] *X Or.* 849f: ἐψηφίσατο δὲ καὶ τιμὰς Ἰόλᾳ τῷ δο<κοῦ>ντι Ἀλεξάνδρῳ τὸ φάρμακον δοῦναι'). Iolas is otherwise attested as Alexander's chief cupbearer (Plu. *Alex.* 74.1); his father was indeed honoured by the Athenians (see D173). The motivation of the decree is problematic: even if it was the case that Alexander was poisoned by his cupbearer, it is hard to believe that the Athenians would have openly praised the assassin. The story about this decree appears to have existed in biographical accounts of Hypereides. For discussion, see Chapter 5.2.3 above. **Date**: after June 323.

X3–7 Fourth-Century decrees in Apsines' *Art of Rhetoric*

Dilts and Kennedy write that 'none of Apsines' quotations are reliable sources for the texts of the authors he cites'.[2] Therefore we cannot follow Apsines' claim of a decree unless there is another, earlier, testimony: they are literary fabrications cited for the sake of rhetorical advice. It is, however, worth listing the probably false decrees accounted for by Apsines relating to this period:

X3 Aeschines' proposal, after the acquittal of Timarchos, to abolish the trierarchic law (Apsines 1.7);

X4 Hypereides' proposal that when Philip was at Elateia, Demosthenes alone should be the adviser to the city and his proposal of a bodyguard for Demosthenes (Apsines 1.9);

---

2 Dilts and Kennedy 1997: xvii.

APPENDIX 2

X5 Demosthenes' proposal that a temple should be dedicated to Philip (Apsines 1.19);

X6 Demosthenes' proposal to dig a canal through the Isthmos (Apsines 1.72);

X7 Aristogeiton's proposal to overlook illegal actions in return for a bribe (Apsines 2.13, 19).

X8 Annual Sacrifices to Sophocles

According to Diogenes, Istros said that the Athenians made a decree that Sophocles was to receive annual sacrifices on account of his virtue (*FGrH* 334 F38: "Ἴστρος δέ φησιν Ἀθηναίους διὰ τὴν τοῦ ἀνδρὸς ἀρετὴν καὶ ψήφισμα πεποιηκέναι κατ' ἔτος αὐτῶι θύειν'). This measure is usually (but hardly definitively) dated to 405; however, Connolly suggests that this could be a cult that started around the time that the statues of the three tragedians were set up, that is during the 330s;[3] however, it may well be a later Hellenistic invention, perhaps even based on the comic parody of the idea. Another Byzantine source says that the Athenians built a *heroon* for him and named him Dexion 'because of his reception of Asklepios' (*TrGF* 4 T69).

X9 Statue of Kallimedon

See Chapter 5.3.2 above.

X10 Decree that Women and Men Should Sit Apart

According to Suda (cited in the Scholion to Aristophanes *Ekklesiazousai* 22), a certain Sphyromachos introduced a decree that women and men should sit apart (Suda, s.v. 'Σφυρόμαχος': 'οὗτος ψήφισμα εἰσηγήσατο, ὥστε τὰς γυναῖκας καὶ τοὺς ἄνδρας χωρὶς καθέζεσθαι'). As Whitehead notes in the online Suda: 'The name, unparalleled, should be Phyromachos. But more important, there can never have been such a decree, since women could not attend the Athenian Assembly. The Aristophanic text is uncertain and does not demonstrably presuppose a decree – on any subject – at all; rather, what may be involved is merely a remark by Ph. involving *hetairai*.'

---

3 Connolly 1998.

X11 Decree for Aristotle

An Athenian honorific decree for Aristotle, transmitted in the work of the Arabian scholar Ibn Abī Usaybiʻa, the text of which suggests that it was made for him as a return for the benefits that he had bestowed upon the Athenians and in particular his interventions with Philip on their behalf. Haake has demonstrated, however, that this decree is a forgery, fabricated by a Hellenistic forger (writing probably in the third, second or first centuries BC) upon which the Arabic scholar drew:[4] it was fabricated originally as part of a biographical defence of Aristotle; as Haake shows, not only did the forger fabricate a decree for Aristotle, but he also developed a story, which aimed to blacken the reputation of Aristotle's opponents.[5]

X12–15 Decrees (and Similar) in Athenaios' *Deipnosophistai*

For discussion of these decrees, see Chapter 5.4.3 above.

X12 Ath. 171d: decree of the Athenian council on the *protenthai*: see BD 8. See Davies 2000: 212–13;

X13 Ath. 234d–f: Athenian decree about *parasitoi* proposed by Alkibiades: see Davies 2000: 215.

X14 Ath. 587c (Polemon F3) and Harpokration, s.v. 'Νεμέας': decree (?) against naming women after four-yearly festivals: see Davies 2000: 215.

X15 Ath. 590d–e: decree banning appeals to pity and the display of men or women on trial: see Davies 2000: 213–14; Filonik 2016: 132–3; Chapter 5.4.3 above.

---

4 Haake 2006: 332–6; 348–50; cf. Haake 2007: 55–60.
5 Haake 2013: 94–6.

Bibliography

Adamidis, V. (2017) *Character Evidence in the Courts of Classical Athens: Rhetoric, Relevance and the Rule of Law.* London and New York.

Allen, D.S. (2005) 'Greek tragedy and law' in *The Cambridge Companion to Greek Law*, eds. M. Gagarin and D. Cohen. Cambridge: 374–93.

(2006) 'Talking about revolution: on political change in fourth-century Athens and historiographic method' in *Rethinking Revolutions through Ancient Greece*, eds. R. Osborne and S. Goldhill. Cambridge: 183–217.

(2010) *Why Plato Wrote.* Oxford.

Alonso Troncoso, V.A. (2013) 'Olympie et la publication des traités internationaux' in *War, Peace and Panhellenic Games*, eds. N. Birgalias, K. Buraselis, P. Cartledge, A. Gartziou-Tatti and M. Dimopoulou. Athens: 209–31.

Alwine, A. (2015) *Enmity and Feuding in Classical Athens.* Austin.

Arnaoutoglou, I. (2003) Θυσίας ἔνεκα καὶ συνουσίας: *Private Religious Associations in Hellenistic Athens.* Athens.

Arnott, W.G. (1996) *Alexis: The Fragments. A Commentary.* Cambridge.

Asmonti, L. (2004) 'Il retore e il gabelliere: il ruolo di Democare di Leuconoe nella transmission dell'ideale democratico', *Acme* 57: 25–42.

Assman, J. (1995) 'Collective memory and cultural identity', trans. J. Czaplicka. *New German Critique* 65: 125–33.

Atkinson, J. (1992) 'Curbing the comedians: Cleon versus Aristophanes and Syracosius' decree', *CQ* 42: 56–64.

(2003) 'Athenian law and the will of the people in the fourth century BC', *Acta Classica* 46: 21–48.

Austin, C. and Olson, S.D. (2004) *Aristophanes' Themophoriazusae: Edited with Introduction and Commentary.* Oxford.

Aviles, D. (2011) '"Arguing against the law": non-literal interpretation in Attic forensic oratory', *Dike* 14: 19–42.

Azoulay, V. and Ismard, P. (2011) *Clisthène et Lycurgue d'Athènes: autour du politique dans la cité classique.* Paris.

Badian, E. (1992) 'The ghost of empire' in W. Eder, ed., *Die Athenische: Demokratie im 4. Jahrhundert v. Chr.* Stuttgart: 79–106

Bakewell, G. (1997) 'Metoikia in the Suplices of Aeschylus', *ClAnt* 16: 209–28.

Bearzot, C. (2003) 'L'uso dei documenti in Tucidide' in *L'uso dei documenti nella storiografia antica*, eds. A.M. Biraschi, P. Desideri, S. Roda and G. Zecchini. Naples: 267–314.

(2014), 'The use of documents in Xenophon's *Hellenica*' in *Between Thucydides and Polybius: The Golden Age of Greek Historiography*, ed. G. Parmeggiani. Washington, DC: 89–114.

Bedernab D.J. (2001) *International Law in Antiquity*. Cambridge.

Behr, C.A. (1981–6) *P. Aelius Aristides: The Complete Works*. 2 vols. Leiden.

Bers, V. (2002) 'What to believe in Demosthenes 57, *Against Eubulides*', *Hyperboreus* 8: 232–9.

(2013) 'Performing the speech in Athenian courts and assembly: adjusting the act to fit the bema?' in *Profession and Performance*, eds. C. Kremmydas, J. Powell and L. Rubinstein. London: 27–40.

Biagi, C. (1785) *Tractatus de Decretis Atheniensium in que Illustratur Singula Decretum Atheniense ex Museo Equitis ac Senatoris Iacobi Nanii Veneti*. Rome.

Biles, Z.P., and Olson, S.D. (2015) *Aristophanes: Wasps*. Oxford.

Blanshard, A. (2004a) 'What counts as the *demos*? Some notes on the relationship between the jury and "the people" in classical Athens', *Phoenix* 58: 28–48.

(2004b) 'Depicting democracy: an exploration of art and text in the law of Eukrates', *JHS* 124: 1–15.

(2007) 'The problems with honouring Samos: an Athenian document relief and its interpretation' in *Art and Inscriptions in the Ancient World*, eds. Z. Newby and R. Leader-Newby. Cambridge: 19–37.

Bleicken, J. (1987) 'Die einheit der athenischen Demokratie in klassischer Zeit', *Hermes* 115: 257–83.

Blok, J. (2017) *Citizenship in Classical Athens*. Cambridge.

Blyth, M. (2002) *The Great Transformations*. Cambridge.

Boegehold, A. (1972) 'The evolution of a public archive at Athens', *AJA* 76: 23–30.

(1996) 'Resistance to change in the law at Athens' in J. Ober and C. Hedrick eds., *Demokratia: A Conversation on Democracies Ancient and Modern*, Princeton: 203–14.

Bolansée, J. (1999) *Hermippos of Smyrna and his Biographical Writings*. Leuven.

Bolmarcich, S. (2007) 'The afterlife of a treaty', *CQ* 57: 13–25.

Bommas, M. (2011) 'Introduction' in M. Bommas ed. *Cultural Memory and Identity in Ancient Societies*. London and New York: 1–9.

Bosworth, A.B. (1990) 'Plutarch, Callisthenes and the Peace of Callias', *JHS* 110: 1–13.

(2000) 'The historical context of Thucydides' funeral oration', *JHS* 120: 1–16.

Bourdieu, P. (1977) *Outline of a Theory of Practice*. Cambridge.

(1979) *La Distinction: critique sociale du jugement*.

(1986) 'The forms of capital' in *Handbook of Theory and Research for the Sociology of Education*, ed. J. Richardson. New York: 241–58

(1991) *Language and Symbolic Power*. Oxford.

(1998) *Practical Reason*. Oxford.

(2010) *Distinction: A Social Critique of the Judgement of Taste*. Oxford.

Bouyssou, G. (2013) 'Parasites/flatteurs et mauvais banquet' in *À la table des rois: luxe et pouvoir dans l'oeuvre d'Athénée*, eds. C. Grandjean, A. Heller and J. Peigney. Rennes: 87–105.

Bowen, A.J. (2013) *Aeschylus: Suppliant Women*. Oxford.

Bowie, E.L. (1970) 'The Greeks and their past in the Second Sophistic', *Past and Present* 46: 3–41.

Braund, D. (2000) 'Learning, luxury and empire: Athenaeus' Roman patron' in *Athenaeus and his World*, eds. D. Braund and J. Wilkins. Exeter: 3–22.

Brauw, M., de (2001) '"Listen to the laws themselves": citations of laws and portrayal of character in Attic oratory', *CJ* 97: 161–76.

Brillant, M. (1911) *Les secrétaires Athéniens*. Paris.

Brock, R. (1998) 'Mythical polypragmosune in Athenian drama and rhetoric' in M. Austin, I. Harries and C. Smith, eds., *Modus Operandi: Essays in Honour of Geoffrey Rickman*. *BICS* Supplement 71. London: 227–38.

Brüggenbrock, C. (2006) *Die Ehre in den Zeiten der Demokratie: Das Verhältnis von athenischer Polis und Ehre in klassischer Zeit*. Frankfurt am Main.

Burian, P. (2007) 'Pelasgus and politics in the Danaid trilogy' in M. Lloyd ed. *Aeschylus*. Oxford: 199–210.

(2011) 'Athenian tragedy as democratic discourse' in *Why Athens? A Reappraisal of Tragic Politics*, ed. D. Carter. Oxford, 95–117.

Burnett, A.P. and Edmondson, C.N. (1961) 'The Chabrias monument in the Athenian Agora', *Hesperia* 30: 74–91.

Byrne, S. (2004) 'Proposers of Athenian state decrees 286–61 BC' in *ΑΤΤΙΚΑΙ ΕΠΙΓΡΑΦΑΙ*, eds. A. Matthaiou with G. Malouchou. Athens: 141–54.

Calhoun, G.M. (1914) 'Documentary frauds in litigation at Athens, *CPh* 9: 134–44.

Cammack, D. (2013) 'Rethinking Athenian democracy', PhD dissertation. Harvard University.

Campa, N.T. (2018) 'Positive freedom and the citizen in Athens', *Polis* 35: 1–32.

Canevaro, M. (2010) 'The naturalisation decree for the Plataeans (Ps.-D. 59.104)', *GRBS* 50: 337–69.

(2011) 'The twilight of *nomothesia*: legislation in early-Hellenistic Athens (322–301)', *Dike* 14: 59–92.

(2013) *The Documents in the Attic Orators: Laws and Decrees in the Public Speeches of the Demosthenic Corpus*. With a chapter by E.M. Harris. Oxford.

(2016a) *Demostene, Contro Leptine: Introduzione, traduzione e commento storico*. Berlin and Boston.

(2016b) 'Making and changing laws in ancient Athens' in *Oxford Handbook of Ancient Greek Law*, eds. E.M. Harris and M. Canevaro. Oxford (Online publication).

(2018) 'Majority rule vs. consensus: the practice of deliberation in the Greek poleis' in *Ancient Greek History and Contemporary Social Sciences*, eds. M. Canevaro, A. Erskine, B. Gray and J. Ober. Edinburgh.

(forthcoming) 'The fortune of the false documents in the Attic orators: early antiquarians and unintentional forgers' in *Falsifications and Authority in Antiquity, the Middle Ages and the Renaissance*, eds. J. Papy and E. Gielen.

Canevaro, M. and Esu, A. (2018) 'Extreme democracy and mixed constitution in theory and practice: *nomophylakia* and fourth-century *nomothesia* in the Aristotelian *Athenaion Politeia*' in *Athenaion Politeiai tra storia, politica e sociologia: Aristotele e Ps-Senofonte, Quaderni di Erga-Logoi*, eds. C. Bearzot, M. Canevaro, T. Gargiulo and E. Poddighe, Milan: 105–45.

Canevaro, M. and Harris, E.M. (2012) 'The documents in Andocides' *On the Mysteries*', *CQ* 62: 98–129.

(2016) 'The authenticity of the documents at Andocides' On the Mysteries 77–79 and 83–8', *Dike* 19: 9–49.

Carawan, E.M. (1985) '*Apophasis* and *eisangelia*: the role of the Areopagus in Athenian political trials', *GRBS* 26:115–39.

(2013) *The Athenian Amnesty and Reconstructing the Law*. Oxford.

(2015) 'The Athenian rule of law', *CR* 65: 175–6.

(2017) 'Decrees in Andocides' *On the Mysteries* and "latent fragments" from Craterus', *CQ* 67: 400–21.

Carey, C. (1994) 'Artless proofs in Aristotle and the orators', *BICS* 39: 95–106.

(1996) '*Nomos* in Attic rhetoric and oratory', *JHS* 116: 33–46.

Cargill, J. (1981) *The Second Athenian Confederacy: Empire or Free Alliance?* Berkeley and London.

Carlsson, S. (2010) *Hellenistic Democracies: Freedom, Independence and Political Procedure in Some East Greek City-States*. Stuttgart.

Carter, D.M. (2007) *The Politics of Greek Tragedy*. Exeter.

(ed.) (2011) *Why Athens? A Reappraisal of Tragic Politics*. Oxford.

(2013) 'Reported assembly scenes in Greek tragedy', *ICS* 38: 230–63.

Carter, L.B. (1986) *The Quiet Athenian*. Oxford.

Ceccarelli, P. (2010) 'Changing contexts: tragedy in the civic and cultural life of Hellenistic city-states' in *Beyond the Fifth Century: Interactions with Greek Tragedy from the Fourth Century BCE to the Middle Ages*, eds. I. Gildenhard and M. Revermann. Berlin and New York: 99–150.

Champion, C. (2018) 'Polybius on "Classical Athenian Imperial Democracy"' in *The Hellenistic Reception of Classical Athenian Democracy and Political Thought*, eds. M. Canevaro and B. Gray. Oxford: 123–38.

Chaniotis, A. (2013) '*Paradoxon, enargeia*, empathy: Hellenistic decrees and Hellenistic oratory' in *Hellenistic Oratory: Continuity and Change*, eds. C. Kremmydas and K. Tempest. Oxford: 201–17.

(2016) 'History as an argument in Hellenistic oratory: the evidence of Hellenistic decrees' in *La rhétorique du pouvoir: une exploration de l'art oratoire délibératif grec*, ed. P. Derron. Fondation Hardt Entretiens 62. Vandoeuvres: 129–74.

Christ, M.R. (1998) *The Litigious Athenian*. Baltimore and London.

(2006) *The Bad Citizen in Classical Athens*. Cambridge.

(2012) *The Limits of Altruism in Democratic Athens*. Cambridge.

Clarke, C. (2008) *Making Time for the Past: Local History and the Polis*. Oxford.

Clements, A. (2014) *Aristophanes' Thesmophoriazusae: Philosophizing Theatre and the Politics of Perception in Late Fifth-Century Athens*. Cambridge.

Cohen, D. (1991) *Law, Sexuality and Society: The Enforcement of Morals in Classical Athens*. Cambridge.

(1995) *Law, Violence and Community in Classical Athens*. Cambridge.

(2003) 'Writing, law and legal practice in the Athenian law courts' in *Written Texts and the Rise of Literate Culture in Ancient Greece*, ed. H. Yunis. Cambridge: 78–96.

Connolly, A. (1998) 'Was Sophocles heroised as Dexion?', *JHS* 118: 1–21.

BIBLIOGRAPHY

Connor, W.R. (1971) *The New Politicians of Fifth Century Athens*. Princeton.

Constantakopoulou, C. (2017) *Aegean Interactions: Delos and its Networks in the Third Century*. Oxford.

Cooper, C.R. (1995) 'Hyperides and the trial of Phryne', *Phoenix* 49: 303–18.

Cribiore, R. (2001) *Gymnastics of the Mind: Greek Education in Hellenistic and Roman Egypt*. Princeton.

Culasso Gastaldi, E. (2014a) '"To destroy the stele": epigraphic reinscription and historical revision in Athens', *AIO Papers* 2, trans. C. Dickman-Wilkes. Originally published as 'Abbattere la stele: riscrittura epigrafica e revisione storica ad Atene', *Cahiers Glotz* 14 (2003) 241–62.

(2014b) '"To destroy the stele", "To remain faithful to the stele": epigraphic text as guarantee of political decision', *AIO Papers* 3, trans. C. Dickman-Wilkes. Originally published as '"Abbattere la stele", "Rimanere fedeli alla stele": il testo epigrafico come garanzia della deliberazione politica' in *Philathenaios: Studies in Honour of Michael J. Osborne*, eds. A. Tamis, C.J. Mackie and S.G. Byrne. Athens (2010): 139–55.

Davies, J.K. (1994a) 'Accounts and accountability in classical Athens' in *Ritual, Finance, Politics: Democratic Accounts Presented to David Lewis*, eds. S. Hornblower and R. Osborne. Oxford: 201–12.

(1994b) 'On the non-usability of the concept of sovereignty in an ancient Greek context' in *Federazioni e federalismo nell'Europa antica*, ed. L. Aigner Foresti. Milan: 51–65.

(1996) 'Documents and "documents" in fourth-century historiography' in *Le IVe Siècle av. J-C: approches historiographiques*, ed. P. Carlier. Nancy and Paris: 29–40.

(2000) 'Athenaeus' use of public documents' in *Athenaeus and his World*, eds. D. Braund and J. Wilkins. Exeter: 203–17.

(2004) 'Athenian fiscal expertise and its influence', *Mediterraneo Antico* 7: 491–512.

(2005) 'The origins of the inscribed Greek stela' in *Writing and Ancient Near Eastern Society: Papers in Honour of Alan R. Millard*, eds. P. Bienkowski, C. Mee and E. Slater. New York: 283–300.

(2015) 'Retrospect and prospect' in *Communities and Networks in the Ancient Greek World*, eds. C. Taylor and K. Vlassopoulos. Oxford: 239–56.

Day, J.W. (1980) *The Glory of Athens: The Popular Tradition as Reflected in the Panatheaicus of Aelius Aristides*. Chicago.

(2010) *Archaic Greek Epigram and Dedication: Representaton and Reperformance*. Cambridge.

De Brauw, M. (2001–2) '"Listen to the laws themselves": citations of laws and portrayal of character in Attic oratory', *CJ* 97: 161–76.

De Laix, R.A. (1973) *Probouleusis at Athens: A Study of a Political Decision-Making*. Berkeley and Los Angeles.

De Tocqueville, A. (2003) *Democracy in America and Two Essays on America*. London and New York.

Deene, M. (2016) 'Who commissioned and paid for the reliefs on honorary *stelai* in classical Athens? Some new thoughts', *ZPE* 198: 75–9.

Delz, J. (1950) *Lukians Kenntnis der Athenischen Antiquitäten*. Freiburg.

Detienne, M. (1998) 'L' espace de la publicité: ses opératures intellectuels dans la cité' in *Les savoirs de l'écriture en grèce ancienne*, ed. M. Detienne. Lille: 29–81.

Develin, R. (1989) *Athenian Officials 684–321 BC*. Cambridge.

Dilts, M.R. and Kennedy, G.A. (1997) *Two Greek Rhetorical Treatises from the Roman Empire: Introduction, Text, and Translation of the* Arts of Rhetoric, *Attributed to Anonymous Seguerianus and to Apsines of Gadara*. Leiden and Boston.

Domingo Gygax, M. (2016) *Benefaction and Rewards in the Ancient Greek City: The Origins of Euergetism*. Cambridge.

Dorjahn, A.P. (1946) *Political Forgiveness in Old Athens: The Amnesty of 403*. Evanston.

Dover, K.J. (1976) 'The freedom of the intellectual in Greek society', *Talanta* 7: 24–54.

(1980) 'The language of classical Attic documentary inscriptions', *Transactions of the Philological Association* 79: 1–14.

Dreher, M. (1995) *Hegemon und Symmachoi: Untersuchungen zum zweiten athenischen Seebund*. Berlin and New York.

Drerup, E. (1898) 'Über die bei den Attischen Rednern eingelegten Urkunden', *Jahrbuch für Classische Philologie Supplementband*, 24: 221–365.

(1923) *Demosthenes im Urteile des Altertums*. Würzburg.

Dunbar, N. (1995) Aristophanes' Birds: *Edited with Introduction and Commentary*. Oxford.

Dyck, A.R. (1985) 'The function and persuasive power of Demosthenes' portrait of Aeschines in the speech "On the Crown"', *G&R* 32: 42–8.

Easterling, P.A. (1985) 'Anachronism in Greek tragedy', *JHS* 105: 1–10.

(1989) 'City settings in Greek poetry', *PCA* 86: 5–17.

(2005) 'The image of the polis in Greek tragedy' in *The Imaginary Polis: Symposium, January 7–10, 2004*, ed. M.H. Hansen. Copenhagen: 49–72.

Edwards, M. (2016) 'Greek political oratory and the canon of ten Attic orators' in *La rhétorique du pouvoir: une exploration de l'art oratoire délibératif grec*, ed. P. Derron. Fondation Hardt Entretiens 62. Vandoeuvres: 15–40.

Ehrenberg, V. (1950), 'The origins of democracy', *Historia* 1: 515–48.

Eidinow, E. (2016) *Envy, Poison and Death: Women on Trial in Classical Athens*. Oxford.

Engels, J. (2008) *Lykurg: Rede gegen Leokrates*. Darmstadt.

Engen, D.T. (2010) *Honor and Profit: Athenian Trade Policy and the Economy and Society of Greece, 415–307 BCE*. Ann Arbor.

Erdas, D. (2002) *Cratero il Macedone: testimonianze e frammenti*. Rome.

Erskine, A. (2018) 'Standing up to the *demos*: Plutarch, Phocion, and the democratic life' in *The Hellenistic Reception of Classical Athenian Democracy and Political Thought*, eds. M. Canevaro and B. Gray. Oxford: 238–59.

Esu, A. (2018) 'Divided power and deliberation: decision-making procedures in the Greek city-states (434–150 BC)', PhD dissertation. Edinburgh.

Euben, J.P. (1990) *The Tragedy of Political Theory: The Road not Taken*. Princeton.

Faraguna, M. (2003) 'I documenti nelle "Vite dei X oratori" dei Moralia plutarchei' in A.M. Biraschi, P. Desideri, S. Roda and G. Zecchini (eds.), *L'uso dei documenti nella storiografia antica*. Naples, 479–503.

(2006) 'Alcibiade, Cratero e gli archivi giudiziari ad Atene' in M. Faraguna and V. Vedaldi Iasbez (eds.), Δύνασθαι διδάσκειν: studi in onore di Filippo Càssola. Trieste: 197–207.

(2015) 'Archives, documents, and legal practices in the Greek polis' in *The Oxford Handbook of Ancient Greek Law*, eds. E.M. Harris and M. Canevaro (Electronic publication).

(2017) 'Documents, public information and the historian: perspectives on fifth-century Athens', *Historika* 7: 23–52.

Farrell, C.A. (2016) 'Xenophon *Poroi* 5: securing a "more just" Athenian hegemony', *Polis* 33: 331–55.

(forthcoming) *The Social and Political Thought of Xenophon of Athens*.

Ferrario, S.B. (2017) 'Xenophon and Greek political thought' in *The Cambridge Companion to Xenophon*, ed. M.A. Flower. Cambridge: 57–83.

Filonik, J. (2016) 'Impiety avenged: rewriting Athenian history' in *Splendide Mendax. Rethinking Fakes and Forgeries in Classical, Late Antique and Early Christian Literature*, eds. E.P. Cueva and J. Martinez. Groningen: 125–40.

Finley, M. (1962) 'The Athenian demagogues', *P&P* 21: 3–24.

(1975) 'The problem of the unity of Greek law' in M. Finley, *The Use and Abuse of History*. London: 134–52 (= 129–42 in *Atti del III Congresso Internazionale della Società italiana di Storia del Diritto*, 1966).

Fisher, N. (1994) 'Sparta re-(de)valued: some Athenian public attitudes to Sparta between Leuctra and the Lamian War' in *The Shadow of Sparta*, eds. S. Hodkinson and A. Powell. Swansea: 347–400.

(2007) 'Lykourgos of Athens: Lakonian by name, Lakoniser by policy?' in *The Contribution of Ancient Sparta to Political Thought and Practice*, eds. N. Birgalias, K. Burasalis and P. Cartledge, Athens: 327–44.

Flaig, E. (2013) 'Die Versammlungsdemokratie am Nadir: Entscheidungstheoretische Überlegungen zum Arginusenprozess', *Historische Zeitschrift* 297: 23–63.

Forrest, W.G. (1963) 'Aristophanes' *Acharnians*', *Phoenix* 17: 1–12.

Forsdyke, S. (2005) 'Revelry and riot in archaic Megara: democratic disorder or ritual reversal?', *JHS* 125: 73–92.

Foster, E. (2017) 'Military defeat in fifth-century Athens: Thucydides and his audience' in *Brill's Companion to Military Defeat in Ancient Mediterranean Society*, eds. J. Clark and B. Turner. Leiden and Boston: 99–122.

Frier, B.W. and Kehoe, P. (2007) 'Law and economic institutions' in *The Cambridge Economic History of the Greco-Roman World*, eds. W. Schiedel, I. Morris and R. Saller. Cambridge: 113–43.

Friis Johansen, H. and Whittle, E.W. (1980) *Aeschylus: The Suppliants*, 3 vols. Copenhagen.

Frost, F. (1961) 'Some documents in Plutarch's Lives', *C&M* 22: 182–94.

Funke, P. (1980) Homonoia und Arche: *Athen und die griechische Staatenwelt vom Ende des Peloponnesischen Krieges bis zum König frieden (404/3–287/6 v. Chr.)*. Wiesbaden.

BIBLIOGRAPHY

Gabrielsen, V. (2015) 'Naval and grain networks and associations in fourth-century Athens' in *Communities and Networks in the Ancient Greek World*, eds. C. Taylor and K. Vlassopoulos. Oxford: 177–205.

Gagarin, M. (2011) *Writing Greek Law*. Cambridge.

Garvie, A.F. (2006) *Aeschylus' Supplices: Play and Trilogy*, 2nd ed. Exeter.

Gauthier, P. (1985) *Les cités grecques et leurs bienfaiteurs, BCH* Suppl. 12. Athens and Paris.

Gehrke, H.-J. (2001) 'Myth, history and collective identity: uses of the past in ancient Greece and beyond' in *The Historian's Craft in the Age of Herodotus*, ed. N. Luraghi. Oxford: 286–313.

Gerolymatos, A. (1986), *Espionage and Treason: A Study of the proxenia in Political and Military Intelligence Gathering in Classical Greece*. Amsterdam.

Giannadaki, I. (2014) 'The time limit (*prothesmia*) in the *graphe paranomon*', *Dike* 17: 15–34.

Giessen, K. (1901) 'Plutarchs Quaestiones graecae und Aristoteles' Politien', *Philologus* 60: 446–71.

Goldhill, S. (1987) 'The Great Dionysia and civic ideology', *JHS* 107: 58–76.

(2000) 'Civic ideology and the problem of difference: the politics of Aeschylean tragedy, once again', *JHS* 120: 34–56.

Gomme, A.W. (1938) 'Aristophanes and politics', *CR* 52: 97–109.

(1956) *A Historical Commentary on Thucydides: The Ten Years' War. Volume III. Books IV–V24*. Oxford.

(1962) *More Essays in Greek History and Literature*. Oxford.

Gotteland, S. (2016) 'Passions et raison dans les prologues de Démosthène', *REG* 129: 1–16.

Gottesman, A. (2014) *Politics and the Street in Democratic Athens*. Cambridge.

Graeber, D. (2001) *Toward an Anthropological Theory of Value: The False Coin of Our Own Dreams*. New York.

Gray, B. (2013) 'The polis becomes humane? *Philanthropia* as a cardinal civic virtue in later Hellenistic honorific epigraphy and historiography', *Studi ellenistici* 27: 137–62.

(2015) Stasis *and Stability: Exile, the* Polis*, and Political Thought, c.404–146 BC*. Oxford.

(2018) 'A later Hellenistic debate about classical Athenian civic ideals? The evidence of epigraphy, historiography and philosophy', in M. Canevaro and B. Gray, eds. *The Hellenistic Reception of Classical Athenian Democracy and Political Thought*. Oxford: 139–76.

Gray, V. (2004) 'Le Socrate de Xénophon et la démocratie', *EPh* 2: 141–76

(2007) *Xenophon on Government*. Cambridge.

Greif, A. (2006) *Institutions and the Path to the Modern Economy: Lessons from Medieval Trade*. Cambridge.

Grethlein, J. (2014) 'The value of the past challenged: myth and ancient history in the Attic orators' in *Valuing the Past in the Greco-Roman World: Proceedings from the*

Penn Leiden Colloquia on Ancient Values VII, eds. C. Pieper and J. Kerr. Leiden: 326–54.

Grieb, V. (2009) *Hellenistiche Demokratie: politische Organisation und Struktur in freien griechischen Poleis nach Alexander dem Grossen*. Stuttgart.

Grote, G. (1849) *A History of Greece*, vol. 5. London.

Guth, D. (2014) 'Rhetoric and historical narrative: the Theban–Athenian alliance of 339 BCE', *Historia* 63: 151–65.

Haake, M. (2004) 'Documentary evidence, literary forgery or manipulation of historical documents? Diogenes Laertius and an Athenian honorary decree for Zeno of Citium', *CQ* 54: 470–83.

(2006) 'Ein athenisches Ehrendekret für Aristoteles? Die Rhetorik eines pseudo-epigraphischen Dokuments und die Logik seiner Geschichte', *Klio* 88: 328–50.

(2007) *Der Philosoph in der Stadt: Untersuchungen zur öffentlichen Rede über Philosophen und Philosophie in den hellenistischen Poleis*. Vestigia 56. Munich.

(2013) 'Illustrating, documenting, making-believe: the use of *psephismata* in Hellenistic biographies of philosophers' in *Inscriptions and Their Uses in Greek and Latin Literature*, eds. P. Liddel and P. Low. Oxford: 79–124.

Haake, M. and Jung, M. (eds.) (2013) *Griechische Heiligtümer als Erinnerungsorte*. Stuttgart.

Habicht, Ch. (1961) 'Falsche Urkunden zur Geschichte Athens in Zeitalter der Perserkriege', *Hermes* 89: 1–35.

(1984) 'Pausanias and the evidence of inscriptions', *ClAnt* 3: 40–56.

(1997) *Athens from Alexander to Antony*, trans. D. Schneider Cambridge, MA and London.

Hagermajer Allen, K. (2003) 'Intercultural exchanges in Attic decrees', *ClAnt* 22: 199–346.

Hakkarainen, M. (1997) 'Private wealth in the Athenian public sphere during the late classical and the early Hellenistic period' in *Early Hellenistic Athens: Symptoms of a Change*, ed. J. Frösén, Papers and Monographs of the Finnish Institute at Athens 6. Helsinki: 1–32.

Hall, E. (1995) 'Lawcourt dramas: the power of performance in in Greek forensic oratory', *BICS* 40: 39–58.

Hammer, D. (2002) *The Iliad as Politics: The Performance of Political Thought*. Oklahoma.

Hanink, J. (2014) *Lycurgan Athens and the Making of Classical Tragedy*. Cambridge.

Hansen, M.H. (1974) *The Sovereignty of the People's Court in Athens in the Fourth Century BC and the Public Action Against Unconstitutional Proposals*. Odense.

(1975) *Eisangelia*. Odense.

(1976) *Apagoge, Endeixis and Ephegesis Against Kakourgoi, Atimoi and Pheugontes in Classical Athens*. Odense.

(1978) '*Demos, ecclesia* and *dicasterion* in classical Athens', *GRBS* 19: 127–46.

(1980) 'Seven hundred *archai* in classical Athens', *GRBS* 21 (1980) 151–73.

(1983) *The Athenian Ecclesia: A Collection of Articles 1976–1983*. Copenhagen.

(1985) 'Athenian *nomothesia*', *GRBS* 26: 345–371.

(1987) *The Athenian Assembly*. Oxford.

(1988) *Three Studies in Athenian Demography*. Copenhagen.

(1989) *The Athenian Ecclesia II: A Collection of Articles 1983–9*. Copenhagen.

(1990) 'Solonian democracy in fourth-century Athens' in *Aspects of Athenian Democracy*, ed. J.R. Fears. Copenhagen: 71–99.

(1991) *The Athenian Democracy in the Age of Demosthenes: Structure, Principles, and Ideology*. Oxford.

(1996) 'Reflections on the number of citizens accommodated in the assembly place on the Pnyx' in B. Forsén and G. Stanton, eds., *The Pnyx in the History of Athens: Proceedings of an International Colloquium Organised by the Finnish Institute at Athens, 7–9 October, 1994*. Papers and Monographs of the Finnish Institute at Athens, 2. Helsinki: 23–33.

(2000) 'Conclusion: the impact of city-state cultures on the world' in M.H. Hansen (ed.), *A Comparative Study of Thirty City-State Cultures*. Copenhagen: 597–623.

(2010) 'The concepts of *demos*, *ekklesia*, and *dikasterion* in classical Athens', *GRBS* 50: 499–536.

(2015) 'Is Patrokleides' decree (Andoc. 1.77–79) a genuine document?', *GRBS* 55: 884–901.

(2016) 'Is Teisamenos' decree (Andoc. 1.83–84) a genuine document?', *GRBS* 56: 34–48.

(2017) '*Nomos ep' andri* in fourth-century Athens: on the law quoted at Andocides 1.87', *GRBS* 57: 268–81.

Harding, P. (1994) *Androtion and the Atthis: The Fragments Translated with Introduction and Commentary*. Oxford.

(2008) *The Story of Athens: The Fragments of the Local Chronicles of Attica*. London and New York.

Harris, D. (1994) 'Freedom of information and accountability: the inventory lists of the Parthenon' in S. Hornblower and R. Osborne (eds.), *Ritual, Finance, Politics: Democratic Accounts Presented to David Lewis*. Oxford: 213–23.

Harris, E.M. (1989) 'Demosthenes' speech against Meidias', *Harvard Studies in Classical Philology* 92: 117–36.

(1994) 'Law and oratory' in *Persuasion: Greek Rhetoric in Action*, ed. I. Worthington. London: 130–50.

(1995) *Aeschines and Athenian Politics*. Oxford.

(2000a) 'The authenticity of Andocides' *De Pace*: a subversive essay' in *Polis and Politics: Studies in Greek History*, ed. P. Flensted-Jensen, T. Nielsen and L. Rubinstein. Copenhagen: 479–506.

(2000b) 'Open texture in Athenian Law', *Dike* 3: 27–78.

(2006a) 'The rule of law in Athenian democracy: reflections on the judicial oath', *Dike* 9: 157–81.

(2006b) *Democracy and the Rule of Law in Classical Athens: Essays on Law, Society, and Politics*. Cambridge.

(2006c) 'Was all criticism of Athenian democracy anti-democratic?' in *Democrazia e anti-democrazia*, ed. U. Bultrighini. Alessandria: 11–24.

(2007) 'Who enforced the law in classical Athens?' in *Symposion 2005*, ed. E. Cantarella. Vienna: 159–76.

(2010) 'Introduction' in *Law and Drama in Ancient Greece*, eds. E.M. Harris, D.F. Leão and P.J. Rhodes. London: 1–24.

(2012–13) 'Review of Gottesman, *Politics and The Street in Democratic Athens*', *Classical Ireland* 19–20: 156–60.

(2013a) *The Rule of Law in Action in Democratic Athens*. Oxford.

(2013b) 'The *Against Meidias* (Dem. 21)' in M. Canevaro, *The Documents in the Attic Orators: Laws and Decrees in the Public Speeches of the Demosthenic Corpus*. Oxford: 209–36.

(2013–14) 'The authenticity of the document at Andocides *On the Mysteries* 96–98', Τεκμήρια 12: 121–53.

(2016a) 'From democracy to the rule of law? Constitutional change in Athens during the fifth and fourth centuries BCE' in *Die Athenische Demokratie im 4. Jahrhundert: Zwischen Modernisierung und Tradition*, ed. C. Tiersch. Berlin: 73–87.

(2016b) 'Alcibiades, the ancestors, liturgies, and the etiquette of addressing the Athenian assembly ' in *The Art of History. Literary Perspectives on Greek and Roman Historiography*, eds. V. Liotsakis and S. Farrington. Berlin and Boston: 145–56.

(2017a) 'Applying the law about the award of crowns to magistrates (Aeschin. 3.9–31 ; Dem. 18.113–117): epigraphic evidence for the legal arguments at the trial of Ctesiphon', *ZPE* 202: 105–17.

(2017b) 'How to "act" in an Athenian court: emotions and forensic performance' in *The Theatre of Justice: Aspects of Performance in Greco-Roman Oratory and Rhetoric*, eds. S. Papaioannou, A. Seraphim and B. de Vela. Leiden and Boston: 223–4)

(2017c) 'Rhetoric and politics' in *The Oxford Handbook of Rhetorical Studies*, ed. M.J. MacDonald. Oxford: 53–61.

(2018) *Demosthenes: Speeches 23–26*. Austin.

Harris, E.M., Leão, D.F. and Rhodes, P.J. (2010) *Law and Drama in Ancient Greece*. London.

Harrison, A.R.W. (1971) *The Law of Athens*, vol. 2. Oxford.

Hartmann, A. (2013) '*Cui vetustas fidem faciat*: inscriptions and other material relics of the past in Graeco-Roman antiquity' in *Inscriptions and their Uses in Greek and Latin Literature*, eds. P. Liddel and P. Low. Oxford: 33–63.

Hedrick, C.W. (1999) 'Democracy and the Athenian epigraphical habit', *Hesperia* 68: 387–439.

(2000) 'For anyone who wishes to see', *AncW* 31: 127–33.

Henderson, J. (1987) *Aristophanes Lysistrata: Edited with Introduction and Commentary*. Oxford.

(2000) *Aristophanes: Birds; Lysistrata; Women at the Thesmophoria*. Cambridge, MA.

(2002) *Aristophanes: Frogs; Assemblywomen; Wealth*. Cambridge, MA.

(2007) 'Drama and democracy' in *The Cambridge Companion to the Age of Pericles*, ed. L.J. Samons. Cambridge: 179–95.

Henry, A.S. (1977) *The Prescripts of Athenian Decrees. Mnemosyne* Suppl. 49. Leiden.

(1996) 'The hortatory intention in Attic state decrees', *ZPE* 112: 105–19.

(1983) *Honours and Privileges in Athenian Decrees: The Principal Formulae of Athenian Honorary Decrees*. Hildesheim and New York.

Herman, G. (1987) *Ritualised Friendship and the Greek City*. Cambridge.

(2006). *Morality and Behaviour in Democratic Athens: A Social History*. Cambridge.

Hesk, J. (2000) *Deception and Democracy in Classical Athens*. Cambridge.

(2012) 'Common knowledge and the contestation of history in some fourth-century Athenian trials' in *Greek Notions of the Past in the Archaic and Classical Eras: History Without Historians*, eds. J. Marincola, L. Llewellyn-Jones and C. Maciver. Edinburgh: 207–26.

Higbie, C. (1999) 'Craterus and the use of inscriptions in ancient scholarship', *TAPhA* 129: 43–83.

(2017) *Collectors, Scholars, and Forgers in the Ancient World: Object Lessons*. Oxford.

Hobart, M. (1975) 'Orators and patrons: two types of political leader in Balinese village society' in *Political Language and Oratory in Traditional Society*, ed. M. Bloch. London, New York and San Francisco: 65–92.

Hobden, F. (2007) 'Imagining past and present: a rhetorical strategy in Aeschines 3, *Against Ctesiphon*', *CQ* 57: 490–501.

Hölkeskamp, K.-J. (1992) 'Written law in archaic Greece', *PCPhS* 38: 97–117.

(2000) '(In-)Schrift und Monument: Zum Begriff des Gesetzes im Archaischen und Klassischen Griechenland', *ZPE* 132: 73–96.

Holton, J. (2018) '*Philanthropia*, Athens, and democracy in Diodorus Siculus: the Athenian debate' in *The Hellenistic Reception of Classical Athenian Democracy and Political Thought*, eds. M. Canevaro and B. Gray. Oxford: 177–207.

Hopkinson, N. (2008) *Lucian: A Selection*. Cambridge.

Hornblower, S. (1996) *A Commentary on Thucydides: Volume II. Books IV–V.24*. Oxford.

(2004) 'This was decided (*edoxe tauta*): the army as polis in Xenophon's *Anabasis* – and elsewhere' in *The Long March: Xenophon and the Ten Thousand*, ed. R.J. Lane Fox. New Haven and London: 243–63.

(2008) *A Commentary on Thucydides: Volume III. Books 5.25–8.109*. Oxford.

(2009) 'Thucydides and the Athenian *boule* (council of five hundred)' in *Greek History and Epigraphy: Essays in Honour of P.J. Rhodes*, eds. L. Mitchell and L. Rubinstein. Swansea: 251–65.

Horváth, L. (2014) *Der Neue Hypereides: Textedition, Studien und Erläuterungen*. Berlin.

Householder, F.W. Jr (1940) 'The mock decrees in Lucian', *TAPhA* 71: 199–219.

Huber, J.D. and Shipan, C.R. (2002) *Deliberate Discretion: The Institutional Foundation of Bureaucratic Autonomy*. Cambridge.

Humphreys, S. (2004) *The Strangeness of the Gods*. Oxford.

Hunt, P. (2010) *War, Peace, and Alliance in Demosthenes' Athens*. Cambridge.

Hunter, V. (1991) 'Gossip and the politics of reputation in classical Athens', *Phoenix* 45: 299–325.

(1994) *Policing Athens: Social Control in the Attic Lawsuits*. Princeton.

BIBLIOGRAPHY

Huntington, S.P. (1968) *Political Order in Changing Societies*. New Haven and London.

Irwin, E. (2005) *Solon and Early Greek Poetry: The Politics of Exhortation*. Cambridge.

Ismard, P. (2015) *La démocratie contre les experts: les esclaves publics en Grèce ancienne*. Paris.

Jackson, C.N. (1919) 'The decree-seller in the Birds: the professional politicians at Athens', *HSCP* 30: 89–102.

Jacob, C. (2013) *The Web of Athenaeus*, trans. A. Papaconstantinou. Washington, DC.

Johnstone, S. (1996) 'Greek oratorical settings and the problem of the Pnyx' in *Theory, Text, Context: Issues in Greek Rhetoric and Oratory*, ed. C. Johnstone. Albany: 97–127.

    (1999) *Disputes and Democracy*. Austin.

Johnstone, S. (2011) *A History of Trust in Ancient Greece*. Chicago and London.

Jones, N. (1987) *Public Organisation in Ancient Greece*. Philadelphia.

    (1999) *The Associations of Classical Athens: The Response to Democracy*. New York and Oxford.

Jovanović, M. and Henrard, K. (2008) 'Sovereignty, statehood and the diversity challenge' in *Sovereignty and Diversity*, eds. M. Jovanović and K. Henrard. Portland: 1–12.

Joyce, C. (2016) 'The Athenian reconciliation agreement of 403 BCE and its legacy for Greek city-states in the classical and Hellenistic Age' in *The Oxford Handbook of Ancient Greek Law*, eds. M. Canevaro and E.M. Harris (Online publication).

    (2018) '*Atimia* and outlawry in archaic and classical Greece', *Polis* 35: 33–60.

Kallet-Marx, L. (1994) 'Money talks: rhetor, demos and the reserve of the Athenian empire' in *Ritual, Finance, Politics: Democratic Accounts Presented to David Lewis*, eds. S.N. Hornblower and R. Osborne. Oxford: 227–51.

Keaney, J.J. (1993) 'Theophrastus on ostracism and the character of his NOMOI' in *Aristote et Athènes: Aristoteles and Athens. Fribourg (Suisse) 23–25 mai 1991*, ed. M. Piérart. Paris: 261–78.

Klaffenbach, G. (1960) *Bemerkungen zum griechischen Urkundenwesen*. Berlin.

Koerner, R. (1993) *Inschriftliche Gesetzestexte der frühen griechischen Polis: Aus dem Nachlass von Reinhard Koerner*, ed. K. Hallof. Cologne.

Konstan, D. (2000) 'Pity and the law in Greek theory and practice', *Dike* 4: 124–45.

Kostakopoulou, D. (2002) 'Floating sovereignty: a pathology or a necessary means of state evolution?', *Oxford Journal of Legal Studies* 22: 135–156.

Kremmydas, C. (2007a) 'P. Berl. 9781: the early reception of Demosthenes 20', *BICS* 50: 19–48.

    (2007b) 'Logical argumentation in Demosthenes' *Against Leptines*' in *Logos: Rational Argument in Classical Rhetoric*, ed. J. Powell. London: 19–34

    (2012) *Commentary on Demosthenes Against Leptines: With Introduction, Text, and Translation*. Oxford.

    (2016) 'Demosthenes' *Philippics* and the art of characterisation for the assembly' in *La rhétorique du pouvoir: une exploration de l'art oratoire délibératif grec*, ed. P. Derron. Fondation Hardt Entretiens 62. Vandoeuvres: 41–70.

BIBLIOGRAPHY

Krentz, P.M. (1989) *Xenophon: Hellenika I–II.3.10*. Warminster.

(2007) 'The oath of Marathon, not Plataea?', *Hesperia* 76: 731–42.

(2009) 'The Athenian treaty in Theopompos F153', *Phoenix* 63: 231–8.

Lalonde, G.V. (1971) 'The publication and transmission of Greek diplomatic documents', Ph D diss. University of Washington.

(1977) 'A Boiotian decree in Athens', *Hesperia* 46: 268–76.

Lambert, S.D. (1998) *The Phratries of Attica*, 2nd ed. Ann Arbor.

(2008) 'Polis and theatre in Lykourgan Athens: the honorific decrees' in Μικρός Ιερομνήμων: Μελέτες εις Μνήμην Michael H. Jameson, eds. A.P. Matthaiou and I. Polinskaya. Athens: 52–85.

(2010) 'Connecting with the past in Lykourgan Athens: an epigraphical perspective' in *Intentional History: Spinning Time in Ancient Greece*, eds. L. Foxhall, H.-J. Gehrke and N. Luraghi. Stuttgart: 225–38.

(2011a) 'What was the point of inscribed honorific decrees in classical Athens?' in *Sociable Man: Essays in Ancient Greek Social Behaviour, in Honour of Nick Fisher*, ed. S.D. Lambert. Cardiff: 193–214.

(2011b) 'Some political shifts in Lykourgan Athens' in *Clisthène et Lycurgue d'Athènes*, ed. V. Azoulay and P. Ismard. Paris: 175–90.

(2012a) *Inscribed Athenian Laws and Decrees 352/1–322/1 BC: Epigraphical Essays*. Leiden.

(2012b) 'Inscribing the past in fourth-century Athens' in *Greek Notions of the Past in the Archaic and Classical Eras: History without Historians*, eds. J. Marincola, L. Llewellyn-Jones and C. MacIver. Edinburgh: 253–75.

(2015) 'The inscribed version of the decree honouring Lykourgos of Boutadai (*IG* II² 457 and 3207)', *AIO Papers* 6.

(2017) 'Two inscribed documents of the Athenian empire: the Chalkis decree and the tribute reassessment decree', *AIO Papers* 8.

(2018) *Inscribed Athenian Laws and Decrees in the Age of Demosthenes: Historical Essays*. Leiden and Boston.

Lane Fox, R.J. (1994) 'Aeschines and Athenian politics' in *Ritual, Finance, Politics: Athenian Democratic Accounts Presented to David Lewis*, eds. S.N. Hornblower and R.G., Osborne. Oxford: 137–55.

(2010) 'Thucydides and documentary history', *CQ* 60: 11–29.

Lanni, A. (1997) 'Spectator sport or serious politics? *Hoi periestekotes* and the Athenian lawcourts', *JHS* 117: 183–9.

(2004) 'Arguing from precedent: modern perspectives on Athenian practice' in *The Law and the Courts in Ancient Greece*, eds. E. Harris and L. Rubinstein. London: 159–71.

(2006) *Law and Justice in the Courts of Classical Athens*. Cambridge.

(2012) 'Social sanctions in classical Athens' in *Symposion 2011*, ed. G. Thür. Vienna: 99–110.

(2016) *Law and Order in Ancient Athens*. Cambridge.

Larfeld, W. (1902–7) *Handbuch der Griechischen Epigraphik*, 2 vols. Leipzig.

Lavelle, B.M. (1988) 'Adikia, the decree of Kannonos, and the trial of the generals', C&M 39: 19–41.

Lawton, C. (1995) Attic Document Reliefs. Oxford.

Leão, D.F. and Rhodes, P.J. (2015) The Laws of Solon: A New Edition with Introduction, trans. and commentary. London and New York.

Leppin, H. (1999) 'Argos: Eine griechische Demokratie des funften Jahrhunderts v. Chr.', Ktema 24: 297–312

Lewis, S. (1996) News and Society in the Greek Polis. London

Liddel, P. (2003) 'The places of publication of Athenian state decrees from the fifth century BC to the third century AD', ZPE 134: 79–93.

(2007) Civic Obligation and Individual Liberty in Ancient Athens. Oxford.

(2008) 'Scholarship and morality: Plutarch's use of inscriptions' in The Unity of Plutarch's Work: 'Moralia' Themes in the 'Lives'. Features of the 'Lives' in the 'Moralia', ed. A. Nikolaidis. Berlin: 125–37.

(2010) 'Epigraphy, legislation, and power within the Athenian empire', BICS 53: 99–128.

(2016) 'The honorific decrees of fourth-century Athens: trends, perceptions, controversies' in Die Athenische Demokratie im 4. Jahrhundert: Zwischen Modernisierung und Tradition, ed. C. Tiersch. Berlin: 335–57.

(2018) 'Exploring inter-community political activity in fourth-century Greece' in Ancient Greek History and the Contemporary Social Sciences, eds. M. Canevaro, A. Erskine, B. Gray and J. Ober.

(forthcoming) 'Rules, practices, narratives: managing decrees and decree-making in classical Athens', in The Institutional History of the Greek Polis. New Approaches, eds. M. Barbato and M. Canevaro.

Livingstone, N. (2016) Athens: The City as University. London.

Loening, T.C. (1987) The Reconciliation Agreement of 403/402 in Athens: Its Content and Application. Hermes Einzelschrift 53. Stuttgart.

Longworth, P. (1969) The Cossacks. London.

Loomis, W.T. (1998) Wages, Welfare Costs and Inflation in Classical Athens. Ann Arbor.

Loraux, N. (2002) The Divided City: On Memory and Forgetting in Ancient Athens, trans. C. Pache with J. Fort. New York.

Lotze, D. (1981) 'Zum Begriff der Demokratie in Aischylos' Hiketiden' in Aischylos und Pindar: Studien zu Werk und Nachwirkung, ed. E.G., Schmidt, Berlin: 207–16.

Lougovaya, J. (2013) 'Inscriptions on the Attic stage' in Inscriptions and their Uses in Ancient Greek and Latin Literature, eds. P. Liddel and P. Low. Oxford: 255–70.

Low, P. (2005) 'Looking for the language of Athenian imperialism', JHS 125: 91–111.

(2007) Interstate Relations in Classical Greece. Cambridge.

(2016) 'Lives from stone: epigraphy and biography in Classical and Hellenistic Greece' in Creative Lives in Classical Antiquity: Poets, Artists and Biography, eds. R. Fletcher and J. Hanink, eds. Cambridge: 147–74.

(forthcoming) 'Remembering, forgetting, and rewriting the past: Athenian inscriptions and collective memory' in Shaping Memory in Ancient Greece: Poetry, Historiography and Epigraphy, eds. C. Constantakopoulou and M. Fragoulaki. London.

Lowndes, V. and Roberts, P. (2013) *Why Institutions Matter: The New Institutionalism in Political Science*. New York.

Luraghi, N. (2010) 'The demos as narrator: public honors and the construction of future and past' in *Intentional History: Spinning Time in Ancient Greece*, eds. L. Foxhall, H.-J. Gehrke and N. Luraghi. Stuttgart: 247–63.

Ma, J. (2003) 'Peer polity interaction in the Hellenistic age', *P&P* 180: 9–39.

(2013) *Statues and Cities: Honorific Portraits and Civic Identity in the Hellenistic World*. Oxford.

MacCormack, N. (2007) *Institutions of Law: An Essay in Legal Theory*. Oxford.

MacDonald, C. (1977) *Cicero: In Catilinam I–IV. Pro Murena. Pro Sulla. Pro Flacco*. Cambridge, MA and London.

MacDowell, D.M. (1962) *Andokides: On the Mysteries*. Oxford.

(1998) 'Andocides' in *Antiphon and Andocides*, ed. M. Gagarin. Austin: 93–170.

(2000) *Demosthenes: On the False Embassy*. Oxford.

(2009) *Demosthenes the Orator*. Oxford.

(2010) 'Aristophanes and Athenian law' in *Law and Drama in Ancient Greece*, eds. E.M. Harris, D.F. Leão and P.J. Rhodes. London: 147–57.

Mack, W. (2015) *Proxeny and Polis: Institutional Networks in the Ancient Greek World*. Oxford.

(2018) '*Vox populi, vox deorum*? The Athenian document reliefs and the theologies of public inscription', *ABSA* 113.

MacLean, B.H. (2002) *An Introduction to Greek Epigraphy of the Hellenistic and Roman Periods from Alexander the Great down to the Reign of Constantine (323 B.C.-A.D. 337)*. Ann Arbor.

Mader, G. (2006) 'Fighting Philip with decrees: Demosthenes and the syndrome of symbolic action', *AJPh* 127: 376–86.

Maidment, K.J. (1952) *Minor Attic Orators I: Antiphon, Andocides*. Cambridge, MA.

Makkink, A.D.J. *Andokides' Eerste Rede*. Amsterdam.

Malouchou, G.E. (2014) 'Τὸ ἐνεπίγραφο βάθρο ἀπὸ Φυλῆς τὸν δημὸν καταγαγόντων', *Ηόρος* 22–5 (2010-13) [2014]: 115–44.

Mansbridge, J.J. (1983) *Beyond Adversary Democracy*. New York.

March, J.G. and Olsen, P.J. (1984) 'The New Institutionalism: organizational factors in political life', *APSR* 78.3: 734–49.

(1989) *Rediscovering Institutions: The Organizational Basis of Politics*. New York.

Marincola, J., Llewellyn-Jones, L. and Maciver, C., eds. (2012) *Greek Notions of the Past in the Archaic and Classical Eras: History Without Historians*. Edinburgh.

Martin, G. (2014) 'Interpreting instability: considerations on the lives of the ten orators', *CQ* 64: 321–36.

(2016) 'The Gods in the Athenian assembly' in *Theologies of Ancient Greek Religion*, eds. E. Eidinow, J. Kindt and R. Osborne. Cambridge: 281–300.

Massar, N. (2006) 'La circulation des décrets dans les cités et entre cités à l'époque hellénistique' in *La circulation de l'information dans les états antiques*, eds. L. Capdetrey and J. Nelis-Clément. Bordeaux: 73–87.

Matthaiou, A.P. (2011) 'The Theozotides decree on the sons of those murdered in the Oligarchy' in *Τὰ ἐν τῆι στήληι γεγραμμένα: Six Greek Historical Inscriptions of the Fifth Century BC* ed. A.P. Matthaiou. Athens: 71–81.

(2017) 'Παρατηρήσεις εἰς ἐκδεδομένα Ἀττικὰ ψηφίσματα (7ο τεῦχος)', *Γραμματεῖον* 6: 11–19.

Mauss, M. (2006) *Techniques Technology and Civilization*. New York and Oxford.

Meiggs, R. (1972) *The Athenian Empire*. Oxford.

Meiggs, R. and Lewis, D.M. (1988) *A Selection of Greek Historical Inscriptions to the End of the Fifth Century BC*, rev. ed. Oxford.

Meritt, B.D., and Traill, J.S. (1974) *Inscriptions: The Athenian Councillors. The Athenian Agora* volume XV. Princeton.

Meyer, E. (2013) 'Inscriptions as honours and the Athenian epigraphical habit', *Historia* 62: 453–505.

(2016) 'Posts, *kurbeis, metopes*: the origins of the Athenian "documentary" stele', *Hesperia* 85: 323–83.

Meyer, J.W. and Rowan, B. (1991) 'Institutionalized organizations: formal structure as myth and ceremony' in *The New Institutionalism in Organizational Analysis*, eds. W.W. Powell and P.J. Di Maggio. Cambridge: 41–62.

Meyer-Laurin, H. (1965) *Gesetz und Billigkeit im Attischen Prozess*. Weimar.

Mhire, J.J. and Frost, B.-P. eds. (2014) *The Political Theory of Aristophanes*. New York.

Miller, J. (2016) 'Euergetism, agonism, and democracy: the hortatory intention in late classical and early Hellenistic Athenian honorific decrees', *Hesperia* 85: 385–435.

Mitchell, L. (1997) *Greeks Bearing Gifts: The Public Use of Private Relationships in the Greek World, 435–323*. Cambridge.

(2006) 'Greek government' in *A Companion to the Classical Greek World*, ed. K. Kinzl. Oxford: 367–86.

Moles, J. (1999) '*Anathema kai ktema*: the inscriptional inheritance of ancient historiography', *Histos* 3: 27–69.

(2011) 'Luke's preface: the Greek decree, classical historiography and Christian redefinitions', *New Testament Studies* 27: 461–82.

Momigliano, A. (1950) 'Ancient history and the antiquarian', *Journal of the Warburg and Courtauld Institutes* 13: 285–315.

Monoson, S. (2000) *Plato's Democratic Entanglements: Perceptions of a Common Humanity*. Princeton.

Moreno, A. (2007) *Feeding the Democracy: The Athenian Grain Supply in the Fifth and Fourth Centuries BC*. Oxford.

Morris, I. (2015) *Foragers, Farmers, and Fossil Fuels: How Human Values Evolve*. Princeton and Oxford.

Moroo, A. (2016) 'The origin and development of acropolis as a place for erecting public decrees: the Periclean building project and its effect on the Athenian epigraphic habit' in *The Parthenon Frieze: Ritual Communication between the Goddess and the Polis*, ed. T. Osada. Vienna: 31-48.

Morwood, J. (2007) *Euripides: Suppliant Women, with Introduction, Translation and Commentary*. Oxford.

Mossé, C. (1979) 'Citoyens actifs et citoyens "passifs" dans les cités grecques: une approche théoretique du problème', *REA* 81: 241–9.

(1989) 'Lycurge l'Athénien: homme du passé ou précurseur de l'avenir?', *QC* 30: 25–36.

Mossman J. (2012) '*Philotimia* and Greekness in Lucian' in *The Lash of Ambition: Plutarch, Imperial Greek Literature and the Dynamics of* Philotimia, eds. G. Roskam, M.De Pourcq and L. Van der Stockt. Paris and Walpole: 169–82.

Müller, F.L. (1997) *Das Problem der Urkunden bei Thukydides: Die Frage der Überlieferungsabsicht durch den Autor*. Stuttgart.

Müller, K.O. (1853) *Fragmenta historicorum Graecorum*, vol. 3. Paris.

Murray, O. (1990) 'Cities of reason' in *The Greek City from Homer to Alexander*, eds. O. Murray and S. Price. Oxford: 1–25.

(1995) 'Forms of sociality' in *The Greeks*, ed. J.-P. Vernant, trans. C. Lambert and T.L. Fagan. Chicago: 218–53.

Nikolaidis, A.G. (2012) 'Aspects of Plutarch's notion of *philotimia*' in *The Lash of Ambition: Plutarch, Imperial Greek Literature and the Dynamics of* Philotimia, eds. G. Roskam, M.De Pourcq and L. Van der Stockt. Paris and Walpole: 31–53.

Ní Mheallaigh, K. (2008) 'Pseudo-documentarism and the limits of ancient fiction', *AJP* 129: 403–31.

(2014) *Reading Fiction with Lucian: Fakes, Freaks and Hyperreality*. Cambridge.

North, D.C. (1990) *Institutions, Institutional Change and Economic Performance*. Cambridge.

Nouhaud, M. (1982) *L'Utilisation de l'histoire par les orateurs attiques*. Paris.

O'Rourke, S. (2007) *The Cossacks*. Manchester and New York.

Ober, J. (1989) *Mass and Elite in Democratic Athens*. Princeton.

(1996) *The Athenian Revolution*. Princeton.

(1998) *Political Dissent in Democratic Athens: Intellectual Critics of Popular Rule*. Princeton.

(2008) *Democracy and Knowledge: Innovation and Learning in Classical Athens*. Princeton.

(2015) *The Rise and Fall of Classical Greece*. London and Princeton.

Oikonomides, A.N. (1986) 'The epigraphical tradition of the decree of Stratocles honoring "post mortem" the orator Lykourgos', *AW* 14: 51–4.

Olick, J.K. (2007) *The Politics of Regret: On Collective Memory and Historical Responsibility*. New York and Oxford.

Oliver, G.J. (2007) 'Space and the visualization of power in the Greek *polis*: the award of portrait statues in decrees in Athens' in *Early Hellenistic Portraiture: Image, Style, Context*, eds. P. Schultz and R. von den Hoff. Cambridge: 181–204.

Olson, S.D. (2010) 'Comedy, politics and society' in *Brill's Companion to the Study of Greek Comedy*, ed. G.W. Dobrov. Leiden and Boston: 35–69.

Oost, S.I. (1977) 'Two notes on Aristophon of Azenia', *CPh* 72: 238–4.

Osborne, M.J. (1974) 'Two Athenian decrees for Delians', *Eranos* 72, 168–84.

(1981–3) *Naturalization in Athens*, 4 vols. Brussels.

(2012) 'Secretaries, *psephismata* and *stelai* in Athens', *Ancient Society* 42: 33–59.

Osborne, R.G. (1985) *Demos: The Discovery of Classical Attica*. Cambridge.

(1999) 'Inscribing democracy' in *Performance Culture in Athenian Democracy*, eds. R. Osborne and S. Goldhill. Cambridge: 341–58.

Ostrom, E. (1986) 'An agenda for the study of institutions', *Public Choice* 48.1: 3–35.

Ostwald, M. (1986) *From Popular Sovereignty to Sovereignty of the Law: Law, Society and Politics in Fifth-Century Athens*. London; Berkeley.

Papadopoulou, T. (2011). *Aeschylus: Suppliants*. Bristol.

Papazarkadas, N. (2009) 'Epigraphy and the Athenian empire: reshuffling the chronological cards' in *Interpreting the Athenian Empire*, eds. J.Ma, N. Papazarkadas and R.C.T. Parker. London: 67–88.

(2014) 'Athens, Sigeion, and the politics of approbation during the Ionian War' in *ΑΘΗΝΑΙΩΝ ΕΠΙΣΚΟΠΟΣ: Studies in Honour of Harold B. Mattingly*, eds. A.P. Matthaiou and R.K. Pitt. Athens: 215–38.

Parker, R.C.T. (1996) *Athenian Religion: A History*. Oxford.

(2005) *Polytheism and Society at Athens*. Oxford.

Pasquino, P. (2010) 'Democracy ancient and modern: divided power' in *Démocratie athénienne: démocratie moderne. Tradition et influences neuf exposés suivis de discussions*, ed. M.H. Hansen. Fondation Hardt Entretiens 56. Vandoeuvres: 1–49.

Patterson, C. (1981) *Pericles' Citizenship Law of 451–50 B.C.*, New York.

Pattoni, M.P. (2017) 'Democraic *paideia* in Aeschylus' *Suppliants*', *Polis* 34: 251–72.

Payen, P. (2014) 'Plutarch the antiquarian' in *A Companion to Plutarch*, ed. M. Beck. Oxford: 235–48.

Pébarthe, C. (2006) *Cité, démocratie et écriture: histoire de l'alphabétisation d'Athènes à l'époque classique*. Paris and Brussels.

Pelling, C. (2000) *Literary Texts and the Greek Historian*. London and New York.

Peters, B.G. (2005) *Institutional Theory in Political Science: The 'New' Institutionalism*. London.

(2008) 'Introduction' in *Debating Institutionalism*, eds. J. Pierre, B. Guy Peters and G. Stoker. Manchester: 1–17.

Petre, Z. (1986) 'Le décret des *Suppliantes* d'Eschyle', *Studii Clasice*, 24, 25–32.

Petrovic, A. (2010) 'True lies of Athenian public epigrams' in *Archaic and Classical Greek Epigram*, eds. M. Baumbach, A. Petrovic and I. Petrovic. Cambridge: 202–15.

(2013) 'Inscribed epigrams in orators and epigrammatic collections' in *Inscriptions and Their Uses in Greek and Latin Literature*, eds. P. Liddel and P. Low. Oxford, 197–213.

Piérart, M. (2000) 'Argos: une autre democratie' in *Polis and Politics: Studies in Greek History*, eds. P. Flensted-Jensen, T. Nielsen and L. Rubinstein. Copenhagen: 296–314.

(2004) 'Qu'est-ce qu'être Argien? Identité civique et régime démocratique à Argos au Ve s. avant J.-C.' in *Poleis e politeiai: esperienze politische, tradizioni letterarie*, *progetti costitutionali. Atti del Convegno Internazionale di Storia Greca, Torino, 29 maggio–31 maggio 2002*, ed. S. Cataldi. Alessandria: 167–85.

Pitcher, L.V. (2005) 'Narrative technique in the *Lives of the Orators*', *CQ* 55: 217–34.

Plassart, A. (1950) *Inscriptions de Délos: périodes de l'amphictyonie ionienne et de l'amphictyonie attico-délienne*. Paris.

Podlecki, A.J. (1966) *The Political Background of Aeschylean Tragedy*. Ann Arbor.

(1986) 'Polis and monarch in early Attic tragedy' in *Greek Tragedy and Political Theory*, ed. J.P., Euben. Los Angeles: 76–100

(1993) 'Κατ' ἀρχῆς γὰς Φιλαίτιος λεώς: the concept of leadership in Aeschylus' in *Tragedy, Comedy and the Polis: Papers from the Greek Drama Conference, Nottingham, 18–20 July 1990*, eds A.H. Sommerstein, S. Halliwell, J. Henderson and B. Zimmermann. Bari: 55–79.

Pope, M. (1988) 'Thucydides and democracy', *Historia* 37: 276–96.

Pownall, F. (2008) 'Theopompos and the public documentation of fifth-century Athens' in *Epigraphy and the Greek Historian*, ed. C. Cooper. Toronto: 119–28.

Preller, L. (1838) *Polemonis Periegetae: Fragmenta*. Leipzig.

Pritchett, W.K. (1996) *Greek Archives, Cults and Topography. Archaia Hellas*, 2. Amsterdam.

Quass, F. (1971) *Nomos und Psephisma*. Munich.

Quillin, J. (2002) 'Achieving amnesty: the role of events, institutions, and ideas', *TAPA* 132: 71–107.

Raaflaub, K. (2004) 'Homer and the beginning of political thought in Greece' in *Ancient Greek Democracy: Readings and Sources*, ed. E. Robinson. Oxford: 28–40.

Rhodes, P.J. (1972) *The Athenian Boule*. Oxford.

(1981) *Commentary on the Aristotelian Athenaion Politeia*. Oxford.

(1984) '*Nomothesia* in fourth-century Athens', *CQ* 35: 55–60.

(1986) 'Political activity in classical Athens', *JHS* 106: 132–44.

(1990) 'The Atthidographers' in *Purposes of History. Studies in Greek Historiography from the 4th to the 2nd centuries BC*, eds. H. Verdin, G. Schepens and E de Keyser. Leuven: 73–81.

(1991) 'The Athenian code of laws, 410–399 BC', *JHS* 111: 87–100.

(1998) 'Enmity in fourth-century Athens' in *Kosmos: Essays in Order, Conflict and Community in Classical Athens*, eds. P. Cartledge, P. Millett and S. von Reden. Canbridge: 144–61.

(2000) 'Who ran democratic Athens?' in *Polis and Politics: Studies in Ancient Greek History Presented to Mogens Herman Hansen on his Sixtieth Birthday, August 20, 2000*, eds. P. Flensted-Jensen, T.H. Nielsen and L. Rubinstein. Copenhagen: 465–77.

(2003a) 'Sessions of *nomothetai* in fourth-century Athens', *CQ* 53: 124–9.

(2003b) 'Nothing to do with democracy: Athenian drama and the *polis*' *JHS* 123: 104–19.

(2004a) 'Aristophanes and the Athenian assembly' in *Law, Rhetoric and Comedy in Classical Athens: Essays in Honour of D.M. MacDowell*, eds. D.L. Cairns and R.A. Knox. Swansea: 223–37.

(2004b) 'The laws of Athens in the Athenaion Politeia' in *Nomos: Direito e Sociedade na Antiguidade Classica*, eds. D.F. Leão, L. Rosseti and M. do Céo Fialho. Madrid: 75–87.

(2006) 'Political activity in democratic Athens', *JHS* 106: 132–44.

(2008) 'Making and breaking treaties in the Greek world' in *War and Peace in Ancient and Medieval History*, eds. P. de Souza and J. France, Cambridge: 6–27.

(2010) 'The "assembly" at the end of Aristophanes' *Knights*' in *Law and Drama in Ancient Greece*, eds. E.M. Harris, D.F. Leão and P.J. Rhodes. London: 158–68.

(2011) 'Appeals to the past in classical Athens' in *Stability and Crisis in the Athenian Democracy. Historia Einzelschriften* 220, ed. G. Herman. Stuttgart: 13–30.

(2013) 'The organisation of Athenian public finance', *G&R* 60: 203–31.

(2014) *Atthis: The Ancient Histories of Athens*. Heidelberg.

(2016a) 'Demagogues and *demos* in Athens', *Polis* 33: 243–64.

(2016b) 'Heraclides of Clazomenae and an Athenian treaty with Persia', *ZPE* 200: 177–86.

Rhodes, P.J., with Lewis, D. (1997) *The Decrees of the Greek States*. Oxford.

Rhodes, P.J. and Osborne, R.G. (2003) *Greek Historical Inscriptions, 404–323 BC*. Oxford.

Richardson, M.B. (2000) 'The location of inscribed laws in fourth-century Athens' in *Polis and Politics: Studies in Ancient Greek History Presented to Mogens Herman Hansen on His Sixtieth Birthday, August 20, 2000*, eds. P. Flensted-Jensen, T.H. Nielsen and L. Rubinstein. Copenhagen: 601–16.

Richardson, M.B. (2015) 'Polis inscriptions and jurors in fourth-century Athens' in *Cities Called Athens: Studies Honoring John McK. Camp II*, eds. K.F. Daly and L.A. Riccardi. Lanham: 351–68.

Roberts, J.T. (1994) *Athens on Trial: The Antidemocratic Tradition in Western Thought*. Princeton.

Robertson, N. (1990) 'The laws of Athens, 410–399 BC: the evidence for review and publication', *JHS* 110: 43–75

Robinson, E.W. (1997) *The First Democracies: Early Popular Government Outside Athens*. Stuttgart.

(2011) *Democracy beyond Athens: Popular Government in the Greek Classical Age*. Cambridge.

Robson, J. (2017) 'Humouring the masses: the theatre audience and the highs and lows of Aristophanic comedy' in L. Grig (ed.), *Popular Culture in the Ancient World*. Cambridge: 66–87.

Roisman, J. (2006) *The Rhetoric of Conspiracy in Ancient Athens*. Berkeley and London.

Roisman, J. and Worthington, I. (2015) *Lives of the Attic Orators: Texts from Pseudo-Plutarch, Photius, and the Suda*. Oxford.

Rosen, K. (1987) 'Ehrendekrete, Biographie und Geschichtsschreibung', *Chiron* 17: 277–92.

Rosenbloom, D. (2012) 'Scripting revolution: democracy and its discontents in late fifth-century drama' in *Crisis on Stage: Tragedy and Comedy in Late Fifth-century Athens*, eds. A. Markantonatos and B. Zimmermann. Berlin: 403–39.

(2014) 'Argos/Mycenae' in *The Encyclopedia of Greek Tragedy*, vol. 1, ed. H.M. Roisman: 127–8.

Rothwell, K.S. (1990) *Politics and Persuasion in Aristophanes'* Ecclesiazusae. *Mnemosyne* Supplement 111. Leiden.

Rubinstein, L. (1998) 'The Athenian political perception of the *idiotes'* in *Kosmos: Essays in Order, Conflict and Community in Classical Athens*, eds. P. Cartledge, P. Millett and S. von Reden. Cambridsge: 125–43.

(2013) 'Spoken words, written submissions, and diplomatic conventions: the importance and impact of oral performance in Hellenistic inter-polis relations' in *Hellenistic Oratory: Continuity and Change*, eds. C. Kremmydas and K. Tempest. Oxford: 165–99.

(2016) 'Envoys and *ethos*: team speaking by envoys in classical Greece' in *La rhétorique du pouvoir oratoire: une exploration de l'art délibératif grec*, ed. P. Derron. Fondation Hardt Entretiens 62. Vandoeuvres: 79–128.

Rydberg-Cox, J. (2003) 'Oral and written sources in Athenian forensic rhetoric', *Mnemosyne* 56: 652–65.

Said, S. (1993) 'Tragic Argos' in *Tragedy, Comedy and the Polis: Papers from the Greek Drama Conference, Nottingham, 18–20 July 1990*, eds. A.H. Sommerstein, S. Halliwell, J. Henderson and B. Zimmermann. Bari: 167–89.

Ste Croix, G.E.M. de (1963) 'The alleged secret pact between Athens and Philip II Concerning Amphipolis and Pydna', *CQ* 13: 110–19.

(1972) *Origins of the Peloponnesian War*. London.

(2004) *Athenian Democratic Origins and Other Essays*, eds. D. Harvey and R. Parker, with the assistance of P. Thonemann. Oxford.

Salmond, P.D. (1996) 'Sympathy for the devil: Chares and Athenian politics', *G&R* 43: 43–53.

Sanders, E. (2006) 'Historical institutionalism' in *The Oxford Handbook of Political Institutions* eds. S.A. Binder, R.A.W. Rhodes and B.A. Rock. Oxford (Electronic Publication).

(2016) 'Persuasion through emotions in Athenian deliberative oratory' in E. Sanders and M. Johncock, eds., *Emotion and Persuasion in Classical Antiquity*. Stuttgart: 57–73.

Saxonhouse, A. (1996) *Athenian Democracy: Modern Mythmakers and Ancient Theorists*. Notre Dame.

Schaps, D. (1979) *The Economic Rights of Women in Ancient Greece*. Edinburgh.

Schmitt Pantel, P. (2014) 'Political traditions in democratic Athens' in *Patterns of the Past:* Epitedeumata *in the Greek Tradition*, eds. A. Moreno and R. Thomas. Oxford: 93–120.

Schoemann, G.F. (1819) *De comitiis Atheniensium: libri tres*. Greifswald.

Scholz, P. (2009) 'Der "gute" Bürger in Lykurgs Rede gegen Leokrates' in *Rollenbilder in der athenischen Demokratie: Medien, Gruppen, Räume im politischen und sozialen System. Beiträge zu einem interdisciplinären Kolloquium in Freiburg i. Br., 24.–25. November 2006*, eds. C. Mann, M. Haake and R. van den Hoff. Weisbaden: 171–92.

BIBLIOGRAPHY

Schuller, W. (1974) 'Wirkungen des ersten attischen Seebunds auf die Herausbildung der athenischen Demokratie' in *Studien zum attischen Seebund. Xenia* 8. Konstanz: 87–101.

Seager, R. (2001) 'Xenophon and democratic Ideology', *CQ* 51: 385–97.

Sealey, R. (1987) *The Athenian Republic: Democracy or Rule of Law?* London.

Serafim, A. (2017) *Attic Oratory and Performance*. London and New York.

Shear, J. (2007) 'The oath of Demophantos and the politics of Athenian identity' in *Horkos: The Oath in Greek Society*, eds. A.H. Sommerstein and J. Fletcher. Exeter: 148–60.

(2011) *Polis and Revolution: Responding to Oligarchy in Classical Athens*. Cambridge.

(2012) 'The politics of the past: remembering revolution at Athens' in *Greek Notions of the Past in the Archaic and Classical Eras: History without Historians*, eds. J. Marincola, L. Llewellyn-Jones and C. MacIver. Edinburgh: 276–300.

Shepherd, A. (2016) 'Aristophanes' Ecclesiazusae and the remaking of the ΠΑΤΡΙΟΣ ΠΟΛΙΤΕΙΑ', *CQ* 66: 463–83.

Sickinger, J.P. (1999a) *Public Records and Archives in Classical Athens*. Chapel Hill and London.

(1999b) 'Literacy, documents, and archives in the ancient Athenian democracy', *American Archivist* 62: 229–46.

(2002) 'Literacy, orality, and legislative procedure in classical Athens' in Epea *and* grammata, *Oral and Written Communication in Ancient Greece*, ed. I Worthington. Leiden and Boston: 147–69.

(2004) 'The laws of Athens: publication, preservation, and consultation' in *The Law and the Courts in Ancient Greece*, eds. E.M. Harris and L. Rubinstein. London: 159–71.

(2007) 'Rhetoric and the law' in *A Companion to Greek Rhetoric*, ed. I. Worthington. Malden and Oxford: 286–302.

(2009) 'Nothing to do with democracy: "formulae of disclosure" and the Athenian epigraphic habit' in *Greek History and Epigraphy: Essays in honour of P.J. Rhodes*, eds. L. Mitchell and L. Rubinstein, Swansea: 87–102.

Sidwell, K. (2014) *Aristophanes the Democrat: The Politics of Satirical Comedy during the Peloponnesian War*. Cambridge.

Simonton, M. (2017) *Classical Greek Oligarchy: A Political History*. Princeton and Oxford.

Slater, N. (1996) 'Literacy and old comedy' in *Voice into Text: Orality and Literacy in Ancient Greece*, ed. I. Worthington. Leiden: 99–112.

Smarczyk, B. (2006) 'Thucydides and epigraphy' in *Brill's Companion to Thucydides*, eds. A. Rengakos and A. Tsakmakis. Leiden and Boston: 495–522.

Sobak, R. (2015) 'Socrates among the shoemakers', *Hesperia* 84: 669–712.

Sommerstein, A. (1983) *Aristophanes: Wasps*. Warminster.

(1990) *Aristophanes: Lysistrata*. Warminster.

(1997) 'The Theatre audience, the demos, and the *Suppliants* of Aeschylus' in *Greek Tragedy and the Historian*, ed. C.B.R. Pelling. Oxford: 63–79.

(1998) *Aristophanes' Ecclesiasuzae: Edited with Translation and Commentary*. Warminster.

(2014a) 'The politics of Greek comedy' in *The Cambridge Companion to Greek Comedy*, ed. M. Revermann. Cambridge: 291–305.

(2014b) 'The authenticity of the Demophantus decree', *CQ* 64: 49–57.

Spatharas, D. (2011) 'Self-praise and envy: from rhetoric to the Athenian courts', *Arethusa* 44: 199–219.

Stadter, P. (1989) *A Commentary on Plutarch's Pericles*. Chapel Hill.

Stanton, G. (1996) 'The shape and size of the Athenian assembly place in its second phase' in B. Forsén and G. Stanton, eds., *The Pnyx in the History of Athens: Proceedings of an International Colloquium Organised by the Finnish Institute at Athens, 7–9 October, 1994*. Papers and Monographs of the Finnish Institute at Athens, 2. Helsinki: 7–21.

Starr, C. (1974) *Political Intelligence in Classical Greece*. Leiden.

Steinbock, B. (2012) *Social Memory in Athenian Public Discourse: Uses and Meanings of the Past*. Michigan.

Steinmo, T., Thelen, K. and Lonstreth, F. eds. (1992) *Structuring Politics: Historical Institutionalism in Comparative Analysis*. Cambridge.

Steiner, D.T. (1994) *The Tyrant's Writ: Myths and Images of Writing in Ancient Greece*. Princeton.

Stephens, S.A. (1983) 'The "Arginusae" theme in Greek rhetorical theory and practice', *The Bulletin of the American Society of Papyrologists* 20: 171–80.

Stockton, D. (1990) *The Classical Athenian Democracy*. Oxford.

Stroud, R. (1998) *The Athenian Grain Tax Law of 374/3 BC*. Hesperia Supplements 29. Princeton

Sundahl, M. (2003) 'The rule of law and the nature of the fourth-century Athenian democracy', *C&M* 54: 127–56.

Szegedy-Maszak, A. (1981) *The Nomoi of Theophrastus*. New York.

Taylor, C. (2007a) 'From the whole citizen body? The sociology of election and lot in Athenian democracy', *Hesperia* 76.2: 323–46.

(2007b) 'A new political world' in *The Anatomy of Cultural Revolution. Athens 430–380 BC*, ed. R.G. Osborne. Cambridge: 72–90.

Taylor, M.C. (2002) 'One hundred heroes of Phyle?', *Hesperia* 71: 377–97.

Teegarden, D.A. (2012) 'The oath of Demophantos, revolutionary mobilization, and the preservation of the Athenian democracy', *Hesperia* 81: 433–65.

(2014) *Death to Tyrants! Ancient Greek Democracy and the Struggle Against Tyranny*. Princeton.

Thelen, K. and Steinmo, S. (1992) 'Historical institutionalism in comparative politics' in *Structuring Politics: Historical Institutionalism in Comparative Analysis*, eds T. Steinmo, K. Thelen and F. Longstreth. Cambridge: 1–32.

Thomas, R. (1989) *Oral Tradition and Written Record in Classical Athens*. Cambridge.

(1992) *Literacy and Orality in Ancient Greece*. Cambridge.

(1994) 'Law and the lawgiver' in *Ritual, Finance, Politics: Democratic Accounts Presented to David Lewis*, eds. S.N. Hornblower and R.G. Osborne. Oxford: 119–33.

Thornton, P.H., Ocasio, W. and Lounsbury, M. (2012) *The Institutional Logics Perspective: A New Appraoch to Culture, Structure, and Process*. Oxford.

Thür, G. (2008) 'The principle of fairness in Athenian legal procedure: thoughts on the *echinos* and *enklema*', *Dike* 11: 51–74.

Timasheff, N.S. (2010) 'Free institutions and the struggle for freedom in Russian history', *Review of Central and East European Law* 35: 7–21.

Tober, D. (2017) 'Greek local historiography and its audiences', *CQ* 67: 460–84.

Todd, S.C. (1990a) 'The purpose of evidence in Athenian courts' in *Nomos: Essays in Athenian Law, Politics and Society*, eds. P. Cartledge, P. Millett and S. Todd. Cambridge: 19–39.

    (1990b) '*Lady Chatterley's Lover* and the Attic orators: the social composition of the Athenian jury', *JHS* 110: 146–73.

    (1990c) 'The use and abuse of the Attic orators', *G&R* 37: 159–78.

    (1993) *The Shape of Athenian Law*. Oxford.

    (1996) 'Lysias Against Nicomachus: the fate of the expert in Athenian law' in L. Foxhall and A.D.E. Lewis, *Greek Law in its Political Setting: Justifications not Justice*. Oxford: 101–31.

    (1998) 'The rhetoric of enmity in the Attic orators' in *Kosmos: Essays in Order, Conflict and Community in Classical Athens*, eds. P. Cartledge, P. Millett and S. von Reden. Cambridge: 162–9.

    (2007) *A Commentary on Lysias, Speeches 1–11*. Oxford.

    (2012) 'The publication of voting-figures in the ancient Greek world: a response to Alberto Maffi' in *Symposion 2011*, eds. B. Legras and G. Thür. Vienna: 33–48.

Too, Y.L. (1995) *The Rhetoric of Identity in Isocrates*. Cambridge.

Tracy, S. (2000) 'Athenian politicians and inscriptions of the years 307-302', *Hesperia* 69: 227–33.

Trevett, J. (1992) *Apollodorus, Son of Pasion*. Oxford.

    (1996a) 'Aristotle's knowledge of Athenian oratory', *CQ* 46: 371–9.

    (1996b) 'Did Demosthenes publish his symbouleutic speeches?', *Hermes* 124: 425–41.

    (1999) 'Demosthenes and Thebes', *Historia* 48: 184–202.

    (2011) *Demosthenes: Speeches 1–17*. Austin.

Tsagalis, C. (2008) *Inscribing Sorrow: Fourth-Century Attic Funerary Epigrams*. Berlin and New York.

Tuplin, C.J. (1998) 'Demosthenes' Olynthiacs and the character of the demegoric corpus', *Historia* 47: 276–320.

    (2005) 'Delian imperialism', *Archaiognosia* 13: 55–111.

Tzifopoulos, Y.Z. (2013) 'Inscriptions as literature in Pausanias' *Exegesis* of Hellas' in *Inscriptions and Their Uses in Greek and Latin Literature*, eds. P. Liddel and P. Low. Oxford: 149–65.

Usher, S. (1999) *Greek Oratory: Tradition and Originality*. Oxford.

Van Effenterre, H. and Ruzé, F. (1994-5) *Nomima: recueil d'inscriptions politiques et juridiques de l'Archaisme Grec*, 2 vols. Rome.

Van Wees, H. (2011) 'Demetrius and Draco: Athens' property classes and population in and before 317 BC', *JHS* 131: 95–114.

Vatri, A. (2017) *Orality and Performance in Classical Attic Prose: A Linguistic Approach.* Oxford.

Veblen, T. (2006) *The Theory of the Leisure Class.* Oxford.

Vlassopoulos, K. (2007a) *Unthinking the Greek Polis': Ancient Greek History Beyond Eurocentrism.* Cambridge.

(2007b) 'Free spaces: identity, experience and democracy in classical Athens', *CQ* 57: 33–52.

Voutiras, E. (1998) 'Athéna dans les cités de Macédoine', *Kernos* 11: 111–29.

Walbank, M.B. (2008) *Fragmentary Decrees from the Athenian Agora: Hesperia* Supplement 38. Athens.

Wallace, M.B. (2003) 'The inscribed copies of the Thirty Years' Peace' in *Lettered Attica: A Day of Attic Epigraphy*, eds. D. Jordan and J. Traill. Athens: 131–4.

Wallace, R.W. (1989) *The Areopagus Council, to 307 BC.* Baltimore and London.

(1994) 'Private lives and public enemies: freedom of thought in classical Athens in *Athenian Identity and Civic Ideology*, eds. A.L. Boegehold and A.C Scafuro. Baltimore: 127–55.

(2012) 'When the Athenians did not enforce their laws' in *Symposion 2011*, ed. G. Thür. Vienna: 115–25.

Wankel, H. (1976) *Demosthenes: Rede für Ktesiphon über den Kranz*, 2 vols. Heidelberg.

Watson, J. (2010) 'The origins of metic status at Athens', *CCJ* 56: 259–78.

Weingast, B. (2002) 'Rational-choice institutionalism' in *Political Science: The State of the Discipline*, eds. I. Katznelson and H.V. Milner. New York and London: 660–92.

Welles, C. Bradford (1934) *Royal Correspondence in the Hellenistic Period: A Study in Greek Epigraphy.* London and Prague.

Welwei, K.-W. (1998) *Die griechische Polis: Verfassung und Gesellschaft in archaischer und klassischer Zeit.* Stuttgart.

West, S. (1985) 'Herodotus' epigraphical interests', *CQ* 35: 278–305.

West, W.C. (1995) 'The decrees of Demosthenes' *Against Leptines'*, *ZPE* 107: 237–47.

Westwood, G. (2017) 'The orator and the ghosts: performing the past in fourth-century Athens' in *A Theatre of Justice: Aspects of Performance in Greco-Roman Oratory and Rhetoric*, eds. A. Serafim, B. da Vela and S. Papaioannou. London: 57–74.

Whitehead, D. (1977) *The Ideology of the Athenian Metic. Cambridge Philological Society Suppl.* 4. Cambridge.

(1983) 'Competitive outlay and community profit: φιλοτιμία in democratic Athens', *C&M* 34: 55–74.

(1986) 'The political career of Aristophon', *CPh* 81: 313–19.

Whittaker, C. (1991) 'Pausanias and his use of inscriptions', *SO* 66: 171–86.

Willey, H. (2016) 'Gods and men in ancient Greek conceptions of lawgiving' in E. Eidinow, J. Kindt and R. Osborne, eds., *Theologies of Ancient Greek Religion.* Cambridge: 176–204.

BIBLIOGRAPHY

Willi, A. (2003) *The Languages of Aristophanes: Aspects of Linguistic Variation in Classical Attic Greek.* Oxford.

Wilson, P. (2009) 'Tragic honours and democracy: neglected evidence for the politics of the Athenian Dionysia', *CQ* 59: 8–29

Wilson, P. and Hartwig, A. (2009) '*IG* I³ 102 and the tradition of proclaiming honours at the tragic *agon* of the Athenian City Dionysia', *ZPE* 169: 17–27.

Wohl, V. (2009) 'Rhetoric of the Athenian citizen' in *The Cambridge Companion to Ancient Rhetoric*, ed. E. Gunderson. Cambridge: 162–77.

(2014) 'Comedy and Athenian law' in *The Cambridge Companion to Greek Comedy*, ed. M. Revermann, Cambridge: 322–5.

Wolpert, A. (2002) *Remembering Defeat: Civil War and Civic Memory in Ancient Athens.* Baltimore and London.

(2003) 'Addresses to the jury in the Attic orators', *AJPh* 124: 537–55.

Worthington, I. (1991) 'Greek oratory, revision of speeches and the problem of historical reliability', *C&M* 42: 55–74.

(2009) '*IG* II² 236 and Philip's Common Peace of 337', in *Greek History and Epigraphy. Essays in honour of P.J. Rhodes*, eds. L. Mitchell and L. Rubinstein. Swansea: 213–23.

Young, J.E. (1993) *The Texture of Memory: Holocaust Memorials and Meaning.* New Haven.

Yunis, H. (1988) 'Law, politics, and the *graphe paranomon* in fourth-century Athens', *GRBS* 29: 361–82.

(1996) *Taming Democracy: Models of Political Rhetoric in Classical Athens.* Ithaca.

(2001) *Demosthenes On the Crown.* Cambridge.

Zeitlin, F. (1986) 'Thebes: theater of self and society in Athenian drama' in *Greek Tragedy and Political Theory*, ed. J. Peter Euben. Berkeley and London: 101–41.

(2000) 'Aristophanes: the performance of eutopia in the Ecclesiazusae' in *Performance Culture and Athenian Democracy*, eds. S. Goldhill and R. Osborne. Cambridge: 167–200.

Zizza, C. (2006) *Le iscrizioni nella Periegesi di Pausania: commento ai testi epigrafici.* Pisa.

Index Locorum

(a) Literary Sources

Aelius Aristides
III *To Plato* 249: 222
VI *The Opposite Argument* 9: 26 n. 48

Aeschines
1.33–5: 36
1.64: 84
1.77–9: 27
1.81: 56
1.88: 88
1.117–18: 171
1.178: 28, 91
1.188: 76
2.13: 36
2.19: 119, 122
2.32–3: 196
2.46: 60
2.53: 122
2.66: 60
2.67: 90
2.68: 22, 23, 76
2.73: 51, 60
2.83–5: 23–4, 90, 122
2.89: 118
2.104: 96, 162–3
2.109–10: 181
2.141: 90, 96, 168
2.142–3: 172
2.160: 81
2.169–70: 64
2.170: 119
2.171: 71
2.176: 90
3.3–4: 27, 36, 84
3.8: 84
3.13: 14
3.25: 89, 94
3.32–6: 63, 111
3.38: 34
3.50: 37, 60, 98

3.54: 90
3.63: 77
3.67: 97 n. 120
3.68: 77
3.73–4: 36, 90, 180
3.75: 60, 84, 90
3.76: 168
3.83: 90
3.92: 98
3.93: 61, 90
3.97–9: 98
3.100: 97
3.103: 37
3.116: 147
3.125–7: 22 n. 29, 82 n. 74
3.142: 96
3.153–5: 98
3.159: 82
3.180: 65, 102
3.183: 136, 147
3.187–8: 49–50, 76, 136, 140
3.191–4: 38, 137
3.194: 81
3.223–4: 90
3.227: 169
3.237: 96
3.243: 88
3.258: 147

Aeschylus
Suppliants 600–24: 207–10

Aineias Tacticus
9.2–3: 171
10.9: 171

Alexis
F 57: 218–19

Andocides
1.45: 114
1.51: 147

300

INDEX LOCORUM

1.82–4: 47–8
1.86: 26
1.88–9: 25, 26
1.95: 141–2
1.108–9: 48
1.115–16: 147
2.23: 101
3.12: 145

Androtion
FGrH 324: 200

Anonymous Seguerianus
3.145: 233
3.188: 234

Apsines of Gadara
Art of Rhetoric: 234–5, 270–1

Aristophanes
Acharnians 530–7: 212
Birds 1037–56: 178, 213–14; 1274–89: 214
Clouds 1016–19: 98, 212; 1198: 229; 1428–9: 212
Ekklesiazousai 1010–13; 216–18
Lysistrata 387–98: 214; 698–705: 214–15
Peace 608–9: 212
Thesmophoriazousai 352–71: 20 n. 23, 215
Wasps 274–8: 212

Aristotle
NE 1134b24: 26; 1137b13–14, 27–32: 25
Politics 1292a6–36: 35; 1299b30–1300a4: 35–6
Rhetoric 1361a28–9: 62; 1361a34–6: 62, 143;
      1384b32–5: 163; 1400a32–6: 47 n. 131, 147

[Aristotle]
Ath. Pol. 14.1: 3 n. 7, 198; 26.2: 35; 29.1–3: 199;
      29.4: 38 n. 101; 34.3: 35 n. 93, 199; 40.2:
      38 n. 101, 50; 41.2: 32–4; 43.3–4: 22 n. 34,
      24 n. 43; 44.2: 22; 45.3: 77; 45.4: 21 n. 25;
      54.3: 32, 93, 110

Athenaios
Deipnosophistai 2d: 225, 171d–e: 228, 272;
      211d–15b: 225–6; 234d–f: 227, 272;
      245b–c: 230; 587c: 272; 590d–f: 230, 272

Cicero
In defence of Flaccus 15–16, 23: 237–8

[Demades]
On the Twelve Years 14–15: 81

Demosthenes/[Demosthenes]
1.17–18: 70 n. 26
3.4–5: 28, 41, 70, 121, 162, 189
3.14–15: 104–5
3.56: 171
4: 110–11
4.45: 169
5.24–5: 70
6.3: 80
7.18: 95, 169
7.25: 70, 92, 95, 112, 169
7.46: 69 n. 22
8.29: 25
8.34–5: 163
8.68–73: 70, 80
8.74–5: 104 n. 146
8.76: 70
9.19: 69
9.36–45: 148
9.41–3: 147
9.42–6: 70
9.71–3: 69
9.76: 69 n. 25
12.8–9: 92, 105
12.10: 135
13.32–3: 105 n. 147, 112
18.37–8: 232
18.63: 65
18.66: 62–3
18.69: 90
18.75: 79
18.79: 78, 79, 117
18.83: 88
18.88: 80
18.102: 57
18.114–15: 88
18.118: 232
18.120–2: 63, 101, 177
18.168: 169
18.173: 79
18.178: 79, 95
18.185: 111
18.188: 78
18.203: 62–3
18.204: 53 n. 152
18.222–3: 65
18.237: 78
18.239: 147
18.248: 79
18.289: 147
18.301–3: 78
19.31: 96

19.34–5: 96
19.47–50: 89, 95
19.61: 67
19.86: 28, 58, 119, 180
19.129: 118–19
19.167: 119
19.179: 30
19.185: 21, 23, 37, 68, 105 n. 149
19.271–2: 54
19.271: 147
19.272: 148
19.276–9: 50 n. 143, 55
20.1: 88
20.3: 14, 43, 85
20.9: 87
20.11–12: 49
20.34: 166
20.36–7: 30, 129, 165, 183
20.52–4: 102 n. 138
20.54–5: 87
20.58: 101–2
20.59: 139
20.60: 87, 101–2
20.64: 43, 86, 102, 143
20.69: 120, 143
20.78: 120
20.81: 165
20.82: 63
20.83: 43
20.84: 120
20.92: 30
20.93–4: 22 n. 34
20.102–3: 43
20.128: 147
20.131: 119–20
20.134–5: 166
20.149: 143
20.159: 122, 142
21.182–3: 84
22.5–6: 36
22.72: 141 n. 106
23.1–2: 88
23.2–3: 104
23.16–17: 61, 98
23.70: 23
23.87: 26
23.104: 84, 164
23.105: 104
23.109: 161
23.111–14: 102
23.118: 85, 102
23.123: 164

23.126: 86, 164
23.140: 164
23.141: 85, 102
23.149–51: 67
23.151: 61 n. 3
23.196–7: 86, 102
23.198: 86
23.199–202: 86
23.201: 189
23.211: 86, 163
23.218: 26
24.11: 115
24.28: 102–3
24.35–6: 34
24.39: 26
24.41–4: 99
24.92–3: 41
24.142–3: 27
24.149: 30
25.37: 84
46.13: 67–8
47.20: 101
47.22–3: 147
47.34: 66, 114, 119
47.64: 141 n. 105
47.71: 147
49.19–20: 30, 66 n. 18
50.3: 61
50.3–8: 66, 105
50.13: 61, 64
50.29: 67
51.1: 115
57.6: 113–14
57.26: 113–14
57.64: 85
57.65: 65
58.30–1: 103, 114
58.34: 85
58.45–7: 84
58.53: 91 n. 102, 179–80
59.2: 65
59.4–6: 80–1
59.43: 82
59.76: 147
59.88: 33
59.90: 170
59.91: 28, 91, 121
59.104–6: 44 n. 119, 54–5, 61

Dinarchus
1.39–40: 55, 76
1.43: 91, 148, 240

INDEX LOCORUM

1.78–80: 90
1.84: 30
1.86: 119, 125
1.94: 90
1.94: 90
1.100–1: 84
2.24–5: 222

Dio Chrysostom
56.10: 35 n. 93

Diodorus Siculus
13.30.7: 196
13.69: 147
13.103.1: 195
14.82.2: 137
15.26.1: 198
15.28.2: 181
15.29.7: 139, 197
15.63.2: 197
16.22.2: 198
16.92.1–2: 180
17.5.3: 197, 206
17.15.1: 270
18.10.2–5: 180, 197
18.18.6: 197

Diogenes Laertius
7.6, 10–12: 202

Harpokration
s.v. *Atimos*: 222
s.v. *Nautodikai*: 225
s.v. *Nemeas*: 272
s.v. *Oxythumia*: 143
s.v. *Procheirotonia*: 23

Hermippos
FGrH 1026 F 46a: 230

Herodotus
1.59.4: 3 n. 7
3.80: 35 n. 92
5.97.3: 190
7.143.1–2: 189
9.5: 53 n. 152, 191

Hypereides
Ath. 22: 26, 31–3: 55, 122, 171
Dem. Fr. 1 col. 1: 30
Diondas 6: 169, 20–1: 106
F 76: 219–20

F 79: 143, 219–20

Isocrates
4 *Panegyrikos* 176, 180: 146
7 *Areop.* 41: 48–9
9 *Evagoras* 57: 101
12 *Panath.* 144: 30 n. 72
16 *Team of Horses* 9
17 *Trapezitikos* 57: 138

Istros
FGrH 334 F38: 271

Krateros
BNJ 342: 223–5

Lucian
Encomium of Demosthenes: 18, 37, 45: 80 n. 70
Menippos 19–20: 236
Parliament of the Gods 14–18: 236
Timon 40–2: 236, 50–2: 236
True History 1.20: 236

Lycurgus
1.12: 161
1.16: 52
1.36: 52
1.41–2: 52–3, 57
1.53: 52
1.76: 146
1.80–1: 146
1.112–15: 53 n 151
1.117–19: 53 n. 151, 147, 148
1.122: 53 n. 151, 191
1.124–6: 50, 142
1.127: 31
1.146: 52
F 18 1b: 89
F 58: 88 n. 95

Lysias
1.30: 147
1.47: 147
2.18: 161
12.73: 35 n. 93
13.71–2: 95 n. 115; 133
13.73: 170
28.5: 67
F 130: 77

Nepos
Thrasybulus 3.2: 200

INDEX LOCORUM

Pausanias
1.23.9: 231
1.29.7: 231
5.23.4: 231

Philochorus
FGrH 328: 199–200

Plato
Ap. 32b: 195
Definitions 415b11: 25
Phdr. 258a–c: 75

Plutarch/[Plutarch]
Alex. 74.1: 205, 270
Cim. 13.4: 224
Dem. 17.1: 203
Dem. 20.3: 80 n. 70, 105 n. 148, 203
Dem. 21.3: 203
Dem. 26.1: 203
Dem. 27.3: 203
Mor. 295c–d: 35 n. 91
Mor. 814a–b: 50
Nic. 1.5: 202
Pel. 7: 186
Per. 10.4–5: 202
Per. 13: 202
Per. 17: 178, 202
Per. 30: 202–3
Per. 32: 203
Phoc. 17.5–6: 269–70
Them. 6.4: 147
Them. 10.4–5: 202
Them. 11.1: 202
X Or. 833d–4b
X Or. 833e–f: 204
X Or. 842c: 94
X Or. 843f: 205 n. 52
X Or. 848e–9a: 89
X Or. 849f: 205, 270
X Or. 850f–1c: 204
X Or. 851f–2e: 204–5

Polemon
F 3 Preller: 226, 272
F 78 Preller: 227–8

Polybius
6.57.1–9: 197
38.13.7: 35 n. 93

Theophrastus
Characters 4.3: 114, 170, 7.8: 114, 117 n. 28

Theopompos
FGrH 115 F 154: 221–2

Thucydides
1.139.1–2: 191
2.37.1: 161
2.61.2: 58
2.64.1: 58
3.36.3: 177 n. 60
3.37.3: 20 n. 23, 193
3.43.4–5: 58
4.118: 191–2
5.18–19: 191
5.29.2–3: 94
5.47: 133 n. 81, 185, 191
5.79: 191
6.8.2: 193
6.61.4–7: 115
8.11: 193

Xenophon
Hell. 1.7.8–36: 22, 39, 194, 1.7.20: 217, 224,
2.1.31–2: 196, 3.5.16: 137, 5.4.37: 196, 6.2.2:
123, 6.55.3: 196, 7.1.1: 23 n. 36, 173, 7.1.14:
111, 173, 7.4.4: 111, 172
Mem. 3.3.11: 62–3, 3.5.5: 62–3
Poroi 3.11: 101 n. 137

(b) Inscriptions
Agora XVI 36: 175–6
Agora XVI 48: 179
IDélos 88: 184
IG I³ 1: 3
IG I³ 8: 4 n. 16, 14 n. 4
IG I³ 83: 133 n. 81
IG I³ 102: 133–4, 140, 224
IG I³ 110: 176 n. 56
IG I³ 125: 133 n. 83
IG I³ 1453: 182, 213
IG I³ 1454: 178, 183
IG II² 6: 47 n. 130, 176 nn. 54–5
IG II² 14: 135, 137
IG II² 20: 135
IG II² 21: 135, 138
IG II² 22: 135, 138
IG II² 33: 135, 139
IG II² 40: 135, 139
IG II² 42: 173
IG II² 43: 127, 128, 139
IG II² 44: 185
IG II² 45: 133 n. 81
IG II² 47: 18 n. 16, 73, 93, 100, 115, 124 n. 49

INDEX LOCORUM

IG II² 55: 185
IG II² 77: 77, 130
IG II² 96: 173
IG II² 107: 124 n. 49, 172, 174
IG II² 109: 172
IG II² 111: 129
IG II² 112: 23 n. 36
IG II² 116: 128, 135, 138, 173
IG II² 120: 128
IG II² 126: 135
IG II² 212: 23 n. 36
IG II² 448: 151 n. 132
IG II² 1623: 82
IG II² 3775: 135, 138
IG II³ 1 292: 23 n. 38, 93, 100, 115 n. 24, 179
IG II³ 1 295: 174
IG II³ 1 297: 168
IG II³ 1 298: 129, 135, 138, 165 n. 18, 174
IG II³ 1 301: 150
IG II³ 1 302: 174
IG II³ 1 304: 130 n. 75, 174
IG II³ 1 306: 12 n. 1, 32, 76, 124
IG II³ 1 308: 135
IG II³ 1 312: 78
IG II³ 1 313: 174
IG II³ 1 316: 128, 174
IG II³ 1 318: 135
IG II³ 1 319: 135, 138
IG II³ 1 320: 31, 142
IG II³ 1 324: 23
IG II³ 1 325: 22
IG II³ 1 325: 22 n. 28
IG II³ 1 337: 19
IG II³ 1 349: 19
IG II³ 1 337: 22 n. 28, 172
IG II³ 1 367: 12 n. 1, 17–19, 21, 100,
    105 n. 150, 124, 130 n. 75,
    166, 179
IG II³ 1 370: 12 n. 1, 115, 124, 151 n. 134
IG II³ 1 399: 99–100, 127
IG II³ 1 416: 127
IG II³ 1 417: 126
IG II³ 1 443: 185

IG II³ 1 452: 166–7
IG II³ 1 469: 32
IG II³ 1 476: 22
IG II³ 1 473: 32
IG II³ 1 516: 126
IG II³ 4 57: 150 n. 129
IG II³ 4 460: 71 n. 35
IKErythrai 30–1: 186
ML 23: 44 n. 119, 221
ML 46: 178
ML 69: 178
ML 70: 139 n. 100
ML 85: 133–4
OR 153: 178
OR 154: 178
OR 155: 182, 213
OR 157: 139 n. 100
OR 178: 135
OR 182: 133–4
RO 2: 118, 172, 180
RO 4: 132 n. 79
RO 6: 135, 137
RO 11: 144
RO 17: 186
RO 22: 127, 128
RO 23: 173
RO 24: 173
RO 25: 32, 128
RO 31: 174
RO 33: 135, 137
RO 39: 129, 184, 186
RO 40: 179, 183
RO 44: 135, 138, 173
RO 47: 135, 138
RO 58: 135
RO 64: 135, 174
RO 76: 135
RO 76: 142
RO 88: 44 n. 119, 146 n. 122, 221
RO 91: 172
SEG XXVIII 85: 132 n. 79, 135, 136
SEG XXXII 43: 135
SEG XL 56: 135, 138

General Index

acropolis, 29, 54, 125, 145, 148, 157, 175, 181, 184, 222, 231, 236, 245
Aelius Aristides, 195, 222, 237
Aeschines, 23, 27, 36, 60, 61, 74, 84, 212, 235
Aeschylus, 207
agora, Athenian, 117, 124, 131, 136, 140, 170, 181
Agoratos, 95, 133
Agyrrhios, 74
Aigina, 163
Aineias Tacticus, 171
Alcibiades, 78, 193, 227
alethestate prophasis, 191
Alexander the Great, 205
Alexis, 218
ambasssadors, 174
Amphipolis, 67, 169
Androtion, 168, 200
announcement of decrees, 63, 111, 233
Anonymous Seguerianus, 233
Antiphon, 224
antiquarian
   interest in decrees, 231
Apatouria, 229
Apollodoros, 61, 81, 121
Apsines of Gadara, 232, 234, 235, 270
Arabic scholarship, 201
Archinos, 199
archive, 10, 110, 120, 140, 243
Areopagus, 161
Arginusae, battle of, 38, 45, 122, 195
Argos, Argives, 207, 208
Aristeides, 77
Aristion, 3, 4, 198
Aristophanes, 220
Aristophon, 73, 168
Aristotle, 25, 35, 60, 163, 189, 201, 233, 234, 272
Arthmios, 53, 54, 70, 147, 221, 224
Arthmios *stele*, 10, 147, 148, 222
assembly (*ekklesia*), 2, 3, 15, 33, 69, 172, 182, 245
atechnoi pisteis, 60, 233
ateleia, 30, 43, 49, 86, 101, 138
Athenaion, 225

Athenaion Politeia, 198
Athenaios, 218, 231, 237
Athenian superiority, 161
Athenogenes, 171
atimia, 72
Atthidography, 200
audiences, non-Athenian, 188
autopsy, lack of evidence for, 137, 144, 192, 224

biblion, 118, 180, 211, 213
biography, 206, 223
Bosporos, Kings of, 166
Bourdieu, P., 5
bribery, 91, 133, 235, 240

Caecilius of Caleacte, 204
Canevaro, M., 232, 233, 269
Chabrias, 74, 120, 158, 165, 197
Chairephilos, 219
Chaironeia, aftermath of, 53, 79, 90, 152, 168, 203
characterisation, 29, 55, 68
Chares, 73
Charidemos, 67, 98, 104, 163
charis, 65, 187
cheirotonia, 14, 36, 208
Cicero, 237
Cimon, 202
citizenship grants, 24, 54, 55, 61, 86, 121, 137, 150, 164
class struggle, 57, 236
Cleon, 193
cleruchies, Athenian, 185
collaboration, political, 18, 73, 82, 94
Comedy, 211–20
communism, by decree, 217
Congress decree, 178, 202
Cornelius Nepos, 200
Cossacks, 2
costs of inscribing, 31, 176
Council (*boule*), 14, 19, 21, 33, 37, 76, 112, 192, 228

306

GENERAL INDEX

crisis, 53
crowns, 88, 100, 124, 153

declamatio, 232
decree-mindedness, 61, 83, 233, 241
decree of Kannonos, 195, 224
decree of Miltiades, 221, 231
decree of Themistocles, 44, 221, 222
decree of the Troizenians, 221
decrees
  abuse of, 213
  Aeschines' use of, 88, 90, 118
  Andocides' use of, 45, 48
  as evidence, 62
  as paradigms, 43, 56, 102, 142, 148, 221
  as proofs, 62, 233
  Athenian *ethos* and, 49
  authority of, 32, 132
  civilisation and, 212
  close attention to, 106, 126, 157, 187
  consequences of, 106
  critique of, 28, 36, 41, 81, 92, 96, 97, 105, 107,
    162, 169, 189
  cultural significance of, 239, 245
  Demosthenes' use in *Against Aristokrates*, 86
  Demosthenes' use in *Against Leptines*, 43
  Demosthenes' use in *Against Leptines*, 88,
    138, 234
  Demosthenes' use in *On the Crown*, 88, 90,
    234
  destruction of, 65, 89, 141
  dissemination of, 120
  enforcement of, 66
  epigraphical publication of, 13, 155, 177, 185
  expenditure upon, 31
  fabricated, 44, 45, 50, 61, 142, 205, 223, 226,
    230, 233, 234, 235, 242, 269, 272
  formulae, 36, 192, 208, 215, 236
  geopolitics and, 46
  honorific, 18, 30, 43, 45, 47, 65, 85, 89, 101, 111,
    127, 145, 150, 164, 166, 180, 201, 236
  humour and, 220, 243
  inanity of, 189
  inscribed
    Ag. XVI 36: 175–6
    Ag. XVI 36: 175
    Ag. XVI 48: 179
    IDelos 88: 184
    IG I³ 1: 3

IG I³ 8: 4, 14
IG I³ 21: 14
IG I³ 102: 133
IG I³ 125: 133
IG I³ 1453: 182, 213
IG I³ 1454: 178, 183
IG I³ 8: 4
IG II² 14: 135
IG II² 20: 135
IG II² 21: 135
IG II² 22: 135
IG II² 33: 135
IG II² 40: 135
IG II² 42: 173
IG II² 43: 127, 128
IG II² 44: 185
IG II² 47: 18, 73, 93, 100, 115
IG II² 55: 185
IG II² 77: 130
IG II² 96: 173
IG II² 107: 174
IG II² 109: 172
IG II² 111: 129, 184
IG II² 116: 128, 135, 173
IG II² 120: 128
IG II² 126: 135
IG II² 286: 208
IG II³ 1 292: 93, 100, 135, 179
IG II³ 1 295: 174
IG II³ 1 298: 174
IG II³ 1 298: 129, 135, 165
IG II³ 1 302: 174
IG II³ 1 304: 100, 174
IG II³ 1 306: 76, 124
IG II³ 1 308: 135
IG II³ 1 312: 78
IG II³ 1 313: 174
IG II³ 1 316: 174
IG II³ 1 318: 135
IG II³ 1 319: 135
IG II³ 1 337: 22, 172
IG II³ 1 352: 22
IG II³ 1 367: 18, 100, 105, 166, 179
IG II³ 1 370: 115, 124
IG II³ 1 399: 100, 127
IG II³ 1 416: 127
IG II³ 1 417: 126
IG II³ 1 443: 185
IG II³ 1 452: 167

IG II³ 1 516: 126
OR 153: 178
OR 154: 178
OR 178: 135
RO 2: 172, 180
RO 4: 132
RO 17: 182, 186
RO 22: 127, 128
RO 23: 44
RO 33: 135
RO 35: 179
RO 39: 184, 186
RO 40: 179, 183
SEG XXVIII 85: 135
intention of, 106, 112, 234
liability for, 56, 86, 92, 246
literary
  BD 5: 168
  BD 8: 229
  D 1: 48, 50, 196
  D 2: 48
  D 5: 38
  D 8: 25, 26
  D 13: 49
  D 14: 225
  D 15: 49, 76, 135, 143
  D 17: 57, 135
  D 19: 31, 50, 142
  D 20: 135, 196
  D 23: 120, 143, 144
  D 24: 101, 135
  D 27: 55
  D 28: 135
  D 29: 135
  D 30: 135
  D 33: 196
  D 37: 196
  D 38: 67
  D 39: 143, 165
  D 40: 135
  D 42: 65
  D 43: 85
  D 44: 55, 76, 81
  D 45: 135
  D 46: 144
  D 47: 122, 144
  D 48: 123, 196
  D 49: 55, 61
  D 54: 143, 144
  D 55: 196
  D 56: 23, 111, 173

D 58: 135
D 59: 85
D 64: 67
D 66: 84, 168
D 67: 28, 61, 66, 105
D 69: 67
D 70: 61, 64
D 71: 164
D 74: 92
D 76: 115
D 83: 135
D 85: 30, 66, 101
D 87: 67
D 88: 115
D 92: 23
D 93: 102
D 94: 61, 85, 104, 163, 234
D 103: 120
D 104: 120
D 105: 58, 119, 180
D 106: 28, 121
D 107: 115, 135, 178, 200
D 108: 69, 111
D 109: 28, 91, 121
D 110: 84, 91, 121
D 111: 28, 112, 200
D 112: 28, 112
D 114: 64, 119
D 115: 80
D 119: 119
D 121: 181
D 122: 68
D 124: 119, 122
D 126: 90, 122, 168, 181
D 127: 77, 90, 181
D 128: 60
D 129: 51, 61
D 130: 95, 120
D 131: 90, 180
D 132: 24, 90, 122
D 134: 89
D 135: 119
D 137: 113
D 138: 56, 122
D 139: 117
D 140: 70, 92, 95, 112
D 142: 92
D 144: 69
D 146: 58, 90
D 147: 61, 90
D 149: 135

GENERAL INDEX

D 151: 78
D 152: 78
D 156: 65
D 158: 80
D 159: 90
D 160: 57
D 161: 90
D 162: 79, 95, 168
D 166: 65
D 167: 52, 57
D 167b: 89
D 168: 52
D 169: 79
D 171: 94, 135
D 172: 135
D 175: 55, 122, 171
D 177: 143
D 178: 135
D 179: 49, 120, 143
D 180: 180
D 182: 90
D 184: 90
D 186: 206
D 187: 84
D 188: 81
D 192: 69
D 193: 90
D 194: 116
D 195: 90, 116, 119, 203
D 198: 90
D 204: 92
D 207: 179
D 209: 103, 114
D 211: 84
D 214: 90
D 223: 82
D 227: 91, 168, 240
D 234: 240
D 237: 84
D 240: 52
X 3: 205
Lycurgus' use of, 43, 52, 53
misleading presentations of, 97, 220
non-Athenians and, 174
of associations, 15
of demes, 15
of tribes, 15
persuasion and, 30
Praxagora's use of, 216
Pseudo-Demosthenes, use of in Philip's
    Letter, 92

rational argument and, 120
reliability of, 62
religion and, 125, 245
resistance to, 187
timelessness of, 87
truth of, 60
dedications, 76
Delos, 167, 185
Demades, 73, 81, 84, 88, 153, 168, 206, 219, 235,
    270
demagogues, 35, 196, 236
Demochares, 78, 204
democracy, 4
    abolition of, 199
    and decrees, 39
    Argive, 209
    extreme, 35, 189, 237
    Plutarch and, 203
    restoration of, 51, 136
    systemic problems of, 107, 189, 200, 237,
        246
    tragedy and, 208
Demon, 203
Demophantos, decree of, 31, 50, 142
Demosthenes, 4, 23, 31, 36, 61, 62, 64, 72, 77,
    79, 83, 84, 94, 117, 153, 168, 203, 212,
    235, 241
diapsephisis, 113
Dinarchus, 76, 84, 119
Diodoros the Periegete, 226
Diodorus Siculus, 197
Diogenes Laertius, 201
Diopeithes, 73
Diopeithes' decree, 203
diplomacy, 35, 244
documents
    and Xenophon, 194
    deployment of, 119, 120, 180,
        199
    drafting of, 93
    inauthentic, 142, 230, 233
    inscribed, 146
    Persian war decrees, 44
    storage of, 117
    Thucydides and, 192
Draco, 29, 34, 148
Drakontides' decree, 203

education, decrees and, 232
eisangelia (impeachment), 15, 84
elite politicians, 73

epigram, 137
epigraphical habit, 4, 32, 45, 62, 76, 155, 185
equality, 207
Erythrai, 4, 186
Eteokarpathians, 178
Euboulos, 73
Euripides, 216
exiles, 172
expertise, 99, 116, 129

fishmongers, 218

generals (strategoi), 114
gossip, 114, 170
graphe nomon me epitedeion thenai, 27, 113
graphe paranomon, 8, 15, 28, 34, 38, 81, 89, 103, 113, 151, 242
Greif, A., 7
gynaecocracy, 218

Hansen, M.H., 25, 33, 59, 69, 154
Harpalos, 240
Harris, E.M., 26, 33, 99, 269
Hegesippos, 73, 95, 169
Heliodoros, 226
heralds (kerykes), 114
Hermai, commemorative, 136
Hermippos of Smyrna, 230
Herodotus, 3, 53, 190, 191, 196
Hieronymos of Kardia, 197
Historical Institutionalism, 7
historiography, 200
homonoia, 46
hortatory clause, 100, 127, 175
humour, 220
Hypereides, 73, 106, 206, 219

Ibn Abī Usaybiʿa, 201
image, Athenian, 56, 188
imperialism, Athenian, 40, 196, 202, 213
inheritance, 103
inscribing costs, 176
inscriptions, appeals for, 177
inscriptions, cited by orators, 149
insecurity, Athenian, 43, 168, 169
Instiutionalism
    Historical Institutionalism, 16, 245
    New Institutionalism, 7, 71, 74, 99
institutions, 7, 25
Iolas, 270
Ionian revolt, 190
Ioulis, 183

Iphikrates, 74, 197
Isocrates, 71, 101
isthmus of Corinth, 235

Kallias, 77
Kallimedon, 218
Keos, Keans, 84, 168, 179, 182, 183, 184, 186
Kephalos, 73, 81
Kersobleptes, 122, 163
kerugma, 207
King's Peace, 87, 146
Kitians, 172
Konon, 120, 143
Krateros, 116, 203, 225
Kritias, 8, 53, 77
Kydias, 163

lability, political, 223
Lambert, S.D., 2, 42, 59, 72, 124, 150
law (nomos), 20, 21, 25, 26
    and rhetoric, 28
    comedy and, 211
    enforcement of, 65
    of Eukrates, 31, 142
    rule of, 29, 34
lawcourt oratory, 92, 98
lawcourts (dikasteria), 33, 113
laws (nomoi)
    and decrees, 28, 30, 32, 33, 91, 216
    inscribed, 29, 147
Leokrates, 43
Leptines, 30
liability, political, 19, 52, 57, 70, 90, 190, 210, 218, 246
liberation, of Greece, 180
lists of traitors, 147, 148
local historiography, 200
logopoioi, 75
Lougovaya, J., 214
Low, P.A., 132
Lucian, 236, 237
Lycurgus, 43, 73, 83, 88, 89, 94, 142, 146, 191, 204, 205
Lykidas, 191

Marathon, battle of, 86
Megara, 35, 100, 163, 191, 200
Megarian decree, 45, 191, 202, 212
Meidias, 74
Melians, Athenian treatment of, 195
memory, collective, 10, 44, 51, 102, 107, 123, 132, 242

GENERAL INDEX

metics, 171, 208
Metroon, 29, 45, 117, 118, 119, 134
Miletos, 4
Miltiades, 77
Miltokythes, 164
mysteries, Eleusinian, 212
Mytilenean debate, 58, 193, 238

Neoptolemos of Parion, 226
Nicias, 202
nomothesia, 8, 15, 20, 34
North, D., 6

oath, 30
Oath of Ephebes, 146, 221
Oath of Plataea, 44, 146, 221
Ober, J., 33
Oiniades, 176
Old Comedy, 211–20
Oinobios, 231
oligarchy, 4, 8, 37
Olynthos and Olynthians, 219
oral dissemination of decrees, 116, 181, 233
Oreos, 37, 163
Osborne, M.J., 127

Pallene, 227
parasitoi, 227
path-dependence, 245
Pausanias, 231
Peace of 392, 145
Peace of 446/5, 231
Peace of Antalkidas, 87, 146
Peace of Callias, 146, 221, 224
Peace of Nicias, 94
Peace of Philokrates, 23, 36, 51, 58, 70, 96, 122, 145, 168, 169, 179
Peisitheides of Delos, 166
Pelasgos, 207
Pellanians, 175
Pelopidas, 186
Peloponnesian war, 40, 191
Pericles, 58, 77, 88, 161, 178, 202, 212, 234
Persian war decrees, 3, 10, 44, 54, 222
Phanodemos, 76
philanthropia, 197
Philip, 24, 36, 68, 70, 105, 180, 201, 203, 235
Philippides, 73
Philochoros, 199, 226
Philokrates, 73
philotimia, 18, 81, 143, 202, 203

Phormio, 68, 128
Phryne, 230
Phrynichos, 224
piety, Athenian, 180
pinax, 211
Piraeus, 129, 138, 144, 165, 183
Pisistratus, 3, 198
Plato, 26, 75
Plutarch, 205, 237
Pnyx, 182
Polemon, 228
Polybius, 197
Poseidonios, 225
probouleuma, 94, 96, 99, 112, 194
probouleusis, 19, 25, 36, 37, 193
procheirotonia, 23
proclamation, 111, 181
proedroi, 14, 19, 22, 23, 24, 27
progymnasmata, 232
proposers, 4, 23, 51, 83
protenthai, 228
proxeny awards, 150, 153
prytaneis, 22, 24, 97, 126, 129, 170, 203, 215
Pythodoros of Delos, 184

reconciliation, Athenian, 51, 131, 200
religious regulations, 152
rhetorical handbooks, 233
Rhodes, P.J., 21

Salamis, battle of, 86, 202
Second Athenian Confederacy, 127, 128, 135, 168, 173, 179, 181, 184, 196
Second Sophistic, 206, 231, 237
secretaries (grammateis), 31, 93, 110, 116, 215
self-interest, political, 108, 189
sexual activity
    decrees about, 217, 230
Shear, J.L., 9, 46, 127, 131
Sicilian expedition, 193, 214
Skionians, Athenian punishment of, 195
social capital, 5
Social War, 45
Socrates, 75
Solon, 26, 29, 34, 148
Sophocles, 271
sovereignty, popular, 33, 34, 36, 208
statues, 52, 53, 86, 88, 137, 138, 144, 145, 148, 153, 204, 218, 231, 236, 240
Steinbock, B., 9
stelai, bronze, 224

stelai, inscribed, 124, 144, 155, 214
stele
   electrum, 236
stele, inscribed, 176
Stephanos, 82
Sthorys of Thasos, 175
summoner *(kleter)*, 115
symbolic capital, 5, 106, 241
symbouleutic oratory, 69, 76, 80, 91, 92, 104,
      106, 110, 163, 169
synegoroi, 65, 80

theatre of Dionysos, 63, 111, 138
Thebans, 9, 55, 96, 137, 198
Themistocles, 77, 190, 202, 234
Themistocles decree, 10
Theopompos, 221
Theozotides, 135, 136
Theseus, 207
thesmothetai, 34
Thirty, the, 8, 35, 118

Thomas, R., 131
Thrasyboulos, 133, 199
Thucydides, 194, 231
Timarchos, 73
time, 62, 86
Timon, 236
Timotheos, 74, 197
tragedy, 211
treaties, 34, 43, 146, 150
tribute, 178
trierarchy, 66, 114
tyranny, 35, 37

voting, 24, 194, 208

women
   decrees and, 214, 215

Xenophon, 38, 62, 122, 171, 197

Zeno, 201